ITIL® Service Operation

London: TSO

Published by TSO (The Stationery Office) and available from:
Online
www.tsoshop.co.uk

Mail, Telephone, Fax & E-mail
TSO
PO Box 29, Norwich, NR3 1GN
Telephone orders/General enquiries: 0870 600 5522
Fax orders: 0870 600 5533
E-mail: customer.services@tso.co.uk
Textphone 0870 240 3701

TSO@Blackwell and other Accredited Agents

Customers can also order publications from:
TSO Ireland
16 Arthur Street, Belfast BT1 4GD
Tel 028 9023 8451 Fax 028 9023 5401

© Crown Copyright 2011

This is a Crown copyright value added product, reuse of which requires a Licence from the Cabinet Office

Applications to reuse, reproduce or republish material in this publication should be sent to The Efficiency & Reform Group Service Desk, Cabinet Office, Rosebery Court, St Andrews Business Park, Norwich, Norfolk NR7 0HS Tel No: (+44) (0)845 000 4999, E-mail: servicedesk@cabinet-office.gsi.gov.uk or complete the application form on the Cabinet Office website, Licensing section.

Copyright in the typographical arrangement and design is vested in The Stationery Office Limited. Applications for reproduction should be made in writing to The Stationery Office Limited, St Crispins, Duke Street, Norwich, NR3 1PD.

The Swirl logo™ is a trade mark of the Cabinet Office
ITIL® is a registered trade mark of the Cabinet Office
PRINCE2® is a registered trade mark of the Cabinet Office
M_o_R® is a registered trade mark of the Cabinet Office
P3O® is a registered trade mark of the Cabinet Office
MSP® is a registered trade mark of the Cabinet Office
MoV™ is a trade mark of the Cabinet Office
MoP™ is a trade mark of the Cabinet Office
The OGC Official Product endorsement logo™ is a trade mark of the Cabinet Office

OGC (former owner of Best Management Practice) and its functions have moved into the Cabinet Office part of HM Government –
www.cabinetoffice.gov.uk

First edition Crown Copyright 2007
Second edition Crown Copyright 2011

First published 2011

ISBN 9780113313075

Printed in the United Kingdom for The Stationery Office
Material is FSC certified and produced using ECF pulp, sourced from fully sustainable forests.
P002425502   c70   07/11   19585   12468

Contents

List of figures

List of tables

Foreword

Back in the 1980s no one truly understood IT service management (ITSM), although it was clear that it was a concept that needed to be explored. Hence a UK government initiative was instigated and ITIL® was born. Over the years, ITIL has evolved and, arguably, is now the most widely adopted approach in ITSM. It is globally recognized as the best-practice framework. ITIL's universal appeal is that it continues to provide a set of processes and procedures that are efficient, reliable and adaptable to organizations of all sizes, enabling them to improve their own service provision.

In the modern world the concept of having a strategy to drive the business forward with adequate planning and design transitioning into day-to-day operation is compelling. Once services have been transitioned into the live environment they need to be monitored, controlled and reviewed as part of service operation. When things go wrong, there should be robust processes in place to record, resolve and ensure that they do not re-occur. The aim of service operation is to ensure that the live operational environment runs as smoothly as possible. Business users and customers interact directly with the operational services and any problems here can have a direct impact on their perception of your business and ultimately to your reputation. In that respect service operation is the most visible part of the service lifecycle. However, it is important that service operation does not drive the lifecycle. Good operational services have been through the stages of strategy, design and transition, and have captured the appropriate metrics in order to maintain the levels of service required.

The principles contained within *ITIL Service Operation* have been proven countless times in the real world. We encourage feedback from business and the ITSM community, as well as other experts in the field, to ensure that ITIL remains relevant. This practice of continual service improvement is one of the cornerstones of the ITIL framework and the fruits of this labour are here before you in this updated edition.

There is an associated qualification scheme so that individuals can demonstrate their understanding and application of the ITIL practices. So whether you are starting out or continuing along the ITIL path, you are joining a legion of individuals and organizations who have recognized the benefits of good quality service and have a genuine resolve to improve their service level provision.

ITIL is not a panacea to all problems. It is, however, a tried and tested approach that has been proven to work.

I wish you every success in your service management journey.

Frances Scarff

Head of Best Management Practice
Cabinet Office

Preface

'The first rule of any technology used in a business is that automation applied to an efficient operation will magnify the efficiency. The second is that automation applied to an inefficient operation will magnify the inefficiency.' Bill Gates

This is the fourth book in the series of five ITIL core publications containing advice and guidance around the activities and processes associated with the five stages of the service lifecycle. The primary purpose of the service operation stage of the service lifecycle is to coordinate, deliver and manage services to ensure that the levels agreed with the business, customers and users are met or exceeded. Service operation is also responsible for the ongoing management of the technology that is used to deliver and support the services.

Service operation accepts the new, modified, retiring or retired services from service transition once the test and acceptance criteria have been met. Service operation then ensures that those new or modified services will meet all of their agreed operational targets, as well as ensuring that all existing services continue to meet all of their targets. This stage of the lifecycle performs the vital day-to-day activities and processes that collect the data and information which are essential to the activities of continual service improvement, the final stage of the service lifecycle.

Service operation is the critical stage of the service lifecycle. It is the stage of the lifecycle where the service really starts to deliver benefit and value to the business, customers and users. A well designed and implemented service and its processes will be of little value if they are poorly supported, operated and managed. Service operation staff should have in place effective processes with supporting tools to allow them an overall view of the service and service operation (rather than just the separate components, such as hardware, software applications and networks). This will enable them to rapidly detect any threats or failures to the service and service quality. Service operation staff act as the 'eyes and ears' for the service provider organization, 24 hours a day, seven days a week, giving early warning of any abnormal situations, especially on 'mission-critical' services.

ITIL Service Operation also provides advice and guidance on application management, technical management and the service desk, the functions within the service operation stage of the lifecycle.

ITIL Service Operation provides essential reading to any member of an IT service provider organization trying to deliver service excellence through outstanding operational performance. Unfortunately, the more effective an organization becomes within service operation, the less it seems to need it. However, ongoing service excellence can only be achieved through continual focus, application and commitment.

Contact information

Full details of the range of material published under the ITIL banner can be found at:

www.best-management-practice.com/IT-Service-Management-ITIL/

If you would like to inform us of any changes that may be required to this publication, please log them at:

www.best-management-practice.com/changelog/

For further information on qualifications and training accreditation, please visit

www.itil-officialsite.com

Alternatively, please contact:

APM Group – The Accreditor Service Desk
Sword House
Totteridge Road
High Wycombe
Buckinghamshire
HP13 6DG
UK
Tel: +44 (0) 1494 458948
Email: servicedesk@apmgroupltd.com

Acknowledgements

2011 EDITION

Authors and mentors

Randy Steinberg
(Migration Technologies Inc.)   Author

Colin Rudd (IT Enterprise
Management Services Ltd (ITEMS))   Mentor

Shirley Lacy (ConnectSphere)   Project mentor

Ashley Hanna (HP)   Technical continuity editor

Other members of the ITIL authoring team

Thanks are due to the authors and mentors who have worked on all the publications in the lifecycle suite and contributed to the content in this publication and consistency across the suite. They are:

David Cannon (HP), Lou Hunnebeck (Third Sky), Vernon Lloyd (Fox IT), Anthony T. Orr (BMC Software), Stuart Rance (HP), and David Wheeldon (David Wheeldon IT Service Management).

Project governance

Members of the project governance team included:

Jessica Barry, APM Group, project assurance (examinations); Marianna Billington, itSMFI, senior user; Emily Egle, TSO, team manager; Janine Eves, TSO, senior supplier; Phil Hearsum, Cabinet Office, project assurance (quality); Tony Jackson, TSO, project manager; Paul Martini, itSMFI, senior user; Richard Pharro, APM Group, senior supplier; Frances Scarff, Cabinet Office, project executive; Rob Stroud, itSMFI, senior user; Sharon Taylor, Aspect Group Inc., adviser to the project board (technical) and the ATO sub-group, and adviser to the project board (training).

For more information on the ATO sub-group see:

www.itil-officialsite.com/News/
ATOSubGroupAppointed.aspx

For a full list of acknowledgements of the ATO sub-group at the time of publication, please visit: www.itil-officialsite.com/Publications/
PublicationAcknowledgements.aspx

Wider team

Change advisory board

The change advisory board (CAB) spent considerable time and effort reviewing all the comments submitted through the change control log and their hard work was essential to this project. Members of the CAB involved in this review included:

David Cannon, Emily Egle, David Favelle, Ashley Hanna, Kevin Holland, Stuart Rance, Frances Scarff and Sharon Taylor.

Once authors and mentors were selected for the 2011 update, a revised CAB was appointed and now includes:

Emily Egle, David Favelle, Phil Hearsum, Kevin Holland and Frances Scarff.

Reviewers

Claire Agutter, IT Training Zone; Valerie Arraj, Compliance Process Partners; Ernest R. Brewster, Independent; David M. Brink, Solutions3; Jeroen Bronkhorst, HP; Tony Brough, DHL Supply Chain; Janaki Chakravarthy, Independent; Christiane Chung Ah Pong, NCS Pte Ltd, Singapore; Mauricio Corona, Pink Elephant and La Salle University; Federico Corradi, Cogitek; Kevin Dorsey, Kaiser Permanente; Jenny Dugmore, Service Matters; Frank Eggert, MATERNA GmbH; David Favelle, UXC Consulting/Lucid IT; Karen Ferris, Macanta Consulting Pty Ltd; Mark Flynn, Felix Maldo Ltd; Ryan Fraser, HP; Kerry Gilmore, Pink Elephant Malaysia; Genevieve Goris, HP Enterprise Services; Detlef Gross, procise GmbH; Horacio Gutiérrez, PSS México; Alex Hernandez, Accenture; Kevin Holland, NHS Connecting for Health; Steve Ingall, iCore-ltd; Brad Laatsch, HP; Chandrika Labru, Tata Consultancy Services; Madhav Lakshminarayanan, Carnegie Mellon University in Qatar; Martin Lewis, Independent; Reginald Lo, Third Sky; Jane McNamara, Lilliard Associates Ltd; Sergio L. Milametto, KPMG LLP (US); Trevor Murray, The Grey Matters; Vinay Nikumbh, Quint Wellington Redwood; Chris Pierce, Metropolitan Police Service; Judit Pongracz, ITeal Consulting; Adam Poppleton,

BrightOak Consultancy Ltd; Paul Reeves, Business Improvement Results; Michael Santifaller, santix AG; Noel Scott, Symantec; Arun Simha, L-3 Communications STRATIS; Helen Sussex, Logica; J.R. Tietsort, Micron Technology; Ken Turbitt, Service Management Consultancy (SMCG) Ltd

2007 EDITION

Chief architect and authors

Thanks are still due to those who contributed to the 2007 edition of Service Operation, upon which this updated edition is based.

Sharon Taylor (Aspect Group Inc)	Chief architect
David Cannon (HP)	Author
David Wheeldon (HP)	Author

All names and organizations were correct at publication in 2007.

For a full list of all those who contributed to the 2007 and 2011 editions of *Service Strategy, Service Design, Service Transition, Service Operation* and *Continual Service Improvement*, please go to

www.itil-officialsite.com/Publications/ PublicationAcknowledgements.aspx

Introduction

1

1 Introduction

ITIL is part of a suite of best-practice publications for IT service management (ITSM).[1] ITIL provides guidance to service providers on the provision of quality IT services, and on the processes, functions and other capabilities needed to support them. ITIL is used by many hundreds of organizations around the world and offers best-practice guidance applicable to all types of organization that provide services. ITIL is not a standard that has to be followed; it is guidance that should be read and understood, and used to create value for the service provider and its customers. Organizations are encouraged to adopt ITIL best practices and to adapt them to work in their specific environments in ways that meet their needs.

ITIL is the most widely recognized framework for ITSM in the world. In the 20 years since it was created, ITIL has evolved and changed its breadth and depth as technologies and business practices have developed. ISO/IEC 20000 provides a formal and universal standard for organizations seeking to have their service management capabilities audited and certified. While ISO/IEC 20000 is a standard to be achieved and maintained, ITIL offers a body of knowledge useful for achieving the standard.

In 2007, the second major refresh of ITIL was published in response to significant advancements in technology and emerging challenges for IT service providers. New models and architectures such as outsourcing, shared services, utility computing, cloud computing, virtualization, web services and mobile commerce have become widespread within IT. The process-based approach of ITIL was augmented with the service lifecycle to address these additional service management challenges. In 2011, as part of its commitment to continual improvement, the Cabinet Office published this update to improve consistency across the core publications.

The ITIL framework is based on the five stages of the service lifecycle as shown in Figure 1.1, with a core publication providing best-practice guidance for each stage. This guidance includes

key principles, required processes and activities, organization and roles, technology, associated challenges, critical success factors and risks. The service lifecycle uses a hub-and-spoke design, with service strategy at the hub, and service design, transition and operation as the revolving lifecycle stages or 'spokes'. Continual service improvement surrounds and supports all stages of the service lifecycle. Each stage of the lifecycle exerts influence on the others and relies on them for inputs and feedback. In this way, a constant set of checks and balances throughout the service lifecycle ensures that as business demand changes with business need, the services can adapt and respond effectively.

In addition to the core publications, there is also a complementary set of ITIL publications providing guidance specific to industry sectors, organization types, operating models and technology architectures.

1.1 CHAPTER SUMMARY

ITIL Service Operation provides best-practice guidance for the service operation stage of the ITIL service lifecycle. Although this publication can be

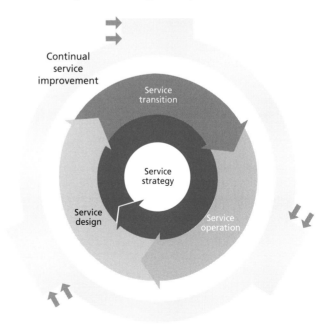

Figure 1.1 The ITIL service lifecycle

---

[1] ITSM and other concepts from this chapter are described in more detail in Chapter 2.

read in isolation, it is recommended that it is used in conjunction with the other core ITIL publications.

1.1.1 Purpose and objectives of service operation

The purpose of the service operation stage of the service lifecycle is to coordinate and carry out the activities and processes required to deliver and manage services at agreed levels to business users and customers. Service operation is also responsible for the ongoing management of the technology that is used to deliver and support services.

Service operation is a critical stage of the service lifecycle. Well-planned and well-implemented processes will be to no avail if the day-to-day operation of those processes is not properly conducted, controlled and managed. Nor will service improvements be possible if day-to-day activities to monitor performance, assess metrics and gather operational data are not systematically conducted during service operation.

Staff involved in the service operation stage of the service lifecycle should have processes and support tools in place that allow them to have an overall view of service operation and delivery (rather than just the separate components, such as hardware, software applications and networks, that make up the end-to-end service from a business perspective). These processes and tools should also detect any threats or failures to service quality.

As services may be provided, in whole or in part, by one or more partner/supplier organizations, the service operation view of the end-to-end service should be extended to encompass external aspects of service provision. When necessary, shared or interfacing processes and tools should be deployed to manage cross-organizational workflows.

The objectives of service operation are to:

- Maintain business satisfaction and confidence in IT through effective and efficient delivery and support of agreed IT services
- Minimize the impact of service outages on day-to-day business activities
- Ensure that access to agreed IT services is only provided to those authorized to receive those services.

1.1.2 Scope

ITIL Service Operation describes the processes, functions, organization and tools used to underpin the ongoing activities required to deliver and support services. The guidance provided in this publication includes:

- **The services themselves** Activities that form part of a service are included in service operation, whether it is performed by the service provider, an external supplier or the user or customer of that service.
- **Service management processes** The ongoing management and execution of the many service management processes that are performed in service operation. Even though a number of ITIL processes (such as change and capacity management) originate at the service design or service transition stage of the service lifecycle, they are in use continually in service operation. Some processes are not included specifically in service operation, such as strategy management for IT services and the actual design process itself. These processes focus more on longer-term planning and improvement activities, which are outside the direct scope of service operation; however, service operation provides input and influences these processes regularly as part of the lifecycle of service management.
- **Technology** All services require some form of technology to deliver them. Managing this technology is not a separate issue, but an integral part of the management of the services themselves. Therefore a large part of *ITIL Service Operation* is concerned with the management of the infrastructure used to deliver services.
- **People** Regardless of what services, processes and technology are managed, they are all about people. It is people who drive the demand for the organization's services and products and it is people who decide how this will be done. Ultimately, it is people who manage the technology, processes and services. Failure to recognize this will result (and has resulted) in the failure of service management activities.

1.1.3 Usage

ITIL Service Operation provides access to proven best practice based on the skill and knowledge of experienced industry practitioners in adopting a standardized and controlled approach to service management. Although this publication can be used and applied in isolation, it is recommended that it is used in conjunction with the other core ITIL publications. All of the core publications need to be read to fully appreciate and understand the overall lifecycle of services and IT service management.

1.1.4 Value to business

Selecting and adopting the best practice as recommended in this publication will assist organizations in delivering significant benefits. Adopting and implementing standard and consistent approaches for service operation will:

- Reduce unplanned labour and costs for both the business and IT through optimized handling of service outages and identification of their root causes.
- Reduce the duration and frequency of service outages which will allow the business to take full advantage of the value created by the services they are receiving.
- Provide operational results and data that can be used by other ITIL processes to improve services continually and provide justification for investing in ongoing service improvement activities and supporting technologies.
- Meet the goals and objectives of the organization's security policy by ensuring that IT services will be accessed only by those authorized to use them.
- Provide quick and effective access to standard services which business staff can use to improve their productivity or the quality of business services and products.
- Provide a basis for automated operations, thus increasing efficiencies and allowing expensive human resources to be used for more innovative work, such as designing new or improved functionality or defining new ways in which the business can exploit technology for increased competitive advantage.

1.1.5 Target audience

ITIL Service Operation is relevant to organizations involved in the development, delivery or support of services, including:

- Service providers, both internal and external

- Organizations that aim to improve services through the effective application of service management and service lifecycle processes to improve their service quality
- Organizations that require a consistent managed approach across all service providers in a supply chain or value network
- Organizations that are going out to tender for their services.

In addition, this publication is relevant to any professional involved in the management of services, particularly:

- IT managers and practitioners
- IT operations and support personnel
- Service desk management and staff
- Technical management staff
- Application management personnel.

1.2 CONTEXT

The context of this publication is the ITIL service lifecycle as shown in Figure 1.1.

The ITIL core consists of five lifecycle publications. Each provides part of the guidance necessary for an integrated approach as required by the ISO/IEC 20000 standard specification. The five publications are:

- *ITIL Service Strategy*
- *ITIL Service Design*
- *ITIL Service Transition*
- *ITIL Service Operation*
- *ITIL Continual Service Improvement*

Each one addresses capabilities having direct impact on a service provider's performance. The core is expected to provide structure, stability and strength to service management capabilities, with durable principles, methods and tools. This serves to protect investments and provide the necessary basis for measurement, learning and improvement. The introductory guide, *Introduction to the ITIL Service Lifecycle*, provides an overview of the lifecycle stages described in the ITIL core.

ITIL guidance can be adapted to support various business environments and organizational strategies. Complementary ITIL publications provide flexibility to implement the core in a diverse range of environments. Practitioners can select complementary publications as needed to provide traction for the ITIL core in a given context, in much the same way as tyres are selected based on the type of vehicle, purpose and road conditions. This is to increase the durability and portability of knowledge assets and to protect investments in service management capabilities.

1.2.1 Service strategy

At the centre of the service lifecycle is service strategy. Value creation begins here with understanding organizational objectives and customer needs. Every organizational asset including people, processes and products should support the strategy.

ITIL Service Strategy provides guidance on how to view service management not only as an organizational capability but as a strategic asset. It describes the principles underpinning the practice of service management which are useful for developing service management policies, guidelines and processes across the ITIL service lifecycle.

Topics covered in *ITIL Service Strategy* include the development of market spaces, characteristics of internal and external provider types, service assets, the service portfolio and implementation of strategy through the service lifecycle. Business relationship management, demand management, financial management, organizational development and strategic risks are among the other major topics.

Organizations should use *ITIL Service Strategy* to set objectives and expectations of performance towards serving customers and market spaces, and to identify, select and prioritize opportunities. Service strategy is about ensuring that organizations are in a position to handle the costs and risks associated with their service portfolios, and are set up not just for operational effectiveness but for distinctive performance.

Organizations already practising ITIL can use *ITIL Service Strategy* to guide a strategic review of their ITIL-based service management capabilities and to improve the alignment between those capabilities and their business strategies. *ITIL Service Strategy* will encourage readers to stop and think about why something is to be done before thinking of how.

1.2.2 Service design

For services to provide true value to the business, they must be designed with the business objectives in mind. Design encompasses the whole IT organization, for it is the organization as a whole that delivers and supports the services. Service design is the stage in the lifecycle that turns a service strategy into a plan for delivering the business objectives.

ITIL Service Design provides guidance for the design and development of services and service management practices. It covers design principles and methods for converting strategic objectives into portfolios of services and service assets. The scope of *ITIL Service Design* is not limited to new services. It includes the changes and improvements necessary to increase or maintain value to customers over the lifecycle of services, the continuity of services, achievement of service levels, and conformance to standards and regulations. It guides organizations on how to develop design capabilities for service management.

Other topics in *ITIL Service Design* include design coordination, service catalogue management, service level management, availability management, capacity management, IT service continuity management, information security management and supplier management.

1.2.3 Service transition

ITIL Service Transition provides guidance for the development and improvement of capabilities for introducing new and changed services into supported environments. It describes how to transition an organization from one state to another while controlling risk and supporting organizational knowledge for decision support. It ensures that the value(s) identified in the service strategy, and encoded in service design, are effectively transitioned so that they can be realized in service operation.

ITIL Service Transition describes best practice in transition planning and support, change management, service asset and configuration management, release and deployment management, service validation and testing, change evaluation and knowledge management. It provides guidance on managing the complexity related to changes to services and service management processes, preventing undesired consequences while allowing for innovation.

ITIL Service Transition also introduces the service knowledge management system, which can support organizational learning and help to improve the overall efficiency and effectiveness of all stages of the service lifecycle. This will enable people to benefit from the knowledge and experience of others, support informed decision-making, and improve the management of services.

1.2.4 Service operation

ITIL Service Operation (this publication) describes best practice for managing services in supported environments. It includes guidance on achieving effectiveness and efficiency in the delivery and support of services to ensure value for the customer, the users and the service provider.

Strategic objectives are ultimately realized through service operation, therefore making it a critical capability. *ITIL Service Operation* provides guidance on how to maintain stability in service operation, allowing for changes in design, scale, scope and service levels. Organizations are provided with detailed process guidelines, methods and tools for use in two major control perspectives: reactive and proactive. Managers and practitioners are provided with knowledge allowing them to make better decisions in areas such as managing the availability of services, controlling demand, optimizing capacity utilization, scheduling of operations, and avoiding or resolving service incidents and managing problems. New models and architectures such as shared services, utility computing, web services and mobile commerce to support service operation are described.

Other topics in *ITIL Service Operation* include event management, incident management, request fulfilment, problem management and access management processes; as well as the service desk, technical management, IT operations management and application management functions.

1.2.5 Continual service improvement

ITIL Continual Service Improvement provides guidance on creating and maintaining value for customers through better strategy, design, transition and operation of services. It combines principles, practices and methods from quality

management, change management and capability improvement.

ITIL Continual Service Improvement describes best practice for achieving incremental and large-scale improvements in service quality, operational efficiency and business continuity, and for ensuring that the service portfolio continues to be aligned to business needs. Guidance is provided for linking improvement efforts and outcomes with service strategy, design, transition and operation. A closed loop feedback system, based on the Plan-Do-Check-Act (PDCA) cycle, is established. Feedback from any stage of the service lifecycle can be used to identify improvement opportunities for any other stage of the lifecycle.

Other topics in *ITIL Continual Service Improvement* include service measurement, demonstrating value with metrics, developing baselines and maturity assessments.

1.3 ITIL IN RELATION TO OTHER PUBLICATIONS IN THE BEST MANAGEMENT PRACTICE PORTFOLIO

ITIL is part of a portfolio of best-practice publications (known collectively as Best Management Practice or BMP) aimed at helping organizations and individuals manage projects, programmes and services consistently and effectively (see Figure 1.2). ITIL can be used in harmony with other BMP products, and international or internal organization standards. Where appropriate, BMP guidance is supported by a qualification scheme and accredited training and consultancy services. All BMP guidance is intended to be tailored for use by individual organizations.

BMP publications include:

- *Management of Portfolios* (MoP™) Portfolio management concerns the twin issues of how to do the 'right' projects and programmes in the context of the organization's strategic objectives, and how to do them 'correctly' in terms of achieving delivery and benefits at a collective level. MoP encompasses consideration of the principles upon which effective portfolio management is based; the key practices in the portfolio definition and delivery cycles, including examples of how they have been applied in real life; and guidance on how to

Figure 1.2 ITIL's relationship with other Best Management Practice guides

implement portfolio management and sustain progress in a wide variety of organizations. Office of Government Commerce (2011). *Management of Portfolios.* TSO, London.

- **Management of Risk (M_o_R®)** M_o_R offers an effective framework for taking informed decisions about the risks that affect performance objectives. The framework allows organizations to assess risk accurately (selecting the correct responses to threats and opportunities created by uncertainty) and thereby improve their service delivery. Office of Government Commerce (2010). *Management of Risk: Guidance for Practitioners.* TSO, London.

- **Management of Value (MoV™)** MoV provides a cross-sector and universally applicable guide on how to maximize value in a way that takes account of organizations' priorities, differing stakeholders' needs and, at the same time, uses resources as efficiently and effectively as possible. It will help organizations to put in place effective methods to deliver enhanced value across their portfolio, programmes, projects and operational activities to meet

the challenges of ever-more competitive and resource-constrained environments. Office of Government Commerce (2010). *Management of Value.* TSO, London.

- **Managing Successful Programmes (MSP®)** MSP provides a framework to enable the achievement of high-quality change outcomes and benefits that fundamentally affect the way in which organizations work. One of the core themes in MSP is that a programme must add more value than that provided by the sum of its constituent project and major activities. Cabinet Office (2011). *Managing Successful Programmes.* TSO, London.

- **Managing Successful Projects with PRINCE2®** PRINCE2 (PRojects IN Controlled Environments, V2) is a structured method to help effective project management via clearly defined products. Key themes that feature throughout PRINCE2 are the dependence on a viable business case confirming the delivery of measurable benefits that are aligned to an organization's objectives and strategy, while ensuring the management of risks, costs and quality.

Office of Government Commerce (2009). *Managing Successful Projects with PRINCE2.* TSO, London.

- ***Portfolio, Programme and Project Offices (P3O®)*** P3O provides universally applicable guidance, including principles, processes and techniques, to successfully establish, develop and maintain appropriate support structures. These structures will facilitate delivery of business objectives (portfolios), programmes and projects within time, cost, quality and other organizational constraints.

 Office of Government Commerce (2008). *Portfolio, Programme and Project Offices.* TSO, London.

1.4 WHY IS ITIL SO SUCCESSFUL?

ITIL embraces a practical approach to service management – do what works. And what works is adapting a common framework of practices that unite all areas of IT service provision towards a single aim – that of delivering value to the business. The following list defines the key characteristics of ITIL that contribute to its global success:

- **Vendor-neutral** ITIL service management practices are applicable in any IT organization because they are not based on any particular technology platform or industry type. ITIL is owned by the UK government and is not tied to any commercial proprietary practice or solution.
- **Non-prescriptive** ITIL offers robust, mature and time-tested practices that have applicability to all types of service organization. It continues to be useful and relevant in public and private sectors, internal and external service providers, small, medium and large enterprises, and within any technical environment. Organizations should adopt ITIL and adapt it to meet the needs of the IT organization and their customers.
- **Best practice** ITIL represents the learning experiences and thought leadership of the world's best-in-class service providers.

ITIL is successful because it describes practices that enable organizations to deliver benefits, return on investment and sustained success. ITIL is adopted by organizations to enable them to:

- Deliver value for customers through services

- Integrate the strategy for services with the business strategy and customer needs
- Measure, monitor and optimize IT services and service provider performance
- Manage the IT investment and budget
- Manage risk
- Manage knowledge
- Manage capabilities and resources to deliver services effectively and efficiently
- Enable adoption of a standard approach to service management across the enterprise
- Change the organizational culture to support the achievement of sustained success
- Improve the interaction and relationship with customers
- Coordinate the delivery of goods and services across the value network
- Optimize and reduce costs.

1.5 CHAPTER SUMMARY

ITIL Service Operation comprises:

- Chapter 2 Service management as a practice
 This chapter explains the concepts of service management and services, and describes how these can be used to create value. It also summarizes a number of generic ITIL concepts that the rest of the publication depends on.

- Chapter 3 Service operation principles
 This chapter describes some of the key principles of service operation that will enable service providers to plan and implement best practice in service operation. These principles are the same irrespective of the organization; however, the approach may need to be tailored to circumstances, including the size of the organization, geographic distribution, culture and available resources. The chapter concludes with a table showing the major inputs and outputs for the service operation lifecycle stage.

- Chapter 4 Service operation processes
 Chapter 4 sets out the processes and activities on which effective service operation depends and how they integrate with the other stages of the lifecycle.

- Chapter 5 Common service operation activities
 Chapter 5 identifies the operational activities required to effectively and efficiently manage IT services on a day-to-day basis to deliver value to

the business. It addresses many of the common operational activities that organizations use to operate their services such as job scheduling, backup and restore, and the management of mainframes, servers, network and desktop.

- Chapter 6 Organizing for service operation
  This chapter identifies the organizational roles and responsibilities that should be considered to manage the service operation lifecycle stage and its associated processes. These roles are provided as guidelines and can be combined to fit into a variety of organizational structures. Examples of organizational structures are also provided.

- Chapter 7 Technology considerations
  ITIL service management practices gain momentum when the right type of technical automation is applied. This chapter provides recommendations for the use of technology in service operation and the basic requirements a service provider will need to consider when choosing service management tools.

- Chapter 8 Implementation of service operation
  For organizations new to ITIL, or those wishing to improve their maturity and service capability, this chapter outlines effective ways to implement the service operation lifecycle stage.

- Chapter 9 Challenges, risks and critical success factors
  It is important for any organization to understand the challenges, risks and critical success factors that could influence their success. This chapter discusses typical examples of these for the service operation lifecycle stage.

- Appendix A Related guidance
  This contains a list of some of the many external methods, practices and frameworks that align well with ITIL best practice. Notes are provided on how they integrate into the ITIL service lifecycle, and when and how they are useful.

- Appendix B Communication in service operation
  Appendix B provides guidance around the kinds of communication that need to take place to provide effective and efficient service operation. Examples include general communication requirements, communication

between shifts, performance reporting, and communications with projects, changes, exceptions, emergencies, users and customers.

- Appendix C Kepner and Tregoe
  This provides an overview of the Kepner and Tregoe method for conducting problem analysis.

- Appendix D Ishikawa diagrams
  This appendix provides an overview of the Ishikawa diagram tool which can systematically identify and present all the possible causes of a particular problem on a chart.

- Appendix E Considerations for facilities management
  Appendix E provides requirements and guidance around the management of physical facilities such as buildings, equipment hosting, power, environmental conditioning, safety, and shipping and receiving.

- Appendix F Physical access control
  This gives detailed guidance on the controls used to provide authorized access to physical facilities. It identifies the kinds of control that can be used, with examples and advantages and disadvantages.

- Appendix G Risk assessment and management
  This appendix contains basic information about several commonly used approaches to the assessment and management of risk.

- Appendix H Pareto analysis
  This contains a technique for analysing and separating important causes of failure from more trivial issues.

- Appendix I Examples of inputs and outputs across the service lifecycle
  This appendix identifies some of the major inputs and outputs between each stage of the service lifecycle.

- References and further reading
  This provides a list of other sources of information that both informed the writing of this publication and can be used for further study and exploration by readers.

- Abbreviations and glossary
  This contains a list of abbreviations and a selected glossary of terms.

Service management as a practice

2

2 Service management as a practice

2.1 SERVICES AND SERVICE MANAGEMENT

2.1.1 Services

Services are a means of delivering value to customers by facilitating the outcomes customers want to achieve without the ownership of specific costs and risks. Services facilitate outcomes by enhancing the performance of associated tasks and reducing the effect of constraints. These constraints may include regulation, lack of funding or capacity, or technology limitations. The end result is an increase in the probability of desired outcomes. While some services enhance performance of tasks, others have a more direct impact – they perform the task itself.

The preceding paragraph is not just a definition, as it is a recurring pattern found in a wide range of services. Patterns are useful for managing complexity, costs, flexibility and variety. They are generic structures useful to make an idea applicable in a wide range of environments and situations. In each instance the pattern is applied with variations that make the idea effective, economical or simply useful in that particular case.

Definition: outcome

The result of carrying out an activity, following a process, or delivering an IT service etc. The term is used to refer to intended results, as well as to actual results.

An outcome-based definition of service moves IT organizations beyond business–IT alignment towards business–IT integration. Internal dialogue and discussion on the meaning of services is an elementary step towards alignment and integration with a customer's business (Figure 2.1). Customer outcomes become the ultimate concern of business relationship managers instead of the gathering of requirements, which is necessary but not sufficient. Requirements are generated for internal coordination and control only after customer outcomes are well understood.

Customers seek outcomes but do not wish to have accountability or ownership of all the associated costs and risks. All services must have a budget when they go live and this must be managed. The service cost is reflected in financial terms such as return on investment (ROI) and total cost of ownership (TCO). The customer will only be exposed to the overall cost or price of a service, which will include all the provider's costs and risk mitigation measures (and any profit margin if appropriate). The customer can then judge the value of a service based on a comparison of cost or price and reliability with the desired outcome.

Definitions

Service: A means of delivering value to customers by facilitating outcomes customers want to achieve without the ownership of specific costs and risks.

IT service: A service provided by an IT service provider. An IT service is made up of a combination of information technology, people and processes. A customer-facing IT service directly supports the business processes of one or more customers and its service level targets should be defined in a service level agreement. Other IT services, called supporting services, are not directly used by the business but are required by the service provider to deliver customer-facing services.

Customer satisfaction is also important. Customers need to be satisfied with the level of service and feel confident in the ability of the service provider to continue providing that level of service – or even improving it over time. The difficulty is that customer expectations keep shifting, and a service provider that does not track this will soon lose business. *ITIL Service Strategy* is helpful in understanding how this happens, and how a service provider can adapt its services to meet the changing customer environment.

Services can be discussed in terms of how they relate to one another and their customers, and can be classified as core, enabling or enhancing.

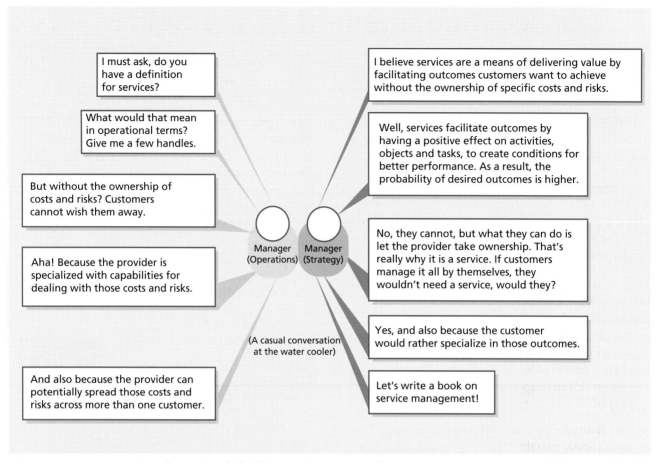

Figure 2.1 Conversation about the definition and meaning of services

Core services deliver the basic outcomes desired by one or more customers. They represent the value that the customer wants and for which they are willing to pay. Core services anchor the value proposition for the customer and provide the basis for their continued utilization and satisfaction.

Enabling services are services that are needed in order for a core service to be delivered. Enabling services may or may not be visible to the customer, but the customer does not perceive them as services in their own right. They are 'basic factors' which enable the customer to receive the 'real' (core) service.

Enhancing services are services that are added to a core service to make it more exciting or enticing to the customer. Enhancing services are not essential to the delivery of a core service, and are added to a core service as 'excitement' factors, which will encourage customers to use the core service more (or to choose the core service provided by one company over those of its competitors).

Services may be as simple as allowing a user to complete a single transaction, but most services are complex. They consist of a range of deliverables and functionality. If each individual aspect of these complex services were defined independently, the service provider would soon find it impossible to track and record all services.

Most service providers will follow a strategy where they can deliver a set of more generic services to a broad range of customers, thus achieving economies of scale and competing on the basis of price and a certain amount of flexibility. One way of achieving this is by using service packages. A service package is a collection of two or more services that have been combined to offer a solution to a specific type of customer need or to underpin specific business outcomes. A service package can consist of a combination of core services, enabling services and enhancing services.

Where a service or service package needs to be differentiated for different types of customer, one or more components of the package can be changed, or offered at different levels of utility and warranty, to create service options. These different service options can then be offered to customers and are sometimes called service level packages.

2.1.2 Service management

When we turn on a water tap, we expect to see water flow from it. When we turn on a light switch, we expect to see light fill the room. Not so many years ago, these very basic things were not as reliable as they are today. We know instinctively that the advances in technology have made them reliable enough to be considered a utility. But it isn't just the technology that makes the services reliable. It is how they are managed.

The use of IT today has become the utility of business. Business today wants IT services that behave like other utilities such as water, electricity or the telephone. Simply having the best technology will not ensure that IT provides utility-like reliability. Professional, responsive, value-driven service management is what brings this quality of service to the business.

Service management is a set of specialized organizational capabilities for providing value to customers in the form of services. The more mature a service provider's capabilities are, the greater is their ability to consistently produce quality services that meet the needs of the customer in a timely and cost-effective manner. The act of transforming capabilities and resources into valuable services is at the core of service management. Without these capabilities, a service organization is merely a bundle of resources that by itself has relatively low intrinsic value for customers.

Definitions

Service management: A set of specialized organizational capabilities for providing value to customers in the form of services.

Service provider: An organization supplying services to one or more internal or external customers.

Organizational capabilities are shaped by the challenges they are expected to overcome. An example of this is provided by Toyota in the 1950s when it developed unique capabilities to overcome the challenge of smaller scale and financial capital compared to its American rivals. Toyota developed new capabilities in production engineering, operations management and managing suppliers to compensate for its inability to afford large inventories, make components, produce raw materials or own the companies that produced them (Magretta, 2002).

Service management capabilities are similarly influenced by the following challenges that distinguish services from other systems of value creation, such as manufacturing, mining and agriculture:

- Intangible nature of the output and intermediate products of service processes: they are difficult to measure, control and validate (or prove)
- Demand is tightly coupled with the customer's assets: users and other customer assets such as processes, applications, documents and transactions arrive with demand and stimulate service production
- High level of contact for producers and consumers of services: there is little or no buffer between the service provider's creation of the service and the customer's consumption of that service
- The perishable nature of service output and service capacity: there is value for the customer from assurance on the continued supply of consistent quality. Providers need to secure a steady supply of demand from customers.

Service management is more than just a set of capabilities. It is also a professional practice supported by an extensive body of knowledge, experience and skills. A global community of individuals and organizations in the public and private sectors fosters its growth and maturity. Formal schemes exist for the education, training and certification of practising organizations, and individuals influence its quality. Industry best practices, academic research and formal standards contribute to and draw from its intellectual capital.

The origins of service management are in traditional service businesses such as airlines, banks, hotels and phone companies. Its practice has grown with the adoption by IT organizations of a service-oriented approach to managing IT applications, infrastructure and processes. Solutions to business problems and support for business models, strategies and operations are increasingly in the form of services. The popularity of shared services and outsourcing has contributed to the increase in the number of organizations that behave as service providers, including internal IT organizations. This in turn has strengthened the practice of service management while at the same time imposed greater challenges.

2.1.3 IT service management

Information technology (IT) is a commonly used term that changes meaning depending on the different perspectives that a business organization or people may have of it. A key challenge is to recognize and balance these perspectives when communicating the value of IT service management (ITSM) and understanding the context for how the business sees the IT organization. Some of these meanings are:

- IT is a collection of systems, applications and infrastructures which are components or sub-assemblies of a larger product. They enable or are embedded in processes and services.
- IT is an organization with its own set of capabilities and resources. IT organizations can be of various types such as business functions, shared services units and enterprise-level core units.
- IT is a category of services utilized by business. The services are typically IT applications and infrastructure that are packaged and offered by internal IT organizations or external service providers. IT costs are treated as business expenses.
- IT is a category of business assets that provide a stream of benefits for their owners, including, but not limited to, revenue, income and profit. IT costs are treated as investments.

Every IT organization should act as a service provider, using the principles of service management to ensure that they deliver the outcomes required by their customers.

> **Definitions**
>
> *IT service management (ITSM):* The implementation and management of quality IT services that meet the needs of the business. IT service management is performed by IT service providers through an appropriate mix of people, process and information technology.
>
> *IT service provider:* A service provider that provides IT services to internal or external customers.

ITSM must be carried out effectively and efficiently. Managing IT from the business perspective enables organizational high performance and value creation.

A good relationship between an IT service provider and its customers relies on the customer receiving an IT service that meets its needs, at an acceptable level of performance and at a cost that the customer can afford. The IT service provider needs to work out how to achieve a balance between these three areas, and communicate with the customer if there is anything which prevents it from being able to deliver the required IT service at the agreed level of performance or price.

A service level agreement (SLA) is used to document agreements between an IT service provider and a customer. An SLA describes the IT service, documents service level targets, and specifies the responsibilities of the IT service provider and the customer. A single agreement may cover multiple IT services or multiple customers.

2.1.4 Service providers

There are three main types of service provider. While most aspects of service management apply equally to all types of service provider, other aspects such as customers, contracts, competition, market spaces, revenue and strategy take on different meanings depending on the specific type. The three types are:

- **Type I – internal service provider** An internal service provider that is embedded within a business unit. There may be several Type I service providers within an organization.
- **Type II – shared services unit** An internal service provider that provides shared IT services to more than one business unit.
- **Type III – external service provider** A service provider that provides IT services to external customers.

ITSM concepts are often described in the context of only one of these types and as if only one type of IT service provider exists or is used by a given organization. In reality most organizations have a combination of IT service providers. In a single organization it is possible that some IT units are dedicated to a single business unit, others provide shared services, and yet others have been outsourced or depend on external service providers.

Many IT organizations who traditionally provide services to internal customers find that they are dealing directly with external users because of the online services that they provide. *ITIL Service Strategy* provides guidance on how the IT organization interacts with these users, and who owns and manages the relationship with them.

2.1.5 Stakeholders in service management

Stakeholders have an interest in an organization, project or service etc. and may be interested in the activities, targets, resources or deliverables from service management. Examples include organizations, service providers, customers, consumers, users, partners, employees, shareholders, owners and suppliers. The term 'organization' is used to define a company, legal entity or other institution. It is also used to refer to any entity that has people, resources and budgets – for example, a project or business.

Within the service provider organization there are many different stakeholders including the functions, groups and teams that deliver the services. There are also many stakeholders external to the service provider organization, for example:

- **Customers** Those who buy goods or services. The customer of an IT service provider is the person or group who defines and agrees the service level targets. This term is also sometimes used informally to mean user – for example, 'This is a customer-focused organization.'
- **Users** Those who use the service on a day-to-day basis. Users are distinct from customers, as some customers do not use the IT service directly.
- **Suppliers** Third parties responsible for supplying goods or services that are required to deliver IT services. Examples of suppliers include commodity hardware and software vendors, network and telecom providers, and outsourcing organizations.

There is a difference between customers who work in the same organization as the IT service provider, and customers who work for other organizations. They are distinguished as follows:

- **Internal customers** These are customers who work for the same business as the IT service provider. For example, the marketing department is an internal customer of the IT organization because it uses IT services. The head of marketing and the chief information officer both report to the chief executive officer. If IT charges for its services, the money paid is an internal transaction in the organization's accounting system, not real revenue.
- **External customers** These are customers who work for a different business from the IT service provider. External customers typically purchase services from the service provider by means of a legally binding contract or agreement.

2.1.6 Utility and warranty

The value of a service can be considered to be the level to which that service meets a customer's expectations. It is often measured by how much the customer is willing to pay for the service, rather than the cost to the service provider of providing the service or any other intrinsic attribute of the service itself.

Unlike products, services do not have much intrinsic value. The value of a service comes from what it enables someone to do. The value of a service is not determined by the provider, but by the person who receives it – because they decide what they will do with the service, and what type of return they will achieve by using the service. Services contribute value to an organization only when their value is perceived to be higher than the cost of obtaining the service.

From the customer's perspective, value consists of achieving business objectives. The value of a service is created by combining two primary elements: utility (fitness for purpose) and warranty (fitness for use). These two elements work together to achieve the desired outcomes upon which the customer and the business base their perceptions of a service.

Utility is the functionality offered by a product or service to meet a particular need. Utility can be summarized as 'what the service does' and can be used to determine whether a service is able to meet its required outcomes or is 'fit for purpose'. Utility refers to those aspects of a service that contribute to tasks associated with achieving outcomes. For example, a service that enables a business unit to process orders should allow sales people to access customer details, stock availability, shipping information etc. Any aspect of the service that improves the ability of sales people to improve the performance of the task of processing sales orders would be considered utility. Utility can therefore represent any attribute of a service that removes, or reduces the effect of, constraints on the performance of a task.

Warranty is an assurance that a product or service will meet its agreed requirements. This may be a formal agreement such as a service level agreement or contract, or a marketing message or brand image. Warranty refers to the ability of a service to be available when needed, to provide the required capacity, and to provide the required reliability in terms of continuity and security. Warranty can be summarized as 'how the service is delivered', and can be used to determine whether a service is 'fit for use'. For example, any aspect of the service that increases the availability or speed of the service would be considered warranty. Warranty can therefore represent any attribute of a service that increases the potential of the business to be able to perform a task. Warranty refers to any means by which utility is made available to the users.

Utility is *what* the service does, and warranty is *how* it is delivered.

Customers cannot benefit from something that is fit for purpose but not fit for use, and vice versa. The value of a service is therefore only delivered when both utility and warranty are designed and delivered. Figure 2.2 illustrates the logic that a service has to have both utility and warranty to create value. Utility is used to improve the performance of the tasks required to achieve an outcome, or to remove constraints that prevent the task from being performed adequately (or both). Warranty requires the service to be available, continuous and secure and to have sufficient capacity for the service to perform at the required level. If the service is both fit for purpose and fit for use, it will create value.

It should be noted that the elements of warranty in Figure 2.2 are not exclusive. It is possible to define other components of warranty, such as usability, which refers to how easy it is for the user to access and use the features of the service to achieve the desired outcomes.

The warranty aspect of the service needs to be designed at the same time as the utility aspect in order to deliver the required value to the business. Attempts to design warranty aspects after a service has been deployed can be expensive and disruptive.

Information about the desired business outcomes, opportunities, customers, utility and warranty of the service is used to develop the definition of a service. Using an outcome-based definition helps to ensure that managers plan and execute all aspects of service management from the perspective of what is valuable to the customer.

2.1.7 Best practices in the public domain

Organizations benchmark themselves against peers and seek to close gaps in capabilities. This enables them to become more competitive by improving their ability to deliver quality services that meet

Figure 2.2 Logic of value creation through services

the needs of their customers at a price their customers can afford. One way to close such gaps is the adoption of best practices in wide industry use. There are several sources for best practice including public frameworks, standards and the proprietary knowledge of organizations and individuals (Figure 2.3). ITIL is the most widely recognized and trusted source of best-practice guidance in the area of ITSM.

Public frameworks and standards are attractive when compared with proprietary knowledge for the following reasons:

■ Proprietary knowledge is deeply embedded in organizations and therefore difficult to adopt, replicate or even transfer with the cooperation of the owners. Such knowledge is often in the form of tacit knowledge which is inextricable and poorly documented.

■ Proprietary knowledge is customized for the local context and the specific needs of the business to the point of being idiosyncratic. Unless the recipients of such knowledge have

matching circumstances, the knowledge may not be as effective in use.

■ Owners of proprietary knowledge expect to be rewarded for their investments. They may make such knowledge available only under commercial terms through purchases and licensing agreements.

■ Publicly available frameworks and standards such as ITIL, LEAN, Six Sigma, COBIT, CMMI, PRINCE2, PMBOK®, ISO 9000, ISO/IEC 20000 and ISO/IEC 27001 are validated across a diverse set of environments and situations rather than the limited experience of a single organization. They are subject to broad review across multiple organizations and disciplines, and vetted by diverse sets of partners, suppliers and competitors.

■ The knowledge of public frameworks is more likely to be widely distributed among a large community of professionals through publicly available training and certification. It is easier for organizations to acquire such knowledge through the labour market.

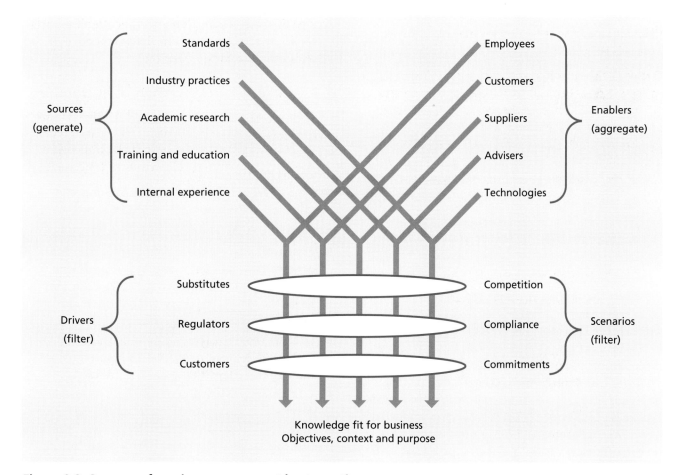

Figure 2.3 Sources of service management best practice

Ignoring public frameworks and standards can needlessly place an organization at a disadvantage. Organizations should cultivate their own proprietary knowledge on top of a body of knowledge based on public frameworks and standards. Collaboration and coordination across organizations become easier on the basis of shared practices and standards. Further information on best practice in the public domain is provided in Appendix A.

2.2 BASIC CONCEPTS

2.2.1 Assets, resources and capabilities

The service relationship between service providers and their customers revolves around the use of assets – both those of the service provider and those of the customer. Each relationship involves an interaction between the assets of each party.

Many customers use the service they receive to build and deliver services or products of their own and then deliver them on to their own customers. In these cases, what the service provider considers to be the customer asset would be considered to be a service asset by their customer.

Without customer assets, there is no basis for defining the value of a service. The performance of customer assets is therefore a primary concern for service management.

> **Definitions**
>
> *Asset:* Any resource or capability.
>
> *Customer asset:* Any resource or capability used by a customer to achieve a business outcome.
>
> *Service asset:* Any resource or capability used by a service provider to deliver services to a customer.

There are two types of asset used by both service providers and customers – resources and capabilities. Organizations use them to create value in the form of goods and services. Resources are direct inputs for production. Capabilities represent an organization's ability to coordinate, control and deploy resources to produce value. Capabilities are typically experience-driven, knowledge-intensive, information-based and firmly embedded within an organization's people, systems, processes

and technologies. It is relatively easy to acquire resources compared to capabilities (see Figure 2.4 for examples of capabilities and resources).

Service providers need to develop distinctive capabilities to retain customers with value propositions that are hard for competitors to duplicate. For example, two service providers may have similar resources such as applications, infrastructure and access to finance. Their capabilities, however, differ in terms of management systems, organization structure, processes and knowledge assets. This difference is reflected in actual performance.

Capabilities by themselves cannot produce value without adequate and appropriate resources. The productive capacity of a service provider is dependent on the resources under its control. Capabilities are used to develop, deploy and coordinate this productive capacity. For example, capabilities such as capacity management and availability management are used to manage the performance and utilization of processes, applications and infrastructure, ensuring service levels are effectively delivered.

2.2.2 Processes

> **Definition: process**
>
> A process is a structured set of activities designed to accomplish a specific objective. A process takes one or more defined inputs and turns them into defined outputs.

Processes define actions, dependencies and sequence. Well-defined processes can improve productivity within and across organizations and functions. Process characteristics include:

- **Measurability** We are able to measure the process in a relevant manner. It is performance-driven. Managers want to measure cost, quality and other variables while practitioners are concerned with duration and productivity.
- **Specific results** The reason a process exists is to deliver a specific result. This result must be individually identifiable and countable.
- **Customers** Every process delivers its primary results to a customer or stakeholder. Customers may be internal or external to the organization, but the process must meet their expectations.

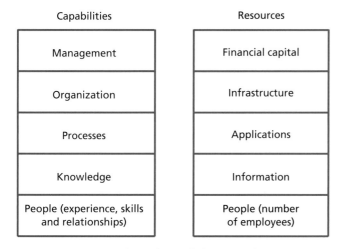

Figure 2.4 *Examples of capabilities and resources*

■ **Responsiveness to specific triggers** While a process may be ongoing or iterative, it should be traceable to a specific trigger.

A process is organized around a set of objectives. The main outputs from the process should be driven by the objectives and should include process measurements (metrics), reports and process improvement.

The output produced by a process has to conform to operational norms that are derived from business objectives. If products conform to the set norm, the process can be considered effective (because it can be repeated, measured and managed, and achieves the required outcome). If the activities of the process are carried out with a minimum use of resources, the process can also be considered efficient.

Inputs are data or information used by the process and may be the output from another process.

A process, or an activity within a process, is initiated by a trigger. A trigger may be the arrival of an input or other event. For example, the failure of a server may trigger the event management and incident management processes.

A process may include any of the roles, responsibilities, tools and management controls required to deliver the outputs reliably. A process

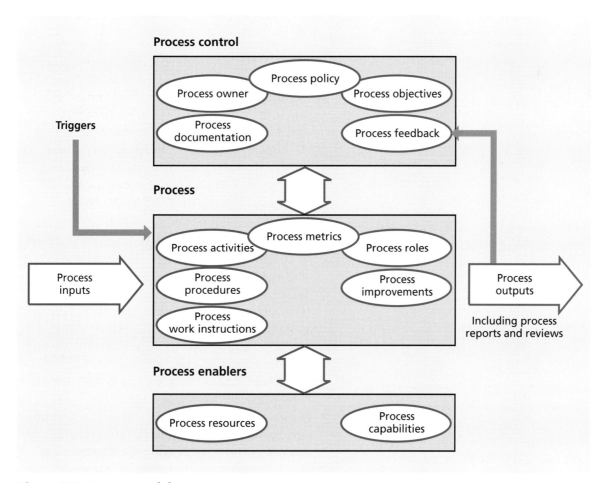

Figure 2.5 *Process model*

may define policies, standards, guidelines, activities and work instructions if they are needed.

Processes, once defined, should be documented and controlled. Once under control, they can be repeated and managed. Process measurement and metrics can be built into the process to control and improve the process as illustrated in Figure 2.5. Process analysis, results and metrics should be incorporated in regular management reports and process improvements.

2.2.3 Organizing for service management

There is no single best way to organize, and best practices described in ITIL need to be tailored to suit individual organizations and situations. Any changes made will need to take into account resource constraints and the size, nature and needs of the business and customers. The starting point for organizational design is strategy. Organizational development for service management is described in more detail in *ITIL Service Strategy* Chapter 6.

2.2.3.1 Functions

A function is a team or group of people and the tools or other resources they use to carry out one or more processes or activities. In larger organizations, a function may be broken out and performed by several departments, teams and groups, or it may be embodied within a single organizational unit (e.g. the service desk). In smaller organizations, one person or group can perform multiple functions – for example, a technical management department could also incorporate the service desk function.

For the service lifecycle to be successful, an organization will need to clearly define the roles and responsibilities required to undertake the processes and activities involved in each lifecycle stage. These roles will need to be assigned to individuals, and an appropriate organization structure of teams, groups or functions will need to be established and managed. These are defined as follows:

- **Group** A group is a number of people who are similar in some way. In ITIL, groups refer to people who perform similar activities – even though they may work on different technologies or report into different organizational structures or even different

companies. Groups are usually not formal organizational structures, but are very useful in defining common processes across the organization – for example, ensuring that all people who resolve incidents complete the incident record in the same way.

- **Team** A team is a more formal type of group. These are people who work together to achieve a common objective, but not necessarily in the same organizational structure. Team members can be co-located, or work in multiple locations and operate virtually. Teams are useful for collaboration, or for dealing with a situation of a temporary or transitional nature. Examples of teams include project teams, application development teams (often consisting of people from several different business units) and incident or problem resolution teams.
- **Department** Departments are formal organizational structures which exist to perform a specific set of defined activities on an ongoing basis. Departments have a hierarchical reporting structure with managers who are usually responsible for the execution of the activities and also for day-to-day management of the staff in the department.
- **Division** A division refers to a number of departments that have been grouped together, often by geography or product line. A division is normally self-contained.

ITIL Service Operation (this publication) describes the following functions in detail:

- **Service desk** The single point of contact for users when there is a service disruption, for service requests, or even for some categories of request for change. The service desk provides a point of communication to users and a point of coordination for several IT groups and processes.
- **Technical management** Provides detailed technical skills and resources needed to support the ongoing operation of IT services and the management of the IT infrastructure. Technical management also plays an important role in the design, testing, release and improvement of IT services.
- **IT operations management** Executes the daily operational activities needed to manage IT services and the supporting IT infrastructure. This is done according to the performance standards defined during service design. IT

operations management has two sub-functions that are generally organizationally distinct. These are IT operations control and facilities management.
- **Application management** Is responsible for managing applications throughout their lifecycle. The application management function supports and maintains operational applications and also plays an important role in the design, testing and improvement of applications that form part of IT services.

The other core ITIL publications do not define any functions in detail, but they do rely on the technical and application management functions described in this publication. Technical and application management provide the technical resources and expertise to manage the whole service lifecycle, and practitioner roles within a particular lifecycle stage may be performed by members of these functions.

2.2.3.2 Roles

A number of roles need to be performed during the service lifecycle. The core ITIL publications provide guidelines and examples of role descriptions. These are not exhaustive or prescriptive, and in many cases roles will need to be combined or separated. Organizations should take care to apply this guidance in a way that suits their own structure and objectives.

Definition: role

A role is a set of responsibilities, activities and authorities granted to a person or team. A role is defined in a process or function. One person or team may have multiple roles – for example, the roles of configuration manager and change manager may be carried out by a single person.

Roles are often confused with job titles but it is important to realize that they are not the same. Each organization will define appropriate job titles and job descriptions which suit their needs, and individuals holding these job titles can perform one or more of the required roles.

It should also be recognized that a person may, as part of their job assignment, perform a single task that represents participation in more than one process. For example, a technical analyst who submits a request for change (RFC) to add

memory to a server to resolve a performance problem is participating in activities of the change management process at the same time as taking part in activities of the capacity management and problem management processes.

See Chapter 6 for more details about the roles and responsibilities described in *ITIL Service Operation*.

2.2.3.3 Organizational culture and behaviour

Organizational culture is the set of shared values and norms that control the service provider's interactions with all stakeholders, including customers, users, suppliers, internal staff etc. An organization's values are desired modes of behaviour that affect its culture. Examples of organizational values include high standards, customer care, respecting tradition and authority, acting cautiously and conservatively, and being frugal.

High-performing service providers continually align the value network for efficiency and effectiveness. Culture through the value network is transmitted to staff through socialization, training programmes, stories, ceremonies and language.

Constraints such as governance, capabilities, standards, resources, values and ethics play a significant role in organizational culture and behaviour. Organizational culture can also be affected by structure or management styles resulting in a positive or negative impact on performance. Organizational structures and management styles contribute to the behaviour of people, process, technology and partners. These are important aspects in adopting service management practices and ITIL.

Change related to service management programmes will affect organizational culture and it is important to prepare people with effective communication plans, training, policies and procedures to achieve the desired performance outcomes. Establishing cultural change is also an important factor for collaborative working between the many different people involved in service management. Managing people through service transitions is discussed at more length in Chapter 5 of *ITIL Service Transition*.

2.2.4 The service portfolio

The service portfolio is the complete set of services that is managed by a service provider and it represents the service provider's commitments and investments across all customers and market spaces. It also represents present contractual commitments, new service development, and ongoing service improvement plans initiated by continual service improvement. The portfolio may include third-party services, which are an integral part of service offerings to customers.

The service portfolio represents all the resources presently engaged or being released in various stages of the service lifecycle. It is a database or structured document in three parts:

■ **Service pipeline** All services that are under consideration or development, but are not yet available to customers. It includes major investment opportunities that have to be traced to the delivery of services, and the value that will be realized. The service pipeline provides a business view of possible future services and is part of the service portfolio that is not normally published to customers.

■ **Service catalogue** All live IT services, including those available for deployment. It is the only part of the service portfolio published to customers, and is used to support the sale and delivery of IT services. It includes a customer-facing view (or views) of the IT services in use, how they are intended to be used, the business processes they enable, and the levels and quality of service the customer can expect for each service. The service catalogue also includes information about supporting services required by the service provider to deliver customer-facing services. Information about services can only enter the service catalogue after due diligence has been performed on related costs and risks.

■ **Retired services** All services that have been phased out or retired. Retired services are not available to new customers or contracts unless a special business case is made.

Service providers often find it useful to distinguish customer-facing services from supporting services:

■ **Customer-facing services** IT services that are visible to the customer. These are normally services that support the customer's business processes and facilitate one or more outcomes desired by the customer.

■ **Supporting services** IT services that support or 'underpin' the customer-facing services. These are typically invisible to the customer, but are

essential to the delivery of customer-facing IT services.

Figure 2.6 illustrates the components of the service portfolio, which are discussed in detail in *ITIL Service Strategy*. These are important components of the service knowledge management system (SKMS) described in section 2.2.5.

2.2.5 Knowledge management and the SKMS

Quality knowledge and information enable people to perform process activities and support the flow of information between service lifecycle stages and processes. Understanding, defining, establishing and maintaining information is a responsibility of the knowledge management process.

Implementing an SKMS enables effective decision support and reduces the risks that arise from a lack of proper mechanisms. However, implementing an SKMS can involve a large investment in tools to store and manage data, information and knowledge. Every organization will start this work in a different place, and have their own vision of where they want to be, so there is no simple answer to the question 'What tools and systems are needed to support knowledge management?' Data, information and knowledge need to be interrelated across the organization. A document management system and/or a configuration management system (CMS) can be used as a foundation for implementation of the SKMS.

Figure 2.7 illustrates an architecture for service knowledge management that has four layers including examples of possible content at each layer. These are:

■ **Presentation layer** Enables searching, browsing, retrieving, updating, subscribing and collaboration. The different views onto the other layers are suitable for different audiences. Each view should be protected to ensure that only authorized people can see or modify the underlying knowledge, information and data.

■ **Knowledge processing layer** Is where the information is converted into useful knowledge which enables decision-making.

■ **Information integration layer** Provides integrated information that may be gathered from data in multiple sources in the data layer.

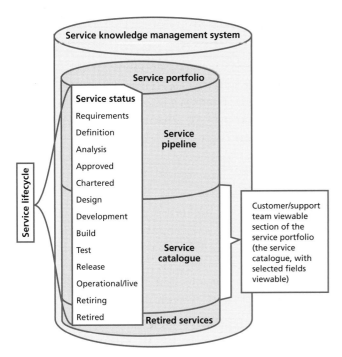

Figure 2.6 The service portfolio and its contents

■ **Data layer**   Includes tools for data discovery and data collection, and data items in unstructured and structured forms.

In practice, an SKMS is likely to consist of multiple tools and repositories. For example, there may be a tool that provides all four layers for the support of different processes or combinations of processes. Various tools providing a range of perspectives will be used by different stakeholders to access this common repository for collaborative decision support.

This architecture is applicable for many of the management information systems in ITIL. A primary component of the SKMS is the service portfolio, covered in section 2.2.4. Other examples include the CMS, the availability management information system (AMIS) and the capacity management information system (CMIS).

2.3 GOVERNANCE AND MANAGEMENT SYSTEMS

2.3.1 Governance

Governance is the single overarching area that ties IT and the business together, and services are one way of ensuring that the organization is able to execute that governance. Governance is what defines the common directions, policies and

rules that both the business and IT use to conduct business.

Many ITSM strategies fail because they try to build a structure or processes according to how they would like the organization to work instead of working within the existing governance structures.

> **Definition: governance**
>
> Ensures that policies and strategy are actually implemented, and that required processes are correctly followed. Governance includes defining roles and responsibilities, measuring and reporting, and taking actions to resolve any issues identified.

Governance works to apply a consistently managed approach at all levels of the organization – first by ensuring a clear strategy is set, then by defining the policies whereby the strategy will be achieved. The policies also define boundaries, or what the organization may not do as part of its operations.

Governance needs to be able to evaluate, direct and monitor the strategy, policies and plans. Further information on governance and service management is provided in Chapter 5 of *ITIL Service Strategy*. The international standard for corporate governance of IT is ISO/IEC 38500, described in Appendix A.

2.3.2 Management systems

A system is a number of related things that work together to achieve an overall objective. Systems should be self-regulating for agility and timeliness. In order to accomplish this, the relationships within the system must influence one another for the sake of the whole. Key components of the system are the structure and processes that work together.

A systems approach to service management ensures learning and improvement through a big-picture view of services and service management. It extends the management horizon and provides a sustainable long-term approach.

By understanding the system structure, the interconnections between all the assets and service components, and how changes in any area will affect the whole system and its constituent parts over time, a service provider can deliver benefits such as:

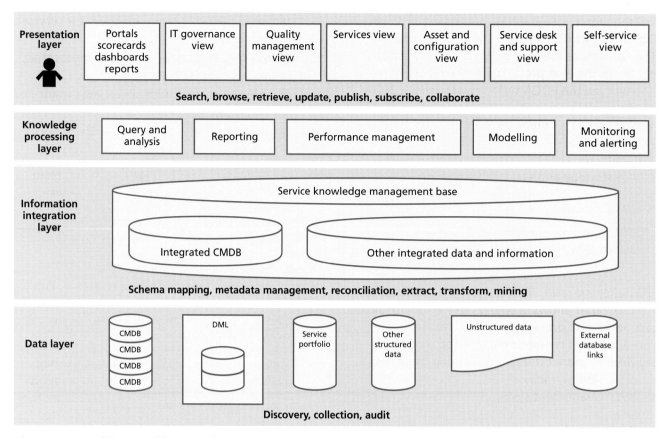

Figure 2.7 Architectural layers of an SKMS

- Ability to adapt to the changing needs of customers and markets
- Sustainable performance
- Better approach to managing services, risks, costs and value delivery
- Effective and efficient service management
- Simplified approach that is easier for people to use
- Less conflict between processes
- Reduced duplication and bureaucracy.

Many businesses have adopted management system standards for competitive advantage and to ensure a consistent approach in implementing service management across their value network. Implementation of a management system also provides support for governance (see section 2.3.1).

Definition: management system (ISO 9001)

The framework of policy, processes, functions, standards, guidelines and tools that ensures an organization or part of an organization can achieve its objectives.

A management system of an organization can adopt multiple management system standards, such as:

- A quality management system (ISO 9001)
- An environmental management system (ISO 14000)
- A service management system (ISO/IEC 20000)
- An information security management system (ISO/IEC 27001)
- A management system for software asset management (ISO/IEC 19770).

Service providers are increasingly adopting these standards to be able to demonstrate their service management capability. As there are common elements between such management systems, they should be managed in an integrated way rather than having separate management systems. To meet the requirements of a specific management system standard, an organization needs to analyse the requirements of the relevant standard in detail and compare them with those that have already been incorporated in the existing integrated management system. Appendix A provides further information on these standards.

ISO management system standards use the Plan-Do Check Act (PDCA) cycle shown in Figure 2.8. The ITIL service lifecycle approach embraces and enhances the interpretation of the PDCA cycle. You will see the PDCA cycle used in the structure of the guidance provided in each of the core ITIL publications. This guidance recognizes the need to drive governance, organizational design and management systems from the business strategy, service strategy and service requirements.

> **Definition: ISO/IEC 20000**
>
> An international standard for IT service management.

ISO/IEC 20000 is an internationally recognized standard that allows organizations to demonstrate excellence and prove best practice in ITSM. Part 1 specifies requirements for the service provider to plan, establish, implement, operate, monitor, review, maintain and improve a service management system (SMS). Coordinated integration and implementation of an SMS, to meet the Part 1 requirements, provides ongoing control, greater effectiveness, efficiency and opportunities for continual improvement. It ensures that the service provider:

- Understands and fulfils the service requirements to achieve customer satisfaction

- Establishes the policy and objectives for service management
- Designs and delivers changes and services that add value for the customer
- Monitors, measures and reviews performance of the SMS and the services
- Continually improves the SMS and the services based on objective measurements.

Service providers across the world have successfully established an SMS to direct and control their service management activities. The adoption of an SMS should be a strategic decision for an organization.

One of the most common routes for an organization to achieve the requirements of ISO/IEC 20000 is by adopting ITIL service management best practices and using the ITIL qualification scheme for professional development.

Certification to ISO/IEC 20000-1 by an accredited certification body shows that a service provider is committed to delivering value to its customers and continual service improvement. It demonstrates the existence of an effective SMS that satisfies the requirements of an independent external audit. Certification gives a service provider a competitive edge in marketing. Many organizations specify a requirement to comply with ISO/IEC 20000 in their contracts and agreements.

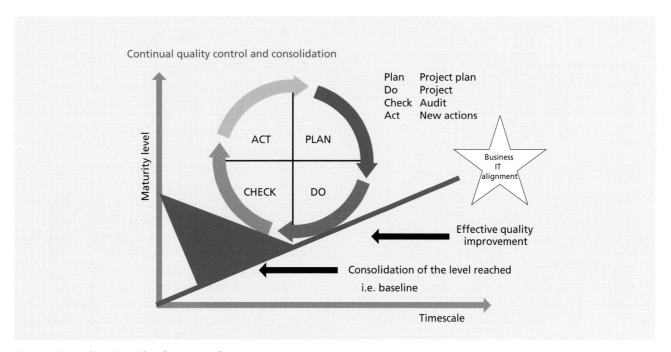

Figure 2.8 Plan-Do-Check-Act cycle

2.4 THE SERVICE LIFECYCLE

Services and processes describe how things change, whereas structure describes how they are connected. Structure helps to determine the correct behaviours required for service management.

Structure describes how process, people, technology and partners are connected. Structure is essential for organizing information. Without structure, our service management knowledge is merely a collection of observations, practices and conflicting goals. The structure of the service lifecycle is an organizing framework, supported by the organizational structure, service portfolio and service models within an organization. Structure can influence or determine the behaviour of the organization and people. Altering the structure of service management can be more effective than simply controlling discrete events.

Without structure, it is difficult to learn from experience. It is difficult to use the past to educate for the future. We can learn from experience but we also need to confront directly many of the most important consequences of our actions.

See Chapter 1 for an introduction to each ITIL service lifecycle stage.

2.4.1 Specialization and coordination across the lifecycle

Organizations need a collaborative approach for the management of assets which are used to deliver and support services for their customers.

Organizations should function in the same manner as a high-performing sports team. Each player in a team and each member of the team's organization who are not players position themselves to

Table 2.1 The processes described in each core ITIL publication

Core ITIL lifecycle publication	Processes described in the publication
ITIL Service Strategy	Strategy management for IT services
	Service portfolio management
	Financial management for IT services
	Demand management
	Business relationship management
ITIL Service Design	Design coordination
	Service catalogue management
	Service level management
	Availability management
	Capacity management
	IT service continuity management
	Information security management
	Supplier management
ITIL Service Transition	Transition planning and support
	Change management
	Service asset and configuration management
	Release and deployment management
	Service validation and testing
	Change evaluation
	Knowledge management
ITIL Service Operation	Event management
	Incident management
	Request fulfilment
	Problem management
	Access management
ITIL Continual Service Improvement	Seven-step improvement process

support the goal of the team. Each player and team member has a different specialization that contributes to the whole. The team matures over time taking into account feedback from experience, best practice, current process and procedures to become an agile high-performing team.

Specialization and coordination are necessary in the lifecycle approach. Specialization allows for expert focus on components of the service but components of the service also need to work together for value. Specialization combined with coordination helps to manage expertise, improve focus and reduce overlaps and gaps in processes. Specialization and coordination together help to create a collaborative and agile organizational architecture that maximizes utilization of assets.

Coordination across the lifecycle creates an environment focused on business and customer outcomes instead of just IT objectives and projects. Coordination is also essential between functional groups, across the value network, and between processes and technology.

Feedback and control between organizational assets helps to enable operational efficiency, organizational effectiveness and economies of scale.

2.4.2 Processes through the service lifecycle

Each core ITIL lifecycle publication includes guidance on service management processes as shown in Table 2.1.

Service management is more effective if people have a clear understanding of how processes interact throughout the service lifecycle, within the organization and with other parties (users, customers, suppliers).

Process integration across the service lifecycle depends on the service owner, process owners, process practitioners and other stakeholders understanding:

- The context of use, scope, purpose and limits of each process
- The strategies, policies and standards that apply to the processes and to the management of interfaces between processes
- Authorities and responsibilities of those involved in each process

- The information provided by each process that flows from one process to another; who produces it; and how it is used by integrated processes.

Integrating service management processes depends on the flow of information across process and organizational boundaries. This in turn depends on implementing supporting technology and management information systems across organizational boundaries, rather than in silos. If service management processes are implemented, followed or changed in isolation, they can become a bureaucratic overhead that does not deliver value for money. They could also damage or negate the operation or value of other processes and services.

As discussed in section 2.2.2, each process has a clear scope with a structured set of activities that transform inputs to deliver the outputs reliably. A process interface is the boundary of the process. Process integration is the linking of processes by ensuring that information flows from one process to another effectively and efficiently. If there is management commitment to process integration, processes are generally easier to implement and there will be fewer conflicts between processes.

Stages of the lifecycle work together as an integrated system to support the ultimate objective of service management for business value realization. Every stage is interdependent as shown in Figure 2.9. See Appendix I for examples of inputs and outputs across the service lifecycle.

The SKMS, described in section 2.2.5, enables integration across the service lifecycle stages. It provides secure and controlled access to the knowledge, information and data that are needed to manage and deliver services. The service portfolio represents all the assets presently engaged or being released in various stages of the lifecycle.

Chapter 1 provides a summary of each stage in the service lifecycle but it is also important to understand how the lifecycle stages work together.

Service strategy establishes policies and principles that provide guidance for the whole service lifecycle. The service portfolio is defined in this lifecycle stage, and new or changed services are chartered.

During the service design stage of the lifecycle, everything needed to transition and operate

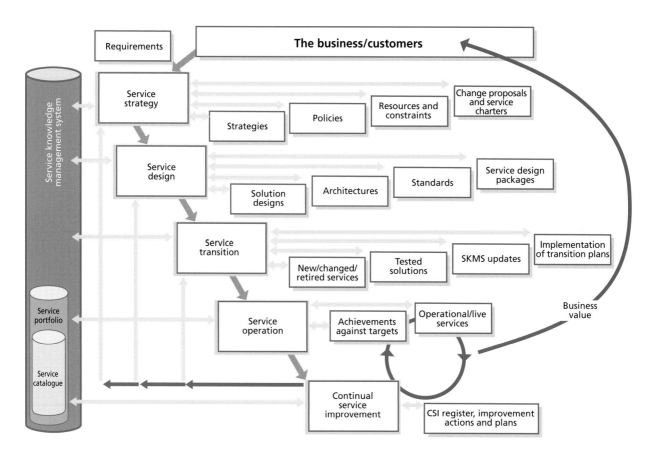

Figure 2.9 Integration across the service lifecycle

the new or changed service is documented in a service design package. This lifecycle stage also designs everything needed to create, transition and operate the services, including management information systems and tools, architectures, processes, measurement methods and metrics.

The activities of the service transition and service operation stages of the lifecycle are defined during service design. Service transition ensures that the requirements of the service strategy, developed in service design, are effectively realized in service operation while controlling the risks of failure and disruption.

The service operation stage of the service lifecycle carries out the activities and processes required to deliver the agreed services. During this stage of the lifecycle, the value defined in the service strategy is realized.

Continual service improvement acts in tandem with all the other lifecycle stages. All processes, activities, roles, services and technology should be measured and subjected to continual improvement.

Most ITIL processes and functions have activities that take place across multiple stages of the service lifecycle. For example:

■ The service validation and testing process may design tests during the service design stage and perform these tests during service transition.

■ The technical management function may provide input to strategic decisions about technology, as well as assisting in the design and transition of infrastructure components.

■ Business relationship managers may assist in gathering detailed requirements during the service design stage of the lifecycle, or take part in the management of major incidents during the service operation stage.

■ All service lifecycle stages contribute to the seven-step improvement process.

Appendix I identifies some of the major inputs and outputs between each stage of the service lifecycle. Chapter 3 of each core ITIL publication provides more detail on the inputs and outputs of the specific lifecycle stage it describes.

Figure 2.10 Continual service improvement and the service lifecycle

The strength of the service lifecycle rests upon continual feedback throughout each stage of the lifecycle. This feedback ensures that service optimization is managed from a business perspective and is measured in terms of the value the business derives from services at any point in time during the service lifecycle. The service lifecycle is non-linear in design. At every point in the service lifecycle, the process of monitoring, assessment and feedback between each stage drives decisions about the need for minor course corrections or major service improvement initiatives.

Figure 2.10 illustrates some examples of the continual feedback system built into the service lifecycle.

Adopting appropriate technology to automate the processes and provide management with the information that supports the processes is also important for effective and efficient service management.

Service operation principles

3

3 Service operation principles

When considering service operation it is tempting to focus only on managing day-to-day activities and technology as ends in themselves. However, service operation exists within a far greater context.

As part of the service lifecycle, service operation is responsible for:

- Executing and performing processes that optimize the cost and quality of services
- Enabling the business to meet its objectives.

As part of the world of technology, service operation is responsible for:

- Effective functioning of components that support services
- Execution of operation control activities to manage and deliver services.

As part of the overall business, service operation is responsible for:

- Delivering services efficiently and at acceptable cost
- Delivering services within prescribed service levels
- Maintaining user satisfaction with IT services.

It is through the service operation lifecycle stage that the business directly sees and receives value from its IT investments. The principles in this chapter are aimed at helping service operation practitioners to recognize this important aspect and to achieve a balance between all of these responsibilities. This balance must focus on effectively managing the day-to-day aspects while maintaining a perspective of the greater context.

3.1 SERVICE OPERATION FUNDAMENTALS

3.1.1 Providing business value through service operation

Each stage in the service lifecycle provides value to business. For example, service value is modelled in service strategy; the cost of the service is designed, predicted and validated in service design and service transition; and measures for optimization

are identified in continual service improvement (CSI). The operation of service is where these plans, designs and optimizations are executed and measured. From a customer viewpoint, service operation is where actual value is seen.

To achieve business value, service operation cannot solely focus on the day-to-day operation and delivery of services. Other challenges exist outside that focus that can put business value at risk:

- Once a service has been designed and tested, it is expected to run within the budgetary and return on investment (ROI) targets established earlier in the lifecycle. In reality, however, very few organizations plan effectively for the costs of ongoing management of services. It is very easy to quantify the costs of a project, but very difficult to quantify what the service will cost after three years of operation.
- It is difficult to obtain funding during the operational stage, to fix design flaws or unforeseen requirements – because this was not part of the original value proposition. In many cases it is only after some time in operation that these problems surface. Most organizations do not have a formal mechanism to review operational services for design and value. This is left to incident and problem management to resolve – as if it is purely an operational issue.
- It is difficult to obtain additional funding for tools or actions (including training) aimed at improving the efficiency of service operation. This is partly because they are not directly linked to the functionality of a specific service and partly because there is an expectation from the customer that these costs should have been built into the cost of the service from the beginning. Unfortunately, the rate of technology change is very high. Shortly after a solution has been deployed that will efficiently manage a set of services, new technology becomes available that can do it faster, cheaper and more effectively.
- Once a service has been operational for some time, it becomes part of the baseline of what the business expects from the IT services. Attempts to optimize the service or to use new

tools to manage it more effectively are seen as successful only if the service has been very problematic in the past. In other words, some services are taken for granted and any action to optimize them is perceived as 'fixing services that are not broken'.

This publication suggests a number of processes, functions and measures aimed at addressing these areas.

3.1.2 Optimizing service operation performance

Service operation is optimized in two ways:

■ **Long-term incremental improvement** This is based on evaluating the performance and output of all service operation processes, technologies, functions and outputs over time. The reports are analysed and a decision made about whether improvement is needed and, if so, how best to implement it through service design and transition. Examples include the deployment of a new set of tools, changes to process designs, reconfiguration of the infrastructure etc. This type of improvement is covered in detail in *ITIL Continual Service Improvement*.

■ **Short-term ongoing improvements** These are the improvements made to working

practices within the processes, functions and technologies that underpin service operation itself. They are generally smaller improvements that are implemented without any change to the fundamental nature of a process or technology. Examples include tuning, workload balancing, personnel redeployment and training etc.

Although both of these are discussed in some detail within the scope of this publication, *ITIL Continual Service Improvement* provides a framework and alternatives within which improvement may be driven as part of the overall support of business objectives. See *ITIL Service Transition* for further detail on the change management process.

3.1.3 Processes within service operation

There are a number of key service operation processes that must link together to provide an effective overall IT support structure. The overall structure is briefly described here and then each of the processes is described in more detail in Chapter 4.

3.1.3.1 Event management

Event management manages events throughout their lifecycle. This lifecycle includes coordination activities to detect events, make sense of them and determine the appropriate control action.

Service: Desktop support

Request types

- Install a desktop
- Move a desktop
- Upgrade a desktop
- Remove a desktop
- Replace a desktop
- Add a keyboard

Service: Email support

Request types
- Add a user
- Delete a user
- Change a password
- Increase a mailbox size
- Add groups of users

Service: Development support

Request types
- Install a developer workstation
- Restore a development environment
- Migrate code from development to test environment
- Install a development server

Figure 3.1 Examples of service requests linked to IT services

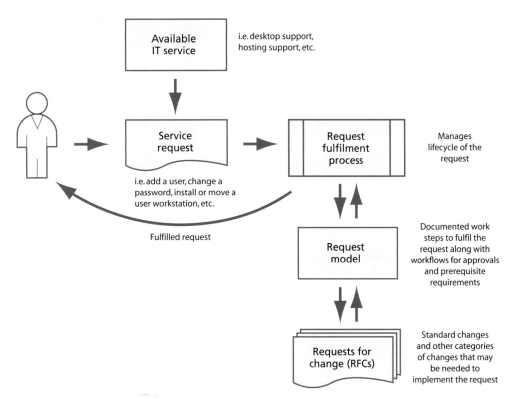

Figure 3.2 Relationship between a service, service request, request model and request for change

3.1.3.2 Incident management

Incident management concentrates on restoring unexpectedly degraded or disrupted services to users as quickly as possible, in order to minimize business impact.

3.1.3.3 Problem management

Problem management involves root cause analysis to determine and resolve the underlying causes of incidents, and proactive activities to detect and prevent future problems/incidents. This also includes the creation of known error records that document root causes and workarounds to allow quicker diagnosis and resolution should further incidents occur.

3.1.3.4 Request fulfilment

Request fulfilment is the process for managing the lifecycle of all service requests. Service requests are managed throughout their lifecycle from initial request to fulfilment using separate request fulfilment records/tables to record and track their status.

Service requests are the mechanism by which users formally request something from an IT service provider. Service requests are transactional and associated with the standard services that a provider is delivering. Examples might include those shown in Figure 3.1.

A service request is associated with a request model that defines any prerequisites, authorizations needed and standard work steps and activities to fulfil it. As part of that request model, standard changes and other types of requests for change (RFCs) may be needed to complete fulfilment actions. Figure 3.2 illustrates the relationship between a service, service request, request model and RFC.

3.1.3.5 Access management

Access management is the process of granting authorized users the rights to use a service, while restricting access to non-authorized users. It is based on being able accurately to identify authorized users and then manage their ability to access services as required for their specific organizational role or job function. Access management has also been called identity or rights management in some organizations. It should fully support the policies designed in the information security management process (see *ITIL Service Design*) with respect to roles, rights and segregation of duties.

3.1.4 Functions within service operation

Processes alone will not result in effective service operation. A stable infrastructure and appropriately skilled people are needed as well. To achieve this, service operation relies on several functions to execute operational tasks. Functions include groups of skilled people who carry out one or more service lifecycle processes and activities. Within service operation, there are four main functions, listed here and discussed in detail in Chapter 6.

3.1.4.1 Service desk

The service desk is the single point of contact for users when there is a service disruption, for service requests, or even for some categories of RFC. The service desk provides a point of communication to the users and a point of coordination for several IT groups and processes.

3.1.4.2 Technical management

Technical management provides detailed technical skills and resources needed to support the ongoing operation of IT services and the management of the IT infrastructure. Technical management also plays an important role in the design, testing, release and improvement of IT services. In small organizations, it is possible to manage this expertise in a single department, but larger organizations are typically split into a number of technically specialized departments.

3.1.4.3 IT operations management

IT operations management executes the daily operational activities needed to manage IT services and the supporting IT infrastructure. This is done according to the performance standards defined during service design. In some organizations this is a single, centralized department, while in others some activities and staff are centralized and some are provided by distributed or specialized departments. IT operations management has two sub-functions that are unique and are generally organizationally distinct. These are:

- **IT operations control** This is generally staffed by shifts of operators which ensures that routine operational tasks are carried out. IT operations control will also provide centralized monitoring and control activities, usually using an operations bridge or network operations centre.

- **Facilities management** This refers to the management of the physical IT environment, usually data centres or computer rooms. In many organizations technical and application management are co-located with IT operations in large data centres.

3.1.4.4 Application management

Application management is responsible for managing applications throughout their lifecycle. The application management function supports and maintains operational applications and also plays an important role in the design, testing and improvement of applications that form part of IT services.

ITIL views application management differently from application development. Within IT, application development is typically focused around internal activities to design, build, test and deploy IT solutions being constructed within the IT organization. Application management takes a much broader view that recognizes the capabilities in today's marketplace to obtain applications from many sources other than the internal IT organization. In addition, it also focuses on the ongoing management and maintenance of applications that takes place once applications have been deployed.

Examples of this broader view take into account all of:

- Applications being developed within the IT organization
- Applications purchased and sourced from a third party
- Applications that may be cloud-based such as Software as a Service (SaaS) solutions (see *ITIL Service Strategy*, section C.2)
- Application maintenance and other activities to manage applications on an ongoing basis
- Application upgrades
- Application licensing and compliance with legal requirements
- Application compliance with other industry requirements such as specialized needs for controls, standards or compliance with disability requirements
- Warranty considerations to ensure that applications can be operated on an ongoing basis at acceptable cost and risk.

Application management may be divided into departments based on the application portfolio of the organization, thus allowing easier specialization and more focused support.

3.2 ACHIEVING BALANCE IN SERVICE OPERATION

Service operation is more than just the repetitive execution of a standard set of procedures or activities. All functions, processes and activities are designed to deliver a specified and agreed level of services, but they have to be delivered in an ever-changing environment.

This forms a conflict between maintaining the status quo and adapting to changes in the business and technological environments. One of service operation's key roles is to deal with this conflict and to achieve a balance between conflicting sets of priorities.

This section highlights some of those key tensions and conflicts. It identifies how IT organizations can recognize that they are suffering from an imbalance by tending more towards one extreme or the other. It also provides some high-level guidelines on how to resolve the conflict and thus move towards a best-practice approach. Every conflict represents an opportunity for growth and improvement.

3.2.1 Internal IT view versus external business view

The most fundamental conflict in all stages of the service lifecycle is between the view of IT as a set of IT services (the external business view) and the view of IT as a set of technology components (internal IT view):

- The external view of IT is the way in which services are experienced by its users and customers. They do not always understand, nor do they wish to care about, the details of what technology is used to manage those services. All they are concerned about is that the services are delivered as required and agreed.
- The internal view of IT is the way in which IT components and systems are managed to deliver the services. Because IT systems are complex and diverse, this often means that the technology is managed by several different teams or departments – each of which is

focused on achieving good performance and availability of 'its' systems.

The whole point of service management is to balance these views to meet the objectives of the organization as a whole. It is critical to structure services around customers. At the same time, it is possible to compromise the quality of services by not thinking about how they will be delivered.

Both views are necessary when delivering services. The organization that focuses only on business requirements without thinking about how they are going to deliver will end up making promises that cannot be kept. The organization that focuses only on internal systems without thinking about what services they support will end up with expensive services that deliver little value.

The potential for role conflict between the external and internal views is the result of many variables, including the maturity of the organization, its management culture, its history etc. This makes a balance difficult to achieve, and most organizations tend more towards one role than the other. Of course, no organization will be totally internally or externally focused, but will find itself in a position along a spectrum between the two. This is illustrated in Figure 3.3.

Table 3.1 outlines some examples of the characteristics of positions at the extreme ends of the spectrum. The purpose of this table is to help organizations identify to which extreme they are closer, not to identify real-life positions to which organizations should aspire.

Building service operation with a balance between internal and external focus requires a long-term, dedicated approach reflected in all stages of the IT

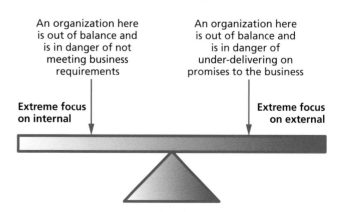

Figure 3.3 Achieving a balance between external and internal focus

Table 3.1 Examples of extreme internal and external focus

	Extreme internal focus	Extreme external focus
Primary focus	Performance and management of IT infrastructure devices, systems and staff, with little regard to the end result on the IT service	Achieving high levels of IT service performance with little regard to how it is achieved
Metrics	Focus on technical performance without showing what this means for services	Focus on external metrics without showing internal staff how these are derived or how they can be improved
	Internal metrics (e.g. network uptime) reported to the business instead of service performance metrics	Internal staff are expected to devise their own metrics to measure internal performance
Customer/user experience	High consistency of delivery, but only delivers a portion of what the business needs	Poor consistency of delivery
		'IT consists of good people with good intentions, but cannot always execute'
	Prefers to have a standard set of services for all business units	Reactive mode of operation
		Prefers to deliver customized services upon request
Operations strategy and design	Standard operations across the board	Multiple delivery teams and multiple technologies
	All new services need to fit into the current architecture and procedures	New technologies require new operations approaches and often new IT operations teams
Procedures and manuals	Focus purely on how to manage the technology, not on how its performance relates to IT services	Focuses primarily on what needs to be done and when and less on how this should be achieved
Cost strategy	Cost reduction achieved purely through technology consolidation	Budget allocated on the basis of which business unit is perceived to have the most need
	Optimization of operational procedures and resources	Less articulate or vocal business units often have inferior services as there is not enough funding allocated to their services
	Business impact of cost cutting often only understood later	
	ROI calculations are focused purely on cost savings or 'payback periods'	
Training	Training is conducted as an apprenticeship, where new operations staff have to learn the way things have to be done, not why	Training is conducted on a project-by-project basis
		There are no standard training courses because operational procedures and technology are constantly changing
Operations staff	Specialized staff, organized according to technical specialty	Generalist staff, organized partly according to technical capability and partly according to their relationship with a business unit
	Staff work on the false assumption that good technical achievement is the same as good customer service	Reliance on 'heroics', where staff go out of their way to resolve problems that could have been prevented by better internal processes

service management (ITSM) service lifecycle. This will require the following:

- An understanding of what services are used by the business and why
- An understanding of the relative importance and impact of those services on the business
- An understanding of how technology is used to provide IT services
- Involvement of service operation in CSI projects that aim to identify ways of delivering more, increase service quality and lower cost
- Procedures and manuals that outline the role of IT operations in both the management of technology and the delivery of IT services
- A clearly differentiated set of metrics to report to the business on the achievement of service objectives; and to report to IT managers on the efficiency and effectiveness of service operation
- All IT operations staff understand exactly how the performance of the technology affects the delivery of IT services and in turn how these affect the business and the business goals
- A set of standard services delivered consistently to all business units and a set of non-standard (sometimes customized) services delivered to specific business units – together with sets of standard operating procedures (SOPs) that can meet both sets of requirements
- A cost strategy aimed at balancing the requirements of different business units with the cost savings available through optimization of existing technology or investment in new technology – and an understanding of the cost strategy by all involved IT resources
- A value-based, rather than cost-based, ROI strategy
- Involvement of IT operations staff in the service design and service transition stages of the service lifecycle
- Input from and feedback to CSI to identify areas where there is an imbalance and the means to identify and enforce improvement
- A clear communication and training plan for business. While many organizations are good at developing communication plans for projects, this often does not extend into their operational stage.

3.2.2 Stability versus responsiveness

No matter how good the functionality of an IT service and no matter how well it has been designed, it will be worth far less if the service components are not available or if they perform inconsistently.

This means that service operation needs to ensure that the IT infrastructure is stable and available as designed. At the same time, service operation needs to recognize that business and IT requirements change.

Some of these changes are evolutionary. For example, the functionality, performance and architecture of a platform may change over a number of years. Each change brings with it an opportunity to provide better levels of service to the business. In evolutionary changes, it is possible to plan how to respond to the change and thus maintain stability while responding to the changes.

Many changes, though, happen very quickly and sometimes under extreme pressure. For example, a business unit unexpectedly wins a contract that requires additional IT services, more capacity and faster response times. The ability to respond to this type of change without impacting other services is a significant challenge.

Many IT organizations are unable to achieve this balance and tend to focus on either the stability of the IT infrastructure or the ability to respond to changes quickly (Figure 3.4).

Table 3.2 outlines some examples of the characteristics of positions at extreme ends of the spectrum. The purpose of this table is to help organizations identify to which extreme they are closer, not to identify real-life positions to which organizations should aspire.

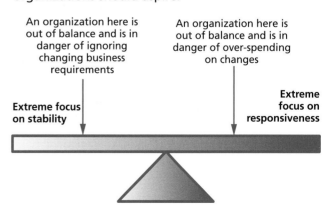

Figure 3.4 Achieving a balance between focus on stability and responsiveness

Table 3.2 Examples of extreme focus on stability and responsiveness

	Extreme focus on stability	Extreme focus on responsiveness
Primary focus	Technology Developing and refining standard IT management techniques and processes	Output to the business Agrees to required changes before determining what it will take to deliver them
Typical problems experienced	IT can demonstrate that it is complying with SOPs and operational level agreements (OLAs), even when there is clear misalignment to business requirements	IT staff are not available to define or execute routine tasks because they are busy on projects for new services
Technology growth strategy	Growth strategy based on analysing existing demand on existing systems New services are resisted and business units sometimes take ownership of 'their own' systems to get access to new services	Technology purchased for each new business requirement Using multiple technologies and solutions for similar solutions, to meet slightly different business needs
Technology used to deliver IT services	Existing or standard technology to be used; services must be adjusted to work within existing parameters	Over-provisioning. No attempt is made to model the new service on the existing infrastructure. New, dedicated technology is purchased for each new project
Capacity management	Forecasts based on projections of current workloads System performance is maintained at consistent levels through tuning and demand management, not by workload forecasting and management	Forecasts based on future business activity for each service individually and do not take into account IT activity or other IT services Existing workloads not relevant

Building an IT organization that achieves a balance between stability and responsiveness in service operation will require the following actions:

- Ensure investment in technologies and processes that are adaptive rather than rigid, e.g. virtual server and application technology and the use of change models (see *ITIL Service Transition*).
- Build a strong service level management (SLM) process which is active from the service design stage to the CSI stage of the service lifecycle.
- Foster integration between SLM and the other service design processes to ensure proper mapping of business requirements to IT operational activities and components of the IT infrastructure. This makes it easier to model the effect of changes and improvements.
- Initiate changes at the earliest appropriate stage in the service lifecycle. This will ensure that both functional (business) and manageability (IT operational) requirements can be assessed and built or changed together.
- Ensure IT involvement in business changes as early as possible in the change process to ensure scalability, consistency and achievability of IT services sustaining business changes.
- Service operation teams should provide input into the ongoing design and refinement of the architectures and IT services (see *ITIL Service Design* and *ITIL Service Strategy*).
- Implement and use SLM to avoid situations where business and IT managers and staff negotiate informal agreements.

3.2.3 Quality of service versus cost of service

Service operation is required consistently to deliver the agreed level of IT service to its customers and users, while at the same time keeping costs and resource utilization at an optimal level. Figure 3.5

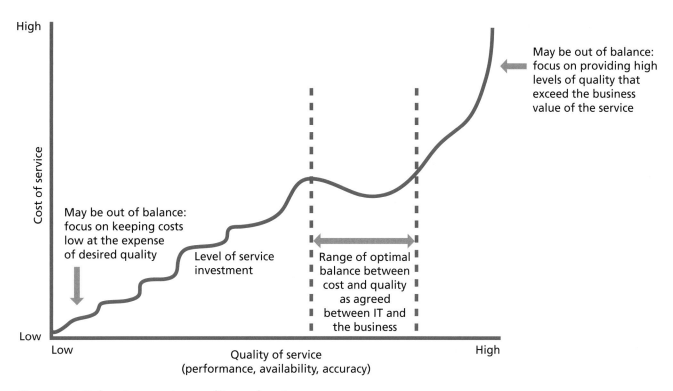

Figure 3.5 Balancing service quality and cost

represents the investment made to deliver a service at increasing levels of quality.

In Figure 3.5, an increase in the level of quality usually results in an increase in the cost of that service, and vice versa. However, the relationship is not always directly proportional:

■ Early in the service's lifecycle it is possible to achieve significant increases in service quality with a relatively small amount of money. For example, improving service availability from 55% to 75% is fairly straightforward and may not require a huge investment.

■ Later in the service's lifecycle, even small improvements in quality are very expensive. For example, improving the same service's availability from 96% to 99.9% may require large investments in high-availability technology and support staff and tools.

While this may seem straightforward, many organizations are under severe pressure to increase the quality of service while reducing their costs. In Figure 3.6, the relationship between cost and quality is sometimes inverse. It is possible (usually inside the range of optimization) to increase quality while reducing costs. This is normally initiated within service operation and carried forward by CSI. Some costs can be reduced

incrementally over time, but most cost savings can be made only once. For example, once a duplicate software tool has been eliminated, it cannot be eliminated again for further cost savings.

Achieving an optimal balance between cost and quality (shown between the dotted lines in Figure 3.5) is a key role of service management. There is no industry standard for what this range should be, because each service will have a different range of optimization, depending on the nature of the service and the type of business objective being met. For example, the business may be prepared to spend more to achieve high availability on a mission-critical service, while it is prepared to live with the lower quality of an administrative tool.

Determining the appropriate balance of cost and quality should be done during the service strategy and service design lifecycle stages, although in many organizations it is left to the service operation teams – many of whom do not generally have all the facts or authority to be able to make this type of decision.

Unfortunately, it is also common to find organizations that are spending vast quantities of money without achieving any clear improvements in quality. Again, CSI will be able to identify the cause of the inefficiency, evaluate the optimal balance for that service and formulate a corrective plan.

Achieving the correct balance is important. Too much focus on quality will result in IT services that deliver more than necessary, at a higher cost, and could lead to a discussion on reducing the price of services. Too much focus on cost will result in IT delivering on or under budget, but putting the business at risk through substandard IT services.

> **Special note: just how far is too much?**
>
> Over the past several years, IT organizations have been under pressure to cut costs. In many cases this resulted in optimized costs and quality. But in other cases, costs were cut to the point where quality started to suffer. At first, the signs were subtle – small increases in incident resolution times and a slight increase in the number of incidents. Over time, though, the situation became more serious as staff worked long hours to handle multiple workloads and services ran on ageing or outdated infrastructure.
>
> There is no simple calculation to determine when costs have been cut too far, but good SLM is crucial to making customers aware of the impact of cutting too far, so recognizing these warning signs and symptoms can greatly enhance an organization's ability to correct this situation.

3.2.3.1 Service level requirements

Service level requirements – together with a clear understanding of the business purpose of the service and the potential risks – will help to ensure that the service is delivered at the appropriate cost. They will also help to avoid 'oversizing' of the service just because budget is available, or 'undersizing' because the business does not understand the manageability requirements of the solution. Either result will cause customer dissatisfaction and even more expense when the solution is re-engineered or retrofitted to the requirements that should have been specified during service design.

Table 3.3 outlines some examples of the characteristics of positions at extreme ends of the cost/quality spectrum. The purpose of this table is to help organizations identify to which extreme they are closer, not to identify real-life positions to which organizations should aspire.

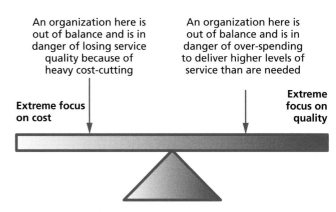

Figure 3.6 Achieving a balance between focus on cost and quality

Achieving a balance will ensure delivery of the level of service necessary to meet business requirements at an optimal (as opposed to lowest possible) cost. This will require the following:

■ A financial management process and tools that can account for the cost of providing IT services; and which model alternative methods of delivering services at differing levels of cost. For example, comparing the cost of delivering a service at 98% availability or at 99.9% availability; or the cost of providing a service with or without additional functionality.

■ Ensuring that decisions around cost versus quality are made by the appropriate managers during service strategy and service design. IT operational managers are generally not equipped to evaluate business opportunities and should only be asked to make financial decisions that are related to achieving operational efficiencies.

3.2.4 Reactive versus proactive

A reactive organization is one which does not act unless it is prompted to do so by an external driver, e.g. a new business requirement, an application that has been developed or escalation in complaints made by users and customers. An unfortunate reality in many organizations is the focus on reactive management mistakenly as the sole means to ensure services that are highly consistent and stable, actively discouraging proactive behaviour from operational staff. The unfortunate irony of this approach is that discouraging effort investment in proactive service management can ultimately increase the effort and cost of reactive activities and further risk stability and consistency in services.

Table 3.3 Examples of extreme focus on quality and cost

	Extreme focus on quality	Extreme focus on cost
Primary focus	Delivering the level of quality demanded by the business regardless of what it takes	Meeting budget and reducing costs
Typical problems experienced	Escalating budgets IT services generally deliver more than is necessary for business success Escalating demands for higher-quality services Use of more support resources and other service assets than necessary to fulfil service demands.	IT limits the quality of service based on their budget availability Escalations from the business to get more service from IT
Financial management	IT usually does not have a method of communicating the cost of IT services. Accounting methods are based on an aggregated method (e.g. cost of IT per user)	Financial reporting is done purely on budgeted amounts. There is no way of linking activities in IT to the delivery of IT services

A proactive organization is always looking for ways to improve the current situation. It will continually scan the internal and external environments, looking for changes that may have potential impact. Proactive behaviour is usually seen as positive, especially because it enables the organization to maintain competitive advantage in a changing environment. However, being too proactive can be expensive and can result in staff being distracted. The need for proper balance in reactive and proactive behaviour often achieves the optimal result (see Figure 3.7).

It is best practice to manage services proactively, but achieving this comes with many challenges:

■ **The maturity of the organization** The longer the organization has been delivering a consistent set of IT services, the more likely it is to understand the relationship between IT and the business and the IT infrastructure and IT services.

■ **The culture of the organization** Some organizations have a culture that is focused on innovation and are more likely to be proactive. Others are more likely to focus on the status quo and as such are likely to resist change and have more reactive focus.

■ **Role of IT and the mandate** The role that IT plays in the business and the mandate that IT has to influence the strategy and tactics of the business are significant. For example, a company where the CIO is a board member is likely to have an IT organization that is far more proactive and responsive than a company where IT is seen as an administrative overhead.

■ **The level of integration of management processes and tools** Higher levels of integration will facilitate better knowledge of opportunities.

■ **The maturity and scope of knowledge management in the organization** This is likely to be seen in organizations that have been able to store and organize historical data effectively – especially availability and problem management data.

From a maturity perspective, it is clear that newer organizations will have different priorities and experiences from a more established organization – what is best practice for a mature organization

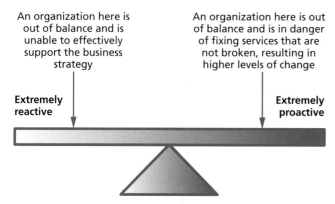

Figure 3.7 Achieving a balance between being too reactive or too proactive

may not suit a younger organization. Therefore an imbalance could result from an organization being either less or more mature. Consider the following:

- Less mature organizations (or organizations with newer IT services or technology) will generally be more reactive, simply because they do not know all the variables involved in running their business and providing IT services.
- IT staff in newer organizations tend to be generalists because it is unclear exactly what is required to deliver stable IT services to the business.
- Incidents and problems in newer organizations are fairly unpredictable because the technology is relatively new and changes quickly.
- More mature organizations tend to be more proactive, simply because they have more data and reporting available and know the typical patterns of incidents and workflows. Thus, they forecast exceptions far more easily.
- Staff working in mature organizations also generally tend to have more established relationships between IT staff and the business and so can be more proactive about meeting changing business requirements – this is especially true when IT is seen as a strategic component of the business.

Table 3.4 outlines some examples of the characteristics of positions at extreme ends of the spectrum. The purpose of this table is to help organizations identify to which extreme they are closer, not to identify real-life positions to which organizations should aspire.

While proactive behaviour in service operation is generally good, there are also times where reactive behaviour is needed. The role of service operation is therefore to achieve a balance between being reactive and proactive. This will require:

- Formal problem management and incident management processes, integrated between service operation and CSI.
- The ability to be able to prioritize technical faults as well as business demands. This needs to be done during service operation, but the mechanisms need to be put in place during service strategy and design. These mechanisms could include incident categorization systems, escalation procedures and tools to facilitate impact assessment for changes.

- Data from configuration and asset management to provide data where required, saving projects time and making decisions more accurate.
- Ongoing involvement of SLM in service operation.

3.3 PROVIDING GOOD SERVICE

All service operation staff must be fully aware that they are there to 'provide service' to the business. They must provide a timely (rapid response and speedy delivery of requirements), professional and courteous service to allow the business to conduct its own activities – so that the commercial customer's needs are met and the business thrives.

It is important that staff are trained not only in how to deliver and support IT services, but also in the manner in which that service should be provided. For example, staff that are capable and deliver service effectively may still cause significant customer dissatisfaction if they are insensitive or dismissive. Conversely, no amount of being nice to a customer will help if the service is not being delivered.

A critical element of being a proficient service provider is placing as much emphasis on recruiting and training staff to develop competency in dealing with and managing customer relationships and interactions as they do on technical competencies for managing the IT environment.

3.4 OPERATION STAFF INVOLVEMENT IN OTHER SERVICE LIFECYCLE STAGES

It is extremely important that service operation staff are involved in activities taking place with other service lifecycle stages where appropriate. Resources must be made available for these activities and the time required should be taken into account, as appropriate.

3.4.1 Operation staff involvement in service strategy

IT operation staff play an important assistance role in supporting service strategy activities. Examples of assistance activities might include:

- Identifying and communicating current operation capabilities, workforce levels and operational staff skills to those developing IT strategies

Table 3.4 Examples of extremely reactive and proactive behaviour

	Extremely reactive	Extremely proactive
Primary focus	Responds to business needs and incidents only after they are reported	Anticipates business requirements before they are reported and problems before they occur
Typical problems experienced	Preparing to deliver new services takes a long time because each project is dealt with as if it is the first Similar incidents occur again and again, as there is no way of trending them Staff turnover is high and morale is generally low, as IT staff keep moving from project to project without achieving a lasting, stable set of IT services	Money is spent before the requirements are stated. In some cases IT purchases items that will never be used because they anticipated the wrong requirements or because the project is stopped IT staff tend to have been in the organization for a long time and tend to assume that they know the business requirements better than the business does
Capacity planning	Wait until there are capacity problems and then purchase surplus capacity to last until the next capacity-related incident	Anticipate capacity problems and spend money on preventing these – even when the scenario is unlikely to happen
IT service continuity planning	No plans exist until after a major event or disaster IT plans focus on recovering key systems, but without ensuring that the business can recover its processes	Over-planning (and over-spending) of IT recovery options. Usually immediate recovery is provided for most IT services, regardless of their impact or priority
Change management	Changes are often not logged, or logged at the last minute as emergency changes Not enough time for proper impact and cost assessments Changes are poorly tested and controlled, resulting in a high number of incidents	Changes are requested and implemented even when there is no real need, i.e. a significant amount of work done to fix items that are not broken

- Gathering and identifying IT operational costs
- Identifying high-level impacts of chosen IT strategies on current operational activities
- Identifying operational constraints that may impact IT strategies such as workforce union restrictions or inadequate physical environment capabilities
- Identifying operational risks for IT strategies being considered.

3.4.2 Operation staff involvement in service design

One key to achieving balance in service operation is an effective set of service design processes. These will provide IT operations management, technical management, application management and service desk with:

- Clear definition of IT service objectives and performance criteria
- Linkage of IT service specifications to the performance of the IT infrastructure

- Definition of operational performance requirements
- A mapping of services and technology
- The ability to model the effect of changes in technology and changes to business requirements
- Appropriate cost models (e.g. customer or service based) to evaluate ROI and cost reduction strategies.

The nature of IT operations management involvement should be carefully positioned. Service design is a stage in the service lifecycle using a set of processes, not a function independent of service operation. As such, many of the people involved in service design may come from IT operations management, technical management and application management.

Service operation involvement in service design activities should be strongly encouraged. Staff should also be measured on their involvement in service design activities – and such activities should be included in job descriptions and roles whenever possible. This will help to ensure continuity between business requirements and technology design and operation and it will also help to ensure that what is designed can also be operated.

3.4.3 Involvement in service transition

IT operations management staff should be involved during service transition to ensure consistency and that both stated business and manageability requirements are met. Examples of assistance activities might include:

- Training activities to learn how to operate a new service or for changes in how an existing service is currently operated
- Participation and review of operational acceptance tests
- Participation in transition planning to identify impacts of transition activities on current operation activities
- Participation in transition tasks such as moving applications and other components from their development environment to the live environment
- Provision of early life support activities for new services or major changes that have been released to the live environment

- Participation in quality assurance activities such as validating operational readiness of a new service or major change to the live environment.

3.4.4 Involvement in continual service improvement

Service operation staff should be involved in supporting CSI activities and identifying improvement opportunities for inclusion in the CSI register. Examples include:

- Ensuring operational data is made available to personnel involved in CSI activities
- Validating accuracy of operational data used to identify improvement opportunities
- Assessing the impact of proposed improvement actions on existing operation activities
- Executing operational tasks to support service monitoring, measurement and reporting activities
- Identifying and promoting operational issues and concerns to CSI staff
- Identifying and proposing improvements that can enhance the performance and quality of the IT services being delivered.

3.5 OPERATIONAL HEALTH

Many organizations find it helpful to compare the monitoring and control of service operation to health monitoring and control.

In this sense, the IT infrastructure is like an organism with vital life signs that can be monitored to check whether it is functioning normally. This means that it is not necessary to monitor continuously every component of every IT system to ensure that it is functioning.

Operational health can be determined by isolating a few important 'vital signs' on devices or services that are defined as critical for the successful execution of a vital business function. This could be the bandwidth utilization on a network segment, or memory utilization on a major server. If these signs are within normal ranges, the system is healthy and does not require additional attention. This reduction in the need for extensive monitoring will result in cost reduction and operational teams and departments that are focused on the appropriate areas for service success.

However, as with organisms, it is important to check systems more thoroughly from time to time, to check for problems that do not immediately affect vital signs. For example a disk may be functioning perfectly, but it could be nearing its mean time between failures (MTBF) threshold. In this case the system should be taken out of service and given a thorough examination or 'health check'. At the same time, it should be stressed that the end result should be the healthy functioning of the service as a whole. This means that health checks on components should be balanced against checks of the 'end-to-end' service. The definition of what needs to be monitored and what is healthy versus unhealthy is defined during service design, especially availability management and SLM.

Operational health is dependent on the ability to prevent incidents and problems by investing in reliable and maintainable infrastructure. This is achieved through good availability design and proactive problem management. At the same time, operational health is also dependent on the ability to identify faults and localize them effectively so that they have minimal impact on the service. This requires strong (preferably automated) incident and problem management.

The idea of operational health has also led to a specialized area called 'self-healing systems'. This is an application of availability, capacity, knowledge, incident and problem management and refers to a system that has been designed to withstand the most severe operating conditions and to detect, diagnose and recover from most incidents and known errors. Self-healing systems are known by different names, for example autonomic systems, adaptive systems and dynamic systems. Characteristics of self-healing systems include:

- Resilience is designed and built into the system, for example multiple redundant disks or multiple processors. This protects the system against hardware failure because it is able to continue operating using the duplicated hardware component.
- Software, data and operating system resilience is also designed into the system, for example mirrored databases (where a database is duplicated on a backup device) and disk-striping technology (where individual bits of data are distributed across a disk array – so that a disk failure results in the loss of only a part

of data, which can be easily recovered using algorithms).

- The ability to shift processing from one physical device to another without any disruption to the service. This could be a response to a failure or because the device is reaching high utilization levels (some systems are designed to distribute processing workloads continuously, to make optimum use of available capacity, which is also known as virtualization).
- Built-in monitoring utilities which enable the system to detect events and to determine whether these represent normal operations or not.
- A correlation engine (see section 4.1.4.4). This will enable the system to determine the significance of each event and also to determine whether there is any predefined response to that event.
- A set of diagnostic tools, such as diagnostic scripts, fault trees and a database of known errors and common workarounds. These are used as soon as an error is detected, to determine the appropriate response.
- The ability to generate a call for human intervention by raising an alert or generating an incident.

While the concept of operational health is not a core concept of service operation, it is often a helpful metaphor to help determine what needs to be monitored and how frequently to perform preventive maintenance.

What and when to monitor for operational health should be determined in service design, tested and refined during service transition and optimized in CSI, as necessary.

3.6 COMMUNICATION

Good communication is needed with other IT teams and departments, with users and internal customers, and between the service operation teams and departments themselves. Issues can often be prevented or mitigated with appropriate communication.

This section aims to summarize the communication that should take place in service operation. This is not a separate process, but a checklist of the type of communications that are required for effective service operation.

An important principle is that all communication must have an intended purpose or a resultant action. Information should not be communicated unless there is a clear audience. In addition, that audience should have been actively involved in determining the need for that communication and what they will do with the information. Further, there should be review of ongoing communications on a periodic basis to validate that they are still required by the audience.

A detailed description of the types of communication typical in service operation is contained in Appendix B, together with a description of the typical audience and the actions that are intended to be taken as a result of each communication. These include:

- Routine operational communication
- Communication between shifts
- Performance reporting
- Communication in projects
- Communication related to changes
- Communication related to exceptions
- Communication related to emergencies
- Training on new or customized processes and service designs
- Communication of strategy, design and transition to service operation teams.

Please note that there is no definitive medium for communication, nor is there a fixed location or frequency. In some organizations communication has to take place in meetings. Other organizations prefer to use email or the communication inherent in their service management tools.

There should therefore be a policy around communication within each team or department and for each process. Although this should be formal, the policy should not be cumbersome or complex. For example, a manager might require that all communications regarding changes must be sent by email. As long as this is specified in the department's SOPs (in whatever form they exist), there is no need to create a separate policy for it.

Although the typical content of communication is fairly consistent once processes have been defined, the means of communication are changing with every new introduction of technology. The list of alternatives is growing and currently includes:

- Email, to traditional clients or mobile devices

- Social media and microblogging services
- Web-based internet relay chat (IRC)
- Short message services messages
- Pagers
- Instant messaging, texting and web-based 'chats'
- Voice over internet protocol (VoIP) utilities that can turn any connected device into an inexpensive communication medium
- Teleconference and virtual meeting utilities have revolutionized meetings which are now held across long distances
- Document-sharing utilities.

The means of communication itself is outside the scope of this publication. However, the following points should be noted:

- Communication is primary and the means of communication must ensure that they serve this goal. For example, the need for secure communication may eliminate the possibility of some of the above means.
- It is possible to use any means of communication as long as all stakeholders understand how and when the communication will take place and indicate their need to continue to use it.

3.6.1 Meetings

Different organizations communicate in different ways. Where organizations are distributed, they will tend to rely on email and teleconferencing facilities. Organizations that have more mature service management processes and tools will tend to rely on the tools and processes for communication (e.g. using an incident management tool to escalate and track incidents, instead of requesting email or telephone calls for updates).

Other organizations prefer to communicate using meetings. However, it is important not to get into the mode whereby the only time work is done, or management is involved, is during a meeting. Also, face-to-face meetings tend to increase costs (e.g. travel, time spent in informal discussions, refreshments etc.), so meeting organizers should balance the value of the meeting with the number and identity of the attendees and the time they will spend in, and getting to, the meeting.

The purpose of meetings is to communicate effectively to a group of people about a common set of objectives or activities. Meetings should be well controlled and brief, and the focus should be on facilitating action. A good rule is not to hold a meeting if the information can be communicated effectively by automated means or where information being communicated is only one way.

A number of factors are essential for successful meetings. Although these may seem to be common sense, they are sometimes neglected:

■ Establish and communicate a clear agenda in advance to allow the audience to prepare and to ensure that the meeting achieves its objective. This also helps the facilitator prevent attendees from 'hijacking' the meeting.

■ Ensure that the rules for participating are understood. Organizations tend to have a formal set of meeting rules, ranging from relatively informal to very formal (e.g. published books such as Roberts Rules of Order that describe procedures, rules, ethics and customs for governing meetings).

■ Make use of 'parking lots' or notes which record issues that are not directly relevant to the purpose of the meeting, but which can be called on if the need for discussion arises.

■ Minutes of the meeting: rules should be set about when minutes are taken. Minutes are used to remind people who are assigned actions and to track the progress of delegated actions. They are also useful in ensuring that cross-functional decisions and actions are tracked and followed through. Minutes of the actions, for whom, the responsible party, and deadline should always be taken, and published within acceptable timeframes.

■ Use techniques to encourage the appropriate level of participation. One technique when discussing improvements, for example, is the 'keep, stop, start' technique. Participants are encouraged to list items that they would like to keep, things that need to be stopped and initiatives or actions that they would like to see started.

Examples of typical meetings are given below.

3.6.1.1 The operations meeting

Operations meetings are normally held between the managers of the IT operational departments,

teams or groups, at the beginning of each business day or week. The purpose of this type of meeting is to make staff aware of any issue relevant to operations (such as change schedules, business events, maintenance schedules etc.) and to provide an opportunity for staff to raise any issues of which they are aware. This is an opportunity to ensure that all departments in a data centre are synchronized.

In geographically dispersed organizations it may not be possible to have a single daily operations meeting. In these cases it is important to coordinate the agenda of the meetings and to ensure that each meeting has two components:

■ The first part of the meeting will cover aspects that apply to the organization as a whole, e.g. new policies or changes that affect all regions and business events that span all regions.

■ The second part of the meeting will cover aspects that apply only to the local region, e.g. local operations schedules, changes to local equipment etc.

The operations meeting is usually chaired by the IT operations manager or a senior operations manager and attended by all managers and supervisors (except those whose shifts are not on duty). It is also helpful to have at least one representative from the service desk at the meeting so that they are aware of any situations that could give rise to incidents.

Opportunities to improve services or processes should be captured, if raised, and forwarded to the team responsible for CSI.

3.6.1.2 Department, group or team meetings

Essentially the same as the operations meeting, these meetings are aimed at a single IT department, group or team. Each manager or supervisor relays the information from the operations meeting that is relevant to their team.

These meetings will also include a more detailed discussion of incidents, problems and changes that are still being worked on, with information about:

■ Progress to date
■ Confirmation of what still needs to be done
■ Estimated completion times
■ Request for additional resources, if required
■ Discussion of potential problems or concerns

- Confirmation of staff availability for roster duties
- Confirmation of holiday schedules.

3.6.1.3 Customer meetings

From time to time it will be necessary to hold meetings with customers, apart from the regular service level review meetings. Examples include:

- **Follow-up after serious incidents** The purpose of these meetings is to repair relationships with the customer, but also to ensure that IT has all the information required to prevent recurrence. Customers also have the opportunity to provide information about unforeseen business impacts. These meetings are helpful in agreeing actions for similar types of incident that may occur in future.
- **A customer forum** This can be used for a range of purposes, including testing ideas for new services or solutions, or gathering requirements for new or revised services or procedures. A customer forum is generally a regular meeting with customers to discuss areas of common concern.
- **Customer meetings** These should be scheduled and held in coordination with business relationship management and the service level manager to ensure that communications to the customer are coordinated and consistent.

3.7 DOCUMENTATION

IT operations management and all of the technical and application management teams and departments are involved in creating and maintaining a range of documents that should be stored in the service knowledge management system (SKMS; see Figure 4.8). These documents are detailed in Chapters 4, 5 and 6 (more information on the SKMS can be found in *ITIL Service Transition*). Documentation activities include the following:

- Participation in the definition and maintenance of process manuals for all processes they are involved in. These will include processes in other stages of the service lifecycle (e.g. capacity management, change management, availability management) as well as for all processes included in the service operation stage.

- Establishing their own technical procedures manuals. These must be kept up to date and new material must be added as it becomes relevant, under change control. It should be remembered that their procedures should always be structured to meet the objectives and constraints defined within higher-level service management processes, such as SLM. For example, a technical procedure for managing servers should always ensure that it aims at achieving the availability and performance levels agreed to in the operational level agreements (OLAs) and service level agreements (SLAs).
- Participation in the creation and maintenance of planning documents, e.g. the capacity and availability plans and the IT service continuity plans.
- Participation in the creation and maintenance of the service portfolio. This will include quantifying costs and establishing the operational feasibility of each proposed service.
- Participation in the definition and maintenance of service management tool work instructions in order to meet reporting requirements.

3.8 SERVICE OPERATION INPUTS AND OUTPUTS

3.8.1 Examples of interfaces to other service lifecycle processes

There are other processes that will be executed or supported during service operation, but which are driven during other stages of the service lifecycle. These will be discussed in more detail in the final part of Chapter 4. Examples of these kinds of interfaces include:

- Change management, which is a major process that should be closely linked to service asset and configuration management and release and deployment management. These topics are primarily covered in *ITIL Service Transition*.
- Capacity and availability management, which are covered in *ITIL Service Design*.
- Financial management for IT services, which is covered in *ITIL Service Strategy*.
- Service catalogue management, which identifies the live IT services that are to be delivered. This process is covered in *ITIL Service Design*.

Table 3.5 Service operation inputs and outputs by lifecycle stage

Lifecycle stage	Service operation inputs (from the lifecycle stages in the first column)	Service operation outputs (to the lifecycle stages in the first column)
Service strategy	Vision and mission Service portfolio Policies Strategies and strategic plans Priorities Financial information and budgets Demand forecasts and strategies Strategic risks	Operating risks Operating cost information for total cost of ownership (TCO) calculations Actual performance data
Service design	Service catalogue Service design packages, including: ■ Details of utility and warranty ■ Operations plans and procedures ■ Recovery procedures Knowledge and information in the SKMS Vital business functions Hardware and software maintenance requirements Designs for service operation processes and procedures SLAs, OLAs and underpinning contracts Security policies	Operational requirements Actual performance data RFCs to resolve operational issues Historical incident and problem records
Service transition	New or changed services Known errors Standard changes for use in request fulfilment Knowledge and information in the SKMS (including the configuration management system) Change schedule	RFCs to resolve operational issues Feedback on quality of transition activities Input to operational testing Actual performance information Input to change evaluation and change advisory board meetings
Continual service improvement	Results of customer and user satisfaction surveys Service reports and dashboards Data required for metrics, key performance indicators (KPIs) and critical success factors (CSFs) RFCs for implementing improvements	Operational performance data and service records Proposed problem resolutions and proactive measures Knowledge and information in the SKMS Achievements against metrics, KPIs and CSFs Improvement opportunities logged in the continual service improvement register

■ Knowledge management, which is covered in *ITIL Service Transition*.

■ IT service continuity, which is covered in *ITIL Service Design*.

■ Service reporting and measurement, which are covered in *ITIL Continual Service Improvement*.

■ SLM, which is covered in *ITIL Service Design*.

■ Information security management, which is covered in *ITIL Service Design*.

3.8.2 Examples of interfaces to other service lifecycle stages

Service operation does not operate standalone, but interacts with all the other service lifecycle stages. Table 3.5 shows the major service operation inputs and outputs, by lifecycle stage. Appendix I provides a summary of the major inputs and outputs between each stage of the service lifecycle.

Service operation processes

4

4 Service operation processes

This chapter sets out the processes and activities on which effective service operation depends. These comprise both lifecycle processes and those almost wholly contained within service operation. Each is described in detail, setting out the key elements of that process or activity.

The topics specifically addressed in this chapter are:

- Event management
- Incident management
- Request fulfilment
- Problem management
- Access management.

Some of these processes are used throughout the service lifecycle, but are addressed in this publication because they are central to effective service operation.

The processes and activities described in this chapter are mostly contained within the service operation stage of the lifecycle, but also support other stages, e.g. validating attainment of the service levels set by the service level management (SLM) process within service design.

The purpose and scope of service operation as a whole are set out in section 1.1.

As a reference, an overview of each process is briefly described here and then in more detail later in the chapter. Please note that the roles for each process and the tools used for each process are described in Chapters 6 and 7, respectively.

Event management is the process that monitors all events that occur through the IT infrastructure to allow for normal operation and also to detect and escalate exception conditions.

Incident management concentrates on restoring unexpectedly degraded or disrupted services to users as quickly as possible, in order to minimize business impact.

Problem management involves root cause analysis to determine and resolve the underlying causes of events and incidents. Reactive activities seek to understand the underlying causes of incidents, create known error records that document root

causes and workarounds, and undertake actions to remove those errors from the IT infrastructure. Known error records are used to document root causes and workarounds and allow quicker diagnosis and resolution if further incidents do occur. Proactive activities undertake efforts to detect and prevent future problems/incidents such that they won't occur in the first place.

Note that without a distinction between incidents and problems, and keeping separate incident and problem records, there is a risk that:

- Incident resolution activities may extend the duration of service outages 'looking for root cause' versus taking direct actions to restore normal state service operation.
- Incident records will be closed too early in the overall support cycle and there will be no actions taken to prevent recurrence – so the same incidents will continue to disrupt the business and have to be fixed over and over again.
- Incident records will be kept open so that root cause analysis can be done and visibility will be lost of when the user's service was actually restored – so SLA targets may not be met even though the service has been restored within users' expectations. This often results in a large number of open incidents, many of which will never be closed unless a periodic 'purge' is undertaken. This can be very demotivating and can prevent effective visibility of current issues.

Separating the two processes and managing through separate incident and problem records allows support staff to meet the rapid restoration objective for incident management while allowing root cause to be investigated and resolved in a separate, parallel problem management process.

Request fulfilment is the process of managing the lifecycle of customer or user service requests from initial request to fulfilment using separate request fulfilment records/tables to record and track their status. Service requests handle all other interactions with users or customers that are not service disruptions. Examples of service requests might include the solicitation of assistance with the acquisition of a service, guidance on how to use a service, request for a password change, adding a user, or moving a user workstation (see section 3.1.3.4 for a more complete description of a service request).

Access management is the process of granting authorized users the rights to use a service, while restricting access to non-authorized users. It is based on being able accurately to identify authorized users and then manage their ability to access services as required for their specific organizational role or job function. Access management has also been called identity or rights management in some organizations. It should fully support the policies designed in the information security management process (see *ITIL Service Design*) with respect to roles, rights and segregation of duties.

4.1 EVENT MANAGEMENT

An event can be defined as any change of state that has significance for the management of a configuration item (CI) or IT service. Events are typically recognized through notifications created by an IT service, CI or monitoring tool.

Effective service operation is dependent on knowing the status of the infrastructure and detecting any deviation from normal or expected operation. This is provided by good monitoring and control systems, which are based on two types of tools:

- Active monitoring tools that poll key CIs to determine their status and availability. Any exceptions will generate an alert that needs to be communicated to the appropriate tool or team for action.
- Passive monitoring tools that detect and correlate operational alerts or communications generated by CIs.

4.1.1 Purpose and objectives

4.1.1.1 Purpose

The purpose of event management is to manage events throughout their lifecycle. This lifecycle of activities to detect events, make sense of them and determine the appropriate control action is coordinated by the event management process.

Event management is therefore the basis for operational monitoring and control. If events are programmed to communicate operational information as well as warnings and exceptions, they can be used as a basis for automating many routine operations management activities, for example executing scripts on remote devices, or submitting jobs for processing, or even dynamically balancing the demand for a service across multiple devices to enhance performance.

4.1.1.2 Objectives

The objectives of the event management process are to:

- Detect all changes of state that have significance for the management of a CI or IT service
- Determine the appropriate control action for events and ensure these are communicated to the appropriate functions
- Provide the trigger, or entry point, for the execution of many service operation processes and operations management activities
- Provide the means to compare actual operating performance and behaviour against design standards and SLAs
- Provide a basis for service assurance and reporting; and service improvement. (This is covered in detail in *ITIL Continual Service Improvement*.)

4.1.2 Scope

Event management can be applied to any aspect of service management that needs to be controlled and which can be automated. This includes:

- Configuration items (CIs):
  - Some CIs will be included because they need to stay in a constant state (e.g. a switch on a network needs to stay on and event management tools confirm this by monitoring responses to 'pings')
  - Some CIs will be included because their status needs to change frequently and event management can be used to automate this and update the configuration management system (CMS) (e.g. the updating of a file server)
- Environmental conditions (e.g. fire and smoke detection)

- Software licence monitoring for usage to ensure optimum/legal licence utilization and allocation
- Security (e.g. intrusion detection)
- Normal activity (e.g. tracking the use of an application or the performance of a server).

The difference between monitoring and event management

Monitoring and event management are closely related, but slightly different in nature. Event management is focused on generating and detecting meaningful notifications about the status of the IT infrastructure and services.

While it is true that monitoring is required to detect and track these notifications, monitoring is broader than event management. For example, monitoring tools will check the status of a device to ensure that it is operating within acceptable limits, even if that device is not generating events.

Put more simply, event management works with occurrences that are specifically generated to be monitored. Monitoring tracks these occurrences, but it will also actively seek out conditions that do not generate events.

4.1.3 Value to business

Event management's value to the business is generally indirect; however, it is possible to determine the basis for its value as follows:

- Event management provides mechanisms for early detection of incidents. In many cases it is possible for the incident to be detected and assigned to the appropriate group for action before any actual service outage occurs.
- Event management makes it possible for some types of automated activity to be monitored by exception – thus removing the need for expensive and resource-intensive real-time monitoring, while reducing downtime.
- When integrated into other service management processes (such as, for example, availability or capacity management), event management can signal status changes or exceptions that allow the appropriate person or team to perform early response, thus improving the performance of the process. This, in turn, will allow the business to benefit

from more effective and more efficient service management overall.

- Event management provides a basis for automated operations, thus increasing efficiencies and allowing expensive human resources to be used for more innovative work, such as designing new or improved functionality or defining new ways in which the business can exploit technology for increased competitive advantage.
- Event management can have a direct bearing on service delivery and customer satisfaction. As an example, an automated teller machine may generate event notifications that indicate the device is running low on cash, potentially avoiding the failure of the cash withdrawal portion of that service and its immediate impact on customer satisfaction.

4.1.4 Policies, principles and basic concepts

4.1.4.1 Policies

Examples of event management policies might include:

- Event notifications should only go to those responsible for the handling of their further actions or decisions related to them. This avoids needless notifications to those not directly involved in processing events. This implies that event notifications must identify which departments, groups or individuals need to respond to events. Event routeing information must be constantly maintained as new events are added or personnel responsibilities change.
- Event management and support should be centralized as much as reasonably possible. This avoids conflicts in management of events. It supports consistent appropriate operational response for new events and changes that may occur in event handling actions. This also ensures that support personnel do not receive event notifications for events that they are not prepared to handle. This implies that a common rule base may need to be built and maintained for directing events. Changes and additions for the rule base will need to be under the control of change management.
- All application events should utilize a common set of messaging and logging standards and protocols wherever possible. This allows for

consistent handling of events. It can also result in faster implementation of new events and their handling actions as well as establish common expectations for how events will be recognized and handled.

■ Event handling actions should be automated wherever possible. This eliminates potential incidents that could be caused by human error. It enforces consistent means for handling events and reduces labour needed to handle them. This implies that a CSI effort should be in place to continuously look for events that can be automated.

■ A standard classification scheme should be in place that references common handling and escalation processes. This supports a consistent approach for taking actions on events in a manner that supports operational and service level objectives. This implies that a common set of actions should be established for each class of event. Operational and service level objectives should be taken into consideration when taking action on recognized events. Actions for events that trigger the notification of incidents and problems should be tied into existing categorization and prioritization policies that have been established by incident and problem management.

■ All recognized events should be captured and logged. This will provide a means for examining incidents, problems and trends after events have occurred. It supports activities to determine root cause analysis when solving complex problems. This implies that a mechanism is in place for logging all events. Adequate storage resources must be in place to support event capture and retention. An efficient means for data manipulation, filtering and reporting should be in place to quickly search and identify events or groups of events to support incident and problem diagnosis activities. Event information should be easily linked with incident and problem records.

4.1.4.2 Principles and basic concepts

Types of events

There are many different types of events, such as informational events, warning events and exception events.

INFORMATIONAL EVENTS

■ A scheduled workload has completed
■ A user has logged in to use an application
■ An email has reached its intended recipient.

WARNING EVENTS

■ A server's memory utilization reaches within 5% of its highest acceptable performance level
■ The completion time of a transaction is 10% longer than normal.

Warning events signify unusual, but not exceptional, operation. These are an indication that the situation may require closer monitoring. In some cases the condition will resolve itself, for example in the case of an unusual combination of workloads – as they are completed, normal operation is restored. In other cases, operator intervention may be required if the situation is repeated or if it continues for too long. These rules or policies are defined in the monitoring and control objectives for that device or service.

EXCEPTION EVENTS

■ A user attempts to log on to an application with the incorrect password
■ An unusual situation has occurred in a business process that may indicate an exception requiring further business investigation (e.g. a web page alert indicates that a payment authorization site is unavailable – impacting financial approval of business transactions)
■ A device's CPU is above the acceptable utilization rate
■ A PC scan reveals the installation of unauthorized software.

Two things are significant about the above examples:

■ Exactly what constitutes informational versus a warning, versus an exception? There is no definitive rule about this. Informational events convey data for use in decision making, warning events tend to convey predictive information that some exception might occur and exception events indicate an abnormal situation that requires action to address. For example, a manufacturer may provide that a benchmark of 75% memory utilization is optimal for application X. However, it is discovered that, under specific conditions, response times begin to degrade above 70% utilization. Thresholds are then set that trigger warning events if utilization is between 70 and 75%. At 75% or higher, an exception event is triggered that will require immediate action, such as adding more memory.

■ Each relies on the sending and receipt of a message of some sort. These are generally referred to as event notifications and they don't just happen without planning. The following sections will explore exactly how events are defined, generated and captured.

Filtering of events

One of the most important principles of event management is achieving the correct level of filtering to focus management and control actions on those events that have significance. This can become complicated by the fact that the significance of events changes. For example, a user logging into a system today is normal, but if that user leaves the organization and tries to log in it is a security breach.

There are several strategies that can be used to obtain the correct level of filtering. These are shown as follows:

■ **Integration** Integrate event management into all service management processes where feasible. This will ensure that only the events significant to these processes are reported.

■ **Design** Design new services with event management in mind. (Section 4.1.4.3 discusses design considerations for events while challenges and risks to be considered when designing events are discussed in more detail in section 4.1.9.)

■ **Trial and error** No matter how thoroughly event management is prepared, there will be classes of events that are not properly filtered. Event management must therefore include a formal process to evaluate the effectiveness of filtering.

■ **Planning** Proper planning is needed for the deployment of event management software across the entire IT infrastructure. This should be regarded as a project with realistic timescales and adequate resources being allocated and protected throughout the duration of the project.

4.1.4.3 Designing for event management

Effective event management is not designed once a service has been deployed into operations. Because event management is the basis for monitoring the performance and availability of a service, the exact targets and mechanisms for monitoring should be specified and agreed during the availability and capacity management processes (see *ITIL Service Design*). Testing and evaluation of designed event mechanisms should be included with activities undertaken during service transition (see *ITIL Service Transition*).

However, this does not mean that event management is designed by a group of remote system developers and then released to operations management together with the system that has to be managed. Nor does it mean that, once designed and agreed, event management becomes static – day-to-day operations will define additional events, priorities, alerts and other improvements that will feed through the continual improvement process back into service strategy, service design etc.

Service operation functions will be expected to participate in the design of the service and how it is measured (see section 3.4).

Key considerations for designing event management can include:

■ What needs to be monitored?
■ What type of monitoring is required (e.g. active or passive; performance or output)?
■ When do we need to generate an event?
■ What type of information needs to be communicated in the event?
■ Who are the messages intended for?
■ Who will be responsible for recognizing, communicating, escalating and taking action on events?

For event management, the specific design areas include the following.

Instrumentation

Instrumentation is the definition of what can be monitored about CIs and the way in which their behaviour can be affected. In other words, instrumentation is about defining and designing exactly how to monitor and control the IT infrastructure and IT services.

Instrumentation is partly about a set of decisions that need to be made and partly about designing mechanisms to execute these decisions. Mechanisms that need to be designed include:

- How will events be generated?
- How will events be classified?
- How will events be communicated and escalated?
- Does the CI already have event generation mechanisms as a standard feature and, if so, which of these will be used? Are they sufficient or does the CI need to be customized to include additional mechanisms or information?
- What data will be used to populate the event record?
- Are events generated automatically or does the CI have to be polled?
- Where will events be logged and stored?
- How will supplementary data be gathered?

Error messaging

Error messaging is important for all components (hardware, software, networks etc.). It is particularly important that all software applications are designed to support event management. This might include the provision of meaningful error messages and/or codes that clearly indicate the specific point of failure and the most likely cause. In such cases the testing of new applications should include testing of accurate event generation.

Technologies now provide the tools for building distributed, web-based, modular and dynamic solutions for managing and monitoring devices, applications and service-driven networks. These can be used to reduce or eliminate the need to include error messaging within the code – allowing a valuable level of normalization and code independence.

Note that a strong interface exists here with the application's design. All applications should be coded in such a way that meaningful and detailed error messages/codes are generated at the exact point of failure – so that these can be included in the event and allow swift diagnosis and resolution of the underlying cause. The need to include and test such error messaging is covered in more detail in *ITIL Service Transition*.

Event detection and alert mechanisms

Good event management design will also include the design and population of the tools used to filter, correlate and escalate events.

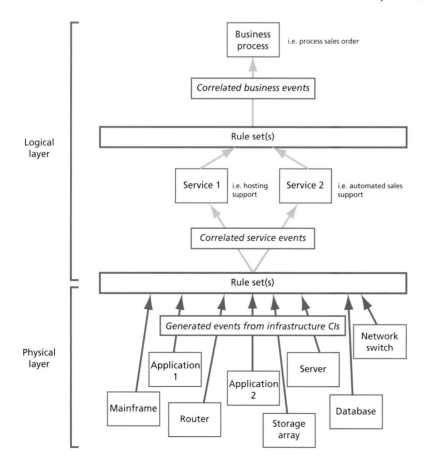

Figure 4.1 Relationship between events for physical infrastructure CIs, services and business processes

The correlation engine specifically will need to be populated with the rules and criteria that will determine the significance and subsequent action for each type of event.

Thorough design of the event detection and alert mechanisms requires the following:

■ Business knowledge in relationship to any business processes being managed via event management
■ Detailed knowledge of the service level requirements of the service being supported by each CI
■ Knowledge of who is going to be supporting the CI
■ Knowledge of what constitutes normal and abnormal operation of the CI
■ Knowledge of the significance of multiple similar events (on the same CI or various similar CIs)
■ An understanding of what they need to know to support the CI effectively
■ Information that can help in the diagnosis of problems with the CI
■ Familiarity with incident prioritization and categorization codes so that if it is necessary to create an incident record, these codes can be provided
■ Knowledge of other CIs that may be dependent on the affected CI, or those CIs on which it depends. Availability of known error information from vendors or from previous experience.

4.1.4.4 Use of event rule sets and correlation engines

A rule set consists of several rules that define how the event messages for a particular event will be processed and evaluated. For example, a warning event may be generated each time a disk log file reaches its capacity, but an exception event will be generated if more than four warning events have been generated. Rules themselves are typically embedded into monitoring and event handling technologies. They consist of Boolean kinds of algorithms to correlate events that have been generated in order to create additional events that need to be communicated. These algorithms can be codified into event management software typically referred to as correlation engines.

Using rule sets to monitor and detect 'end to end' service events

Event technologies are generally architected to produce events for CIs within the IT infrastructure. This provides notification for changes in operational state and status of those CIs; however, there may be a desire to also generate events from a business or service perspective that have meaning for business users. For example, technologies may generate events that communicate individual status for each hardware and software CI that participates in delivery of an email service, yet fail to communicate whether the email service is actually sending and receiving messages from an acceptable user perspective. This requires a complete understanding of how the business views its IT services, how the business views 'end to end' to achieve outcomes from those services, and which CIs underpin the delivery of those business outcomes.

Services and business processes represent a logical abstraction from parts of the physical IT infrastructure. For this reason, many technologies include rule set capabilities that allow for the creation of events for these logical abstractions. Events generated from physical infrastructure CIs utilize rule sets to correlate and generate logical events that have meaning for end users and customers. Figure 4.1 illustrates the relationship between events for physical infrastructure CIs and how these can be abstracted for services and business processes.

A best practice is to establish the required events, rule sets and correlations as a service is being designed (see *ITIL Service Design*). This prevents the more reactive and expensive practice of engineering monitoring and event solutions after a service has already gone into live production.

4.1.5 Process activities, methods and techniques

Figure 4.2 is a high-level and generic representation of event management. It should be used as a reference and definition point, rather than an actual event management flow chart. Each activity in this process is described below.

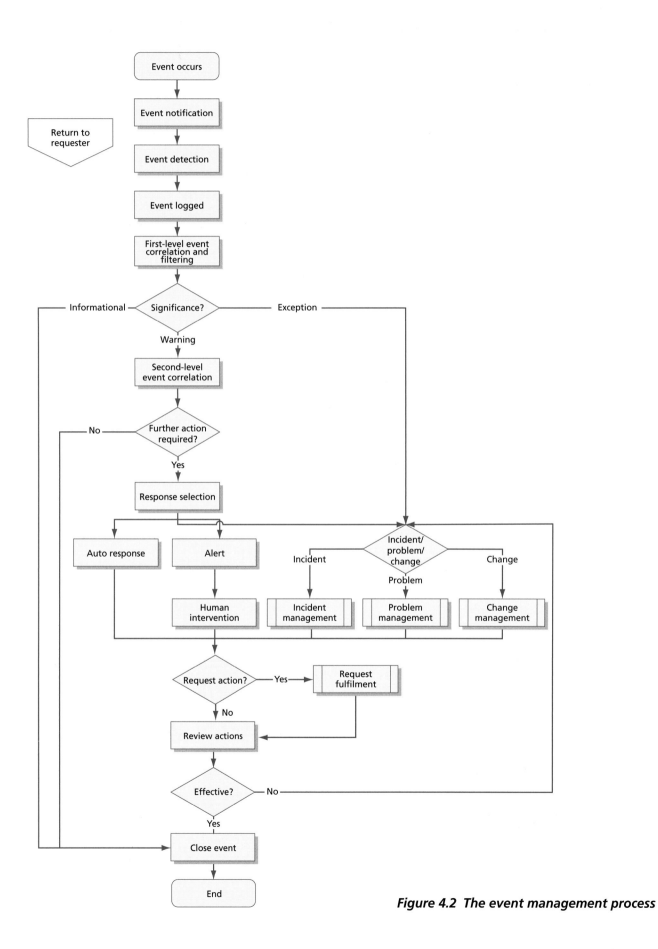

Figure 4.2 The event management process

4.1.5.1 Event occurs

Events occur continuously, but not all of them are detected or registered. It is therefore important that everybody involved in designing, developing, managing and supporting IT services and the IT infrastructure that they run on understands what types of event need to be detected.

Event design details are discussed in section 4.1.4.3, while challenges with designing events are discussed in section 4.1.9.1.

4.1.5.2 Event notification

Most CIs are designed to communicate certain information about themselves in one of two ways:

- A device is interrogated by a management tool, which collects certain targeted data. This is often referred to as polling.
- The CI generates a notification when certain conditions are met. The ability to produce these notifications has to be designed and built into the CI, for example a programming hook inserted into an application.

Event notifications can be proprietary, in which case only the manufacturer's management tools can be used to detect events. Most CIs, however, generate event notifications using an open standard such as simple network management protocol (SNMP).

Many CIs are configured to generate a standard set of events, based on the designer's experience of what is required to operate the CI, with the ability to generate additional types of event by 'turning on' the relevant event generation mechanism. For other CI types, some form of 'agent' software will have to be installed in order to initiate the monitoring. Often this monitoring feature is free, but sometimes there is a cost to the licensing of the tool.

The service design process should define which events need to be generated and then specify how this can be done for each type of CI. During service transition, the event generation options would be set and tested.

In many organizations, however, defining which events to generate is done by trial and error. System managers use the standard set of events as a starting point and then tune the CI over time, to

include or exclude events as required. The problem with this approach is that it only takes into account the immediate needs of the staff managing the device and does not facilitate good planning or improvement. In addition, it makes it very difficult to monitor and manage the service over all devices and staff. One approach to combating this problem is to review the set of events as part of continual improvement activities.

A general principle of event notification is that the more meaningful the data it contains and the more targeted the audience, the easier it is to make decisions about the event. Operators are often confronted by coded error messages and have no idea how to respond to them or what to do with them. Meaningful notification data and clearly defined roles and responsibilities need to be articulated and documented during service design and service transition (see also sections 4.1.5 and 4.1.11.1). If roles and responsibilities are not clearly defined, in a wide alert no one knows who is doing what and this can lead to things being missed or duplicated efforts.

4.1.5.3 Event detection

Once an event notification has been generated, it will be detected by an agent running on the same system, or transmitted directly to a management tool specifically designed to read and interpret the meaning of the event.

4.1.5.4 Event logged

There should be a record of the event and any subsequent actions. The event can be logged as an event record in the event management tool or it can simply be left as an entry in the system log of the device or application that generated the event. If this is the case, though, there needs to be a standing order for the appropriate operations management staff to check the logs on a regular basis and clear instructions about how to use each log. It should also be remembered that the event information in the logs may not be meaningful until an incident occurs; and where the technical management staff use the logs to investigate where the incident originated. This means that the event management procedures for each system or team need to define standards about how long events are kept in the logs before being archived and deleted.

4.1.5.5 First-level event correlation and filtering

The purpose of first-level event correlation and filtering is to decide whether to communicate the event to a management tool or to ignore it. If ignored, the event will usually be recorded in a log file on the device, but no further action will be taken.

The reason for filtering is that it is not always possible to turn event notification off, even though a decision has been made that it is not necessary to generate that type of event. A first-level correlation will be performed as needed if it is decided that only the first in a series of repeated event notifications will be transmitted.

During the filtering step, the first level of correlation is performed, i.e. the determination of whether the event is informational, a warning, or an exception (see next step). This correlation is usually done by an agent or correlation engine that resides on the CI or on a server to which the CI is connected.

This step may not always require events to be correlated. For some CIs, every event is significant and moves directly into a management tool's correlation engine, even if it is duplicated. Also, it may not have been possible to turn off all unwanted event notifications.

4.1.5.6 Significance of events

Every organization will have its own categorization of the significance of an event, but it is suggested that at least these three broad categories be represented.

Informational

This refers to an event that does not require any action and does not represent an exception. They are typically stored in the system or service log files and kept for a predetermined period. Informational events are typically used to check on the status of a device or service, or to confirm the successful completion of an activity. Informational events can also be used to generate statistics (such as the number of users logged on to an application during a certain period) and as input into investigations (such as which jobs completed successfully before the transaction processing queue hung). Examples of informational events include:

- A user logs onto an application
- A job in the batch queue completes successfully
- A device has come online
- A transaction is completed successfully.

Warning

A warning is an event that is generated when a service or device has reached a threshold that indicates a situation must be checked and appropriate actions taken to prevent an exception. Warnings are not typically raised for a device failure, although there is some debate about whether the failure of a redundant device is a warning or an exception (because the service is still available). A good rule is that every failure should be treated as an exception, because the risk of an incident impacting the business is much greater. Examples of warnings are:

- Memory utilization on a server is currently at 65% and increasing. If it reaches 75%, response times will be unacceptably long and the OLA for that department will be breached.
- The collision rate on a network has increased by 15% over the past hour.

Exception

An exception means that a service or device is currently operating abnormally (however that has been defined). Typically, this means that an OLA and SLA have been breached and the business is being impacted. Exceptions could represent a total failure, impaired functionality or degraded performance. Note, however, that an exception does not always represent a failure or abnormal operation. For example, an exception could be generated when an unauthorized device is discovered on the network. This can be managed by raising either an incident record or an RFC (or even both), depending on the organization's incident and change management policies. Examples of exceptions include:

- A server is down
- Response time of a standard transaction across the network has slowed to more than 15 seconds
- More than 150 users have logged on to the general ledger application concurrently
- A segment of the network is not responding to routine requests.

4.1.5.7 Second-level event correlation

If an event is a warning, a decision has to be made about exactly what the significance is and what actions need to be taken to deal with it. It is here that the meaning of the event is determined.

Correlation is normally done by a 'correlation engine', usually part of a management tool that compares the event with a set of criteria and rules in a prescribed order. These criteria are often called business rules, although they are generally fairly technical. The idea is that the event may represent some impact on the business and the rules can be used to determine the level and type of business impact.

A correlation engine is programmed according to the performance standards created during service design and any additional guidance specific to the operating environment.

Examples of what correlation engines will take into account for warning events might include:

■ Number of similar events (e.g. this is the third time that the same user has logged in with the incorrect password, a business application reports that there has been an unusual pattern of usage of a mobile telephone that could indicate that the device has been lost or stolen)
■ Number of CIs generating similar events
■ Whether a specific action is associated with the code or data in the event
■ Whether the event represents an exception
■ A comparison of utilization information in the event with a maximum or minimum standard (e.g. has the device exceeded a threshold?)
■ Whether additional data is required to investigate the event further, and possibly even a collection of that data by polling another system or database
■ Categorization of the event
■ Assigning a priority level to the event.

4.1.5.8 Further action required?

If the second-level correlation activity recognizes an event, a response will be required.

There are many different types of responses, each designed specifically for the task it has to initiate. Examples can include:

■ Generating a record in the incident management system, thus initiating the incident management process
■ Generating an RFC, thus initiating the change management process
■ An authorized RFC that has been implemented but caused the event, or from an unauthorized change that has been detected – in either case this will be referred to change management for investigation
■ Scripts that execute specific actions, such as submitting batch jobs or rebooting a device
■ Paging systems that will notify a person or team of the event by mobile phone
■ Database actions that restrict access of a user to specific records or fields, or that create or delete entries in the database.

4.1.5.9 Response selection

At this point in the process, there are a number of response options available. It is important to note that the response options can be chosen in any combination. For example, it may be necessary to preserve the log entry for future reference, but at the same time escalate the event to an operations management staff member for action.

The options in the flow chart are examples. Different organizations will have different options, and they are sure to be more detailed. For example, there will be a range of auto responses for each different technology. The process of determining which one is appropriate and how to execute it are not represented in this flow chart. Some of the options available are listed below.

Auto response

Some events are understood well enough that the appropriate response has already been defined and automated. This is normally as a result of good design or of previous experience (usually problem management). The response will initiate the action and then evaluate whether it was completed successfully. If not, an incident or problem record will be created. Examples of auto responses include:

■ Rebooting a device
■ Restarting a service
■ Submitting a job into batch
■ Changing a parameter on a device

■ Locking a device or application to protect it against unauthorized access.

Note that locking a device may result in denial of service to authorized users, which could be exploited by a deliberate attacker – so great care should be taken when deciding whether this is an appropriate automated action. Where this response is used it may be prudent to also combine this with a call for human intervention, so that the automated action can be swiftly checked and approved.

Alert and human intervention

If the event requires human intervention, it will need to be escalated. The purpose of the alert is to ensure that the person with the skills appropriate to deal with the event is notified. The alert will contain all the information necessary for that person to determine the appropriate action – including reference to any documentation required (e.g. user manuals). It is important to note that this is not necessarily the same as the functional escalation of an incident, where the emphasis is on restoring service within an agreed time (which may require a variety of activities). The alert requires a person, or team, to perform a specific action, possibly on a specific device and possibly at a specific time, e.g. changing a toner cartridge in a printer when the level is low.

Incident, problem or change?

Some events will represent a situation where the appropriate response will need to be handled through the incident, problem or change management process. These are discussed below, but it is important to note that a single event may initiate any one or a combination of these three processes – for example, a non-critical server failure is logged as an incident, but as the underlying cause is not known, a problem record is created to determine the root cause and resolution and an RFC is logged to relocate the workload onto an alternative server while the problem is resolved.

Open an RFC

There are two places in the event management process where an RFC can be created:

■ **When an exception occurs** For example, a scan of a network segment reveals that two new devices have been added without the

necessary authorization. A way of dealing with this situation is to open an RFC, which can be used as a vehicle for the change management process to deal with the exception (as an alternative to the more conventional approach of opening an incident that would be routed via the service desk to change management). Investigation by change management is appropriate here because unauthorized changes imply that the change management process was not effective.

■ **Correlation identifies that a change is needed** In this case the event correlation activity determines that the appropriate response to an event is for something to be changed. For example, a performance threshold has been reached and a parameter on a major server needs to be tuned. How does the correlation activity determine this? It was programmed to do so either in the service design process or because this has happened before and problem management or operations management updated the correlation engine to take this action.

Open an incident record

As with an RFC, an incident can be generated immediately when an exception is detected, or when the correlation engine determines that a specific type or combination of events represents an incident. When an incident record is opened, as much information as possible should be included – with links to the events concerned and if possible a completed diagnostic script.

Open or link to a problem record

It is rare for a problem record to be opened without related incidents (for example as a result of a service failure analysis (see *ITIL Service Design*) or maturity assessment, or because of a high number of retry network errors, even though a failure has not yet occurred). In most cases this step refers to linking an incident to an existing problem record. This will assist the problem management teams to reassess the severity and impact of the problem, and may result in a changed priority to an outstanding problem. Event management technologies can also be used to evaluate the impact of incidents and raise problem records automatically, to allow root cause analysis to start immediately.

Special types of incident

In some cases an event will indicate an exception that does not directly impact any IT service; for example a redundant air conditioning unit fails, or there is an unauthorized entry to a data centre. Guidelines for these events are as follows:

■ An incident should be logged using an incident model that is appropriate for that type of exception, e.g. an operations incident or security incident (see section 4.2.4.2 for more details of incident models).

■ The incident should be escalated to the group that manages that type of incident.

■ As there is no outage, the incident model used should reflect that this was an operational issue rather than a service issue. The statistics would not normally be reported to customers or users, unless they can be used to demonstrate that the money invested in redundancy was a good investment.

■ These incidents should not be used to calculate downtime, and can in fact be used to demonstrate how proactive IT has been in making services available.

4.1.5.10 Review actions

With thousands of events being generated every day, it is not possible formally to review every individual event. However, it is important to check that any significant events or exceptions have been handled appropriately, or to track trends or counts of event types etc. In many cases this can be done automatically, for example polling a server that had been rebooted using an automated script to see that it is functioning correctly.

In cases where events have initiated an incident, problem and/or change, the action review should not duplicate any reviews that have been done as part of those processes. Rather, the intention is to ensure that the handover between the event management process and other processes took place as designed and that the expected action did indeed take place. This will ensure that incidents, problems or changes originating within operations management do not get lost between the teams or departments.

The review will also be used as input into continual improvement and the evaluation and audit of the event management process.

4.1.5.11 Close event

Some events will remain open until a certain action takes place, for example an event that is linked to an open incident. However, most events are not 'opened' or 'closed'.

Informational events are simply logged and then used as input to other processes, such as backup and storage management. Auto-response events will typically be closed by the generation of a second event. For example, a device generates an event and is rebooted through auto response – as soon as that device is successfully back online, it generates an event that effectively closes the loop and removes the first event.

It is sometimes very difficult to relate open and closed events if they are in different formats. It is suggested that devices in the infrastructure produce these events in the same format and specify the change of status. This allows the correlation step in the process to easily match open and close notifications.

In the case of events that generated an incident, problem or change, these should be formally closed with a link to the appropriate record from the other process.

4.1.6 Triggers, inputs, outputs and interfaces

4.1.6.1 Triggers

Event management can be initiated by any type of change in state. The key is to define which of these state changes need to be acted upon. Examples of triggers might include:

■ Exceptions to any level of CI performance defined in the design specifications, OLAs or SOPs

■ Exceptions to an automated procedure or process, e.g. a routine change that has been assigned to a build team has not been completed in time

■ An exception within a business process that is being monitored by event management

■ The completion of an automated task or job

■ A status change in a server or database CI

■ Access of an application or database by a user or automated procedure or job

■ A situation where a device, database or application etc. has reached a predefined threshold of performance.

4.1.6.2 Inputs

Inputs to the event management process will mostly come from service design and service transition. Examples of these may include:

■ Operational and service level requirements associated with events and their actions
■ Alarms, alerts and thresholds for recognizing events
■ Event correlation tables, rules, event codes and automated response solutions that will support event management activities
■ Roles and responsibilities for recognizing events and communicating them to those that need to handle them
■ Operational procedures for recognizing, logging, escalating and communicating events.

4.1.6.3 Outputs

Examples of outputs from event management may include:

■ Events that have been communicated and escalated to those responsible for further action
■ Event logs describing what events took place and any escalation and communication activities taken to support forensic, diagnosis or further CSI activities
■ Events that indicate an incident has occurred
■ Events that indicate the potential breach of an SLA or OLA objective
■ Events and alerts that indicate completion status of deployment, operational or other support activities
■ Populated SKMS with event information and history.

4.1.6.4 Interfaces

Event management can interface to any process that requires monitoring and control, especially those that do not require real-time monitoring, but which do require some form of intervention following an event or group of events. Examples of interfaces with other processes are listed below for each service lifecycle stage.

Service design

■ **Service level management**   Event management can play an important role in ensuring that potential impact on SLAs is detected early and any failures are rectified as soon as possible so that impact on service targets is minimized.
■ **Information security management**   Interface with business applications and/or business processes to allow potentially significant business events to be detected and acted upon (e.g. a business application reports abnormal activity on a customer's account that may indicate some sort of fraud or security breach).
■ **Capacity and availability management**   These processes are critical in defining what events are significant, what appropriate thresholds should be and how to respond to them. In return, event management will improve the performance and availability of services by responding to events when they occur and by reporting on actual events and patterns of events to determine (by comparison with SLA targets and key performance indicators (KPIs)) if there is some aspect of the infrastructure design or operation that can be improved.

Service transition

■ **Service asset and configuration management**   This process (covered in more detail in *ITIL Service Design* and *ITIL Service Transition*) is able to use events to determine the current status of any CI in the infrastructure. Comparing events with the authorized baselines in the CMS will help to determine whether there is unauthorized change activity taking place in the organization (see *ITIL Service Transition*). In addition, this process can use event management to determine the lifecycle status of assets. For example, an event could be generated to signal that a new asset has been successfully configured and is now operational.
■ **Knowledge management**   Events can be a rich source of information that can be processed for inclusion in knowledge management systems. For example, patterns of performance can be correlated with business activity and used as input into future design and strategy decisions.
■ **Change management**   Interfaces with change management to identify conditions that may require a response or action.

Service operation

- **Incident and problem management** Interfaces with activities to resolve incidents and problems to identify conditions that may require a response or action.
- **Access management** Events can be used to detect unauthorized access attempts and security breaches.

4.1.7 Information management

Key information involved in event management includes the following:

- Messages, such as SNMP messages, which are a standard way of communicating technical information about the status of components of an IT infrastructure.
- Databases, such as management information bases of IT devices that contain information about that device, including its operating system, basic input/output system (BIOS) version, configuration of system parameters etc. The ability to interrogate these databases and compare them to a norm is critical to being able to generate events.
- Vendor's monitoring tools agent software.
- Correlation engines contain detailed rules to determine the significance and appropriate response to events. Details on this are provided in section 4.1.5.7.

There is no standard event record for all types of event. The exact contents and format of the record depend on the tools being used, what is being monitored (e.g. a server and the change management tools will have very different data and probably use a different format). However, there is some key data that is usually required from each event to be useful in analysis. It should typically include the:

- Device
- Component
- Type of failure
- Date/time
- Parameters in exception
- Unique identifier to allow for tracking of the event across the event management infrastructure and correlation into the other ITSM processes like incident, problem and change
- Value.

4.1.8 Critical success factors and key performance indicators

The following list includes some sample critical success factors (CSFs) for event management. Each organization should identify appropriate CSFs based on its objectives for the process. Each sample CSF is followed by a small number of typical KPIs that support the CSF. These KPIs should not be adopted without careful consideration. Each organization should develop KPIs that are appropriate for its level of maturity, its CSFs and its particular circumstances. Achievement against KPIs should be monitored and used to identify opportunities for improvement, which should be logged in the continual service improvement (CSI) register for evaluation and possible implementation.

- **CSF** Detecting all changes of state that have significance for the management of CIs and IT services
  - **KPI** Number and ratio of events compared with the number of incidents
  - **KPI** Number and percentage of each type of event per platform or application versus total number of platforms and applications underpinning live IT services (looking to identify IT services that may be at risk for lack of capability to detect their events)
- **CSF** Ensuring all events are communicated to the appropriate functions that need to be informed or take further control actions
  - **KPI** Number and percentage of events that required human intervention and whether this was performed
  - **KPI** Number of incidents that occurred and percentage of these that were triggered without a corresponding event
- **CSF** Providing the trigger, or entry point, for the execution of many service operation processes and operations management activities
  - **KPI** Number and percentage of events that required human intervention and whether this was performed
- **CSF** Provide the means to compare actual operating performance and behaviour against design standards and SLAs
  - **KPI** Number and percentage of incidents that were resolved without impact to the business (indicates the overall effectiveness

of the event management process and underpinning solutions)

- **KPI** Number and percentage of events that resulted in incidents or changes
- **KPI** Number and percentage of events caused by existing problems or known errors (this may result in a change to the priority of work on that problem or known error)
- **KPI** Number and percentage of events indicating performance issues (for example, growth in the number of times an application exceeded its transaction thresholds over the past six months)
- **KPI** Number and percentage of events indicating potential availability issues (e.g. failovers to alternative devices, or excessive workload swapping)
- **CSF** Providing a basis for service assurance, reporting and service improvement
  - **KPI** Number and percentage of repeated or duplicated events (this will help in the tuning of the correlation engine to eliminate unnecessary event generation and can also be used to assist in the design of better event generation functionality in new services)
  - **KPI** Number of events/alerts generated without actual degradation of service/functionality (false positives – indication of the accuracy of the instrumentation parameters, important for CSI).

4.1.9 Challenges and risks

4.1.9.1 Challenges

There are a number of challenges that might be encountered:

- An initial challenge may be to obtain funding for the necessary tools and effort needed to install and exploit the benefits of the tools. In order to obtain the necessary funding a compelling business case should be prepared showing how the benefits of effective event management can far outweigh the costs – giving a positive ROI.
- One of the greatest challenges is setting the correct level of filtering. Setting the level of filtering incorrectly can result in either being flooded with relatively insignificant events, or not being able to detect relatively important events until it is too late.

- Deploying the necessary monitoring agents across the entire IT infrastructure may be a difficult and time-consuming activity requiring an ongoing commitment over quite a long period – there is a danger that other activities may arise that could divert resources and delay the deployment.
- Automated monitoring activities can generate additional network traffic that might have negative impacts on planned capacity levels of the network. This might lead to actions that reduce frequency of polling or communication between agents and the system resulting in less traffic, but could delay identification of events.
- Acquiring the necessary skills can be time-consuming and costly.
- Deploying event management tools without setting up processes to operate them, processes to deploy monitors and agents to new CIs, and processes to update filters, correlation rules or triggers can put the value of these tool investments at risk.

4.1.9.2 Risks

The key risks are really those already mentioned above:

- Failure to obtain adequate funding
- Ensuring the correct level of filtering
- Failure to maintain momentum in deploying the necessary monitoring agents across the IT infrastructure.

If any of these risks are not addressed it could adversely impact on the success of event management.

4.2 INCIDENT MANAGEMENT

In ITIL terminology, an 'incident' is defined as an unplanned interruption to an IT service or reduction in the quality of an IT service or a failure of a CI that has not yet impacted an IT service (for example failure of one disk from a mirror set).

Incident management is the process responsible for managing the lifecycle of all incidents. Incidents may be recognized by technical staff, detected and reported by event monitoring tools, communications from users (usually via a telephone call to the service desk), or reported by third-party suppliers and partners.

4.2.1 Purpose and objectives

4.2.1.1 Purpose

The purpose of incident management is to restore normal service operation as quickly as possible and minimize the adverse impact on business operations, thus ensuring that agreed levels of service quality are maintained. 'Normal service operation' is defined as an operational state where services and CIs are performing within their agreed service and operational levels.

4.2.1.2 Objectives

The objectives of the incident management process are to:

- Ensure that standardized methods and procedures are used for efficient and prompt response, analysis, documentation, ongoing management and reporting of incidents
- Increase visibility and communication of incidents to business and IT support staff
- Enhance business perception of IT through use of a professional approach in quickly resolving and communicating incidents when they occur
- Align incident management activities and priorities with those of the business
- Maintain user satisfaction with the quality of IT services.

4.2.2 Scope

Incident management includes any event which disrupts, or which could disrupt, a service. This includes events which are communicated directly by users, either through the service desk or through an interface from event management to incident management tools.

Incidents can also be reported and/or logged by technical staff (if, for example, they notice something untoward with a hardware or network component they may report or log an incident and refer it to the service desk). This does not mean, however, that all events are incidents. Many classes of events are not related to disruptions at all, but are indicators of normal operation or are simply informational (see section 4.1).

Although both incidents and service requests are reported to the service desk, this does not mean that they are the same. Service requests do not represent a disruption to agreed service, but are a way of meeting the customer's needs and may

be addressing an agreed target in an SLA. Service requests are dealt with by the request fulfilment process (see section 4.3).

4.2.3 Value to business

The value of incident management includes:

- The ability to reduce unplanned labour and costs for both the business and IT support staff caused by incidents.
- The ability to detect and resolve incidents which results in lower downtime to the business, which in turn means higher availability of the service. This means that the business is able to exploit the functionality of the service as designed.
- The ability to align IT activity to real-time business priorities. This is because incident management includes the capability to identify business priorities and dynamically allocate resources as necessary.
- The ability to identify potential improvements to services. This happens as a result of understanding what constitutes an incident and also from being in contact with the activities of business operational staff.
- The service desk can, during its handling of incidents, identify additional service or training requirements found in IT or the business.

Incident management is highly visible to the business, and it is therefore easier to demonstrate its value than most areas in service operation. For this reason, incident management is often one of the first processes to be implemented in service management projects. The added benefit of doing this is that incident management can be used to highlight other areas that need attention – thereby providing a justification for expenditure on implementing other processes.

4.2.4 Policies, principles and basic concepts

4.2.4.1 Policies

Examples of incident management policies might include:

- Incidents and their status must be timely and effectively communicated. This implies that a good service desk function is in place to coordinate communication about incidents to those impacted by them as well as those working to resolve them. The audience receiving communications about incidents must be considered to ensure that communications are in business terms or the right level of technical terms where appropriate.

- Incidents must be resolved within timeframes acceptable to the business. This implies that agreed service levels, operational levels and underpinning contracts (UCs) are in place, quick access is available to incident, known error and configuration information, and appropriate technology support is in place to efficiently record, classify, prioritize and diagnose incidents. Appropriate resources to work the incident should be made available and adequate access to needed technologies and resources should also be provided to work the issues and develop plans to meet expected service levels.

- Customer satisfaction must be maintained at all times. This implies that adequate customer-oriented and technically trained support staff with the correct skill levels are effectively utilized at all stages of the process.

- Incident processing and handling should be aligned with overall service levels and objectives. This ensures that incident management activities support service levels and objectives by prioritizing those activities based on actual business need. It implies that required service levels and objectives are already understood and agreed to by the business.

- All incidents should be stored and managed in a single management system. Status and detailed information on the incident should be recorded and updated on a timely basis in incident records. This provides a definitive recognized source for incident information and supports easier access for reporting and investigation efforts. Technologies used to support this system should be well integrated throughout the business and interface easily to other service management technologies that use or provide incident-related information.

- All incidents should subscribe to a standard classification schema that is consistent across the business enterprise. This provides for faster access to incident and troubleshooting information. It provides better support for problem management diagnostic and proactive trending activities. It implies that a well defined

and communicated set of incident classification categories is in place. Service desk and incident handling staff are aware of what categories exist and the ability to enter non-standard categories for incidents is highly restricted.

- Incident records should be audited on a regular basis to ensure they have been entered and categorized correctly. This ensures that incident information is accurate, correctly categorized and can be trusted by other support areas. This implies that incident records are audited by an independent source for accuracy and completeness. Feedback mechanisms should be in place to communicate audit findings and issues to incident handling staff.

- All incident records should utilize a common format and set of information fields wherever possible (see section 4.2.5.2). This ensures that all required information about incidents is made available in a common format to support incident management activities and is easily shared across other support areas dependent on incident information.

- A common and agreed set of criteria for prioritizing and escalating incidents should be in place wherever possible (see sections 4.2.5.4 and 4.2.5.6). This ensures that accepted means are in place for prioritizing and escalating incidents based on agreed policies and not solely determined by individuals within the IT support organization. This implies that criteria for prioritizing and escalating incidents are established in advance, well communicated, and agreed to by both IT and the business.

4.2.4.2 Principles and basic concepts

There are some basic things that need to be taken into account and decided when considering incident management. These are covered in this section.

Timescales

Timescales must be agreed for all incident handling stages (these will differ depending upon the priority level of the incident), based upon the overall incident response and resolution targets within SLAs, and captured as targets within OLAs and UCs. All support groups should be made fully aware of these timescales. Service management tools should be used to automate timescales and escalate the incident as required based on predefined rules.

Incident models

Many incidents are not new – they involve dealing with something that has happened before and may well happen again. For this reason, many organizations will find it helpful to predefine 'standard' incident models and apply them to appropriate incidents when they occur.

An incident model is a way of predefining the steps that should be taken to handle a process (in this case a process for dealing with a particular type of incident) in an agreed way. Support tools can then be used to manage the required process. This will ensure that 'standard' incidents are handled in a predefined path and within predefined timescales.

Incidents which would require specialized handling can be treated in this way (for example, security-related incidents can be routed to information security management and capacity- or performance-related incidents that would be routed to capacity management).

The incident model should include:

- The steps that should be taken to handle the incident
- The chronological order these steps should be taken in, with any dependencies or co-processing defined
- Responsibilities; who should do what
- Precautions to be taken before resolving the incident such as backing up data, configuration files, or steps to comply with health and safety related guidelines
- Timescales and thresholds for completion of the actions
- Escalation procedures; who should be contacted and when
- Any necessary evidence-preservation activities (particularly relevant for security- and capacity-related incidents).

The models should be input to the incident handling support tools in use and the tools should then automate the handling, management and escalation of the process. Incident models should be stored in the SKMS.

Major incidents

A separate procedure, with shorter timescales and greater urgency, must be used for 'major' incidents. A definition of what constitutes a major incident must be agreed and ideally mapped onto the overall incident prioritization scheme – such that they will be dealt with through this separate procedure.[2]

Where necessary, the major incident procedure should include the establishment of a separate major incident team under the direct leadership of the incident manager, formulated to concentrate on this incident alone to ensure that adequate resources and focus are provided to finding a swift resolution. If the service desk manager is also fulfilling the role of incident manager (say in a small organization), then a separate person may need to be designated to lead the major incident investigation team – so as to avoid conflict of time or priorities – but should ultimately report back to the incident manager.

If the cause of the incident needs to be investigated at the same time, then the problem manager would be involved as well, but the incident manager must ensure that service restoration and underlying cause are kept separate. Throughout, the service desk would ensure that all activities are recorded and users are kept fully informed of progress. While the service desk may be accountable for ensuring that the incident/major incident record is always up-to-date, responsibility may also lie elsewhere (such as with the other technical teams).

Incident status tracking

Incidents should be tracked throughout their lifecycle to support proper handling and reporting on the status of incidents. Within the incident management system, status codes may be linked to incidents to indicate where they are in relation to the lifecycle. Examples of these might include:

- **Open** An incident has been recognized but not yet assigned to a support resource for resolution
- **In progress** The incident is in the process of being investigated and resolved
- **Resolved** A resolution has been put in place for the incident but normal state service operation has not yet been validated by the business or end user

---

[2] People sometimes use loose terminology and/or confuse a major incident with a problem. In reality, an incident remains an incident for ever – it may grow in impact or priority to become a major incident, but an incident never 'becomes' a problem. A problem is the underlying cause of one or more incidents and remains a separate entity always!

■ **Closed** The user or business has agreed that the incident has been resolved and that normal state operations have been restored.

Expanded incident lifecycle

ITIL Service Design and *ITIL Continual Service Improvement* describe the expanded incident lifecycle which can be used to help understand all contributions to the impact of incidents and to plan for how these could be controlled or reduced.

4.2.5 Process activities, methods and techniques

The process activities to be followed during the management of an incident are shown in Figure 4.3, and include the following steps.

4.2.5.1 Incident identification

While work cannot begin on dealing with an incident until it is known that an incident has occurred, it is usually unacceptable, from a business perspective, to wait until a user is impacted and contacts the service desk. As far as possible, all key components should be monitored so that failures or potential failures are detected early. This means that the incident management process can be started quickly. Ideally, incidents should be resolved before they have an impact on users!

Please see section 4.1 for further details.

4.2.5.2 Incident logging

All incidents must be fully logged and date/ time stamped, regardless of whether they are raised through a service desk telephone call, automatically detected via an event alert, or from any other source.[3]

All relevant information relating to the nature of the incident must be logged so that a full historical record is maintained – and so that if the incident has to be referred to other support group(s), they will have all relevant information to hand to assist them.

The information needed for each incident can include:

■ Unique reference number

■ Incident categorization (often broken down into between two and four sub-categories)
■ Incident urgency
■ Incident impact
■ Incident prioritization
■ Date/time recorded
■ Name/ID of the person and/or group recording the incident
■ Method of notification (telephone, automatic, email, in person etc.)
■ Name/department/phone/location of user
■ Call-back method (telephone, mail etc.)
■ Description of symptoms
■ Incident status (active, waiting, closed etc.)
■ Related CI
■ Support group/person to which the incident is allocated
■ Related problem/known error
■ Activities undertaken to resolve the incident and when these took place
■ Resolution date and time
■ Closure category
■ Closure date and time.

Note that if the service desk does not work 24/7 and responsibility for first-line incident logging and handling passes to another group, such as IT operations or network support, out of service desk hours, then these staff need to be equally rigorous about logging of incident details. Full training and awareness needs to be provided to such staff on this issue.

As further activities to resolve an incident occur, the incident record should be updated with relevant information and details so that a full history is maintained. Examples of this might include changing the categorization or priority once further diagnosis or escalation activities have occurred.

4.2.5.3 Incident categorization

Part of the initial logging must be to allocate suitable incident categorization coding so that the exact type of incident is recorded. This will be important later when looking at incident types/ frequencies to establish trends for use in problem management, supplier management and other ITSM activities.

Note that the check for service requests in this process does not imply that service requests are

---

[3] If service desk and/or support staff visit the customers to deal with one incident, they may be asked to deal with further incidents 'while they are there'. It is important that if this is done, a separate incident record is logged for each additional incident handled, to ensure that a historical record is kept and credit is given for the work undertaken.

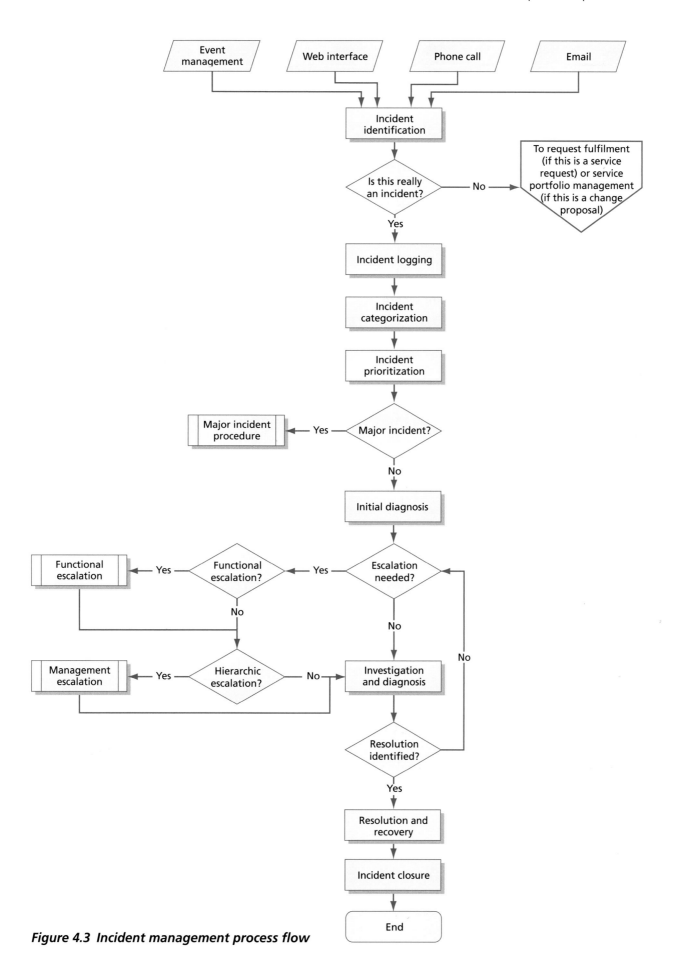

Figure 4.3 Incident management process flow

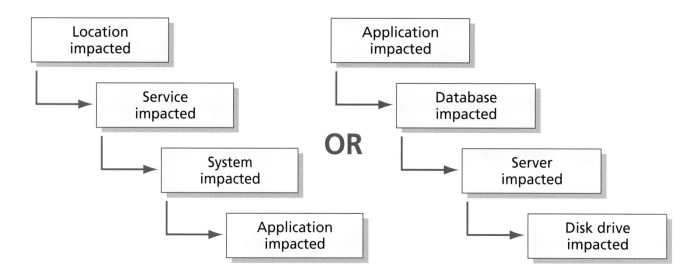

Figure 4.4 Multi-level incident categorization

incidents. This is simply recognition of the fact that service requests are sometimes incorrectly logged as incidents (e.g. a user incorrectly enters the request as an incident from the web interface). This check will detect any such requests and ensure that they are passed to the request fulfilment process. Incident categorization may change throughout the lifecycle of an incident. For example, upon discovery and logging of the incident, initial categories may reflect symptoms (e.g. 'service unavailable' or 'performance slow'). Upon later analysis, categories may reflect the actual CIs at fault such as 'server' or 'disk drive'. For this reason, multi-level categorization can be used to identify multiple levels of categories that can be associated with an incident. The capability to track chosen categories as they change throughout the lifecycle of an incident may also prove useful when looking for potential improvements.

Multi-level categorization is available in most tools – usually to three or four levels of granularity. For example, an incident may be categorized as shown in Figure 4.4.

All organizations are unique and it is therefore difficult to give generic guidance on the categories an organization should use, particularly at the lower levels. However, there is a technique that can be used to assist an organization achieve a correct and complete set of categories – if they are starting from scratch! The steps involve:

1   Hold a brainstorming session among the relevant support groups, involving the service

desk supervisor and incident and problem managers.

2   Use this session to decide the 'best guess' top-level categories, ideally with the customer in mind, so that service (or worst case, application) heads the list – and include an 'other' category. Set up the relevant logging tools to use these categories for a trial period.

3   Use the categories for a short trial period (long enough for several hundred incidents to fall into each category, but not too long that an analysis will take too long to perform).

4   Perform an analysis of the incidents logged during the trial period. The number of incidents logged in each higher-level category will confirm whether the categories are worth having – and a more detailed analysis of the 'other' category should allow identification of any additional higher-level categories that will be needed.

5   A breakdown analysis of the incidents within each higher-level category should be used to decide the lower-level categories that will be required.

6   Review and repeat these activities after a further period of, say, one to three months and again review regularly to ensure that they remain relevant. Be aware that any significant changes to categorization may cause some difficulties for incident trending or management reporting, so they should be stabilized unless changes are genuinely required.

If an existing categorization scheme is in use, but is not thought to be working satisfactorily, the basic idea of the technique suggested above can be used to review and amend the existing scheme.

It is worth noting that sometimes the details available at the time an incident is logged may be incomplete, misleading or incorrect. It is therefore important that the categorization of the incident is checked, and updated if necessary, at call closure time (in a separate closure categorization field, so as not to corrupt the original categorization) (see section 4.2.5.9).

4.2.5.4 Incident prioritization

Another important aspect of logging every incident is to agree and allocate an appropriate prioritization code, as this will determine how the incident is handled both by support tools and support staff.

Prioritization can normally be determined by taking into account both the urgency of the incident (how quickly the business needs a resolution) and the level of business impact it is causing. An indication of impact is often (but not always) the number of users being affected. In some cases, and very importantly, the loss of service to a single user can have a major business impact – it all depends upon who is trying to do what – so numbers alone are not enough to evaluate overall priority! Other factors that can also contribute to impact levels are:

- Risk to life or limb
- The number of services affected – may be multiple services
- The level of financial losses

Table 4.1 Simple priority coding system

Impact				
Urgency		High	Medium	Low
	High	1	2	3
	Medium	2	3	4
	Low	3	4	5

Priority code	Description	Target resolution time
1	Critical	1 hour
2	High	8 hours
3	Medium	24 hours
4	Low	48 hours
5	Planning	Planned

- Effect on business reputation
- Regulatory or legislative breaches.

An effective way of calculating these elements and deriving an overall priority level for each incident is given in Table 4.1.

In all cases, clear guidance – with practical examples – should be provided for all support staff to enable them to determine the correct urgency and impact levels, so the correct priority is allocated. Such guidance should be produced during service level negotiations.

However, it must be noted that there will be occasions when, because of particular business expediency, normal priority levels have to be overridden. When a user is adamant that an incident's priority level should exceed normal guidelines, the service desk should comply with such a request – and if it subsequently turns out to be incorrect this can be resolved as an off-line management level issue, rather than a dispute occurring with the user while the incident is being reported.

Some organizations may also recognize VIPs (high-ranking executives, officers, diplomats, politicians etc.) whose incidents would be handled on a higher priority than normal – but in such cases this is best catered for and documented within the guidance provided to the service desk staff on how to apply the priority levels, so they are all aware of the agreed rules for VIPs, and who falls into this category. A better practice would be to formally recognize VIP priorities as an additional service option (the 'gold' level of service, for example) that is documented as part of the service catalogue tied to differentiated service levels.

It should be noted that an incident's priority may be dynamic – if circumstances change, or if an incident is not resolved within SLA target times, then the priority must be altered to reflect the new situation. Changes to priority that might occur throughout the management of an incident should be recorded in the incident record to provide an audit trail of why the priority was changed.

Note that some tools may have constraints that make it difficult automatically to calculate performance against SLA targets if a priority is changed during the lifetime of an incident. However, if circumstances do change, the change in priority should be made – and if necessary manual adjustments made to reporting tools. Ideally, tools with such constraints should not be selected.

4.2.5.5 Initial diagnosis

If the incident has been routed via the service desk, the service desk analyst must carry out initial diagnosis, typically while the user is still on the telephone – if the call is raised in this way – to try to discover the full symptoms of the incident and to determine exactly what has gone wrong and how to correct it. It is at this stage that diagnostic scripts and known error information can be most valuable in allowing earlier and accurate diagnosis.

If possible, the service desk analyst can resolve an incident while the user is still on the telephone – and close the incident if the resolution and recovery are agreed to be successful.

If the service desk analyst cannot resolve the incident while the user is still on the telephone, but there is a prospect that the service desk may be able to do so within the agreed time limit without help from other support groups, the analyst should inform the user of their intentions, give the user the incident reference number and attempt to find a resolution.

Incident matching procedure

Many incidents are regularly experienced and the appropriate resolution actions are well known. However, it is necessary to have a procedure for matching incident classification data against that for problems and known errors. Successful matching gives efficient and quick access to proven resolution actions, reducing the time it takes to restore service back to users. The process of classification and matching allows incident management to be carried out more quickly and minimizes the need for escalation to other support staff.

Effective use of incident matching ensures that incidents are not redundantly being investigated for resolution over and over each time. A procedure can be developed to help service desk and other support staff match incidents to find resolutions quickly where possible. An example of an incident-matching procedure is shown in Figure 4.5.

4.2.5.6 Incident escalation

Functional escalation

As soon as it becomes clear that the service desk is unable to resolve the incident itself (or when target times for first-point resolution have been exceeded – whichever comes first), the incident must be immediately escalated for further support.

If the organization has a hierarchy of support groups with more time or specialist skills that the service desk believes can resolve the incident, it should refer the incident to the appropriate next level support group in that hierarchy. If it is obvious that the incident will require deeper technical knowledge – or a support group has not been able to resolve the incident within agreed target times (whichever comes first), the incident must be immediately escalated to the next appropriate support group in the hierarchy. The rules for escalation and handling of incidents must be agreed in OLAs and UCs with internal and external support groups, respectively.

Some incidents may require multiple support groups to resolve. Support groups may be internal, but they may also be third parties such as software suppliers or hardware manufacturers or maintainers. The rules for handling of incidents across support groups and between third-party support providers must also be agreed in OLAs and UCs with each support group, respectively.

Note that incident ownership remains with the service desk! Regardless of where an incident is referred to during its life, ownership of the incident must remain with the service desk at all times. The service desk remains responsible for tracking progress, keeping users informed and ultimately for incident closure.

Hierarchic escalation

If incidents are of a serious nature (for example, high-priority incidents) the appropriate IT managers must be notified, for informational purposes at least. Hierarchic escalation is also used if the 'investigation and diagnosis' and 'resolution and recovery' steps are taking too long or proving too difficult. Hierarchic escalation should continue up the management chain so that senior managers are aware and can be prepared and take any necessary action, such as allocating additional resources or involving suppliers/maintainers.

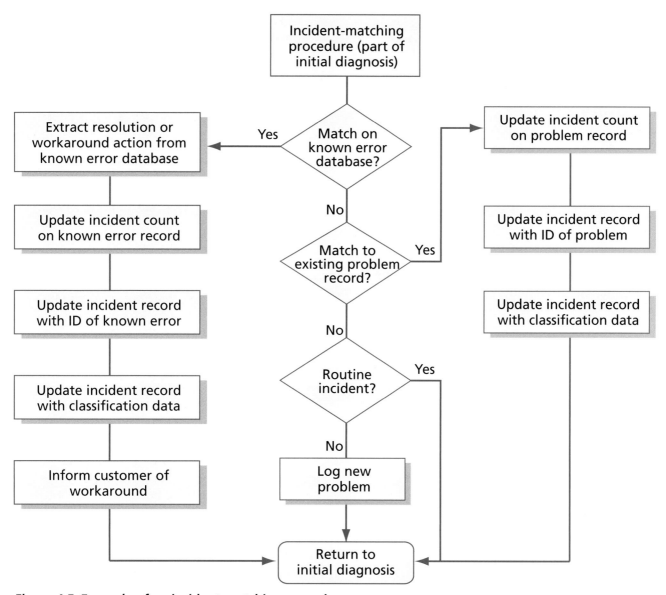

Figure 4.5 Example of an incident-matching procedure

Hierarchic escalation is also used when there is contention about who the incident is allocated to.

Hierarchic escalation can, of course, be initiated by the affected users or customer management, as they see fit – that is why it is important that IT managers are made aware so that they can anticipate and prepare for any such escalation.

The exact levels and timescales for both functional and hierarchic escalation need to be agreed, taking into account SLA targets, and embedded within support tools which can then be used to police and control the process flow within agreed timescales. The service desk should keep the user informed of any relevant escalation that takes place and ensure the incident record is updated accordingly to keep a full history of actions.

Note regarding allocation of staff for handling incidents

There may be many incidents in a queue with the same priority level, so it will be the job of the service desk and/or incident management staff initially, in conjunction with managers of the various support groups to which incidents are escalated, to decide the order in which incidents should be picked up and actively worked on. These managers must ensure that incidents are dealt with in true business priority order and that staff are not allowed to arbitrarily choose the incidents they will address!

4.2.5.7 Investigation and diagnosis

A reported incident is likely to require some degree of investigation and diagnosis. Each of the support groups involved with the incident handling will investigate and diagnose what has gone wrong – and all such activities (including details of any actions taken to try to resolve or recreate the incident) should be fully documented in the incident record so that a complete historical record of all activities is maintained at all times.

Note that valuable time can often be lost if investigation and diagnostic action (or indeed resolution or recovery actions) are performed serially. Where possible, such activities should be performed in parallel to reduce overall timescales – and support tools should be designed and/ or selected to allow this. However, care should be taken to coordinate activities, particularly resolution or recovery activities, otherwise the actions of different groups may conflict or further complicate a resolution!

This investigation is likely to include such actions as:

■ Establishing exactly what has gone wrong or is being sought by the user
■ Understanding the chronological order of events
■ Confirming the full impact of the incident, including the number and range of users affected
■ Identifying any events that could have triggered the incident (e.g. a recent change, some user action?)
■ Detailed knowledge searches looking for previous occurrences by searching incident/ problem records and/or known error databases (KEDBs) or manufacturers'/suppliers' error logs or knowledge databases. These matches may not have been obvious during initial diagnosis.

4.2.5.8 Resolution and recovery

When a potential resolution has been identified, this should be applied and tested. The specific actions to be undertaken and the people who will be involved in taking the recovery actions may vary, depending upon the nature of the fault, but could involve:

■ Asking the user to undertake directed activities on their own desktop or remote equipment

■ The service desk implementing the resolution either centrally (say, rebooting a server) or remotely using software to take control of the user's desktop to diagnose and implement a resolution
■ Specialist support groups being asked to implement specific recovery actions (e.g. network support reconfiguring a router)
■ A third-party supplier or maintainer being asked to resolve the fault.

Even when a resolution has been found, sufficient testing must be performed to ensure that recovery action is complete and that normal state service operation has been restored. Note that in some cases it may be necessary for two or more groups to take separate, though perhaps coordinated, recovery actions for an overall resolution to be implemented. In such cases incident management must coordinate the activities and liaise with all parties involved.

Regardless of the actions taken, or who does them, the incident record must be updated accordingly with all relevant information and details so that a full history is maintained.

The resolving group should pass the incident back to the service desk for closure action.

4.2.5.9 Incident closure

The service desk should check that the incident is fully resolved and that the users are satisfied and willing to agree the incident can be closed. The service desk should also check the following:

■ **Closure categorization**   Check and confirm that the initial incident categorization was correct or, where the categorization subsequently turned out to be incorrect, update the record so that a correct closure categorization is recorded for the incident – seeking advice or guidance from the resolving group(s) as necessary.
■ **User satisfaction survey**   Carry out a user satisfaction call-back or email survey for the agreed percentage of incidents.
■ **Incident documentation**   Chase any outstanding details and ensure that the incident record is fully documented so that a full historic record at a sufficient level of detail is complete.
■ **Ongoing or recurring problem?**   Determine (in conjunction with resolver groups) whether the

incident was resolved without the root cause being identified. In this situation, it is likely that the incident could recur and require further preventive action to avoid this. In all such cases, determine if a problem record related to the incident has already been raised. If not, raise a new problem record in conjunction with the problem management process so that preventive action is initiated.

■ **Formal closure** Formally close the incident record.

Note that some organizations may choose to utilize an automatic closure period on specific, or even all, incidents (e.g. incident will be automatically closed after two working days if no further contact is made by the user). Where this approach is to be considered, it must first be fully discussed and agreed with the users – and widely publicized so that all users and IT staff are aware of this. It may be inappropriate to use this method for certain types of incidents, such as major incidents or those involving VIPs etc.

4.2.5.10 Rules for reopening incidents

Despite all adequate care, there will be occasions when incidents recur even though they have been formally closed. The choice made must consider its effect on data collection, so the reoccurrence and associated work is clearly recorded and accurately reported. Because of such cases, it is wise to have predefined rules about if and when an incident can be reopened. It might make sense, for example, to agree that if the incident recurs within one working day then it can be reopened – but that beyond this point a new incident must be raised, but linked to the previous incident(s).

The exact time threshold/rules may vary between individual organizations, but clear rules should be agreed and documented and guidance given to all service desk staff so that uniformity is applied.

4.2.6 Triggers, inputs, outputs and interfaces

4.2.6.1 Triggers

Incidents can be triggered in many ways. The most common route is when a user rings the service desk or completes a web-based incident-logging screen, but increasingly incidents are raised automatically via event management tools. Technical staff may notice potential failures and raise an incident, or

ask the service desk to do so, so that the fault can be addressed. Some incidents may also arise at the initiation of suppliers – who may send some form of notification of a potential or actual difficulty that needs attention.

4.2.6.2 Inputs

Examples of inputs to the incident management process may include:

■ Information about CIs and their status
■ Information about known errors and their workarounds
■ Communication and feedback about incidents and their symptoms
■ Communication and feedback about RFCs and releases that have been implemented or planned for implementation
■ Communication of events that were triggered from event management
■ Operational and service level objectives
■ Customer feedback on success of incident resolution activities and overall quality of incident management activities
■ Agreed criteria for prioritizing and escalating incidents.

4.2.6.3 Outputs

Examples of outputs from the incident management process may include:

■ Resolved incidents and actions taken to achieve their resolution
■ Updated incident management records with accurate incident detail and history
■ Updated classification of incidents to be used to support proactive problem management activities
■ Raising of problem records for incidents where an underlying cause has not been identified
■ Validation that incidents have not recurred for problems that have been resolved
■ Feedback on incidents related to changes and releases
■ Identification of CIs associated with or impacted by incidents
■ Satisfaction feedback from customers who have experienced incidents
■ Feedback on level and quality of monitoring technologies and event management activities

■ Communications about incident and resolution history detail to assist with identification of overall service quality.

4.2.6.4 Interfaces

Examples of interfaces with incident management are listed below for each service lifecycle stage.

Service design

■ **Service level management**   The ability to resolve incidents in a specified time is a key part of delivering an agreed level of service. Incident management enables SLM to define measurable responses to service disruptions. It also provides reports that enable SLM to review SLAs objectively and regularly. In particular, incident management is able to assist in defining where services are at their weakest, so that SLM can define actions as part of the service improvement plan (SIP) (see *ITIL Continual Service Improvement* for more details). SLM defines the acceptable levels of service within which incident management works, including:

  ● Incident response times
  ● Impact definitions
  ● Target fix times
  ● Service definitions, which are mapped to users
  ● Rules for requesting services
  ● Expectations for providing feedback to users.

■ **Information security management**   Providing security-related incident information as needed to support service design activities and gain a full picture of the effectiveness of the security measures as a whole based on an insight into all security incidents. This is facilitated maintaining log and audit files and incident records.

■ **Capacity management**   Incident management provides a trigger for performance monitoring where there appears to be a performance problem. Capacity management may develop workarounds for incidents.

■ **Availability management**   Availability management will use incident management data to determine the availability of IT services and look at where the incident lifecycle can be improved.

Service transition

■ **Service asset and configuration management**   This process provides the data used to identify and progress incidents. One of the uses of the CMS is to identify faulty equipment and to assess the impact of an incident. The CMS also contains information about which categories of incident should be assigned to which support group. In turn, incident management can maintain the status of faulty CIs. It can also assist service asset and configuration management to audit the infrastructure when working to resolve an incident.

■ **Change management**   Where a change is required to implement a workaround or resolution, this will need to be logged as an RFC and progressed through change management. In turn, incident management is able to detect and resolve incidents that arise from failed changes.

Service operation

■ **Problem management**   For some incidents, it will be appropriate to involve problem management to investigate and resolve the underlying cause to prevent or reduce the impact of recurrence. Incident management provides a point where these are reported. Problem management, in return, can provide known errors for faster incident resolution through workarounds that can be used to restore service.

■ **Access management**   Incidents should be raised when unauthorized access attempts and security breaches have been detected. A history of incidents should also be maintained to support forensic investigation activities and resolution of access breaches.

4.2.7 Information management

Most information used in incident management comes from the following sources.

4.2.7.1 Incident management tools

These contain information about:

■ Incident and problem history
■ Incident categories
■ Action taken to resolve incidents

- Diagnostic scripts which can help first-line analysts to resolve the incident, or at least gather information that will help second- or third-line analysts resolve it faster.

4.2.7.2 Incident records

These include the following data:

- Unique reference number
- Incident classification
- Date and time of recording and any subsequent activities
- Name and identity of the person recording and updating the incident record
- Name/organization/contact details of affected user(s)
- Description of the incident symptoms
- Details of any actions taken to try to diagnose, resolve or recreate the incident
- Incident category, impact, urgency and priority
- Relationship with other incidents, problems, changes or known errors
- Closure details, including time, category, action taken and identity of person closing the record
- Other logged data about the incident (see section 4.2.5.2)
- Service catalogue, which can include the following data:
  - Key service delivery objectives, levels and targets
  - Information about the service in terms that the customer and users understand
  - Information that can be used for communicating with customers and users.

Incident management also requires access to the CMS. This will help it to identify the CIs affected by the incident and also to estimate the impact of the incident.

The KEDB provides valuable information about possible resolutions and workarounds. This is discussed in detail in section 4.4.7.2.

4.2.8 Critical success factors and key performance indicators

The following list includes some sample CSFs for incident management. Each organization should identify appropriate CSFs based on its objectives for the process. Each sample CSF is followed by a small number of typical KPIs that support the CSF. These KPIs should not be adopted without careful consideration. Each organization should develop KPIs that are appropriate for its level of maturity, its CSFs and its particular circumstances. Achievement against KPIs should be monitored and used to identify opportunities for improvement, which should be logged in the CSI register for evaluation and possible implementation.

- **CSF** Resolve incidents as quickly as possible minimizing impacts to the business
  - **KPI** Mean elapsed time to achieve incident resolution or circumvention, broken down by impact code
  - **KPI** Breakdown of incidents at each stage (e.g. logged, work in progress, closed etc.)
  - **KPI** Percentage of incidents closed by the service desk without reference to other levels of support (often referred to as 'first point of contact')
  - **KPI** Number and percentage of incidents resolved remotely, without the need for a visit
  - **KPI** Number of incidents resolved without impact to the business (e.g. incident was raised by event management and resolved before it could impact the business)
- **CSF** Maintain quality of IT services
  - **KPI** Total numbers of incidents (as a control measure)
  - **KPI** Size of current incident backlog for each IT service
  - **KPI** Number and percentage of major incidents for each IT service
- **CSF** Maintain user satisfaction with IT services
  - **KPI** Average user/customer survey score (total and by question category)
  - **KPI** Percentage of satisfaction surveys answered versus total number of satisfaction surveys sent
- **CSF** Increase visibility and communication of incidents to business and IT support staff
  - **KPI** Average number of service desk calls or other contacts from business users for incidents already reported
  - **KPI** Number of business user complaints or issues about the content and quality of incident communications
- **CSF** Align incident management activities and priorities with those of the business

- **KPI** Percentage of incidents handled within agreed response time (incident response-time targets may be specified in SLAs, for example, by impact and urgency codes)
- **KPI** Average cost per incident
- **CSF** Ensure that standardized methods and procedures are used for efficient and prompt response, analysis, documentation, ongoing management and reporting of incidents to maintain business confidence in IT capabilities
  - **KPI** Number and percentage of incidents incorrectly assigned
  - **KPI** Number and percentage of incidents incorrectly categorized
  - **KPI** Number and percentage of incidents processed per service desk agent
  - **KPI** Number and percentage of incidents related to changes and releases.

It is also helpful to break down and categorize incident metrics by category, timeframe, impact, urgency, service impacted, location and priority and compare these with previous periods. This can provide input to problem management, CSI and other processes seeking to identify issues, problem trends or other situations.

Reports should be produced under the authority of the incident manager, who should draw up a schedule and distribution list, in collaboration with the service desk and support groups handling incidents. Distribution lists should at least include IT services management and specialist support groups. Consider also making the data available to users and customers, for example via SLA reports.

4.2.9 Challenges and risks

4.2.9.1 Challenges

The following challenges will exist for successful incident management:

- The ability to detect incidents as early as possible. This will require the configuration of event management tools, the education of the users reporting incidents, and the use of specialized service desk groups (see section 6.3.3.5).
- Convincing all staff (technical teams as well as users) that all incidents must be logged, and encouraging the use of self-help web-based capabilities (which can speed up assistance and reduce resource requirements).

- Availability of information about problems and known errors. This will enable incident management staff to learn from previous incidents and also to track the status of resolutions.
- Integration into the CMS to determine relationships between CIs and to refer to the history of CIs when performing first-line support.
- Integration into the SLM process. This will help incident management to correctly assess the impact and priority of incidents and assists in defining and executing escalation procedures. SLM will also benefit from the information learned during incident management, for example in determining whether service level performance targets are realistic and achievable.

4.2.9.2 Risks

The risks to successful incident management are actually similar to some of the challenges and the reverse of some of the CSFs mentioned above. They include:

- Being inundated with incidents that cannot be handled within acceptable timescales due to a lack of available or properly trained resources
- Unintended backlog of incidents created by inadequate support tools to raise alerts and prompt progress
- Lack of adequate and/or timely information sources because of inadequate tools or lack of integration
- Mismatches in objectives or actions because of poorly aligned or non-existent OLAs and/or UCs.

4.3 REQUEST FULFILMENT

The term 'service request' is used as a generic description for many different types of demands that are placed upon the IT organization by the users. Many of these are typically requests for small changes that are low risk, frequently performed, low cost etc. (e.g. a request to change a password, a request to install an additional software application onto a particular workstation, a request to relocate some items of desktop equipment) or may be just a request for information.

Their scale and frequent, low-risk nature means that they are better handled by a separate process, rather than being allowed to congest and obstruct the normal incident and change management processes. Effective request fulfilment has a very important role in maintaining end user satisfaction with the services they are receiving and can directly impact how well IT is perceived throughout the business.

Section 3.1.3.4 provides more details around service requests and their relationship to IT services, request models, and changes.

4.3.1 Purpose and objectives

4.3.1.1 Purpose

Request fulfilment is the process responsible for managing the lifecycle of all service requests from the users.

4.3.1.2 Objectives

The objectives of the request fulfilment process are to:

- Maintain user and customer satisfaction through efficient and professional handling of all service requests
- Provide a channel for users to request and receive standard services for which a predefined authorization and qualification process exists
- Provide information to users and customers about the availability of services and the procedure for obtaining them
- Source and deliver the components of requested standard services (e.g. licences and software media)
- Assist with general information, complaints or comments.

4.3.2 Scope

The process needed to fulfil a request will vary depending upon exactly what is being requested, but can usually be broken down into a set of activities that have to be performed. For each request, these activities should be documented into a request model and stored in the SKMS.

Some organizations will be comfortable letting the service requests be handled through their incident management process (and tools) – with service requests being handled as a particular type of 'incident' (using a high-level categorization system to identify those 'incidents' that are in fact service requests). Note, however, that there is a significant difference here – an incident is usually an unplanned event, whereas a service request is usually something that can and should be planned!

Therefore, in an organization where large numbers of service requests have to be handled, and where the actions to be taken to fulfil those requests are very varied or specialized, it may be appropriate to handle service requests as a completely separate work stream – and to record and manage them as a separate record type. This is essential if reporting is desired that more accurately separates incidents from requests.

This may be particularly appropriate if the organization has chosen to widen the scope of the service desk to expand upon just IT-related issues and use the desk as a focal point for other types of service request– for example, a request to service a photocopier or even going so far as to include, for example, building management issues, such as a need to replace a light fitting or repair a leak in the plumbing.

Note that ultimately it will be up to each organization to decide and document which service requests it will handle through the request fulfilment process and which will have to go through other processes such as business relationship management for dealing with requests for new or changed services (see *ITIL Service Strategy*). There will always be grey areas which prevent generic guidance from being usefully prescribed.

4.3.3 Value to business

The value of the request fulfilment process includes:

- The ability to provide quick and effective access to standard services that business staff can use to improve their productivity or the quality of business services and products.
- The ability to effectively reduce the bureaucracy involved in requesting and receiving access to existing or new services, thus also reducing the cost of providing these services.
- The ability to increase the level of control over requested services through a centralized fulfilment function. This in turn can help reduce costs through centralized negotiation with suppliers, and can also help to reduce the cost of support.

4.3.4 Policies, principles and basic concepts

4.3.4.1 Policies

Examples of request fulfilment policies might include:

■ The activities used to fulfil a request should follow a predefined process flow (a model) devised to include the stages needed to fulfil the request, the individuals or support groups involved, target timescales and escalation paths. This ensures that requests are fulfilled in a consistent and efficient manner. It implies that all types of requests for any given service are identified in advance and their fulfilment flows considered during service design.

■ The ownership of service requests should reside with a centralized function such as the service desk, which monitors, escalates, despatches and often fulfils the user request. This provides the benefit of a single point of contact for requesting and receiving information about service requests and their status.

■ Service requests that impact CIs should usually be satisfied by implementing a standard change (see *ITIL Service Transition* for further details on standard changes). This ensures that change management does not lose track of changes that may be introduced to CIs through request fulfilment activities.

■ All requests should be logged, controlled, coordinated, promoted and managed throughout their lifecycle via a single system. This supports a consistent and repeatable approach for handling service requests and reduces the potential for lost requests and conflicts that might arise during handling of requests.

■ All requests should be authorized before their fulfilment activities are undertaken. This ensures that resources are efficiently used only for authorized requests. This implies that requests are tied to access management activities and the information security policy (see *ITIL Service Design*).

■ Fulfilment of requests should take place under an agreed set of criteria for determining their priority that is aligned with overall service levels and objectives. This ensures that request fulfilment activities support service levels and objectives by prioritizing those activities based on actual business need. It implies that required service levels and objectives for different types of requests are already understood and agreed to by the business.

■ Clear communication for making requests and determining their status must be in place. This implies that a single point of contact is in place which can be used to request the service and obtain its status. This is often provided by the service desk or through a web-based interface, but could be through an automated request directly into the request fulfilment or procurement system.

4.3.4.2 Principles and basic concepts

There are some basic things that need to be taken into account and decided when considering request fulfilment. These are covered in this section.

Request models

Some service requests will occur frequently and will require handling consistently in order to meet agreed service levels. To assist this, many organizations will wish to create predefined request models (which typically include one or more standard changes in order to complete fulfilment activities). This is similar in concept to the idea of incident models already described in incident management, but applied to service requests.

Menu selection

Request fulfilment offers great opportunities for self-help practices, where users can generate a service request using technology that links into service management tools. Ideally, users should be offered a 'menu'-type selection via a web-based interface or request portal so that they can select and input details of service requests from a predefined list. In this way, appropriate expectations can be set by giving target delivery and/or implementation targets/dates (in line with SLA targets). Where organizations are offering a self-help IT support capability to the users, it would make sense to combine this with a request fulfilment system as described.

Specialist web tools to offer this type of 'shopping basket' experience can be used together with interfaces directly to the back-end integrated ITSM tools, or other more general business process automation or enterprise resource planning (ERP) tools that may be used to manage the request fulfilment activities.

Request status tracking

Requests should be tracked throughout their lifecycle to support proper handling and reporting on the status of requests. Within the request fulfilment system, status codes may be linked to requests to indicate where they are in relation to the lifecycle. Examples of these might include:

- Draft – a request is created in the draft state. This could be used to record a request without submitting to the request fulfilment process.
- In review – requests that have been authorized and are under review by those that will be performing fulfilment activities for them.
- Suspended – fulfilment activities for the request have been suspended.
- Waiting authorization – the service request has been submitted for authorization.
- Rejected – the request has been rejected.
- Cancelled – the request is no longer required by the user.
- In progress – the request is in the process of being fulfilled.
- Completed – the request has been fulfilled.
- Closed – the user has agreed that the request has been fulfilled and the request has been closed.

Prioritizing requests

All service requests should follow a standard set of criteria for assessing their priority. This can be done by considering request impact and urgency in a similar manner as described for incident management (see section 4.2).

Escalating requests

In some situations, it may be necessary to escalate requests to resolve certain situations or take further actions that are not part of the standard set of fulfilment activities. Examples of these kinds of situations might be:

- A request was misrouted to the wrong function or set of resources for fulfilment
- An SLA for fulfilling a request may be in jeopardy
- A user disagrees that the request has been fulfilled to their entire satisfaction
- A request has been used in lieu of a more complicated requirement.

Development of request models should consider the likelihood of situations where escalation may be needed and include predefined escalation paths and activities to deal with them.

Financial approval

One important extra step that is likely to be needed when dealing with a service request is that of financial approval.

Most requests will have some form of financial implications, regardless of the type of commercial arrangements in place. The cost of fulfilling the service request must first be established. It may be possible to agree fixed prices for 'standard' requests – and prior approval for such requests may be given as part of the organization's overall annual financial management. In all other cases, an estimate of the cost must be produced and submitted to the user for financial approval (the user may need to seek approval up their management/financial chain). If approval is given, in addition to fulfilling the request, the process must also include charging (billing or cross-charging) for the work done – if charging is in place.

Other approvals

In some cases further approvals may be needed – such as compliance-related or wider business approval. Request fulfilment must have the ability to define and check such approvals where needed. Procedures for obtaining required approvals should be included as part of the request fulfilment models to save time in processing the service request.

Coordination of fulfilment activities

The actual fulfilment activity will depend upon the nature of the service request. Some simpler requests may be completed by the service desk, acting as first-line support, while others will have to be forwarded to specialist groups and/or suppliers for fulfilment.

Some organizations may have specialist fulfilment groups (to 'pick, pack and despatch'), or may have outsourced some fulfilment activities to a third-party supplier(s). The service desk should monitor and chase progress and keep users informed throughout, regardless of the actual fulfilment source.

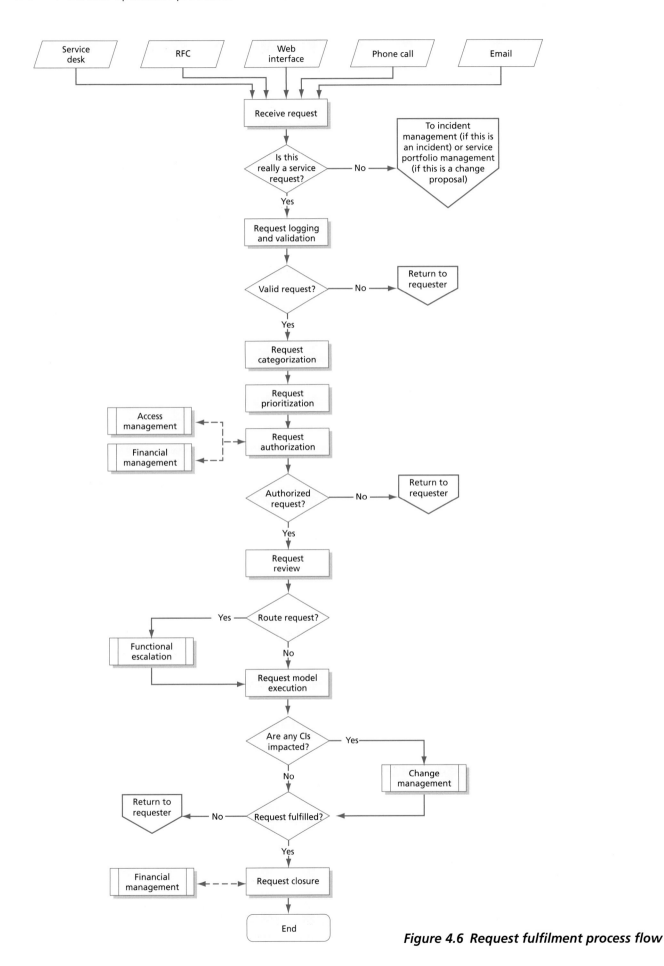

Figure 4.6 Request fulfilment process flow

Closure

When the service request has been fulfilled it must be referred back to the service desk for closure. The service desk should go through a closure process that checks to see whether the user is satisfied with the outcome.

4.3.5 Process activities, methods and techniques

The process to be followed during the management of a request is shown in Figure 4.6. The process includes the following steps.

4.3.5.1 Receive request

Fulfilment work on service requests should not begin until a formalized request has been received. Service requests should mostly come from the service desk, but it is not unusual to have requests that come in from other sources such as RFCs, email, an automated web ordering interface or phone call. Standard forms and records should be used to capture request information so that they can be more easily processed, with minimal need to go back to requesters for more information.

Initially, it must be determined whether the request might actually be an incident or a request for new or changed service features. In some cases, it is possible that an incident has taken place, but is being reported as a service request. For example, a user may have experienced an outage with their desktop, but has directly asked for replacement hardware versus reporting the outage as an incident. If it has been determined that the request is really an incident, the service request, and any related information provided with it, should be forwarded to incident management.

In other cases, the request may actually be a request for new or changed service features. This can come from a user or customer who is asking for a new service or requesting something new that is an addition to the agreed standard services available to them. In this case, the service request can be passed to business relationship management, who may invoke the change management or service portfolio management processes (see *ITIL Service Strategy*) to properly review the need and business case for the service change.

4.3.5.2 Request logging and validation

All service requests must be fully logged and date/time stamped, regardless of whether they are raised through a service desk, RFC, telephone call or email.

Note that if service desk and/or support staff visit the customers to deal with one service request, they may be asked to deal with further requests 'while they are there'. It is important that if this is done, a separate request record is logged for each additional request handled, to ensure that a historical record is kept and credit is given for the work undertaken.

All relevant information relating to the nature of the request must be logged so that a full historical record is maintained – and so that if the request has to be referred to other support group(s), they will have all relevant information to hand to assist them.

The information needed for a service request is likely to include:

- Unique reference number
- Request categorization (often broken down into sub-categories including which service the request is being asked for)
- Request urgency
- Request impact
- Request prioritization
- Date/time recorded
- Name/ID of the person and/or group making the request
- Method of notification (telephone, web interface, RFC, email, in person etc.)
- Name/department/phone/location of user
- Budget centre in case a charge is associated
- User 'hours of working' (e.g. 9–5 weekdays)
- Call-back method (telephone, mail etc.)
- Description of request
- Request status (in progress, waiting authorization, closed etc.)
- Related CIs
- Support group/person to which the service request will be allocated
- Fulfilment date and time
- Closure date and time.

In some cases there may be agreement of 24/7 service through an SLA with the customer even though the service desk does not work 24/7. In these cases, responsibility for request logging and handling may pass to another group such as IT operations or network support when the service desk is not available. These groups need to be equally rigorous about logging of request details. Full training and awareness needs to be provided to such staff on this issue.

As further activities to fulfil a request occur, the request record should be updated accordingly, with relevant information and details so that a full history is maintained. Examples of this might include changing the request status or closure date and time once fulfilment activities have been completed.

Requests must also be initially validated. This includes validating the source of the request and that the request is within the scope of the IT services being offered. Note that automation tools for service catalogues may include features that assist with this task by publishing available types of service request and making these accessible online to users. These tools ensure that the source of the request is valid and that only valid types of request are issued. In addition, later authorization steps can also be automated through these kinds of tools.

4.3.5.3 Request categorization

Part of the initial logging must be to allocate suitable request categorization coding so that the exact type of the request is recorded. This will be important later when looking at request types/frequencies to establish trends for use in determining how services are being used, which requests are the most frequently asked for and other ITSM activities.

Examples of typical categories of requests might include:

- By service – categorizing the request by the service it is part of. For example, a request to establish a new user email account may be part of an email service.
- By activity – categorizing the request by the type of activity it is undertaking. Examples might include password reset, desktop installation or printer cartridge replacement.
- By type – categorizing the request by what kind of request it is, such as an informational request versus a standard change.

- By function – categorizing the request by which function will be used to perform the fulfilment activities for it.
- By CI type – categorizing the request by the types of CIs that it impacts.

4.3.5.4 Request prioritization

Another important aspect of logging every request is to agree and allocate an appropriate prioritization code, as this will determine how the service request is handled both by support tools and support staff.

Prioritization can normally be determined by taking into account both the urgency of the request (how quickly the business needs to have it fulfilled) and the level of impact it is causing. An indication of impact is often (but not always) the number of users being affected. In some cases, and very importantly, a request to a single user can have a major business impact – it all depends upon who is trying to do what – so numbers alone are not enough to evaluate overall priority! Other factors that can also contribute to impact levels are:

- The number of services impacted by fulfilment activities
- The number of users or business units impacted by fulfilment activities
- Whether the requester is at an executive level of the business or a lower level administrative function
- The level of financial gain or loss if the request is fulfilled or not fulfilled
- Effect on business reputation if the request is not fulfilled
- Regulatory or legislative fines or penalties if the request is not fulfilled.

An effective way of calculating these elements and deriving an overall priority level for each type of request is to use Table 4.1 (as described in section 4.2.5.4).

In all cases, clear guidance – with practical examples – should be provided for all support staff to enable them to determine the correct urgency and impact levels, so the correct priority is allocated. Such guidance should be produced during service level negotiations.

There will be occasions when, because of particular business expediency, normal priority levels have to be overridden. When a user is adamant that a service request priority level should exceed normal guidelines, the service desk should comply with such a request – and if it subsequently turns out to be incorrect this can be resolved as an offline management level issue, rather than a dispute occurring when the user is on the telephone.

Some organizations may also recognize VIPs (high-ranking executives, officers, diplomats, politicians etc.) whose service requests would be handled as a higher priority than normal – but in such cases this is best catered for and documented within the guidance provided to the service desk staff on how to apply the priority levels, so they are all aware of the agreed rules for VIPs, and who falls into this category. Ideally, VIP priorities and service levels should be formally recognized as having differentiated service levels (for example the 'gold' delivery option for a service request versus the 'standard' delivery option that may be available to others). This approach removes the ambiguity around VIP needs and provides transparency for services and costs specific to VIP users.

4.3.5.5 Request authorization

No work should take place to fulfil a request until it has been properly authorized. Simple authorizations can take place via the service desk alone or as pre-authorized requests based on the request type. In some cases, a more rigorous authorization may be needed from other sources before any work can proceed, such as through access management to determine whether the requester is truly authorized to make the request, or financial management to authorize any charges or costs associated with fulfilling the request.

A service request that cannot be properly authorized should be returned to the requester with the reason for the rejection and the request record also updated to indicate the rejection status.

4.3.5.6 Request review

At this stage, the request is reviewed to determine the proper function that will fulfil it. In many cases, the service desk function may perform all needed fulfilment activities (such as fulfilling a request for information). In other cases, the requests may be escalated to other functions that perform specialized activities to fulfil them. As requests are reviewed, escalated and acted upon, the request

records should be updated to reflect the current request status.

Automated tools may also be used to capture, log, analyse and fulfil requests without human intervention. An example of this might be a website where users can issue self-help requests that automatically reset passwords for user accounts or provision equipment such as cellular telephones.

4.3.5.7 Request model execution

As functions undertake activities to fulfil a request, a request model should be used that documents a standard process flow, roles and responsibilities for fulfilling it. This ensures that a repeatable and consistent set of actions are always undertaken for each request type that minimize the risks for delays or failures as requests are fulfilled.

As functions receive and analyse requests, the appropriate request model should be chosen based on the type of request being fulfilled. The process steps and activities indicated in the model are then executed by the function to fulfil the request.

Request models may be described as process steps and activities that can be:

- Stored as reference documents that can be accessed as part of the SKMS
- Stored through specialized configurations within automated workflow tools
- Stored through code elements and configurations as part of web-based self-help solutions.

Any service requests that impact CIs in the live environment should also be authorized through change management. In many cases, these will be standard changes. Use of these ensures that change management is kept aware of all changes that have taken place, including those triggered by request fulfilment.

4.3.5.8 Request closure

Once service request activities have been completed, the service desk should be notified of the completion status. The service desk should then check that the request has been fulfilled and that users are satisfied and willing to agree that the request can be closed. The service desk should also check the following:

- **Financial requirements** Financial management may need to be notified of any costs incurred by fulfilment activities or if requesters are to be billed for them.
- **Closure categorization** Check and confirm that the request categorization was correct, or where the categorization subsequently turned out to be incorrect, update the record so that a correct closure categorization is recorded for the request – seeking advice or guidance from the fulfilment group(s) as necessary.
- **User satisfaction survey** Carry out a user satisfaction call-back or email survey for the agreed percentage of requests.
- **Request documentation** Chase any outstanding details and ensure that the request record is fully documented so that a full historic record at a sufficient level of detail is complete.
- **Formal closure** Formally close the request record.

Note that some organizations may choose to use an automatic closure period on specific, or even all, requests (e.g. request will be automatically closed after two working days if no further contact is made by the user). Where this approach is to be considered, it must first be fully discussed and agreed with the users – and widely publicized so that all users and IT staff are aware of this.

4.3.5.9 Rules for reopening requests

It is wise to have predefined rules about if and when a closed service request can be reopened. It might make sense, for example, to agree that if the request needs to be reopened within one working day then it can be reopened – but that beyond this point a new service request must be raised.

The exact time threshold/rules may vary between individual organizations, but clear rules should be agreed and documented and guidance given to all service desk staff so that uniformity is applied. The impact on data tracking and reporting should be considered when establishing these rules.

4.3.6 Triggers, inputs, outputs and interfaces

Most requests will be triggered through either a user calling the service desk or a user completing some form of self-help web-based input screen to make their request. The latter will often involve selection from a portfolio of available request types.

4.3.6.1 Inputs

Examples of inputs to the request fulfilment process can include:

- Work requests
- Authorization forms
- Service requests
- RFCs
- Requests from various sources such as phone calls, web interfaces or email
- Request for information.

4.3.6.2 Outputs

Examples of outputs from the request fulfilment process may include:

- Authorized/rejected service requests
- Request fulfilment status reports
- Fulfilled service requests
- Incidents (rerouted)
- RFCs/standard changes
- Asset/CI updates
- Updated request records
- Closed service requests
- Cancelled service requests.

4.3.6.3 Interfaces

Examples of primary interfaces with request fulfilment are listed below for each service lifecycle stage.

Service strategy

- **Financial management for IT services** Interfaces may be needed if costs for fulfilling requests need to be reported and recovered.

Service design

- **Service catalogue management** This process will need to be tightly linked with request fulfilment to ensure that available requests are well communicated to users and linked with the services in the catalogue that they support. Changes to available requests must be synchronized with service catalogue management activities.

Service transition

- **Release and deployment management** Some requests will be for the deployment of new or upgraded components that can be automatically deployed. In such cases a 'release' can be predefined, built and tested but only deployed upon request by those who want the 'release'.
- **Service asset and configuration management** Upon deployment, the CMS will have to be updated to reflect changes that may have been made as part of fulfilment activities. Asset lifecycle information, asset tags and other related information may also need to be updated for fulfilment activities involving moves, additions and changes to service assets. Where appropriate, software licence checks/updates will also be necessary.
- **Change management** Where a change is required to fulfil a request, it will need to be logged as an RFC and progressed through change management.

Service operation

- **Incident and problem management** Many service requests may come in via the service desk and may be initially handled through the incident management process. Some organizations may choose that all requests are handled via this route, but others may choose to have a separate process, for reasons already discussed earlier in this chapter. Where appropriate, it will be necessary to relate service requests issued by IT to any incidents or problems that created the need for the requests.
- **Access management** This process may be involved with request fulfilment activities to ensure that those making requests are authorized to do so in accordance with the information security policy. In addition, the output of fulfilment activities may produce information or results that are sensitive.

4.3.7 Information management

Request fulfilment is dependent on information from formal service requests which can include:

- What service is being requested
- Who requested and authorized the service
- Which process will be used to fulfil the request

- Who it was assigned to and what action was taken
- The date and time when the request was logged as well as the date and time of all actions taken
- Closure details
- RFCs: In some cases the request fulfilment process will be initiated by an RFC. This is typical where the service request relates to a CI
- The service portfolio, to enable the scope of agreed service requests to be identified
- Security policies that prescribe any controls to be executed or adhered to when providing the service, e.g. ensuring that the requester is authorized to access the service, or that the software is licensed.

4.3.8 Critical success factors and key performance indicators

The following list includes some sample CSFs for request fulfilment. Each organization should identify appropriate CSFs based on its objectives for the process. Each sample CSF is followed by a small number of typical KPIs that support the CSF. These KPIs should not be adopted without careful consideration. Each organization should develop KPIs that are appropriate for its level of maturity, its CSFs and its particular circumstances. Achievement against KPIs should be monitored and used to identify opportunities for improvement, which should be logged in the CSI register for evaluation and possible implementation.

- **CSF** Requests must be fulfilled in an efficient and timely manner that is aligned to agreed service level targets for each type of request
  - **KPI** The mean elapsed time for handling each type of service request
  - **KPI** The number and percentage of service requests completed within agreed target times
  - **KPI** Breakdown of service requests at each stage (e.g. logged, work in progress, closed etc.)
  - **KPI** Percentage of service requests closed by the service desk without reference to other levels of support (often referred to as 'first point of contact')
  - **KPI** Number and percentage of service requests resolved remotely or through automation, without the need for a visit

- **KPI** Total numbers of requests (as a control measure)
- **KPI** The average cost per type of service request
- **CSF** Only authorized requests should be fulfilled
  - **KPI** Percentage of service requests fulfilled that were appropriately authorized
  - **KPI** Number of incidents related to security threats from request fulfilment activities
- **CSF** User satisfaction must be maintained
  - **KPI** Level of user satisfaction with the handling of service requests (as measured in some form of satisfaction survey)
  - **KPI** Total number of incidents related to request fulfilment activities
  - **KPI** The size of current backlog of outstanding service requests.

4.3.9 Challenges and risks

4.3.9.1 Challenges

The following challenges will exist for successful request fulfilment:

- Clearly defining and documenting the type of requests that will be handled within the request fulfilment process (and those that will either go through the service desk and be handled as incidents or those that will need to go through formal change management), so that all parties are absolutely clear on the scope.
- Establishing self-help front-end capabilities that allow the users to interface successfully with the request fulfilment process. These tools may provide an efficient front-end interface to the users. It is essential that these integrate with the back-end fulfilment tools, often managed through incident or change management.
- Service level targets will need to be agreed and communicated for each type of request. Establishing targets may get more complicated when considering varying types of users such as VIPs, executive management and lower level administrative staff.
- The costs for fulfilling requests must also be agreed. This may be done as part of the SLM process. Any variances of the services must also be defined with differences in costs for these identified.

- Agreements will need to be in place for which services will be standardized and who is authorized to request them. Consideration should also be given to outcomes of service requests to ensure they do not violate the information security policy. An example of this might be a request fulfilment activity that produces sensitive information such as customer financial data.
- Information about what requests are available will need to be easily accessible. This implies that available service requests are published to users as part of the service catalogue. It is important that this part of the service catalogue be easily accessed, perhaps on the intranet, and should be recognized as the first source of information for users seeking access to a service.
- Requests will need to follow a predefined standard fulfilment procedure. This implies that a documented request model be in place that communicates a predefined process flow for each of the services being requested. This should also include all procurement policies, roles and responsibilities, which functions will be assigned to execute the model, and the ability to generate purchase orders and work orders.
- Request fulfilment has a very high impact on user satisfaction. Requests that are managed poorly, dropped or not addressed on a timely basis will project a poor image of the IT organization and their ability to get things done. Therefore, great attention to user satisfaction must be maintained. This implies that service requests are processed in a timely manner. Ongoing feedback should be in place to monitor user satisfaction with the handling of requests.

4.3.9.2 Risks

Risks that may be encountered with request fulfilment include:

- Poorly defined scope, where people are unclear about exactly what the process is expected to handle
- Poorly designed or implemented user interfaces so that users have difficulty raising the requests that they need

- Badly designed or operated back-end fulfilment processes that are incapable of dealing with the volume or nature of the requests being made
- Inadequate monitoring capabilities so that accurate metrics cannot be gathered.

4.4 PROBLEM MANAGEMENT

Problem management is the process responsible for managing the lifecycle of all problems. ITIL defines a 'problem' as the underlying cause of one or more incidents.

4.4.1 Purpose and objectives

4.4.1.1 Purpose

The purpose of problem management is to manage the lifecycle of all problems from first identification through further investigation, documentation and eventual removal. Problem management seeks to minimize the adverse impact of incidents and problems on the business that are caused by underlying errors within the IT Infrastructure, and to proactively prevent recurrence of incidents related to these errors. In order to achieve this, problem management seeks to get to the root cause of incidents, document and communicate known errors and initiate actions to improve or correct the situation.

4.4.1.2 Objectives

The objectives of the problem management process are to:

- Prevent problems and resulting incidents from happening
- Eliminate recurring incidents
- Minimize the impact of incidents that cannot be prevented.

4.4.2 Scope

Problem management includes the activities required to diagnose the root cause of incidents and to determine the resolution to those problems. It is also responsible for ensuring that the resolution is implemented through the appropriate control procedures, especially change management and release and deployment management.

Problem management will also maintain information about problems and the appropriate workarounds and resolutions, so that the organization is able to reduce the number and impact of incidents over time. In this respect, problem management has a strong interface with knowledge management, and tools such as the KEDB will be used for both.

Although incident and problem management are separate processes, they are closely related and will typically use the same tools, and may use similar categorization, impact and priority coding systems. This will ensure effective communication when dealing with related incidents and problems.

The problem management process has both reactive and proactive aspects:

- Reactive problem management is concerned with solving problems in response to one or more incidents.
- Proactive problem management is concerned with identifying and solving problems and known errors before further incidents related to them can occur again.
- While reactive problem management activities are performed in reaction to specific incident situations, proactive problem management activities take place as ongoing activities targeted to improve the overall availability and end user satisfaction with IT services. Examples of proactive problem management activities might include conducting periodic scheduled reviews of incident records to find patterns and trends in reported symptoms that may indicate the presence of underlying errors in the infrastructure.
- Conducting major incident reviews where review of 'How can we prevent the recurrence?' can provide identification of an underlying cause or error.
- Conducting periodic scheduled reviews of operational logs and maintenance records identifying patterns and trends of activities that may indicate an underlying problem might exist.
- Conducting periodic scheduled reviews of event logs targeting patterns and trends of warning and exception events that may indicate the presence of an underlying problem.
- Conducting brainstorming sessions to identify trends that could indicate the existence of underlying problems.
- Using check sheets to proactively collect data on service or operational quality issues that may help to detect underlying problems.

Reactive and proactive problem management activities are generally conducted within the scope of service operation. A close relationship exists between proactive problem management activities and CSI lifecycle activities that directly support identifying and implementing service improvements. Proactive problem management supports those activities through trending analysis and the targeting of preventive action. Identified problems from these activities will become input to the CSI register used to record and manage improvement opportunities.

Further information on CSI activities can be found in *ITIL Continual Service Improvement*.

4.4.3 Value to business

The value of problem management includes:

- Higher availability of IT services by reducing the number and duration of incidents that those services may incur. Problem management works together with incident management and change management to ensure that IT service availability and quality are increased. When incidents are resolved, information about the resolution is recorded. Over time, this information is used to speed up the resolution time and identify permanent solutions, reducing the number and resolution time of incidents.
- Higher productivity of IT staff by reducing unplanned labour caused by incidents and creating the ability to resolve incidents more quickly through recorded known errors and workarounds.
- Reduced expenditure on workarounds or fixes that do not work.
- Reduction in cost of effort in fire-fighting or resolving repeat incidents.

4.4.4 Policies, principles and basic concepts

4.4.4.1 Policies

Examples of problem management policies might include:

- Problems should be tracked separately from incidents. This will provide clear separation between many problem management activities that are proactive and incident management activities that are mostly reactive. This implies

that technology capabilities may need to be in place to track problems separately from incidents.

- All problems should be stored and managed in a single management system. This provides a definitive recognized source for problem information and supports easier access for reporting and investigation efforts. It implies that problem management records are kept. Supporting technologies should be well integrated throughout the business and interface easily to other service management technologies that use or provide problem-related information.
- All problems should subscribe to a standard classification schema that is consistent across the business enterprise. This provides for faster access to problem and investigative information. It provides better support for problem management diagnostic and proactive trending activities. It implies that a well defined and communicated set of problem classification categories is in place.

4.4.4.2 Principles and basic concepts

There are some important concepts of problem management that must be taken into account from the outset. These include:

Reactive and proactive problem management activities

Both reactive and proactive problem management activities seek to raise problems, manage them through the problem management process, find the underlying causes of the incidents they are associated with and prevent future recurrences of those incidents. The difference between reactive and proactive problem management lies in how the problem management process is triggered:

- With reactive problem management, process activities will typically be triggered in reaction to an incident that has taken place. Reactive problem management complements incident management activities by focusing on the underlying cause of an incident to prevent its recurrence and identifying workarounds when necessary.
- With proactive problem management, process activities are triggered by activities seeking to improve services. One example might be trend analysis activities to find common underlying

causes of historical incidents that took place to prevent their recurrence. Proactive problem management complements CSI activities by helping to identify workarounds and improvement actions that can improve the quality of a service.

By redirecting the efforts of an organization from reacting to large numbers of incidents to preventing incidents, an organization provides a better service to its customers and makes more effective use of the available resources within the IT support organization.

Problem models

Many problems will be unique and will require handling in an individual way – but it is conceivable that some incidents may recur because of dormant or underlying problems (for example, where the cost of a permanent resolution will be high and a decision has been taken not to go ahead with an expensive solution but to 'live with' the problem).

As well as creating a known error record in the KEDB (see section 4.4.5.7) to ensure quicker diagnosis, the creation of a problem model for handling such problems in the future may be helpful. This is very similar in concept to the idea of incident or request models described in previous chapters, but applied to problems.

Incidents versus problems

An incident is an unplanned interruption to an IT service or reduction in the quality of an IT service. A problem presents a different view of an incident by understanding its underlying cause, which may also be the cause of other incidents. Incidents do not 'become' problems. While incident management activities are focused on restoring services to normal state operations, problem management activities are focused on finding ways to prevent incidents from happening in the first place. It is quite common to have incidents that are also problems.

The rules for invoking problem management during an incident can vary and are at the discretion of individual organizations. Some general situations where it may be desired to invoke problem management during an incident might include situations where:

- Incident management cannot match an incident to existing problems and known errors

- Trend analysis of logged incidents reveals an underlying problem might exist
- A major incident has occurred where problem management activities need to be undertaken to identify the root cause
- Other IT functions identify that a problem condition exists
- The service desk may have resolved an incident but has not determined a definitive cause and suspects that it is likely to recur
- Analysis of an incident by a support group which reveals that an underlying problem exists, or is likely to exist
- A notification from a supplier that a problem exists that has to be resolved.

4.4.4.3 Problem analysis techniques

There are many problem analysis, diagnosis and solving techniques available and much research has been done in this area. Examples of frequently used techniques are given below.

Chronological analysis

When dealing with a difficult problem, there may be conflicting reports about exactly what has happened and when. It is therefore very helpful briefly to document all events in chronological order, to provide a timeline of events. This often makes it possible to see which events may have been triggered by others – or to discount any claims that are not supported by the sequence of events.

Pain value analysis

This is where a broader view is taken of the impact of an incident or problem, or incident/problem type. Instead of just analysing the number of incidents/problems of a particular type in a particular period, a more in-depth analysis is done to determine exactly what level of pain has been caused to the organization/business by these incidents/problems. A formula can be devised to calculate this pain level. Typically this might include taking into account:

- The number of people affected
- The duration of the downtime caused
- The cost to the business (if this can be readily calculated or estimated).

By taking all of these factors into account, a much more detailed picture of those incidents/problems or incident/problem types that are causing most pain can be determined, to allow a better focus on those things that really matter and deserve the highest priority when determining resolution actions.

Kepner and Tregoe

Charles Kepner and Benjamin Tregoe developed a useful way of problem analysis that can be used formally to investigate deeper-rooted problems. They defined the following stages:

- Defining the problem
- Describing the problem in terms of identity, location, time and size
- Establishing possible causes
- Testing the most probable cause
- Verifying the true cause.

The method is described in more detail in Appendix C.

Brainstorming

It can often be valuable to gather together the relevant people, either physically or by electronic means, and to 'brainstorm' the problem, with people throwing in ideas on what the potential cause may be and potential actions to resolve the problem. Brainstorming sessions can be very constructive and innovative but it is equally important that someone, perhaps the problem manager, documents the outcome and any agreed actions and keeps a degree of control in the session(s).

5-Whys

This simple yet highly effective approach is helpful as a way to get to the underlying root cause of a problem. It works by starting out with a description of what event took place and then asking 'why this occurred'. The resulting answer is given, followed by another round of 'why this occurred'. Usually by the fifth iteration, a true root cause will have been found.

Fault isolation

This approach involves re-executing the transactions or events that led to a problem in a careful stepwise fashion, one CI at a time, until the CI at fault is identified. The re-execution effort moves to the first CI encountered at the start of the transaction or event, which is then checked for correct operation. The effort then moves to

the next CI in the chain of events, which in turn is checked, the next CI and then the next until a fault is encountered. If the fault cannot be recreated, a variation of this technique can be tried that involves interrogating the healthy state of the CIs involved with the transaction or event. For example, if one CI is deemed to be at fault, all other CIs in the transaction or event path from source to destination are probed for health.

Affinity mapping

This technique can be used to organize large amounts of data (ideas, opinions, issues) into groupings based on common characteristics. It is typically performed in a brainstorming session with key support staff. Key concepts, such as potential solutions, are written on individual cards and stuck to a wall or whiteboard. Participants and/or the facilitator should then move the cards so that they are grouped by similar traits. A 'header' should then be developed for each group for future identification. Each of the cards under the 'header' should be examined for potential of a root cause that may underlie all of them.

Hypothesis testing

This method can be used to generate a list of possible root causes based on educated guessing and then determining whether each hypothesis is true or false. Educated guesses may relate to relationships between variables or potential root causes of a problem. Using information gathered from incidents and other operational information, a team is assembled to brainstorm a list of potential causes that may be underlying the incidents being studied. Each cause is then converted into testable statements or hypotheses and assigned to one or more support staff. Further data should then be gathered as needed for each assigned statement and an appropriate analysis performed to accept or reject each hypothesis.

Technical observation post

In some cases problems may be linked to incidents that occur intermittently for unknown reasons or causes. This approach consists of a prearranged gathering of specialist technical support staff from within the IT support organization brought together to focus on a specific problem. Its purpose is to monitor events, real-time as they occur, with the specific aim of catching and identifying the specific situation and possible causes for the problem.

Ishikawa diagrams

Kaoru Ishikawa (1915–1989), a leader in Japanese quality control, developed a method of documenting causes and effects that can be useful in helping identify where something may be going wrong, or be improved. Such a diagram is typically the outcome of a brainstorming session where problem solvers can offer suggestions. The main goal is represented by the trunk of the diagram, and primary factors are represented as branches. Secondary factors are then added as stems, and so on. Creating the diagram stimulates discussion and often leads to increased understanding of a complex problem. An example diagram is given in Appendix D.

Pareto analysis

This is a technique for separating the most important potential causes of failures from more trivial issues. Details of this approach are given in Appendix H.

Table 4.2 may be helpful in identifying the kinds of situations that each technique shown above might be used for.

4.4.4.4 Errors detected in the development environment

It is rare for any new applications, systems or software releases to be completely error-free. It is more likely that during testing of such new applications, systems or releases a prioritization system will be used to eradicate the more serious faults, but it is possible that minor faults are not rectified – often because of the balance that has to be maintained between delivering new functionality to the business as quickly as possible and ensuring totally fault-free code or components.

Where a decision is made to release something into the live environment that includes known deficiencies, these should be logged as known errors in the KEDB, together with details of workarounds or resolution activities. There should be a formal step in the testing sign-off that ensures this handover always takes place (see *ITIL Service Transition*).

Experience has shown that if this does not happen, it will lead to far higher support costs when the users start to experience the faults and

Table 4.2 Problem situations and the most useful techniques for identifying root causes

Problem situation	Suggested analysis techniques
Complex problems where a sequence of events needs to be assembled to determine exactly what happened	Chronological analysis Technical observation post
Uncertainty over which problems should be addressed first	Pain value analysis Brainstorming
Uncertain whether a presented root cause is truly the root cause	5-Whys Hypothesis testing
Intermittent problems that appear to come and go and cannot be recreated or repeated in a test environment	Technical observation post Kepner–Tregoe Hypothesis testing Brainstorming
Uncertainty over where to start for problems that appear to have multiple causes	Pareto analysis Kepner–Tregoe Ishikawa diagrams Brainstorming
Struggling to identify the exact point of failure for a problem	Fault isolation Ishikawa diagrams Kepner–Tregoe Affinity mapping Brainstorming
Uncertain where to start when trying to find root cause	5-Whys Kepner–Tregoe Brainstorming Affinity mapping

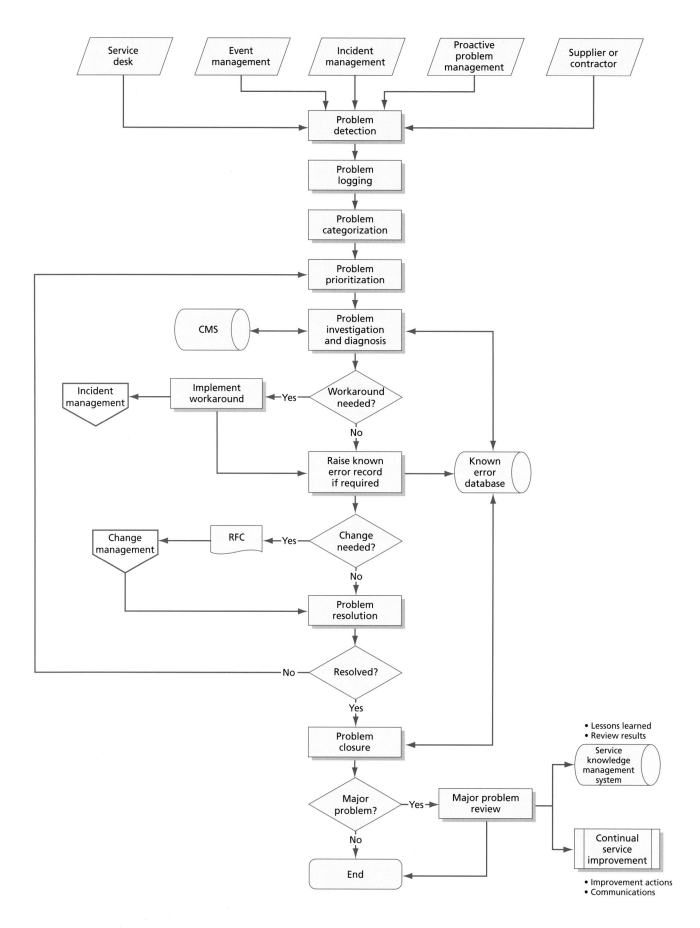

Figure 4.7 Problem management process flow

raise incidents that have to be re-diagnosed and resolved all over again!

4.4.5 Process activities, methods and techniques

The problem management process flow for handling a recognized problem is shown in Figure 4.7. This is a simplified chart to show the normal process flow, but in reality some of the states may be iterative or variations may have to be made in order to handle particular situations. For example, proactive problem management activities may raise new problem records which in turn can become input to this process flow.

4.4.5.1 Problem detection

It is likely that multiple ways of detecting problems will exist in all organizations. These can include triggers for reactive and proactive problem management:

Reactive problem management triggers:

- Suspicion or detection of a cause of one or more incidents by the service desk, resulting in a problem record being raised – the desk may have resolved the incident but has not determined a definitive cause and suspects that it is likely to recur, so will raise a problem record to allow the underlying cause to be resolved. Alternatively, it may be immediately obvious from the outset that an incident, or incidents, has been caused by a major problem, so a problem record will be raised without delay.
- Analysis of an incident by a technical support group which reveals that an underlying problem exists, or is likely to exist.
- Automated detection of an infrastructure or application fault, using event/alert tools automatically to raise an incident which may reveal the need for a problem record.
- A notification from a supplier or contractor that a problem exists that has to be resolved.

Proactive problem management triggers:

- Analysis of incidents that result in the need to raise a problem record so that the underlying fault can be investigated further.
- Trending of historical incident records to identify one or more underlying causes that if removed, can prevent their recurrence. In

this case, a problem record is raised once the underlying trend or cause is discovered.
- Activities taken to improve the quality of a service that result in the need to raise a problem record to identify further improvement actions that should be taken.

Frequent and regular analysis of incident and problem data must be performed to identify any trends as they become discernible. This will require meaningful and detailed categorization of incidents/problems and regular reporting of patterns and areas of high occurrence. 'Top ten' reporting, with drill-down capabilities to lower levels, is useful in identifying trends.

Further details of how detected trends should be handled are included in *ITIL Continual Service Improvement*.

4.4.5.2 Problem logging

Regardless of the detection method, all the relevant details of the problem must be recorded so that a full historic record exists. This must be date and time stamped to allow suitable control and escalation.

A cross-reference must be made to the incident(s) which initiated the problem record – and all relevant details must be copied from the incident record(s) to the problem record. It is difficult to be exact, as cases may vary, but typically this will include details such as:

- User details
- Service details
- Equipment details
- Date/time initially logged
- Priority and categorization details
- Incident description
- Incident record numbers or other cross-reference
- Details of all diagnostic or attempted recovery actions taken.

4.4.5.3 Problem categorization

Problems should be categorized in the same way as incidents (and it is advisable to use the same coding system) so that the true nature of the problem can be easily traced in the future and meaningful management information can be obtained. This also allows for incidents and problems to be more readily matched.

4.4.5.4 Problem prioritization

Problems should be prioritized the same way using the same reasons as incidents. The frequency and impact of related incidents must also be taken into account. The coding system described earlier in Table 4.1 (which combines incident impact with urgency to give an overall priority level) can also be used to prioritize problems. Definition and guidance should be provided to support staff on what constitutes a problem, and the related service targets for each priority code level in the table.

Problem prioritization should also take into account the severity of the problems. Severity in this context refers to how serious the problem is from a service or customer perspective as well as an infrastructure perspective, for example:

■ Can the system be recovered, or does it need to be replaced?

■ How much will it cost?

■ How many people, with what skills, will be needed to fix the problem?

■ How long will it take to fix the problem?

■ How extensive is the problem (e.g. how many CIs are affected)?

4.4.5.5 Problem investigation and diagnosis

At this stage, an investigation should be conducted to try to diagnose the root cause of the problem – the speed and nature of this investigation will vary depending upon the impact, severity and urgency of the problem – but the appropriate level of resources and expertise should be applied to finding a resolution commensurate with the priority code allocated and the service target in place for that priority level.

There are a number of useful problem-solving techniques that can be used to help diagnose and resolve problems, and these should be used as appropriate. Such techniques have been described in more detail in section 4.4.4.

The CMS must be used to help determine the level of impact and pinpoint and diagnose the exact point of failure. The KEDB should also be accessed and problem-matching techniques (such as keyword searches) should be used to see if the problem has occurred before and, if so, to find the resolution.

It is often valuable to try to recreate the failure to understand what has gone wrong, and then try various ways of finding the most appropriate and cost-effective resolution to the problem. It may be possible to recreate the problem in a test environment that mirrors the live environment. This allows for investigation and diagnosis activities to proceed effectively without causing further disruption to users.

4.4.5.6 Workarounds

In some cases it may be possible to find a workaround to the incidents caused by the problem – a temporary way of overcoming the difficulties. For example, a manual amendment may be made to an input file to allow a program to complete its run successfully and allow a billing process to complete satisfactorily, but it is important that work on a permanent resolution continues where this is justified – in this example the reason for the file becoming corrupted in the first place must be found and corrected to prevent this happening again.

When a workaround is found, it is therefore important that the problem record remains open and details of the workaround are documented within the problem record.

In some cases there may be multiple workarounds associated with a problem. As problem investigation and diagnosis activities carry on, there may be a series of improvements that do not resolve the problem, but lead to a progressive improvement in the quality of the workarounds available. These may impact on the prioritization of the problem as successive workaround solutions may reduce the impact of future related incidents, either by reducing their likelihood or improving the speed of their resolution.

4.4.5.7 Raising a known error record

A known error is defined as a problem with a documented root cause and workaround. The known error record should identify the problem record it relates to and document the status of actions being taken to resolve the problem, its root cause and workaround. All known error records should be stored in the KEDB. The KEDB and the way it should be used are described in more detail in section 4.4.7.2.

As soon as the diagnosis is complete, and particularly where a workaround has been found (even though it may not yet be a permanent resolution), a known error record must be raised and placed in the KEDB so that if further incidents or problems arise, they can be identified and the service restored more quickly. In some cases it may be advantageous to raise a known error record even earlier in the overall process, even though the diagnosis may not be complete or a workaround found. This might be used for information purposes or to identify a root cause or workaround that appears to address the problem but hasn't been fully confirmed. Therefore, it is inadvisable to set a concrete procedural point for exactly when a known error record must be raised. It should be done as soon as it becomes useful to do so!

4.4.5.8 Problem resolution

Once a root cause has been found and a solution to remove it has been developed, it should be applied to resolve the problem. In reality, safeguards may be needed to ensure that the resolution does not cause further difficulties. If any change in functionality is required, an RFC should be raised and authorized before the resolution can be applied. If the problem is very serious and an urgent fix is needed for business reasons, then an emergency RFC should be raised. The resolution should be applied only when the change has been authorized and scheduled for release. In the meantime, the KEDB should be used to help resolve quickly any further occurrences of the incidents/ problems that occur.

There may be some problems for which a business case for resolution cannot be justified (e.g. where the impact is limited but the cost of resolution would be extremely high). In such cases a decision may be taken to leave the problem record open but to use a workaround description in the known error record to detect and resolve any recurrences quickly. Care should be taken to use the appropriate code to flag the open problem record so that it does not count against the performance of the team performing the process and so that unauthorized rework does not take place.

In some cases, workarounds may be in place to mitigate the impacts of the problem without a final resolution being found. In this event, the problem should be re-prioritized based on the impact of the workarounds applied and investigative and diagnostic activities should be continued.

4.4.5.9 Problem closure

When a final resolution has been applied, the problem record should be formally closed – as should any related incident records that are still open. A check should be performed at this time to ensure that the record contains a full historical description of all events – and if not, the record should be updated.

The status of any related known error record should be updated to show that the resolution has been applied.

4.4.5.10 Major problem review

After every major problem (as determined by the organization's priority system), and while memories are still fresh, a review should be conducted to learn any lessons for the future. Specifically, the review should examine:

- Those things that were done correctly
- Those things that were done wrong
- What could be done better in the future
- How to prevent recurrence
- Whether there has been any third-party responsibility and whether follow-up actions are needed.

Such reviews can be used as part of training and awareness activities for support staff – and any lessons learned should be documented in appropriate procedures, work instructions, diagnostic scripts or known error records. The problem manager facilitates the session and documents any agreed actions.

Major problem reviews can also be a source of input to proactive problem management through identification of underlying causes that may be discovered in the course of the review (see section 4.4.2 for more details about proactive problem management).

The knowledge gained from the review should be incorporated into a service review meeting with the business customer to ensure the customer is aware of the actions taken and the plans to prevent future major incidents from occurring. This helps to improve customer satisfaction and assure the business that service operation is handling major incidents responsibly and actively working to prevent their future recurrence.

4.4.6 Triggers, inputs, outputs and interfaces

4.4.6.1 Triggers

With reactive problem management, the vast majority of problem records will be triggered in reaction to one or more incidents, and many will be raised or initiated via service desk staff. Other problem records, and corresponding known error records, may be triggered in testing, particularly the latter stages of testing such as user acceptance testing/trials (UAT), if a decision is made to go ahead with a release even though some faults are known. Suppliers may trigger the need for some problem records through the notification of potential faults or known deficiencies in their products or services (e.g. a warning may be given regarding the use of a particular CI and a problem record may be raised to facilitate investigation by technical staff of the condition of such CIs within the organization's IT infrastructure).

With proactive problem management, problem records may be triggered by identification of patterns and trends in incidents when reviewing historical incident records. A review of other sources such as operation logs, operation communications or event logs may also proactively trigger problem records when the appearance of an underlying issue becomes apparent.

4.4.6.2 Inputs

Examples of inputs to the problem management process may include:

- Incident records for incidents that have triggered problem management activities
- Incident reports and histories that will be used to support proactive problem trending
- Information about CIs and their status
- Communication and feedback about incidents and their symptoms
- Communication and feedback about RFCs and releases that have been implemented or planned for implementation
- Communication of events that were triggered from event management
- Operational and service level objectives
- Customer feedback on success of problem resolution activities and overall quality of problem management activities

- Agreed criteria for prioritizing and escalating problems
- Output from risk management and risk assessment activities.

4.4.6.3 Outputs

Examples of outputs from the problem management process may include:

- Resolved problems and actions taken to achieve their resolution
- Updated problem management records with accurate problem detail and history
- RFCs to remove infrastructure errors
- Workarounds for incidents
- Known error records
- Problem management reports
- Output and improvement recommendations from major problem review activity.

4.4.6.4 Interfaces

The primary relationship between incident and problem management has been discussed in detail in section 4.4.4. Examples of other key interfaces are listed below for each service lifecycle stage.

Service strategy

- **Financial management for IT services** Assists in assessing the impact of proposed resolutions or workarounds, as well as pain value analysis. Problem management provides management information about the cost of resolving and preventing problems, which is used as input into the budgeting and accounting systems and total cost of ownership calculations.

Service design

- **Availability management** Is involved with determining how to reduce downtime and increase uptime. As such, it has a close relationship with problem management, especially the proactive areas. Much of the management information available in problem management will be communicated to availability management.
- **Capacity management** Some problems will require investigation by capacity management teams and techniques, e.g. performance issues. Capacity management will also help in assessing proactive measures. Problem management provides management information relative

to the quality of decisions made during the capacity planning process.

- **IT service continuity management** Problem management acts as an entry point into IT service continuity management where a significant problem is not resolved before it starts to have a major impact on the business.
- **Service level management** The occurrence of incidents and problems affects the level of service delivery measured by SLM. Problem management contributes to improvements in service levels, and its management information is used as the basis of some of the SLA review components. SLM also provides parameters within which problem management works, such as impact information and the effect on services of proposed resolutions and proactive measures.

Service transition

- **Change management** Problem management ensures that all resolutions or workarounds that require a change to a CI are submitted through change management through an RFC. Change management will monitor the progress of these changes and keep problem management advised. Problem management is also involved in rectifying the situation caused by failed changes.
- **Service asset and configuration management** Problem management uses the CMS to identify faulty CIs and also to determine the impact of problems and resolutions.
- **Release and deployment management** This process is responsible for deploying problem fixes out into the live environment. It also assists in ensuring that the associated known errors are transferred from the development KEDB into the live known error database. Problem management will help resolve problems caused by faults during the release process.
- **Knowledge management** The SKMS can be used to form the basis for the KEDB and hold or integrate with the problem records.

Continual service improvement

- **The seven-step improvement process** The occurrence of incidents and problems provides a basis for identifying opportunities for service improvement and adding them to the

CSI register. Proactive problem management activities may also identify underlying problems and service issues that if addressed, can contribute to increases in service quality and end user/customer satisfaction.

4.4.7 Information management

Most information used in problem management comes from the following sources:

4.4.7.1 Configuration management system

The CMS will hold details of all of the components of the IT infrastructure, as well as the relationships between these components. It will act as a valuable source for problem diagnosis and for evaluating the impact of problems (e.g. if this disk is down, what data is on that disk; which services use that data; which users use those services?). As it will also hold details of previous activities, it can also be used as a valuable source of historical data to help identify trends or potential weaknesses – a key part of proactive problem management.

4.4.7.2 Known error database

The purpose of a KEDB is to allow storage of previous knowledge of incidents and problems – and how they were overcome – to allow quicker diagnosis and resolution if they recur.

The known error record should hold exact details of the fault and the symptoms that occurred, together with precise details of any workaround or resolution action that can be taken to restore the service and/or resolve the problem. An incident count will also be useful to determine the frequency with which incidents are likely to recur and influence priorities etc.

It should be noted that a business case for a permanent resolution for some problems may not exist. For example, if a problem does not cause serious disruption and a workaround exists and/or the cost of resolving the problem far outweighs the benefits of a permanent resolution, then a decision may be taken to tolerate the problem. However, it will still be desirable to diagnose and implement a workaround as quickly as possible, which is where the KEDB can help.

It is essential that any data put into the database can be quickly and accurately retrieved. The problem manager should be fully trained and familiar with the search methods/algorithms used by the selected database and should carefully ensure that when new records are added, the relevant search key criteria are correctly included.

Care should be taken to avoid duplication of records (i.e. the same problem described in two or more ways as separate records). To avoid this, the problem manager should be the only person able to enter a new record. Other support groups should be encouraged to propose new records, but these should be vetted by the problem manager before entry to the KEDB. In large organizations where a single KEDB is used (recommended) with problem management staff in multiple locations, a procedure must be agreed to ensure that duplication of KEDB records cannot occur. This may involve designating just one staff member as the central KEDB manager.

The KEDB should be used during the incident and problem diagnosis phases to try to speed up the resolution process – and new records should be added as quickly as possible when a new problem has been identified and diagnosed.

All support staff should be fully trained and conversant with the value that the KEDB can offer

and the way it should be used. They should be able readily to retrieve and use data.

The KEDB is part of the CMS and may be part of a larger SKMS illustrated in Figure 4.8. Note that SCMIS stands for supplier and contract management information system. More information on the SKMS can be found in *ITIL Service Transition*.

4.4.8 Critical success factors and key performance indicators

The following list includes some sample CSFs for problem management. Each organization should identify appropriate CSFs based on its objectives for the process. Each sample CSF is followed by a small number of typical KPIs that support the CSF. These KPIs should not be adopted without careful consideration. Each organization should develop KPIs that are appropriate for its level of maturity, its CSFs and its particular circumstances. Achievement against KPIs should be monitored and used to identify opportunities for improvement, which should be logged in the CSI register for evaluation and possible implementation.

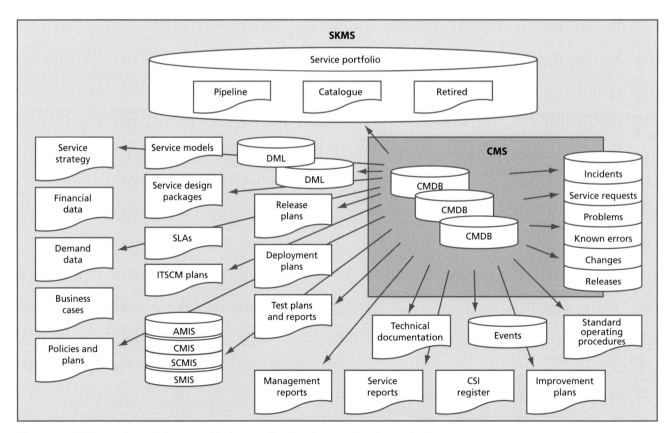

Figure 4.8 Examples of data and information in the service knowledge management system

■ **CSF** Minimize the impact to the business of incidents that cannot be prevented

● **KPI** The number of known errors added to the KEDB

● **KPI** The percentage accuracy of the KEDB (from audits of the database)

● **KPI** Percentage of incidents closed by the service desk without reference to other levels of support (often referred to as 'first point of contact')

● **KPI** Average incident resolution time for those incidents linked to problem records

■ **CSF** Maintain quality of IT services through elimination of recurring incidents

● **KPI** Total numbers of problems (as a control measure)

● **KPI** Size of current problem backlog for each IT service

● **KPI** Number of repeat incidents for each IT service

■ **CSF** Provide overall quality and professionalism of problem handling activities to maintain business confidence in IT capabilities

● **KPI** The number of major problems (opened and closed and backlog)

● **KPI** The percentage of major problem reviews successfully performed

● **KPI** The percentage of major problem reviews completed successfully and on time

● **KPI** Number and percentage of problems incorrectly assigned

● **KPI** Number and percentage of problems incorrectly categorized

● **KPI** The backlog of outstanding problems and the trend (static, reducing or increasing?)

● **KPI** Number and percentage of problems that exceeded their target resolution times

● **KPI** Percentage of problems resolved within SLA targets (and the percentage that are not!)

● **KPI** Average cost per problem.

It is also helpful to break down and categorize problem metrics by category, time frame, impact, urgency, service impacted, location and priority and compare these with previous periods. This can provide input to CSI and other processes seeking to identify issues, problem trends or other situations.

4.4.9 Challenges and risks

4.4.9.1 Challenges

The following challenges will exist for successful problem management:

■ A major dependency for problem management is the establishment of an effective incident management process and tools. This will ensure that problems are identified as soon as possible and that as much work is done on pre-qualification as possible. A critical challenge exists in making sure that the two processes have formal interfaces and common working practices.

■ The skills and capabilities for problem resolution staff to identify the true root cause of incidents is sometimes a challenge. Many times, support staff will describe the root cause based on symptoms or resolution actions taken. The techniques described in section 4.4.4 can be used to help determine the true underlying cause of an incident. Creating a focus around 'why did this happen?' or 'what can be done to prevent the incident from happening again?' can also be helpful.

■ The ability to relate incidents to problems can be a challenge if the tools used to record incidents are different from those of problems. In some cases, incident tools might exist with no capabilities to track problems separately.

■ The ability to integrate problem management activities with the CMS to determine relationships between CIs and to refer to the history of CIs when performing problem support activities.

■ Ensuring that problem management is able to use all knowledge and service asset and configuration management resources available to investigate and resolve problems.

■ Ensuring that ongoing training of technical staff in both technical aspects of their job as well as the business implications of the services they support and the processes they use is in place.

■ The ability to have a good working relationship between the second- and third-line staff working on problem support activities and first-line staff.

■ Making sure that business impact is well understood by all staff working on problem resolution.

4.4.9.2 Risks

The risks to successful problem management are actually similar to some of the challenges and the reverse of some of the CSFs mentioned above. They include:

- Being inundated with problems that cannot be handled within acceptable timescales due to a lack of available or properly trained resources
- Problems being bogged down and not progressed as intended because of inadequate support tools for investigation
- Lack of adequate and/or timely information sources because of inadequate tools or lack of integration
- Problem support staff that may not be properly trained to investigate problems, find their underlying causes or identify appropriate actions to remove errors
- Mismatches in objectives or actions because of poorly aligned or non-existent OLAs and/or UCs.

4.5 ACCESS MANAGEMENT

Access management is the process of granting authorized users the right to use a service, while preventing access to non-authorized users. It has also been referred to as rights management or identity management in different organizations.

4.5.1 Purpose and objectives

4.5.1.1 Purpose

The purpose of access management is to provide the right for users to be able to use a service or group of services. It is therefore the execution of policies and actions defined in information security management.

4.5.1.2 Objectives

The objectives of the access management process are to:

- Manage access to services based on policies and actions defined in information security management (see *ITIL Service Design*)
- Efficiently respond to requests for granting access to services, changing access rights or restricting access, ensuring that the rights being provided or changed are properly granted
- Oversee access to services and ensure rights being provided are not improperly used.

4.5.2 Scope

Access management is effectively the execution of the policies in information security management, in that it enables the organization to manage the confidentiality, availability and integrity of the organization's data and intellectual property.

Access management ensures that users are given the right to use a service, but it does not ensure that this access is available at all agreed times – this is provided by availability management.

Access management is a process that is executed by all technical and application management functions and is usually not a separate function. However, there is likely to be a single control point of coordination, usually in IT operations management or on the service desk.

Access management can be initiated by a service request.

4.5.3 Value to business

The value of access management includes:

- Ensuring that controlled access to services will allow the organization to maintain effective confidentiality of its information
- Ensuring that employees have the right level of access to execute their jobs effectively
- Reducing errors made in data entry or in the use of a critical service by an unskilled user (e.g. production control systems)
- Providing capabilities to audit use of services and to trace the abuse of services
- Providing capabilities to revoke access rights when needed on a timely basis – an important security consideration
- Providing and demonstrating compliance with regulatory requirements (e.g. SOX, HIPAA and COBIT).

4.5.4 Policies, principles and basic concepts

4.5.4.1 Policies

Examples of access management policies might include:

- Access management administration and associated activities should be guided and directed by the policies and controls as defined in the information security policy (see *ITIL Service Design*).

■ Access management should log and track accesses to use of services and ensure rights being provided are appropriately used. This implies that appropriate access logging and tracking capabilities are in place with controls to raise events for unauthorized access and abuse of services.

■ Access management should maintain access to services in alignment with changes in personnel events such as transfers and terminations. This implies that communications are in place with human resource functions to notify IT about personnel events and changes on a timely basis.

■ Access management should maintain an accurate history of who has accessed, or tried to access, services. This provides information to those conducting auditing and compliance activities. It also helps others who may be involved with security forensic activities when investigating security breaches. It implies that records are maintained showing what access rights have been granted to which services and by whom.

■ Procedures for handling, escalating and communicating security events should be clearly defined and documented in accordance with the information security policy (see *ITIL Service Design*). This implies that those performing access management activities fully understand the information security policy and procedures for handling security events.

4.5.4.2 Principles and basic concepts

Access management is the process that enables users to use the services that are documented in the service catalogue. It comprises the following basic concepts:

■ Access refers to the level and extent of a service's functionality or data that a user is entitled to use.

■ Identity refers to the information about them that distinguishes them as an individual and which verifies their status within the organization. By definition, the identity of a user is unique to that user. (This is covered in more detail in section 4.5.7.1.)

■ Rights (also called privileges) refer to the actual settings whereby a user is provided access to a service or group of services. Typical rights, or levels of access, include read, write, execute, change, delete.

■ Services or service groups. Most users do not use only one service, and users performing a similar set of activities will use a similar set of services. Instead of providing access to each service for each user separately, it is more efficient to be able to grant each user – or group of users – access to the whole set of services that they are entitled to use at the same time. (This is discussed in more detail in section 4.5.7.2.)

■ Directory services refer to specific types of tools that are used to manage access and rights. These are discussed in section 5.7.

4.5.5 Process activities, methods and techniques

The process to be followed during the management of an access request is shown in Figure 4.9. The process includes the following steps.

4.5.5.1 Request access

Access (or restriction) can be requested using one of any number of mechanisms, including:

■ A service request generated by the human resource system. This is generally done whenever a person is hired, promoted, transferred or when they leave the company

■ An RFC

■ A service request submitted via the request fulfilment system

■ By executing a pre-authorized script or option (e.g. downloading an application from a staging server as and when it is needed).

Rules for requesting access are normally documented as part of the request fulfilment model associated with requests for access and may also be described in the service catalogue.

4.5.5.2 Verification

Access management needs to verify every request for access to an IT service from two perspectives:

■ That the user requesting access is who they say they are

■ That they have a legitimate requirement for that service.

The first perspective is usually achieved by the user providing their user name and password. Depending on the organization's security policies, the use of the user name and password are usually accepted as proof that the person is a legitimate

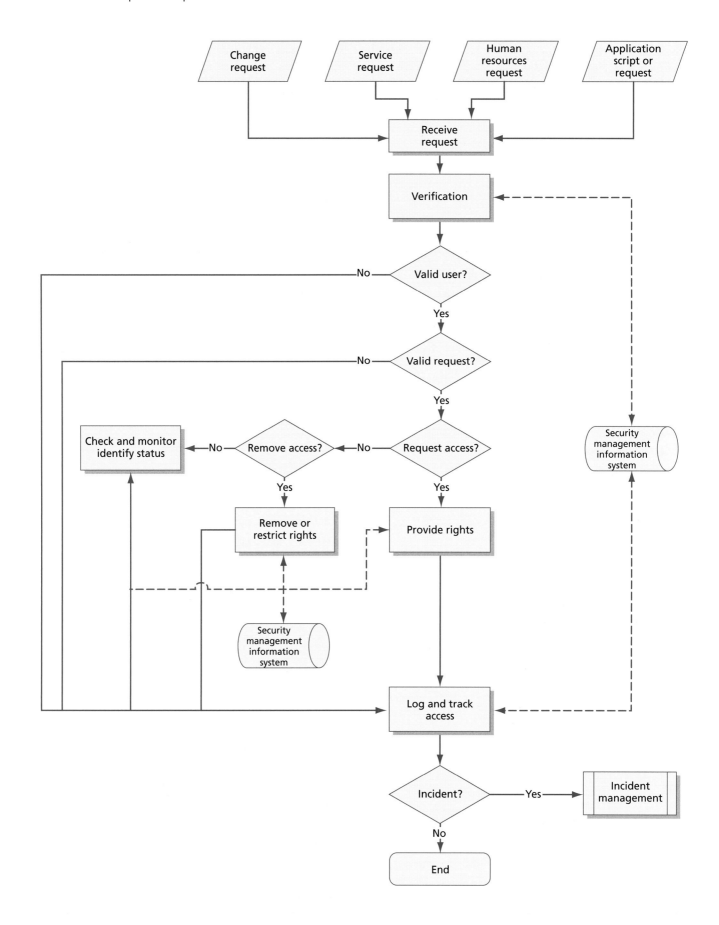

Figure 4.9 Access management process flow

user. However, for more sensitive services further authentication may be required (biometric, use of an electronic access key, encryption device, database of secret questions and answers known only to the user etc.).

The second perspective will require some independent verification, other than the user's request. For example:

- Notification from human resources that the person is a new employee and requires both a user name and access to a standard set of services
- Notification from human resources that the user has been promoted and requires access to additional resources
- Authorization from an appropriate (defined in the process) manager
- Submission of a service request (with supporting evidence) through the service desk
- Submission of an RFC (with supporting evidence) through change management, or execution of a predefined standard change
- A policy stating that the user may have access to an optional service if they need it.

For new services the change record should specify which users or groups of users will have access to the service. Access management will then check to see that all the users are still authorized and automatically provide access as specified in the RFC.

4.5.5.3 Provide rights

Access management does not decide who has access to which IT services. Rather, access management executes the policies and regulations defined during service strategy and service design. Access management enforces decisions to restrict or provide access, rather than making the decision.

As soon as a user has been verified, access management will provide that user with rights to use the requested service. In most cases this will result in a request to every team or department involved in supporting that service to take the necessary action. If possible, these tasks should be automated.

The more roles and groups that exist, the more likely that role conflict will arise. Role conflict in this context refers to a situation where two specific roles or groups, if assigned to a single user, will

create issues with separation of duties or conflict of interest. Examples of this include:

- One role requires detailed access, while another role prevents that access
- Two roles allow a user to perform two tasks that should not be combined (e.g. a contractor can log their time sheet for a project and then approve all payment on work for the same project).

Role conflicts can be avoided by careful creation of roles and groups, but more often they are caused by policies and decisions made outside of service operation – either by the business or by different project teams working during service design. In each case the conflict must be documented and escalated to the stakeholders to resolve.

Whenever roles and groups are defined, it is possible that they could be defined too broadly or too narrowly. There will always be users who need something slightly different from the predefined roles. In these cases, it is possible to use standard roles and then add or subtract specific rights as required – similar to the concept of baselines and variants in service asset and configuration management (see *ITIL Service Transition*). However, the decision to do this is not in the hands of individual operational staff members. Each exception should be coordinated by access management and approved through the originating process.

Access management should perform a regular review of the roles and groups that it has created and manage to ensure that they are appropriate for the services that IT delivers and supports – and obsolete or unwanted roles/groups should be removed.

4.5.5.4 Check and monitor identity status

As users work in the organization, their roles change and so also do their needs to access services. Examples of changes include:

- **Job changes** In this case the user will possibly need access to different or additional services.
- **Promotions or demotions** The user will probably use the same set of services, but will need access to different levels of functionality or data.
- **Transfers** In this situation, the user may need access to exactly the same set of services, but

in a different region with different working practices and different sets of data.

- **Resignation or death** Access needs to be completely removed to prevent the user name being used as a security loophole.

- **Retirement** In many organizations, an employee who retires may still have access to a limited set of services, including benefits systems or systems that allow them to purchase company products at a reduced rate.

- **Disciplinary action** In some cases the organization will require a temporary restriction to prevent the user from accessing some or all of the services that they would normally have access to. There should be a feature in the process and tools to do this, rather than having to delete and reinstate the user's access rights.

- **Dismissals** Where an employee or contractor is dismissed, or where legal action is taken against a customer (for example for defaulting on payment for products purchased on the internet), access should be revoked immediately. In addition, access management, working together with information security management, should take active measures to prevent and detect malicious action against the organization from that user.

Access management should understand and document the typical user lifecycle for each type of user and use it to automate the process. Access management tools should provide features that enable a user to be moved from one state to another, or from one group to another, easily and with an audit trail.

4.5.5.5 Log and track access

Access management should not only respond to requests. It is also responsible for ensuring that the rights they have provided are being properly used.

In this respect, access monitoring and control must be included in the monitoring activities of all technical and application management functions and all service operation processes.

Exceptions should be handled by incident management, possibly using incident models specifically designed to deal with abuse of access rights. Note that the visibility of such actions should be restricted. Making this information

available to all who have access to the incident management system will expose vulnerabilities.

Information security management plays a vital role in detecting unauthorized access and comparing it with the rights that were provided by access management. This will require access management involvement in defining the parameters for use in intrusion detection tools.

Access management may also be required to provide a record of access for specific services during forensic investigations. If a user is suspected of breaches of policy, inappropriate use of resources, or fraudulent use of data, access management may be required to provide evidence of dates, times and even content of that user's access to specific services. This is normally provided by the operational staff of that service, but working as part of the access management process.

4.5.5.6 Remove or restrict rights

Just as access management provides rights to use a service, it is also responsible for revoking those rights. Again, this is not a decision that it makes on its own. Rather, it will execute the decisions and policies made during service strategy and design and also decisions made by managers in the organization.

Removing access is usually done in the following circumstances:

- Death
- Resignation
- Dismissal
- When the user has changed roles and no longer requires access to the service
- Transfer or travel to an area where different regional access applies.

In other cases it is not necessary to remove access, but just to provide tighter restrictions. These could include reducing the level, time or duration of access. Situations in which access should be restricted include:

- When the user has changed roles or been demoted and no longer requires the same level of access
- When the user is under investigation, but still requires access to basic services, such as email. In this case their email may be subject to additional scanning (but this would need to be

handled very carefully and in full accordance with the organization's security policy)

■ When a user is away from the organization on temporary assignment and will not require access to that service for some time.

4.5.6 Triggers, inputs, outputs and interfaces

4.5.6.1 Triggers

Access management is triggered by a request for a user or users to access a service or group of services. This could originate from any of the following:

■ **An RFC** This is most frequently used for large-scale service introductions or upgrades where the rights of a significant number of users need to be updated as part of the project.

■ **A service request** This is usually initiated through the service desk, or directly into the request fulfilment system, and executed by the relevant technical or application management teams.

■ **A request from human resources** A request from the appropriate human resources management personnel (which should be channelled via the service desk) is usually generated as part of the process for hiring, promoting, relocating and termination or retirement.

■ **A request from a manager** This could come from the manager of a department, who could be performing a human resources role, or who could have made a decision to start using a service for the first time.

4.5.6.2 Inputs

Examples of inputs to access management may include:

■ Information security policies (from service design)

■ Operational and service level requirements for granting access to services, performing access management administrative activities and responding to access management related events

■ Authorized RFCs to access rights

■ Authorized requests to grant or terminate access rights.

4.5.6.3 Outputs

Examples of outputs from access management may include:

■ Provision of access to IT services in accordance with information security policies

■ Access management records and history of access granted to services

■ Access management records and history where access has been denied and the reasons for the denial

■ Timely communications concerning inappropriate access or abuse of services.

4.5.6.4 Interfaces

Access management can interface to many processes that request or interface with IT services. Appropriate controls and rights to services should be assured in accordance with the information security policy. Examples of interfaces with other processes are listed below for each service lifecycle stage.

Service strategy

■ **Demand management** This process helps to identify the necessary resource levels to handle expected volumes of requests for access

■ **Strategy management for IT services** It may be determined that some access management activities (especially for larger organizations) could be handled more efficiently within individual business organizations rather than in a centralized access management function.

Service design

■ **Information security management** This process provides the security and data protection policies and tools needed to execute access management. Interfaces should also be in place with human resource processes to verify the user's identity as well as to ensure they are entitled to the services being requested.

■ **Service catalogue management** This process provides methods and means by which users can access different IT services, service descriptions and views that they are authorized for.

■ **IT service continuity management** Interfaces may be needed to manage access to services in the event of a major business disruption or in conditions where services have been temporarily sourced from alternative locations.

- **SLM**   This process maintains the agreements for access to each service. This will include the criteria for who is entitled to access each service, what the cost of that access will be, if appropriate, and what level of access will be granted to different types of user (e.g. managers or staff).

Service transition

- **Change management**   This process controls the actual requests for access. This is because any request for access to a service is a change, although it is usually processed as a standard change or service request (possibly using a model) once the criteria for access have been agreed through SLM.
- **Service asset and configuration management**   Interfaces to this process are needed to identify data storage and interrogate CIs to determine current access details.

Service operation

- **Request fulfilment**   This process provides methods and means by which users can request access to the standard services that are available to them.

4.5.7 Information management

4.5.7.1 Identity

The identity of a user is the information about them that distinguishes them as an individual and which verifies their status within the organization. By definition, the identity of a user is unique to that user. Because there are cases where two users share a common piece of information (e.g. they have the same name), identity is usually established using more than one piece of information, for example:

- Name
- Address
- Contact details, e.g. telephone, email address etc.
- Physical documentation, e.g. driver's licence, passport, marriage certificate etc.
- Numbers that refer to a document or an entry in a database, e.g. employee number, tax number, government identity number, driver's licence number etc.
- Biometric information, e.g. fingerprints, retinal images, voice recognition patterns, DNA etc.
- Expiration date (if relevant).

A user identity is provided to anyone with a legitimate requirement to access IT services or organizational information. These could include:

- Employees
- Contractors
- Vendor staff (e.g. account managers, support personnel etc.)
- Customers (especially when purchasing products or services over the internet).

Most organizations will verify a user's identity before they join the organization by requesting a subset of the above information. The more secure the organization, the more types of information are required and the more thoroughly they are checked.

Many organizations will be faced with the need to provide access rights to temporary or occasional staff or contractors/suppliers. The management of access to such personnel often proves problematic – closing access after use is often as difficult to manage, or more so, than providing access initially. Well-defined procedures between IT and human resources should be established that include fail-safe checks to ensure access rights are removed immediately they are no longer justified or required.

When a user is granted access to an application, it should already have been established by the organization (usually the human resources or security department) that the user is who they say they are.

At this point, all that information is filed and the file is associated with a corporate identity, usually an employee or contractor number and an identity that can be used to access corporate resources and information, usually a user identity or 'user name' and an associated password.

4.5.7.2 Users, groups, roles and service groups

While each user has an individual identity, and each IT service can be seen as an entity in its own right, it is often helpful to group them together so that they can be managed more easily. Sometimes the terms 'user profile', 'user template' or 'user role' are used to describe this type of grouping.

Most organizations have a standard set of services for all individual users, regardless of their position or job (excluding customers, who do not have any visibility to internal services and processes). These will include services such as messaging, office automation, desktop support, telephony etc. New users are automatically provided with rights to use these services.

However, most users also have some specialized role that they perform. For example, in addition to the standard services, the user also performs a marketing management role, which requires that they have access to some specialized marketing and financial modelling tools and data.

Some groups may have unique requirements, such as field or home workers who may have to dial in or use virtual private network connections, with security implications that may have to be more tightly managed.

To make it easier for access management to provide the appropriate rights, it uses a catalogue of all the roles in the organization and which services support each role. This catalogue of roles should be compiled and maintained by access management in conjunction with human resources and will often be automated in the directory services tools (see section 5.7).

In addition to playing different roles, users may also belong to different groups. For example, all contractors are required to log their time sheets in a dedicated time card system, which is not used by employees. Access management will assess all the roles that a user plays as well as the groups that they belong to and ensure that they provide rights to use all associated services.

Role-based access control techniques may also be used by access management to authenticate and authorize users for specific operations. With these techniques, access is assigned to specific roles versus directly to users. Through this approach, users are indirectly authenticated and authorized through the roles they are assigned to.

Note that all data held on users will be subject to data protection legislation (this exists in most geographic locations in some form or other) so should be handled and protected as part of the organization's security procedures.

4.5.8 Critical success factors and key performance indicators

The following list includes some sample CSFs for access management. Each organization should

identify appropriate CSFs based on its objectives for the process. Each sample CSF is followed by a small number of typical KPIs that support the CSF. These KPIs should not be adopted without careful consideration. Each organization should develop KPIs that are appropriate for its level of maturity, its CSFs and its particular circumstances. Achievement against KPIs should be monitored and used to identify opportunities for improvement, which should be logged in the CSI register for evaluation and possible implementation.

- **CSF** Ensuring that the confidentiality, integrity and availability of services are protected in accordance with the information security policy
  - **KPI** Percentage of incidents that involved inappropriate security access or attempts at access to services
  - **KPI** Number of audit findings that discovered incorrect access settings for users that have changed roles or left the company
  - **KPI** Number of incidents requiring a reset of access rights
  - **KPI** Number of incidents caused by incorrect access settings
- **CSF** Provide appropriate access to services on a timely basis that meets business needs
  - **KPI** Percentage of requests for access (service request, RFC etc.) that were provided within established SLAs and OLAs
- **CSF** Provide timely communications about improper access or abuse of services on a timely basis
  - **KPI** Average duration of access-related incidents (from time of discovery to escalation).

4.5.9 Challenges and risks

4.5.9.1 Challenges

Challenges for successful access management can include:

- Monitoring and reporting on access activity as well as incidents and problems related to access
- Verifying the identity of a user (that the person is who they say they are)
- Verifying the identity of the approving person or body
- Verifying that a user qualifies for access to a specific service

- Linking multiple access rights to an individual user
- Determining the status of users at any time (e.g. to determine whether they are still employees of the organization when they log on to a system)
- Managing changes to a user's access requirements
- Restricting access rights to unauthorized users
- Building and maintaining a database of all users and the rights that they have been granted.

4.5.9.2 Risks

Examples of risks that may exist with access management might include:

- Lack of appropriate supporting technologies to manage and control access to services, which in turn can result in a dependency on error-prone manual tasks for operating access controls
- Controlling access from 'back door' sources such as application interfaces and changes to firewall rules for special needs
- Managing and controlling access to services by external third-party suppliers
- Lack of management support for access management activities and controls
- Ensuring that necessary levels of access to services and the necessary management controls are provided in a manner that does not unnecessarily hinder the ability of users to conduct business.

If any of these risks is not addressed it could adversely impact on the success of access management.

Common service operation activities

5

5 Common service operation activities

Chapter 4 dealt with the processes required for effective service operation and Chapter 6 will deal with the organizational aspects. This chapter focuses on a number of operational activities that ensure that technology is aligned with the overall service and process objectives. These activities are sometimes described as processes, but in reality they are sets of specialized technical activities all aimed at ensuring that the technology required to deliver and support services is operating effectively and efficiently.

These activities will usually be technical in nature – although the exact technology will vary depending on the type of services being delivered. This publication will focus on the activities required to manage operational day-to-day delivery of IT services.

Figure 5.1 illustrates the steps involved in maturing from a technology-centric organization to an organization that harnesses technology as part of its business strategy. Figure 5.1 further outlines the role of technology managers in organizations of differing maturity. The diagram is not comprehensive, but it does provide examples of the way in which technology is managed in each type of organization. The bold headings indicate the major role played by IT in managing technology. The text in the rows describes the characteristics of an IT organization at each level.

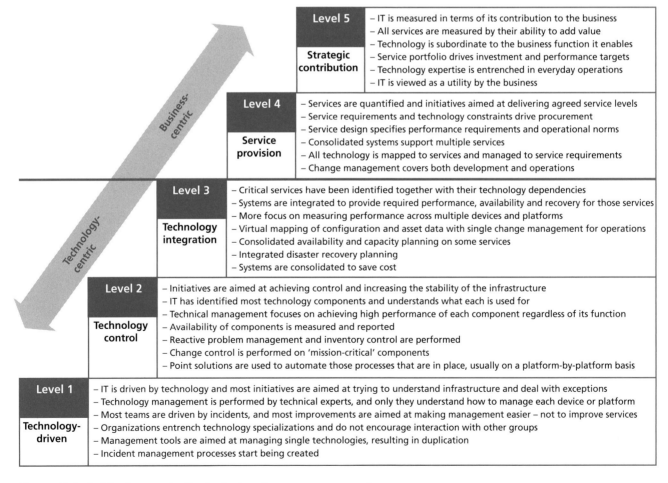

Figure 5.1 Achieving maturity in technology management

Important note on managing technology

It is tempting to divorce the concept of service management from the management of the infrastructure that is used to deliver those services.

In reality, it is impossible to achieve quality services without aligning and 'gearing' every level of technology (and the people who manage it) to the services being provided. Service management involves people, process and technology.

In other words, the common service operation activities are not about managing the technology for the sake of having good technology performance. They are about achieving performance that will integrate the technology component with the people and process components to achieve service and business objectives. See Figure 5.1 for examples of how technology is managed in maturing organizations

The purpose of Figure 5.1 is as follows:

- This chapter focuses on technical management activities, but there is no single way of representing them. A less mature organization will tend to see these activities as ends in themselves, not a means to an end. A more mature organization will tend to subordinate these activities to higher-level service management objectives. For example, the server management team will move from an insulated department, focused purely on managing servers, to a team that works closely with other technology managers to find ways of increasing their value to the business.
- To make and reinforce the point that there is no 'right' way of grouping and organizing the departments that perform these services. Some readers might interpret the headings in this chapter as the names of departments, but this is not the case. The aim of this chapter is to identify the typical technical activities involved in service operation. Organizational aspects are discussed in Chapter 6.
- The service operation activities described in the rest of this chapter are not typical of any one of the levels of maturity. Rather, the activities are usually all present in some form at all levels. They are just organized and managed differently at each level.

In some cases a dedicated group may handle all of a process or activity while in other cases processes or activities may be shared or split between groups. However, by way of broad guidance, the following sections list the required activities under the functional groups most likely to be involved in their operation. This does not mean that all organizations have to use these divisions. Smaller organizations will tend to assign groups of these activities (if they are needed at all) to single departments, or even individuals.

Finally, the purpose of this chapter is not to provide a detailed analysis of all the activities. They are specialized, and detailed guidance is available from the platform vendors and other, more technical, frameworks; new categories will be added continually as technology evolves. This chapter simply aims to highlight the importance and nature of technology management for service management in the IT context.

5.1 MONITORING AND CONTROL

The measurement and control of services is based on a continual cycle of monitoring, reporting and subsequent action. This cycle is discussed in detail in this section because it is fundamental to the delivery, support and improvement of services.

It is also important to note that, although this cycle takes place during service operation, it provides a basis for setting strategy, designing and testing services and achieving meaningful improvement. It is also the basis for SLM measurement. Therefore, although monitoring is performed by service operation functions, it should not be seen as a purely operational matter. All stages of the service lifecycle should ensure that measures and controls are clearly defined, executed and acted upon.

5.1.1 Definitions

5.1.1.1 Monitoring

Monitoring refers to the activity of observing a situation to detect changes that happen over time. In the context of service operation, this implies the following:

- Using tools to monitor the status of key CIs and key operational activities

12333

- Ensuring that specified conditions are met (or not met) and, if not, to raise an alert to the appropriate group (e.g. the availability of key network devices)
- Ensuring that the performance or utilization of a component or system is within a specified range (e.g. disk space or memory utilization)
- To detect abnormal types or levels of activity in the infrastructure (e.g. potential security threats)
- To detect unauthorized changes (e.g. introduction of software)
- To ensure compliance with the organization's policies (e.g. inappropriate use of email)
- To track outputs to the business and ensure that they meet quality and performance requirements
- To track any information used to measure key performance indicators (KPIs).

5.1.1.2 Reporting
Reporting refers to the analysis, production and distribution of the output of the monitoring activity. In the context of service operation, this implies the following:

- Using tools to collate the output of monitoring information that can be disseminated to various groups, functions or processes
- Interpreting the meaning of that information
- Determining where that information would best be used
- Ensuring that decision makers have access to the information that will enable them to make decisions
- Routeing the reported information to the appropriate person, group or tool.

5.1.1.3 Control
Control refers to the process of managing the utilization or behaviour of a device, system or service. It is important to note, however, that simply manipulating a device is not the same as controlling it. Control requires three conditions:

- The action must ensure that the outcome conforms to a defined standard or norm
- The conditions prompting the action must be defined, understood and confirmed
- The action must be defined, approved and appropriate for these conditions.

In the context of service operation, control implies the following:

- Using tools to define what conditions represent normal operations or abnormal operations
- Regulate performance of devices, systems or services
- Measure availability by initiating corrective action, which could be automated (e.g. reboot a device remotely or run a script), or manually (e.g. notify operations staff of the status).

5.1.2 Monitor control loops
The most common model for defining control is the monitor control loop. Although it is a simple model, it has many complex applications within ITSM. This section will define the basic concepts of the monitor control loop model and subsequent sections will show how important these concepts are for the service lifecycle.

Figure 5.2 outlines the basic principles of control. A single activity and its output are measured using a predefined norm, or standard, to determine whether it is within an acceptable range of performance or quality. If not, action is taken to rectify the situation or to restore normal performance.

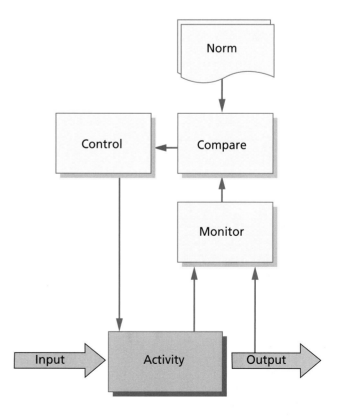

Figure 5.2 The monitor control loop

Typically there are two types of monitor control loops:

- Open loop systems are designed to perform a specific activity regardless of environmental conditions. For example, a backup can be initiated at a given time and frequency – and will run regardless of other conditions.
- Closed loop systems monitor an environment and respond to changes in that environment. For example, in network load balancing a monitor will evaluate the traffic on a circuit. If network traffic exceeds a certain range, the control system will begin to route traffic across a backup circuit. The monitor will continue to provide feedback to the control system, which will continue to regulate the flow of network traffic between the two circuits.

To help clarify the difference, solving capacity management through over-provisioning is open loop; a load-balancer that detects congestion/failure and redirects capacity is closed loop.

5.1.2.1 Complex monitor control loop

The monitor control loop in Figure 5.2 is a good basis for defining how operations management works, but within the context of ITSM the situation is far more complex. Figure 5.3 illustrates a process consisting of three major activities. Each one has an input and an output, and the output becomes an input for the next activity.

In this diagram, each activity is controlled by its own monitor control loop, using a set of norms for that specific activity. The process as a whole also has its own monitor control loop, which spans all the activities and ensures that all norms are appropriate and are being followed.

In Figure 5.3 there is a double feedback loop. One loop focuses purely on executing a defined standard, and the second evaluates the performance of the process and also the standards whereby the process is executed. An example of this would be if the first set of feedback loops at the bottom of the diagram represented individual stations on an assembly line and the higher-level loop represented quality assurance.

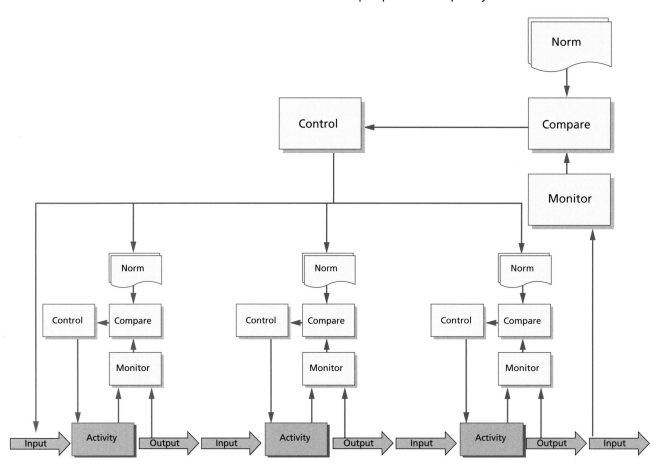

Figure 5.3 Complex monitor control loop

The complex monitor control loop is a good organizational learning tool (Argyris, 1976). The first level of feedback at individual activity level is concerned with monitoring and responding to data (single facts, codes or pieces of information). The second level is concerned with monitoring and responding to information (a collection of a number of facts about which a conclusion may be drawn). Refer to *ITIL Service Transition* for a full discussion on data, information, knowledge and wisdom.

All of this is interesting theory, but does not explain how the monitor control loop concept can be used to operate IT services. And especially – who defines the norm? Based on what has been described so far, monitor control loops can be used to manage:

- The performance of activities in a process or procedure. Each activity and its related output can potentially be measured to ensure that problems with the process are identified before the process as a whole is completed. For example, in incident management, the service desk monitors whether a technical team has accepted an incident in a specified time. If not, the incident is escalated. This is done well before the target resolution time for that incident because the aim of escalating that one activity is to ensure the process as a whole is completed in time.
- The effectiveness of a process or procedure as a whole. In this case the 'activity' box represents the entire process as a single entity. For example, change management will measure the success of the process by checking whether a change was implemented on time, to specification and within budget.
- The performance of a device. For example, the 'activity' box could represent the response time of a server under a given workload.
- The performance of a series of devices. For example, the end user response time of an application across the network.

To define how to use the concept of monitor control loops in service management, the following questions need to be answered:

- How do we define what needs to be monitored?
- What are the appropriate thresholds for each of these?

- How will monitoring be performed (manual or automated)?
- What represents normal operation?
- What are the dependencies for normal state service operation?
- What are the dependencies for monitoring and controlling?
- How frequently should the measurement take place?
- Do we need to perform active measurement to check whether the item is within the norm or do we wait until an exception is reported (passive measurement)?
- Is IT operations management the only function that performs monitoring?
- If not, how are the other instances of monitoring related to operations management?
- If there are multiple loops, which processes are responsible for each loop?

The following sections will expand on the concept of monitor control loops and demonstrate how these questions are answered.

5.1.2.2 The ITSM monitor control loop

In ITSM, the complex monitor control loop can be represented as shown in Figure 5.4.

Figure 5.4 can be used to illustrate the control of a process or of the components used to deliver a service. In this diagram the word 'activity' implies that it refers to a process. To apply it to a service, an 'activity' could also be a 'CI'. There are a number of significant features in Figure 5.4:

- Each activity in a service management process (or each component used to provide a service) is monitored as part of the service operation processes. The operational team or department responsible for each activity or component will apply the monitor control loop as defined in the process, and using the norms that were defined during the service design processes. The role of operational monitoring and control is to ensure that the process or service functions exactly as specified, which is why they are primarily concerned with maintaining the status quo.
- The norms and monitoring and control mechanisms are defined in service design, but they are based on the standards and architectures defined during service strategy.

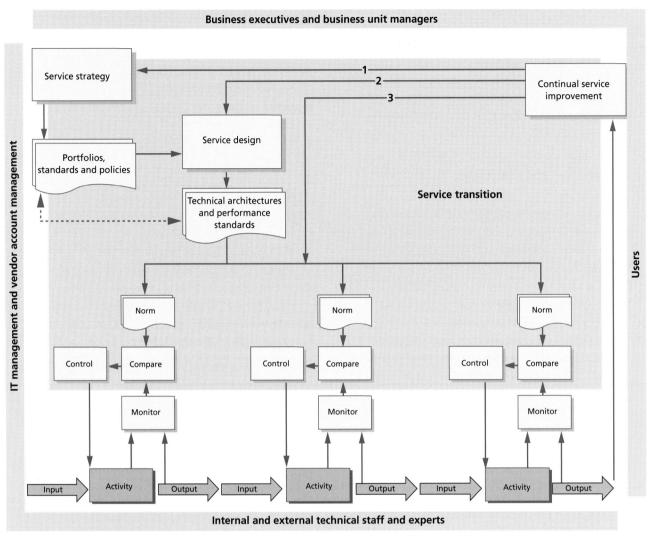

Figure 5.4 The ITSM monitor control loop

Any changes to the organization's service strategy, architecture, service portfolios or service level requirements will precipitate changes to what is monitored and how it is controlled.

■ The monitor control loops are placed within the context of the organization. This implies that service strategy will primarily be executed by business and IT executives with support from vendor account managers. Service design acts as the bridge between service strategy and service operation and will typically involve representatives from all groups. The activities and controls will generally be executed by IT staff (sometimes involving users) and supported by IT managers and the vendors. Service improvement spans all areas, but primarily represents the interests of the business and its users. Notice that the second level of monitoring in this complex monitor control

loop is performed by the CSI activities through service strategy and service design. These relationships are represented by the numbered arrows in Figure 5.4 as follows:

● *Arrow 1* In this case CSI has recognized that the service will be improved by making a change to the service strategy. This could be the result of the business needing a change to the service portfolio, or that the architecture does not deliver what was expected.

● *Arrow 2* In this case the service level requirements need to be adjusted. It could be that the service is too expensive; or that the configuration of the infrastructure needs to be changed to enhance performance; or because operations management is unable to maintain service quality in the current architecture.

● *Arrow 3*   In this case the norms specified in service design are not being adhered to. This could be because they are not appropriate or executable, or because of a lack of education or a lack of communication. The norms and the lack of compliance need to be investigated and action taken to rectify the situation.

Service transition provides a major set of checks and balances in these processes. It does so as follows:

■ For new services, service transition will ensure that the technical architectures are appropriate; and that the operational performance standards can be executed. This in turn will ensure that the service operation teams or departments are able to meet the service level requirements.

■ For existing services, change management will manage any of the changes that are required as part of a control (e.g. tuning), as well as any changes represented by the arrows labelled 1, 2 and 3. Although service transition does not define strategy and design services *per se*, it provides coordination and assurance that the services are working, and will continue to work, as planned.

5.1.2.3 Defining what needs to be monitored

The definition of what needs to be monitored is based on understanding the desired outcome of a process, device or system. IT should focus on the service and its impact on the business, rather than just the individual components of technology. The first question that needs to be asked is 'What are we trying to achieve?'

5.1.2.4 Internal and external monitoring and control

At the outset, it will become clear that there are two levels of monitoring:

■ **Internal monitoring and control**   Most teams or departments are concerned about being able to execute effectively and efficiently the tasks that have been assigned to them. Therefore, they will monitor the items and activities that are directly under their control. This type of monitoring and control focuses on activities that are self-contained within that team or department. For example, the service desk

Why is the ITSM monitor control loop covered under service operation?

Figure 5.4 represents monitoring and control for the whole of ITSM. Some readers of *ITIL Service Operation* may feel that it would be more suitably covered in *ITIL Service Strategy*.

However, monitoring and control can only effectively be deployed when the service is operational. This means that the quality of the entire set of ITSM processes depends on how they are monitored and controlled in service operation.

The implications of this are as follows:

■ Service operation staff are not the only people with an interest in what is monitored and how they are controlled.

■ While service operation is responsible for monitoring and control of services and components, they are acting as stewards of a very important part of the set of ITSM monitoring and control loops.

■ If service operation staff define and execute monitoring and control procedures in isolation, none of the service management processes or functions will be fully effective. This is because the service operation functions will not support the priorities and information requirements of the other processes, e.g. attempting to negotiate an SLA when the only data available is page-swap rates on a server and detailed bandwidth utilization of a network.

manager will monitor the volume of calls to determine how many staff need to be available to answer the telephone.

■ **External monitoring and control**   Although each team or department is responsible for managing its own area, they do not act independently. Every task that they perform, or device that they manage, has an impact on the success of the organization as a whole. Each team or department will also be controlling items and activities on behalf of other groups, processes or functions. For example, the server management team will monitor the CPU performance on key servers and perform workload balancing so that a critical application is able to stay within performance thresholds set by application management.

The distinction between internal and external monitoring is an important one. If service operation focuses only on internal monitoring, it will have very well-managed infrastructure, but no way of understanding or influencing the quality of services. If it focuses only on external monitoring, it will understand how poor the service quality is, but will have no idea what is causing it or how to change it.

In reality, most organizations have a combination of internal and external monitoring, but in many cases these are not linked. For example, the server management team knows exactly how well the servers are performing and the service level manager knows exactly how the users perceive the quality of service provided by the servers. However, neither of them knows how to link these metrics to define what level of server performance represents good quality service. This becomes even more confusing when server performance that is acceptable in the middle of the month is not acceptable at month-end.

5.1.2.5 Defining objectives for monitoring and control

Many organizations start by asking the question 'What are we managing?'. This will invariably lead to a strong internal monitoring system, with very little linkage to the real outcome or service that is required by the business.

The more appropriate question is 'What is the end result of the activities and equipment that my team manages?' Therefore the best place to start when defining what to monitor is to determine the required outcome.

The definition of monitoring and control objectives should ideally start with the definition of the service level requirements documents (see *ITIL Service Design*). These will specify how the customers and users will measure the performance of the service, and are used as input into the service design processes. During service design, various processes will determine how the service will be delivered and managed. For example, capacity management will determine the most appropriate and cost-effective way to deliver the levels of performance required. Availability management will determine how the infrastructure can be configured to provide the fewest points of failure.

If there is any doubt about the validity or completeness of objectives, the COBIT framework provides a comprehensive, high-level set of objectives as a checklist. More information on COBIT is provided in section A.5 in Appendix A.

The service design process will help to identify sets of inputs for defining operational monitoring, control norms and mechanisms. Key activities to accomplish this can include:

- Working with customers and users to determine how the output of the service will be measured. This will include measurement mechanisms, frequency and sampling. This part of the service design will focus specifically on the functional requirements.
- Identification of key CIs, how they should be configured and what level of performance and availability is required in order to meet the agreed service levels.
- Working with the developers and vendors of the CIs that make up each service to identify any constraints or limitations in those components.
- Instrumentation of each service so that it can be monitored to generate meaningful events. All support and delivery teams and departments may be needed to identify what information will help them to execute their role effectively.

All of this means that a very important part of defining what service operation monitors and how it exercises control is to identify the stakeholders of each service.

Stakeholders can be defined as anyone with an interest in the successful delivery and receipt of IT services. Each stakeholder will have a different perspective of what it will take to deliver or receive an IT service. Service operation will need to understand each of these perspectives in order to determine exactly what needs to be monitored and what to do with the output.

Service operation will therefore rely on SLM to define exactly who these stakeholders are and how they contribute to or use the service. This is discussed more fully in *ITIL Service Design* and *ITIL Continual Service Improvement*.

Note on internal and external monitoring objectives

The required outcome could be internal or external to the service operation functions, although it should always be remembered that an internal action will often have an external result. For example, consolidating servers to make them easier to manage may result in a cost saving, which will affect the SLM negotiation and review cycle as well as the financial management processes.

5.1.2.6 Types of monitoring strategies

There are many different types of monitoring strategies and different situations in which each will be used. This section focuses on some of the different types of monitoring that can be performed and when they would be appropriate.

Active versus passive monitoring

Active monitoring refers to the ongoing 'interrogation' of a device or system to determine its status. This type of monitoring can be resource intensive and is usually reserved to proactively monitor the availability of critical devices or systems; or as a diagnostic step when attempting to resolve an incident or diagnose a problem.

Passive monitoring is more common and refers to generating and transmitting events to a 'listening device' or monitoring agent. Passive monitoring depends on successful definition of events and instrumentation of the system being monitored (see section 4.1).

Reactive versus proactive monitoring

Reactive monitoring is designed to request or trigger action following a certain type of event or failure. For example, server performance degradation may trigger a reboot, or a system failure will generate an incident. Reactive monitoring is not only used for exceptions. It can also be used as part of normal operations procedures, for example a batch job completes successfully, which prompts the scheduling system to submit the next batch job.

Proactive monitoring is used to detect patterns of events which indicate that a system or service may be about to fail. Proactive monitoring is generally used in more mature environments where these patterns have been detected previously, often several times. Proactive monitoring tools are therefore a means of automating the experience of seasoned IT staff and are often created through the proactive activities of the problem management process (see section 4.4). Please note that reactive and proactive monitoring could be active or passive, as per Table 5.1.

Table 5.1 Active and passive reactive and proactive monitoring

	Active	Passive
Reactive	Used to diagnose which device is causing the failure and under what conditions (e.g. 'ping' a device, or run and track a sample transaction through a series of devices) Requires knowledge of the infrastructure topography and the mapping of services to CIs Requires capability to simulate service workloads and demand volumes	Detects and correlates event records to determine the meaning of the events and the appropriate action (e.g. a user logs in three times with the incorrect password, which represents a security exception and is escalated through information security management procedures) Requires detailed knowledge of the normal operation of the infrastructure and services
Proactive	Used to determine the real-time status of a device, system or service – usually for critical components or following the recovery of a failed device to ensure that it is fully recovered (i.e. is not going to cause further incidents)	Event records are correlated over time to build trends for proactive problem management Patterns of events are defined and programmed into correlation tools for future recognition

5.1.2.7 Continuous measurement versus exception-based measurement

Continuous measurement is focused on monitoring a system in real time to ensure that it complies with a performance norm (for example, an application server is available for 99.9% of the agreed service hours). The difference between continuous measurement and active monitoring is that active monitoring does not have to be continuous. However, as with active monitoring, this is resource-intensive and is usually reserved for critical components or services. In most cases the cost of the additional bandwidth and processor power outweighs the benefit of continuous measurement. In these cases monitoring will usually be based on sampling and statistical analysis (e.g. the system performance is reported every 30 seconds and extrapolated to represent overall performance). In these cases, the method of measurement will have to be documented and agreed in the OLAs to ensure that it is adequate to support the service reporting requirements (see *ITIL Continual Service Improvement*).

Exception-based measurement does not measure the real-time performance of a service or system, but detects and reports against exceptions. For example, an event is generated if a transaction does not complete, or if a performance threshold is reached. This is more cost-effective and easier to measure, but could result in longer service outages. Exception-based measurement is used for less critical systems or on systems where cost is a major issue. It is also used where IT tools are not able to determine the status or quality of a service (e.g. if printing quality is part of the service specification, the only way to measure this is physical inspection – often performed by the user rather than IT staff). Where exception-based measurement is used, it is important that both the OLA and the SLA for that service reflect this, as service outages are more likely to occur, and users are often required to report the exception.

Performance versus output

There is an important distinction between the reporting used to track the performance of components or teams or departments used to deliver a service and the reporting used to demonstrate the achievement of service quality objectives.

IT managers often confuse these by reporting to the business on the performance of their teams or departments (e.g. number of calls taken per service desk analyst), as if that were the same thing as quality of service (e.g. incidents solved within the agreed time).

Performance monitoring and metrics should be used internally by the service management to determine whether people, process and technology are functioning correctly and to standard.

Users and customers would rather see reporting related to the quality and performance of the service.

Although service operation is concerned with both types of reporting, the primary concern of this publication is performance monitoring, whereas monitoring of service quality (or output-based monitoring) is discussed in detail in *ITIL Continual Service Improvement*.

5.1.2.8 Monitoring in test environments

As with any IT infrastructure, a test environment will need to define how it will use monitoring and control. These controls are more fully discussed in *ITIL Service Transition*.

A test environment consists of infrastructure, applications and processes that have to be monitored, managed and controlled just as any other environment. It is tempting to think that the test environment does not need rigorous monitoring and control because it is not a live environment. However, this argument is not valid. If a test environment is not properly monitored and controlled, there is a danger of running the tests on equipment that deviates from the standards defined in service design. If decisions are made to utilize different levels of monitoring in the test environment from the live environment (sometimes based on cost or performance reasons), then the risks of these decisions need to be carefully weighed up.

Monitoring items being tested

The results of testing need to be accurately tracked and checked. It is also important that any monitoring tools which have been built into new or changed services are also tested.

5.1.2.9 Reporting and action

It has been said that a report alone creates awareness, but that a report with an action plan achieves results. Practical experience has shown that there is more reporting in dysfunctional organizations than in effective organizations. This is because reports are not being used to initiate predefined action plans, but rather:

- To shift the blame for an incident
- To try to find out who is responsible for making a decision
- As input to creating action plans for future occurrences.

In dysfunctional organizations a lot of reports are produced that no one has the time to look at or query.

Monitoring without control is irrelevant and ineffective. Monitoring should always be aimed at ensuring that service and operational objectives are being met. This means that unless there is a clear purpose for monitoring a system or service, it should not be monitored.

This also means that when monitoring is defined, so too should any required actions. For example, being able to detect that a major application has failed is not sufficient. The relevant application management team should also have defined the exact steps that it will take when the application fails.

In addition, it should also be recognized that action may need to be taken by different people. For example, a single event (such as an application failure) may trigger action by the application management team (to restore service), the users (to initiate manual processing) and management (to determine how this event can be prevented in future).

The implications of this principle are outlined in more detail in relation to event management (see section 4.1).

5.1.2.10 Service operation audits

Regular audits must be performed on the service operation processes and activities to ensure:

- They are being performed as intended
- There is no circumvention
- They are still fit for purpose, or to identify any required changes or improvements.

Service operation managers may choose to perform such audits themselves, but ideally some form of independent element to the audits is preferable.

The organization's internal IT audit team or department may be asked to be involved; some organizations may choose to engage third-party consultancy/audit/assessment companies so that an entirely independent expert view is obtained.

Service operation audits are part of the ongoing measurement that takes place as part of CSI and are discussed in more detail in *ITIL Continual Service Improvement*.

5.1.2.11 Measurement, metrics and key performance indicators

This section has focused primarily on the monitoring and control as a basis for service operation. Other sections have covered some basic metrics that could be used to measure the effectiveness and efficiency of a process.

Although this publication is not primarily about measurement and metrics, it is important that organizations using these guidelines have robust measurement techniques and metrics that support the objectives of their organization. This section is a summary of these concepts.

Measurement

- Measurement refers to any technique used to evaluate the extent, dimension or capacity of an item in relation to a standard or unit.
- Extent refers to the degree of compliance or completion (e.g. are all changes formally authorized by the appropriate authority?)
- Dimension refers to the size of an item (e.g. the number of incidents resolved by the service desk)
- Capacity refers to the total capability of an item (e.g. the maximum number of standard transactions that can be processed by a server per minute).

Measurement only becomes meaningful when it is possible to measure the actual output or dimensions of a system, function or process against a standard or desired level (e.g. the server must be capable of processing a minimum of 100 standard transactions per minute). This needs to be defined in service design, and refined over time through CSI, but the measurement itself takes place during service operation.

Metrics

Metrics refer to the quantitative, periodic assessment of a process, system or function, together with the procedures and tools that will be used to make these assessments and the procedures for interpreting them.

This definition is important because it not only specifies what needs to be measured, but also how to measure it, what the acceptable range of performance will be and what action will need to be taken as a result of normal performance or an exception. From this, it is clear that any metric given in the previous section is a very basic one and will need to be applied and expanded within the context of each organization before it can be effective.

Key performance indicators

A KPI refers to a specific, agreed level of performance that will be used to measure the efficiency, effectiveness and cost-effectiveness of a process, IT service or activity.

5.1.2.12 Interfaces to other service lifecycle practices

Operational monitoring and continual service improvement

This section has focused on operational monitoring and reporting, but monitoring also forms the starting point for CSI. This is covered in *ITIL Continual Service Improvement*, but key differences are outlined here.

Quality is the key objective of monitoring for CSI. Monitoring will therefore focus on the effectiveness of a service, process, tool, organization or CI. The emphasis is not on assuring real-time service performance; rather it is on identifying where improvements can be made to the existing level of service, or IT performance.

Monitoring should focus on detecting exceptions and resolutions. For example, the CSI activities are not as interested in whether an incident was resolved, but whether it was resolved within the agreed time and whether future incidents can be prevented.

If an SLA is consistently met over time, the CSI activities may also be interested in determining whether that level of performance can be sustained at a lower cost or whether it needs to be upgraded to an even better level of performance. The CSI activities may require input from regular performance reports.

Monitoring data can be quite large and voluminous when looking at the entire IT service infrastructure. Because the CSI activities are generally focused on targeted service improvements, requirements for specific subsets of monitoring data might be needed at any given time. The subsets of data can be determined by input from the business or obtained through improvements to technology.

This has two main implications:

- Monitoring for CSI will change over time. There may be interest in monitoring the email service one quarter and then moving on to look at human resources systems in the next quarter.
- This means that service operation and CSI need to build a process which will help them to agree on what areas need to be monitored and for what purpose.

5.2 IT OPERATIONS

5.2.1 Console management/operations bridge

The console management/operations bridge function handles a structured set of activities that centrally coordinate management of events, incidents, routine operational activities, and reporting on the status or performance of technology components.

Observation and monitoring of the IT infrastructure can occur from a centralized console to which all system events are routed. Historically, this involved monitoring the master operations console of one or more mainframes – but these days it is more likely to involve monitoring of server farms, storage devices, power racks, virtualized processing environments, security infrastructure, network components, applications, databases or any other CIs from a single location known as the operations bridge.

The console management/operations bridge function can be used to pull together all of the critical observation points within the IT infrastructure so that they can be monitored and managed from a centralized location with minimal effort. The CIs being monitored are likely to be physically dispersed and may be located in centralized computer facilities, dispersed within the user community, or both.

This function also combines many activities, which might include managing consoles, event handling, first-line network management, job scheduling and out-of-hours support (covering for the service desk and/or second-line support groups if they do not work 24/7). In some organizations, the service desk is part of the console management/operations bridge function.

The physical location and layout of the facilities used to underpin this function need to be carefully designed to give the correct accessibility and visibility of all relevant screens and devices to authorized personnel. However, this will become a very sensitive area where controlled access and tight security will be essential.

Smaller organizations may not have a separate console management/operations bridge function, but there will certainly still be the need to manage consoles, usually combined with other technical roles. For example, a single team of technical staff might manage the network, servers and applications. Part of their role will be to monitor the consoles for those systems – often using virtual consoles so that they can perform the activity from any location. It should be noted that these virtual consoles are powerful tools and, if used in insecure locations or over unsecured connections, could represent a significant security threat.

5.2.2 Job scheduling

IT operations will perform standard routines, queries or reports delegated to it as part of delivering services; or as part of routine housekeeping delegated by technical and application management teams.

Job scheduling involves defining and initiating job-scheduling software packages to run batch and real-time work. This will normally involve daily, weekly, monthly, annual and ad hoc schedules to meet business needs.

In addition to the initial design, or periodic redesign, of the schedules, there are likely to be frequent amendments or adjustments to make during which job dependencies have to be identified and accommodated. There will also be a role to play in defining alerts and exception reports to be used for monitoring/checking job schedules. Change management plays an important role

in assessing and validating major changes to schedules, as well as creating standard change procedures for more routine changes.

Run-time parameters and/or files have to be received (or expedited if delayed) and input, and all run-time logs have to be checked and any failures identified.

If failures do occur, then re-runs will have to be initiated, under the guidance of the appropriate business units, often with different parameters or amended data/file versions. This will require careful communications to ensure correct parameters and files are used.

Many organizations are faced with increasing overnight batch schedules which can, if they overrun the overnight batch slot, adversely impact upon the online day services – so are seeking ways of utilizing maximum overnight capacity and performance, in conjunction with capacity management. This is where workload management techniques can be useful, such as:

■ Rescheduling of work to avoid contention on specific devices or at specific times and improve overall throughput
■ Migration of workloads to alternative platforms/environments to gain improved performance and/or throughput (virtualization capabilities make this far more achievable by allowing dynamic, automated migration)
■ Careful timing and 'interleaving' of jobs to gain maximum utilization of available resources.

> **An example of job scheduling improving overall processing performance**
>
> One large organization that was faced with batch overrun/utilization problems identified that, due to human nature where people were seeking to be 'tidy', all jobs were being started on the hour or at 15-minute intervals during the hour (i.e. *n* o'clock, 15 minutes past, half past, 15 minutes to, etc.).
>
> By rescheduling work so that it started as soon as other work finished, and staggering the start times of other work, it was able to gain significant reductions in contention and achieve much quicker overall processing, which resolved its problems without a need for upgrades.

Job scheduling has become a highly complex activity, including any number of variables, such as time sensitivity, critical and non-critical dependencies, workload balancing, failure and resubmission etc. As a result, most operations rely on job scheduling tools that allow IT operations to schedule jobs for the optimal use of technology to achieve service level objectives.

The latest generation of scheduling tools allows for a single toolset to schedule and automate technical and service management process activities (such as change scheduling). While this is a good opportunity for improving efficiency, it also represents a greater single point of failure. Organizations using this type of tool will generally use other non-integrated solutions as agents and also as a backup in case the main toolset fails.

5.2.3 Backup and restore

Backup and restore is essentially a component of good IT service continuity planning. As such, service design should ensure that there are solid backup strategies for each service and service transition should ensure that these are properly tested.

In addition, regulatory requirements specify that certain types of organization (such as financial services or listed companies) must have a formal backup and restore strategy in place and that this strategy is executed and audited. The exact requirements will vary from country to country and by industry sector. This should be determined during service design and built into the service functionality and documentation.

The only point of taking backups is that they may need to be restored at some point. For this reason it is not as important to define how to back a system up as it is to define what components are at risk and how to effectively mitigate that risk.

There are any number of tools available for backup and restore, but it is worth noting that features of storage technologies used for business data are being used for backup/restore (e.g. snapshots). There is therefore an increasing degree of integration between backup and restore activities and those of storage and archiving (see section 5.5).

5.2.3.1 Backup

The organization's data has to be protected and this will include backup (copying) and storage of data in remote locations where it can be protected – and used should it need to be restored due to loss, corruption or implementation of IT service continuity plans.

An overall backup strategy must be agreed with the business, covering:

- What data has to be backed up and the frequency and intervals to be used.
- How many generations of data have to be retained – this may vary by the type of data being backed up, or what type of file (e.g. data file or application executable).
- The type of backup (full, partial, incremental) and checkpoints to be used.
- The locations to be used for storage (likely to include disaster recovery sites) and rotation schedules.
- The mechanisms that will be used to validate that data is truly readable on the backup media after backup has been performed.
- Transportation methods (e.g. file transfer via the network, physical transportation on magnetic media).
- Testing/checks to be performed, such as test-reads, test restores, check-sums etc.
- Recovery point objective. This describes the point to which data will be restored after recovery of an IT service. This may involve loss of data. For example, a recovery point objective of one day may be supported by daily backups, and up to 24 hours of data may be lost. Recovery point objectives for each IT service should be negotiated, agreed and documented in OLAs, SLAs and UCs.
- Recovery time objective. This describes the maximum time allowed for recovery of an IT service following an interruption. The service level to be provided may be less than normal service level targets. Recovery time objectives for each IT service should be negotiated, agreed and documented in OLAs, SLAs and UCs.
- Validating that the backups will work if they need to be restored. Even if there are no error codes generated, there may be several reasons why the backup cannot be restored. A good backup strategy and operations procedure will minimize the risk of this happening. Backup

procedures should include a verification step to ensure that the backups are complete and that they will work if a restore is needed. Where any backup failures are detected, recovery actions must be initiated.

There is also a need to procure and manage the necessary media (disks, tapes, CDs etc.) to be used for backups, so that there is no shortage of supply.

Where automated devices are being used, pre-loading of the required media will be needed in advance. When loading and clearing media returned from off-site storage it is important there is a procedure for verifying that these are the right ones. This will prevent the most recent backup being overwritten with faulty data, and then having no valid data to restore. After successful backups have been taken, the media must be removed for storage.

The actual initiation of the backups might be automated, or carried out from the operations bridge.

Some organizations may utilize operations staff to perform the physical transportation and racking of backup copies to/from remote locations; in other cases this may be handed over to other groups such as internal security staff or external contractors.

If backups are being automated or performed remotely, then event monitoring capabilities should be considered so that any failures can be detected early and rectified before they cause problems. In such cases IT operations has a role to play in defining alerts and escalation paths.

In all cases, IT operations staff must be trained in backup (and restore) procedures, which must be well documented in the organization's IT operations procedures manual. Any specific requirements or targets should be referenced in OLAs or UCs where appropriate, while any user or customer requirements or activity should be specified in the appropriate SLA.

5.2.3.2 Restore

A restore can be initiated from a number of sources, ranging from an event that indicates data corruption, through to a service request from a user or customer logged at the service desk. A restore may be needed in the case of:

- Corrupt data
- Lost data

- Remediation (back-out) after a failed change
- An IT service continuity situation
- Historical data required for forensic investigation.

The steps to be taken can include:

- Location of the appropriate data/media
- Checking the authorization of the user/customer to get access to the data
- Transportation or transfer back to the physical recovery location
- Agreement on the checkpoint recovery point and the specific location for the recovered data (disk, directory, folder etc.)
- Actual restoration of the file/data (copy-back and any roll-back/roll-forward needed to arrive at the agreed checkpoint)
- Checking to ensure successful completion of the restore – with further recovery action if needed until success has been achieved
- User/customer sign-off.

5.2.4 Print and output management

Many services consist of generating and delivering information in printed or electronic form. Ensuring the right information gets to the right people, with full integrity, requires formal control and management.

Print (physical) and output (electronic) facilities and services need to be formally managed because:

- They often represent the tangible output of a service. The ability to measure that this output has reached the appropriate destination is therefore very important (e.g. checking whether files with financial transaction data have actually reached a bank through a file transfer protocol, FTP service).
- Physical and electronic output often contains sensitive or confidential information. It is vital that the appropriate levels of security are applied to both the generation and the delivery of this output.

Many organizations will have centralized bulk printing requirements which IT operations must handle.

In addition to the physical loading and reloading of paper and the operation and care of the printers, other activities may be needed, such as:

■ Agreement and setting of pre-notification of large print runs and alerts to prevent excessive printing by rogue print jobs

■ Physical control of high-value stationery such as company cheques or certificates etc.

■ Management of the physical and electronic storage required to generate the output. In many cases IT will be expected to provide archives for the printed and electronic materials

■ Control of all printed material so as to adhere to data protection legislation and regulation, e.g. HIPAA (Health Insurance Portability and Accountability Act) in the USA, or FSA (Financial Services Authority) in the UK.

Where print and output services are delivered directly to the users, it is important that the responsibility for maintaining the printers or storage devices is clearly defined. For example, most users assume that cleaning and maintenance of printers must be performed by IT. If this is not the case, this must be clearly stated in the SLA.

5.3 SERVER AND MAINFRAME MANAGEMENT AND SUPPORT

Servers and mainframes are used in most organizations to provide flexible and accessible services from hosting applications or databases, operating high-volume transaction systems, running client/server services, storage, print and file management. Successful management of servers and mainframes is therefore essential for successful service operation.

The ways in which server and mainframe management teams are organized are quite diverse. In some organizations:

■ Mainframe management is a single, highly specialized team that manages all aspects from daily operations through to system engineering, separate from server teams who perform similar functions.

■ In other organizations, the activities are performed by several teams or departments, with engineering and third-level support being provided by one set of teams and daily operations being combined with the rest of IT operations (and very probably managed through the operations bridge).

Server and mainframe support activities

Note that the support activities for servers are generally the same as those for mainframes. Although the technologies and skill sets needed are different in how support activities are actually performed, the types of activity needed to support these are essentially similar.

The procedures and activities that must be undertaken by mainframe and server team(s) or department(s) (separate teams may be needed where different technology platforms are used, i.e. mainframe OS, UNIX, Wintel etc.), include:

■ Operating system support: Support and maintenance of the appropriate operating system(s) and related utility software (e.g. failover software) including patch management and involvement in defining backup and restore policies.

■ Licence management for all server CIs, especially operating systems, utilities and any application software not managed by the application management teams.

■ Third-level support for all server and/or server operating system-related incidents, including diagnosis and restoration activities. This will also include liaison with third-party hardware support contractors and/or manufacturers as needed to escalate hardware-related incidents.

■ Procurement advice: Advice and guidance to the business on the selection, sizing, procurement and usage of servers and related utility software to meet business needs.

■ System security: Control and maintenance of the access controls and permissions within the relevant server environment(s) as well as appropriate system and physical security measures. These include identification and application of security patches, access management (see section 4.5) and intrusion detection.

■ Definition and management of virtual servers. This implies that any server that has been designed and built around a common standard can be used to process workloads from a range of applications or users. Server management will be required to set these standards and then ensure that workloads are appropriately balanced and distributed. They are also responsible for being able to track which workload is being processed by which server so that they are able to deal with incidents effectively.

■ Capacity and performance: Provide information and assistance to capacity management to help achieve optimum throughput, utilization and performance from the available servers. This is discussed in more detail in *ITIL Service Design*, but includes providing guidance on, and installation and operation of, virtualization software so as to achieve value for money by obtaining the highest levels of performance and utilization from the minimal number of servers.

Other routine activities include:

■ Defining standard builds for servers as part of the provisioning process. This is covered in more detail in *ITIL Service Design* and *ITIL Service Transition*.

■ Building and installing new servers as part of ongoing maintenance or for the provision of new services. This is discussed in more detail in *ITIL Service Transition*.

■ Setting up and managing clusters, which are aimed at building redundancy, improving service performance and making the infrastructure easier to manage.

■ Ongoing maintenance. This typically consists of replacing servers or 'blades' on a rolling schedule to ensure that equipment is replaced before it fails or becomes obsolete. This results in servers that are not only fully functional, but also capable of supporting evolving services.

■ Decommissioning and disposal of old server equipment. This is often done in conjunction with the organization's environmental policies for disposal.

■ Interfacing to hardware (H/W) support; arranging maintenance, agreeing slots, identifying H/W failure, liaison with H/W engineering.

■ Providing assistance in writing batch and job scripts.

5.4 NETWORK MANAGEMENT

As most IT services are dependent on connectivity, network management will be essential to deliver services and also to enable service operation staff to access and manage key service components.

Network management will have overall responsibility for all of the organization's own local area networks (LANs), metropolitan area networks (MANs) and wide area networks (WANs), and will also be responsible for liaising with third-party network suppliers.

Their role will include the following activities:

■ Initial planning and installation of new networks/network components; maintenance and upgrades to the physical network infrastructure. This is done through service design and service transition.

■ Third-level support for all network-related activities, including investigation of network issues (e.g. pinging or trace route and/or use of network management software tools – although it should be noted that pinging a server does not necessarily mean that the service is available!) and liaison with third parties as necessary. This also includes the installation and use of 'sniffer' tools, which analyse network traffic, to assist in incident and problem resolution.

■ Maintenance and support of network operating system and middleware software including patch management, upgrades etc.

■ Monitoring of network traffic to identify failures or to spot potential performance or bottleneck issues.

■ Reconfiguring or rerouteing of traffic to achieve improved throughput or better balance – definition of rules for dynamic balancing/ routeing.

■ Network security (in liaison with the organization's information security management) including firewall management, access rights, password protection etc.

■ Assigning and managing IP addresses, domain name systems (DNSs, which convert the name of a service to its associated IP address) and dynamic host configuration protocol (DHCP) systems, which enable access and use of the DNS.

■ Managing firewalls and secure gateways.

■ Managing internet service providers (ISPs).

■ Implementing, monitoring and maintaining intrusion detection systems on behalf of information security management. They will also be responsible for ensuring that there is no denial of service to legitimate users of the network.

■ Updating service asset and configuration management as necessary by documenting CIs, status, relationships etc.

Network management is also frequently responsible, often in conjunction with desktop support, for remote connectivity issues such as dial-in, dial-back and virtual private network facilities provided to home workers, remote workers or suppliers.

Some network management teams or departments will also have responsibility for voice/telephony, including the provision and support for exchanges, lines, circuits, automatic call distribution (ACD), statistical software packages etc. and for voice over internet protocol (VoIP), quality of service and remote monitoring systems.

At the same time, many organizations see VoIP and telephony as specialized areas and have teams dedicated to managing this technology. Their activities will be similar to those described above.

Managing VoIP as a service

Many organizations have experienced performance and availability problems with their VoIP solutions, in spite of the fact that there seems to be more than adequate bandwidth available. This results in dropped calls and poor sound quality. This is usually because of variations in bandwidth utilization during the call, which is often the result of utilization of the network by other users, applications or other web activity. This has led to the differentiation between measuring the bandwidth available to initiate a call (service access bandwidth, SAB) and the amount of bandwidth that must be continuously available during the call (service utilization bandwidth, SUB). Care should be taken in differentiating between these when designing, managing or measuring VoIP or similar services.

5.5 STORAGE AND ARCHIVE

Many services require the storage of data for a specific time and also for that data to be available off-line for a certain period after it is no longer used. This is often due to regulatory or legislative requirements, but also because history and audit data are invaluable for a variety of purposes, including marketing, product development, forensic investigations etc.

A separate team or department may be needed to manage the organization's data storage technology such as:

■ Storage devices, such as disks, controllers, tapes etc.
■ Network attached storage (NAS), which is storage attached to a network and accessible by several clients.
■ Storage area networks (SANs), designed to attach computer storage devices such as disk array controllers and tape libraries. In addition to storage devices, a SAN will also require the management of several network components, such as hubs, cables etc.
■ Direct attached storage (DAS), which is a storage device directly attached to a server.
■ Content addressable storage (CAS), which is storage that is based on retrieving information based on its content rather than location. The focus in this type of system is on understanding the nature of the data and information stored, rather than on providing specific storage locations.

Regardless of what type of storage systems are being used, storage and archiving will require management of the infrastructure components as well as the policies related to where data is stored, for how long, in what form and who may access it. Specific responsibilities will include:

■ Definition of data storage policies and procedures
■ File storage naming conventions, hierarchy and placement decisions
■ Design, sizing, selection, procurement, configuration and operation of all data storage infrastructure
■ Maintenance and support for all utility and middleware data storage software
■ Liaison with information lifecycle management team(s) or governance teams to ensure compliance with freedom of information, data protection and IT governance regulations
■ Involvement with definition and agreement of archiving policy
■ Housekeeping of all data storage facilities
■ Archiving data according to rules and schedules defined during service design. The storage teams or departments will also provide input into the definition of these rules and will

provide reports on their effectiveness as input into future design

■ Retrieval of archived data as needed (e.g. for audit purposes, for forensic evidence, or to meet any other business requirements)

■ Management of archiving technologies and, if needed, migration from one (outdated) technology to a newer archiving technology in order to be able to restore data over a long period of time (e.g. 10 years for legal requirements)

■ Third-line support for storage and archive-related incidents.

5.6 DATABASE ADMINISTRATION

Database administration must work closely with key application management teams or departments – and in some organizations the functions may be combined or linked under a single management structure. Organizational options include:

■ Database administration being performed by each application management team for all the applications under its control

■ A dedicated department that manages all databases, regardless of type or application

■ Several departments, each managing one type of database, regardless of what application they are part of.

Database administration works to ensure the optimal performance, security and functionality of databases that they manage. Database administrators typically have the following responsibilities:

■ Creation and maintenance of database standards and policies

■ Initial database design, creation, testing

■ Management of the database availability and performance; resilience, sizing, capacity volumetrics etc.

■ Resilience may require database replication, which would be the responsibility of database administration

■ Ongoing administration of database objects: indexes, tables, views, constraints, sequences, snapshots and stored procedures; page locks – to achieve optimum utilization

■ The definition of triggers that will generate events, which in turn will alert database

administrators about potential performance or integrity issues with the database

■ Performing database housekeeping – the routine tasks that ensure the databases are functioning optimally and securely, e.g. tuning, indexing etc.

■ Monitoring of usage; transaction volumes, response times, concurrency levels etc.

■ Generating reports: these could be reports based on the data in the database, or reports related to the performance and integrity of the database

■ Identification, reporting and management of database security issues; audit trails and forensics

■ Assistance in designing database backup, archiving and storage strategy

■ Assistance in designing database alerts and event management

■ Provision of third-level support for all database-related incidents.

5.7 DIRECTORY SERVICES MANAGEMENT

A directory service is a specialized software application that manages information about the resources available on a network and which users have access to. It is the basis for providing access to those resources and for ensuring that unauthorized access is detected and prevented (see section 4.5 for detailed information on access management).

Directory services view each resource as an object of the directory server and assign it a name. Each name is linked to the resource's network address, so that users don't have to memorize confusing and complex addresses.

Directory services are usually based on the OSI's X.500 standard and commonly use protocols such as Directory Access Protocol (DAP) or Lightweight Directory Access Protocol (LDAP). LDAP is used to support user credentials for application login and often includes internal and external user/customer data which is especially good for extranet call logging. Because LDAP is a critical operational tool, and generally kept up to date, it is also a good source of data and verification for the CMS.

Directory services management refers to the process that is used to manage directory services. Its activities include:

- Working as part of service design and service transition to ensure that new services are accessible and controlled when they are deployed
- Locating resources on a network (if these have not already been defined during service design)
- Tracking the status of those resources and providing the ability to manage those resources remotely
- Managing the rights of specific users or groups of users to access resources on a network
- Defining and maintaining naming conventions to be used for resources on a network
- Ensuring consistency of naming and access control on different networks in the organization
- Linking different directory services throughout the organization to form a distributed directory service, i.e. users will only see one logical set of network resources (this is called distribution of directory services)
- Monitoring events on the directory services, such as unsuccessful attempts to access a resource, and taking the appropriate action where required
- Maintaining and updating the tools used to manage directory services.

5.8 DESKTOP AND MOBILE DEVICE SUPPORT

As most users access IT services using desktops, laptops and mobile computing devices, it is key that these are supported to ensure the agreed levels of availability and performance of services.

Desktop and mobile device support will have overall responsibility for all of the organization's desktop, laptop and mobile device hardware, software and peripherals. Specific responsibilities will include:

- Desktop and mobile computing policies and procedures, for example licensing policies, use of laptops, desktops or mobile devices for personal purposes, USB lockdown etc.
- Designing and agreeing standard desktop and device images
- Service maintenance including deployment of releases, upgrades, patches and hot-fixes (in conjunction with release and deployment management; see *ITIL Service Transition* for further details)

- Design and implementation of desktop and mobile device archiving/rebuild policies (including policies relating to cookies, favourites, templates, personal data, security etc.)
- Third-level support of desktop and mobile device related incidents, including desk-side visits where necessary or replacing devices with reconfigured images and data when needed
- Support for connectivity issues (in conjunction with network management) to home workers, mobile staff etc.
- Configuration control and audit of all desktop, laptop and mobile device equipment (in conjunction with service asset and configuration management and IT audit).

5.9 MIDDLEWARE MANAGEMENT

Middleware is software that connects or integrates software components across distributed or disparate applications and systems. Middleware enables the effective transfer of data between applications, and is therefore key to services that are dependent on multiple applications or data sources.

A variety of technologies are currently used to support program-to-program communication, such as object request brokers, message-oriented middleware, remote procedure calls and point-to-point web services. Newer technologies are emerging all the time, for example enterprise service bus (ESB), which enables programs, systems and services to communicate with each other regardless of the architecture and origin of the applications. This is especially being used in the context of deploying service-oriented architectures (SOAs).

Middleware management can be performed as part of an application management function (where it is dedicated to a specific application) or as part of a technical management function (where it is viewed as an extension to the operating system of a specific platform).

Functionality provided by middleware includes:

- Providing transfer mechanisms for data from various applications or data sources
- Sending work to another application or procedure for processing

- Transmitting data or information to other systems, such as sourcing data for publication on websites (e.g. publishing incident status information)
- Releasing updated software modules across distributed environments
- Collation and distribution of system messages and instructions, for example events or operational scripts that need to be run on remote devices
- Multicast set-up with networks (multicast is the delivery of information to a group of destinations simultaneously using the most efficient delivery route)
- Managing queue sizes.

Middleware management is the set of activities that are used to manage middleware. These include:

- Working as part of service design and transition to ensure that the appropriate middleware solutions are chosen and that they can perform optimally when they are deployed
- Ensuring the correct operation of middleware through monitoring and control
- Detecting and resolving incidents related to middleware
- Maintaining and updating middleware, including licensing, and installing new versions
- Defining and maintaining information about how applications are linked through middleware. This should be part of the CMS (see *ITIL Service Transition*).

5.10 INTERNET/WEB MANAGEMENT

Many organizations conduct much of their business through the internet and are therefore heavily dependent upon the availability and performance of their websites. In such cases a separate internet/web support team or department will be desirable and justified.

The responsibilities of such a team or department incorporate both intranet and internet and are likely to include:

- Management and operation of firewalls and secure gateways
- Management and operation of secured sub-networks (e.g. the DMZ or demilitarized zone) used to provide a secure perimeter between

secured IT infrastructures and larger untrusted networks
- Defining architectures for internet and web services
- The specification of standards for development and management of web-based applications, content, websites and web pages. This will typically be done during service design
- Design, testing, implementation and maintenance of websites. This will include the architecture of websites and the mapping of content to be made available
- In many organizations, web management will include the editing of content to be posted onto the web
- Maintenance of all web development and management applications
- Liaison and advice to web-content teams within the business. Content may reside in applications or storage devices, which implies close liaison with application management and other technical management teams
- Liaison with and supplier management of ISPs, hosts, third-party monitoring or virtualization organizations etc. In many organizations the ISPs are managed as part of network management
- Third-level support for internet/web-related incidents
- Support for interfaces with back-end and legacy systems. This will often mean working with members of the application development and management teams to ensure secure access and consistency of functionality
- Monitoring and management of website performance and including: heartbeat testing, user experience simulation, benchmarking, on-demand load balancing, virtualization
- Website availability, resilience and security. This will form part of the overall information security management of the organization.

5.11 FACILITIES AND DATA CENTRE MANAGEMENT

Facilities management refers to the management of the physical environment of IT operations, usually located in data centres or computer rooms. This is a vast and complex area and this publication will provide an overview of its key role and activities. A more detailed overview is contained in

Appendix E. Data centre requirements (e.g. space, heat, cooling etc.) should be considered in the service design stage (see *ITIL Service Design*).

In many respects facilities management could be viewed as a function in its own right. However, because this publication is focused on where IT operations are housed, it will cover facilities management specifically as it relates to the management of data centres and as a subset of the IT operations management function.

The main components of facilities management are as follows:

- Building management, which refers to the maintenance and upkeep of the buildings that house the IT staff and data centre. Typical activities include cleaning, waste disposal, parking management and access control.
- Equipment hosting, which ensures that all special requirements are provided for the physical housing of equipment and the teams that support them.
- Power management, which refers to managing the sourcing and utilization of power sources used to keep the facility functional. This definition of power management has a number of implications, which are discussed in Appendix E. Note that information about power utilization is important for planning the capacity of both new services and new buildings.
- Building management systems, which include the specification, maintenance and monitoring of environmental conditions such as smoke detection, fire suppression, water, heating and cooling systems, etc.
- Safety is concerned with compliance to all legislation, standards and policies relative to the safety of employees.
- Physical access control refers to ensuring that the facility is only accessed by authorized personnel and that any unauthorized access is detected and managed. This is discussed in more detail in Appendix F.
- Shipping and receiving refers to the management of all equipment, furniture, mail etc. that leaves or enters the building. It ensures that only appropriate items are entering or leaving the building and that they are routed to the correct party.

- Involvement in contract management of the various suppliers and service providers involved in the facility.
- Maintenance refers to regular, scheduled upkeep of the facility, as well as the detection and resolution of problems with the facility.

Important note regarding data centres

Data centres are generally specialized facilities and, while they use and benefit from generic facilities management disciplines, they need to adapt these. For example layout, heating and conditioning, power planning and many other aspects are all managed uniquely in data centres.

This means that, although data centres may be facilities owned by an organization, they are better managed under the authority of IT operations, although there may be a functional reporting line between IT and the department that manages other facilities for the organization.

5.11.1 Data centre strategies

Managing a data centre is far more than hosting an open space where technical groups install and manage equipment, using their own approaches and procedures. It requires an integrated set of processes and procedures involving all IT groups at every stage of the service lifecycle. Data centre operations are governed by strategic and design decisions for management and control and are executed by operators. This requires a number of key factors to be put in place:

- **Data centre automation** Specialized automation systems that reduce the need for manual operators and which monitor and track the status of the facility and all IT operations at all times.
- **Policy-based management** This is where the rules of automation and resource allocation are managed by policy, rather than having to go through complex change procedures every time processing is moved from one resource to another.
- **Real time services** 24 hours a day, 7 days a week.
- **Capacity management of environmental factors** Physical environment factors such as floor space, cooling and power need to be managed in terms of their available capacities

and workloads to ensure that shortfalls in these areas do not create incidents or generate unplanned costs.

■ **Standardization of equipment** This provides greater ease of management, more consistent levels of performance and a means of providing multiple services across similar technology. Standardization also reduces the variety of technical expertise required to manage equipment in the data centre and to provide services.

■ **SOAs** These define where service components can be reused, interchanged and replaced very quickly and with no impact on the business. This will make it possible for the data centre to be highly responsive in meeting changing business demands without having to go through lengthy and involved re-engineering and re-architecting.

■ **Virtualization** This means that IT services are delivered using an ever-changing set of equipment, geared to meet current demand. For example, an application may run on a dedicated device together with its database during high-demand times, but shifted to a shared device with its database on a remote device during non-peak times – all automated and automatic. This will mean even greater cost savings as any equipment can be used at any time, without any human intervention, except to perform maintenance and replace failed equipment. The IT infrastructure is more resilient because any component is backed up by any number of similar components, any of which could take over a failed component's workload automatically.

Remote monitoring, control and management equipment and systems will be essential to manage a virtualized environment, as many services will not be linked to any one specific piece of equipment.

Unified management systems have become more important as services run across multiple locations and technologies. Today it is important to define what actions need to be taken and what systems will perform that action. This means investing in solutions that will allow infrastructure managers to simply specify what outcome is required, and allowing the management system to calculate the best combination of tools and actions to achieve the outcome.

5.12 OPERATIONAL ACTIVITIES OF PROCESSES COVERED IN OTHER LIFECYCLE STAGES

5.12.1 Change management

Change management is primarily covered in *ITIL Service Transition*, but there are some aspects that service operation staff will be involved with on a day-to-day basis. These include:

■ Using the change management process for standard, operational-type changes by raising and submitting RFCs as needed to address service operation issues

■ Participating in change advisory board (CAB) or emergency change advisory board (ECAB) meetings to ensure that service operation risks, issues and views are taken into account

■ Implementing changes as directed by change management where they involve a service operation component or services

■ Backing out changes as directed by change management where they involve a service operation component or services

■ Assisting with activities to move physical assets to their assigned locations within the data centre

■ Helping define and maintain change models relating to service operation components or services

■ Receiving change schedules and ensuring that all service operation staff are made aware of and are prepared for all relevant changes

■ Coordinating efforts with design activities to ensure that service operation requirements and concerns are addressed when planning and designing new or changed services.

5.12.2 Service asset and configuration management

Service asset and configuration management is primarily covered in *ITIL Service Transition*, but there are some aspects that service operation staff will be involved with on a day-to-day basis. Examples of these include:

■ Informing service asset and configuration management of any discrepancies found between any CIs and the CMS

■ Making any amendments necessary to correct any discrepancies, under the authority of service asset and configuration management, where they involve any service operation components or services

■ Labelling and tagging physical assets (e.g. serial numbers and bar codes) so they can be easily identified

■ Assisting with audit activities to validate existence and location of service assets.

Responsibility for updating the CMS remains with service asset and configuration management, but in some cases operations staff might be asked, under the direction of service asset and configuration management, to update relationships, or even to add new CIs or mark CIs as 'disposed' in the CMS, if these updates are related to operational activities actually performed by operations staff. Operations staff may also assist service asset and configuration management activities by communicating changes in state or status with CIs impacted by incidents.

5.12.3 Release and deployment management

Release and deployment management is primarily covered in *ITIL Service Transition*, but there are some aspects that service operation staff will be involved with on a day-to-day basis. These may include:

■ Actual implementation actions regarding the deployment of new releases, under the direction of release and deployment management, where they relate to service operation components or services

■ Participation in the planning stages of major new releases to advise on service operation issues

■ The physical handling of CIs from/to the definitive media library (DML) as required to fulfil their operational roles – while adhering to relevant release and deployment management procedures, such as ensuring that all items are properly booked out and back in

■ Participation in activities to back out unsuccessful releases when these occur.

5.12.4 Capacity management

Capacity management is primarily covered in *ITIL Service Design*. Although many of these activities are of a strategic or longer-term planning nature, there are a number of operational capacity management activities that must be performed on a regular ongoing basis as part of service operation.

5.12.4.1 Capacity and performance monitoring

All components of the IT infrastructure should be continually monitored (in conjunction with event management) so that any potential problems or trends can be identified before failures or performance degradation occurs. Ideally, such monitoring should be automated and thresholds should be set so that exception alerts are raised in good time to allow appropriate avoidance or recovery action to be taken before there is an adverse impact. The components and elements to be monitored will vary depending upon the infrastructure in use, but will typically include:

■ CPU utilization (overall and broken down by system/service usage)

■ Memory utilization

■ I/O rates (physical and buffer) and device utilization

■ Queue length (maximum and average)

■ File store utilization (disks, partitions, segments)

■ Applications (throughput rates, failure rates)

■ Databases (utilization, record locks, indexing, contention)

■ Network transaction rates, error and retry rates

■ Transaction response time

■ Batch duration profiles

■ Internet/intranet site/page hit rates

■ Internet response times (external and internal to firewalls)

■ Number of system/application log-ons and concurrent users

■ Number of network nodes in use, and utilization levels.

There are different kinds of monitoring tool needed to collect and interpret data at each level. For example, some tools will allow performance of business transactions to be monitored, while others will monitor CI behaviour.

Event management must set up and calibrate alarm thresholds (where necessary in conjunction with capacity management, as it is often event monitoring tools that may be used) so that the correct alert levels are set and that any filtering is established as necessary so that only meaningful events are raised. Without such filtering it is possible that 'information only' alerts can obscure more significant alerts that require immediate attention. In addition, it is possible for serious failures to cause 'alert storms' due to very high volumes of repeat alerts, which again must be filtered so that the most meaningful messages are not obscured.

Thresholds themselves should be identified during service design (see *ITIL Service Design*) and set and managed through event management. Unless these are properly designed and communicated during the instrumentation process, it will be difficult to determine which level of performance is appropriate for each CI.

Also, most thresholds are not constant. They typically consist of a number of related variables. For example, the maximum number of concurrent users before response time slows will vary depending on what other jobs are active on the server. This knowledge is often only gained by experience, which means that correlation engines have to be continually tuned and updated through the process of CSI.

It may be appropriate to use external third-party monitoring capabilities for some CIs or components of the IT infrastructure (e.g. key internet sites/ pages). Capacity management should be involved in helping specify and select any such monitoring capabilities and in integrating the results or any alerts with other monitoring and handling systems.

Event management must work with all appropriate support groups to make decisions on where capacity and performance alarms are routed and on escalation paths and timescales. Alerts should be logged to the service desk as well as to appropriate support staff, so that appropriate incident records can be raised and there is a permanent record of the event – and service desk staff have a view of how well the support group(s) are dealing with the fault and can intervene if necessary.

Manufacturers' claimed performance capabilities and agreed service level targets, together with actual historical monitored performance and capacity data, should be used to set alert levels. This may need to be an iterative process initially, performing some trial-and-error adjustments until the correct levels are achieved.

Example of capacity management activities related to service operation

Capacity management is involved in all lifecycle stages, including service operation, and helps to address day-to-day operational challenges such as:

■ Has the organization enough service desk staff to handle the rate of incidents?
■ Can the CAB structure handle the number of changes it is being asked to review and authorize?
■ Are the support tools able to handle the volume of data being gathered?

5.12.4.2 Handling capacity and performance incidents

If an alert is triggered, or an incident is raised at the service desk, caused by a current or ongoing capacity or performance management issue, capacity management support personnel must become involved to identify the cause and find a resolution. Working together with appropriate technical support groups, and alongside problem management personnel, all necessary investigations must be performed to detect exactly what has gone wrong and what is needed to correct the situation.

It may be necessary to switch to more detailed monitoring during the investigation phase to determine the exact cause. Monitoring is often set at a 'background' level during normal circumstances, because of the large amount of data that can be generated and to avoid placing too high a burden on the IT infrastructure – but when specific difficulties are being investigated more detailed monitoring may be needed to pinpoint the exact cause.

When a solution, or potential solution, has been found for a capacity or performance related problem, any changes necessary to resolve it must be authorized via formal change management before implementation. If the fault is causing serious disruption and an urgent resolution is needed, the emergency change process should be used. It is very important that no 'tuning' takes place without submission through change management, as even apparently small adjustments can often have very large cumulative effects – sometimes across the entire IT infrastructure.

5.12.4.3 Capacity and performance trends

Capacity management has a role to play in identifying any capacity or performance trends as they become discernible. Service operation should include activities for logging and collecting performance data and information relating to performance incidents to provide a basis for problem and capacity management trend analysis activities. Further details of actions needed to address such trends are included in *ITIL Continual Service Improvement*.

5.12.4.4 Storage of capacity management data

Large amounts of data are usually generated through capacity and performance monitoring. Monitoring of meters and tables of just a few kilobytes each can quickly grown into huge files if many components are being monitored at relatively short intervals. Another problem with very short-term monitoring is that it is not possible to gather meaningful information without looking over a longer period. For example, a single snapshot of a CPU will show the device to be either 'busy' or 'idle', but a summary over, say, a 5-minute period will show the average utilization level over that period. This is a much more meaningful measure of whether the device is able to work comfortably, or whether potential performance problems are likely to occur.

In any organization it is likely that the monitoring tools used will vary greatly – with a combination of system-specific tools, many of them part of the basic operating system, and specialist monitoring tools being used. In order to coordinate the data being generated and allow the retention of meaningful data for analysis and trending purposes, some form of central repository for holding this summary data is needed: a capacity management information system.

The format, location and design of such a database should be planned and implemented in advance (see *ITIL Service Design* for further details) but there will be some operational aspects to handle, such as database housekeeping and backups.

5.12.4.5 Modelling and applications sizing

Modelling and/or sizing of new services and/or applications must, where appropriate, be done during the design and transition stages (see *ITIL Service Design* and *ITIL Service Transition*). However, the service operation functions have a role to play in evaluating the accuracy of the predictions and feeding back any issues or discrepancies.

5.12.5 Demand management

Demand management is primarily covered in *ITIL Service Strategy*. Demand management is the name given to a number of techniques that can be used to modify demand for a particular resource or service. Some techniques for demand management can be planned in advance, and these are covered in more detail in *ITIL Service Strategy*. However, there are other aspects of demand management that are of a more operational nature, requiring shorter-term action.

If, for example, the performance of a particular service is causing concern, and short-term restrictions on concurrency of users are needed to allow performance improvements for a smaller restricted group, then service operation functions will have to take action to implement such restrictions, usually accompanied by concurrent action to implement the logging-out of users who have been inactive for an agreed period of time to free up resources for others.

There may be occasions where optimization of infrastructure resources is needed to maintain or improve performance or throughput. This can often be done through demand management, as activities such as:

■ Rescheduling a particular service or workload to run at a different time of day, day of the week etc. (usually away from peak-times to off-peak windows), which will often mean having to make adjustments to job-scheduling software
■ Moving a service or workload from one location or set of CIs to another – often to balance utilization or traffic
■ Technical virtualization: setting up and using virtualization systems to allow movement of processing around the infrastructure to give better performance/resilience in a dynamic fashion

- Limiting or moving demand for resources through demand management techniques (see above and also *ITIL Service Strategy*).

It will only be possible to manage demand effectively if there is a good understanding of which workloads exist, which will run at what time and how much resource utilization each workload places upon the IT infrastructure. Diligent monitoring and analysis of workloads is therefore needed on an ongoing operational basis.

5.12.6 Availability management

Availability management is primarily covered in *ITIL Service Design*. During service design and service transition, IT services are designed for availability and recovery. Service operation is responsible for actually making the IT service available to the specified users at the required time and at the agreed levels.

During service operation the IT teams and users are in the best position to detect whether services actually meet the agreed requirements and whether the design of these services is effective.

What seems like a good idea during the design stage may not actually be practical or optimal. The actual experience of the users and operational functions during service operation can provide primary input into the ongoing improvement of existing services and the design.

However, there are a number of challenges with gaining access to this knowledge:

- Most of the experiences of the operational teams and users are either informal, or spread across multiple sources.
- The process for collecting and collating this data needs to be formalized.
- Users and operational staff are usually fully occupied with their regular activities and tasks and it is very difficult for them to be involved in regular planning and design activities. One argument often made here is that if design is improved, the operational teams will be less busy resolving problems and will therefore have more time to be involved in design activities. However, practice shows that as soon as staff are freed up, they often become the target of workforce reduction exercises.

Having said this, there are three key opportunities for operational staff to be involved in availability

improvement, because these are generally viewed as part of their ongoing responsibility:

- Review of maintenance activities. Service design will define detailed maintenance schedules and activities, which are required to keep IT services functioning at the required level of performance and availability. Regular comparison of actual maintenance activities and times with the plans will highlight potential areas for improvement. One of the sources of this information is a review of whether service maintenance objectives were met and if not, why not.
- Major problem reviews. Problems could be the result of any number of factors, one of which is poor design. Problem reviews therefore may include opportunities to identify improvements to the design of IT services, which will include availability and capacity improvement.
- Involvement in specific initiatives using techniques such as service failure analysis (SFA), component failure impact analysis (CFIA), or fault tree analysis (FTA), or as members of technical observation (TO) activities – either as part of the follow-up to major problems or as part of an ongoing service improvement plan (SIP), in collaboration with dedicated availability management staff. These availability management techniques are explained in more detail in *ITIL Service Design*.

There may be occasions when operational staff themselves need downtime of one or more services to enable them to conduct their operational or maintenance activities; this may impact on availability if not properly scheduled and managed. In such cases they must liaise with SLM and availability management staff, who will negotiate with the business/users, often using the service desk to perform this role, to agree and schedule such activities.

5.12.7 Knowledge management

Knowledge management is primarily covered in *ITIL Service Transition*. It is vitally important that all data and information that can be useful for future service operation activities are properly gathered, stored and assessed. Relevant data, metrics and information should be passed up the management chain and to other service lifecycle stages so that it can feed into the knowledge and wisdom layers of the organization's SKMS, the structures of which have to be defined in service strategy and service design and refined in CSI (see other ITIL publications in this series).

Key repositories of service operation, which have been frequently mentioned elsewhere, are the CMS and the KEDB, but this must be widened out to include documentation from all of the service operation teams and departments, such as operations manuals, procedures manuals, work instructions etc.

5.12.8 Financial management for IT services

Financial management for IT services is primarily covered in *ITIL Service Strategy*. Service operation staff must participate in and support the overall IT budgeting and accounting system, and may be actively involved in any charging system that is in place. Proper planning is necessary so that capital expenditure (CAPEX) and operational expenditure (OPEX) budget estimates can be prepared and agreed in good time to meet the budgetary cycles.

The service operation manager must also be involved in regular (at least monthly) reviews of expenditure against budgets, as part of the ongoing IT budgeting and accounting process. Any discrepancies must be identified and necessary adjustments made. All committed expenditure must go through the organization's purchase order system so that commitments can be accrued and proper checks must be made on all goods received so that invoices and payments can be correctly authorized, or discrepancies investigated and rectified.

It should be noted that some proposed cost reductions by the business may actually increase IT costs, or at least unit costs. Care should therefore be taken to ensure that IT is involved in discussing all cost-saving measures and contribute to overall decisions. Financial management is covered in detail in *ITIL Service Strategy*.

5.12.9 IT service continuity management

IT service continuity management is primarily covered in *ITIL Service Design*. Service operation functions are responsible for the testing and execution of system and service recovery plans as determined in the IT service continuity plans for the organization. In addition, managers of all service operation functions must participate in key

coordination and recovery teams as they have been outlined in those continuity plans.

This is discussed in detail in *ITIL Service Strategy* and *ITIL Service Design* and will not be repeated here, except to indicate that it is important that service operation functions be involved in the following areas:

- Risk assessment, using its knowledge of the infrastructure and techniques such as CFIA and access to information in the CMS to identify single points of failure or other high-risk situations
- Execution of any risk management measures that are agreed, e.g. implementation of countermeasures, or increased resilience to components of the infrastructures etc.
- Assistance in writing the actual recovery plans for systems and services under its control
- Participation in testing of the plans (such as involvement in off-site testing, simulations etc.) on an ongoing basis under the direction of the IT service continuity manager
- Ongoing maintenance of the plans under the control of the IT service continuity manager and change management
- Participation in training and awareness campaigns to ensure that they are able to execute the plans and understand their roles in a disaster
- The service desk will play a key role in communicating with staff, customers and users during an actual disaster
- Assistance with testing and execution of system and service recovery plans.

5.12.10 Information security management

Information security management as a process is covered in *ITIL Service Design*. Information security management has overall responsibility for setting policies, standards and procedures to ensure the protection of the organization's assets, data, information and IT services. Service operation teams play a role in executing these policies, standards and procedures and will work closely with the teams or departments responsible for information security management.

Service operation teams cannot take ownership of information security management, as this would represent a conflict. There needs to be segregation of roles between the groups defining and managing the process and the groups executing specific activities as part of ongoing operation. This will help protect against breaches to security measures, as no single individual should have control over two or more phases of a transaction or operation. Information security management should assign responsibilities to ensure a cross-check of duties.

Key service operation team support activities for information security management can include:

■ **Policing and reporting** This will involve operation staff performing specific policing activities such as the checking of system journals, logs, event/monitoring alerts etc., intrusion detection and/or reporting of actual or potential security breaches. This is done in conjunction with information security management to provide a check and balance system to ensure effective detection and management of security issues.

Service operation staff are often first to detect security events and are in the best position to be able to shut down and/or remove access to compromised systems. Particular attention will be needed in the case of third-party organizations that require physical access into the organization. Service operation staff may be required to escort visitors into sensitive areas and/or control their access. They may also have a role to play in controlling network access to third parties, such as hardware maintainers dialling in for diagnostic purposes etc.

■ **Technical assistance** Some technical support may need to be provided to IT security staff to assist in investigating security incidents and producing reports or in gathering forensic evidence for use in disciplinary action or criminal prosecutions. Technical advice and assistance may also be needed regarding potential security improvements (e.g. setting up appropriate firewalls or access/password controls).

The use of event, incident, problem and service asset and configuration management information can be relied on to provide accurate chronologies of security-related investigations.

■ **Operational security control** For operational reasons, technical staff will often need to have privileged access to key technical areas (e.g. root system passwords, physical access to data centres or communications rooms, etc). It

is therefore essential that adequate controls and audit trails are kept of all such privileged activities so as to deter and detect any security events.

Physical controls need to be in place for all secure areas with logging in/out of all staff. Where third-party staff or visitors need access, it may be service operation staff that are responsible for escorting and managing the movement of such personnel.

In the case of privileged systems access, this needs to be restricted to only those people whose need to access the system has been verified – and withdrawn immediately when that need no longer exists. An audit trail must be maintained of who has had access and when, and of all activities performed using those access levels.

■ **Screening and vetting** All service operation staff should be screened and vetted to a security level appropriate to the organization in question.

Suppliers and third-party contractors should also be screened and vetted – both the organizations and the specific personnel involved. Many organizations have started using police or government agency background checks, especially where contractors will be working with classified systems. Where necessary, appropriate non-disclosure and confidentiality agreements must be put in place.

■ **Training and awareness** All service operation staff should be given regular and ongoing training and awareness of the organization's security policy and procedures. This should include details of disciplinary measures in place. In addition, any security requirements should be specified in the employee's contract of employment.

■ **Documented policies and procedures** Service operation documented procedures must include all relevant information relating to security issues – extracted from the organization's overall security policy documents. Consideration should be given to the use of handbooks to assist in getting the security messages out to all relevant staff.

5.2.11 Service level management

Service level management (SLM) as a process is covered in *ITIL Service Design*. SLM is the process responsible for negotiating SLAs, and ensuring that these are met. It monitors and reports on service levels, and holds regular customer reviews. Service operation teams play a role in executing monitoring activities through the event management process that can provide early detection of service level breaches. Incident management priorities and required resolution targets should be guided by service level targets. Problem management activities contribute to the improved attainment of service level targets. SLM also maintains the agreements used by access management to provide access to services while request fulfilment activities may be bounded by agreed service targets.

5.13 IMPROVEMENT OF OPERATIONAL ACTIVITIES

All service operation staff should be constantly looking for areas in which process improvements can be made to give higher IT service quality and/or performed in a more cost-effective way. Opportunities for improvement will be included in the CSI register for review and prioritization. This might include some of the following activities:

- **Automation of manual tasks** Any tasks which have to be carried out manually, particularly those that have to be regularly repeated, are likely to be more time-consuming, costly and error prone than those that can be systemized and automated. All tasks should be examined for potential automation to reduce effort and costs and to minimize potential errors.

  A judgement must be made on the costs of the automation and the likely benefits that will result.

- **Reviewing makeshift activities or procedures** Because of the pragmatic nature of service operation, it may sometimes happen that makeshift activities or processes are introduced to address short-term operational expediencies. There is a danger that such practices can be continued and become the 'norm', leading to ongoing inefficiencies. Where any makeshift activities or procedures do have to be introduced it is important that these are reviewed as soon as the immediate expediency is overcome, and that they are either dispensed with or replaced by efficient agreed processes for the longer term.

- **Operational audits** Regular audits should be conducted of all service operation processes to ensure that they are working satisfactorily.

- **Using incident and problem management** Problem and incident management provide a rich source of operational improvement opportunities. These processes are discussed in detail in Chapter 4.

- **Communication** It should go without saying that good communication about changing requirements, technology and processes will result in improvement in service operation. However, communication is often neglected. Service operation improvement is dependent on formal and regular communication between teams responsible for design, support and operation of services.

- **Education and training** Service operation teams should understand the importance of what they do on a daily basis. Education is required to ensure that staff understand what business functions or services are supported by their activities. This will encourage greater care and attention to detail and will also help service operation teams to better identify business priorities.

Training programmes should ensure that all staff have the appropriate skills for the technology or applications they are managing. Training should always be provided when new technology is introduced, or when existing technology is changed.

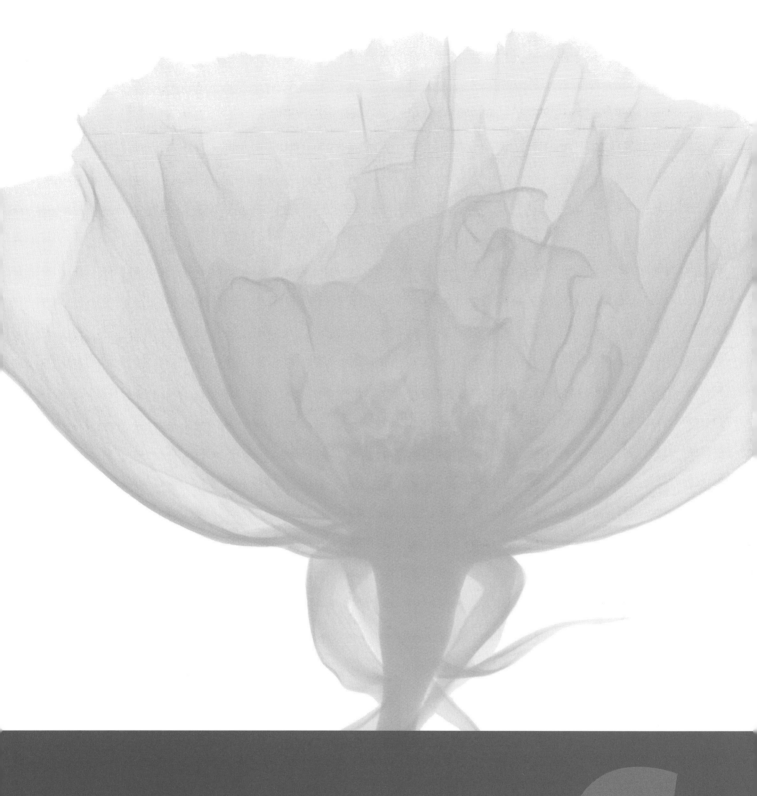

Organizing for service operation

6 Organizing for service operation

This chapter describes the general concepts of organizing for service management in relation to service operation and related practices. It includes generic roles, responsibilities and competencies that apply across the service lifecycle and specific aspects for the processes described in this publication.

Section 2.2.3 describes the basic concepts of organization, function, group, team, department, division and role that are used in this chapter.

6.1 ORGANIZATIONAL DEVELOPMENT

There is no single best way to organize, and best practices described in ITIL need to be tailored to suit individual organizations and situations. Any changes made will need to take into account resource constraints and the size, nature and needs of the business and customers. The starting point for organizational design is strategy. Organization development for service management is described in more detail in Chapter 6 of *ITIL Service Strategy*.

6.2 FUNCTIONS

A function is a team or group of people and the tools or other resources they use to carry out one or more processes or activities. In larger organizations, a function may be broken out and performed by several departments, teams and groups, or it may be embodied within a single organizational unit (e.g. a service desk). In smaller organizations, one person or group can perform multiple functions (e.g. a technical management department could also incorporate the service desk function).

For service operation to be successful, an organization will need to clearly define the roles and responsibilities required to undertake the processes and activities identified in Chapters 4 and 5. These roles will need to be assigned to individuals, and an appropriate organization structure of teams, groups or functions established and managed.

This chapter describes the following main functions: service desk, technical management, IT operations management and application

management. Technical management and application management provide the technical resources and expertise to manage the whole service lifecycle, and practitioner roles within service operation may be performed by members of these functions.

6.2.1 Functions and activities

Functions carry out one or more processes and activities. Activities consist of a set of actions designed to achieve a particular result. They are usually defined as part of processes or plans, and are documented in procedures.

Chapter 5 introduced a number of common service operation activities. Because of the technical nature and specialization of these activities, the teams, groups or departments that perform them are often given names that correspond to the particular activities. For example, network management could be performed by a network management department. This, however, is by no means a rule. There are a number of options available in mapping activities to a team or department, for example:

- One activity could be performed by several teams or departments, e.g. if an organization has five major application support departments, each supporting a different set of applications, each of these departments could perform database administration for its particular applications.
- One department could perform several activities, e.g. the network management department could be responsible for managing the network, directory services management and server management.
- An activity could be performed by groups, e.g. security administration can be performed by any person with responsibility for managing an application, server, middleware or desktop.

These organizational decisions are influenced by a number of factors, such as:

- **The size and location of the organization** Smaller, less distributed organizations will tend to combine these functions, whereas large, decentralized organizations may have several teams or departments performing the same activity (e.g. per region).

- **The complexity of technology used in the organization** The higher the number of different technologies used, the more likely there are to be several different teams, each doing something similar, but in a different context (e.g. UNIX server management and Windows server management).

- **The availability of skills** Where technical skills are scarce, it is common for organizations to use generalists to perform multiple groups of activities – although in some cases security considerations make this very difficult. For example, an organization working on classified or secret projects may have to hire expensive, specialized resources even when that means relocating them or contracting through security-cleared suppliers.

- **The culture of the organization** Some organizations prefer to work in highly specialized environments, while others tend to prefer the flexibility of generalist staff.

- **The financial situation of the organization** This will determine how many people, with what type of skill, can be employed and how they will be organized.

As a result of these factors, it is impossible for this publication to prescribe an appropriate organizational structure that will fit every situation, but the following sections list the required activities under the functional groups most likely to be involved in their operation. Note that this does not mean that all organizations have to use these divisions. Smaller organizations will tend to combine activities into single departments, or even individuals – if they are needed at all.

Ideally, a service provider organization should be able to demonstrate that it has management control of all of the ITSM processes, even if some of those process activities are being executed by external service providers. As a guide, management control of a process can consist of:

- Knowledge and control of inputs
- Knowledge, use and interpretation of outputs
- Definition and measurement of metrics
- Demonstration of objective evidence of accountability for process functionality
- Definition measurement and review of process improvements.

Special note on outsourcing

These organizational considerations are likely to be most relevant to internal IT organizations. The situation becomes even more complex when some or all of a particular activity or function are outsourced to an external service provider. Prime opportunities for outsourcing have been the service desk, IT operations control, facilities management, and network operations. Examples of the key points to consider when outsourcing are:

- Regardless of who is performing the activity, the company contracting the external service provider is still responsible for ensuring it is performed to a standard that will support the delivery of services to their customers and users.

- Outsourcing to solve an organization's problems or as an alternative to good service management processes rarely works. The best results are obtained if service management practices are in place before outsourcing and then extended to activities and interfaces between the IT organization and its suppliers via agreements and contracts.

- Outsourcing works best when there is active involvement by both organizations. If the staff and managers of the customer organization disengage, the external service provider is unlikely to be successful, simply because nobody understands the organization better than the people who work there.

- The external service provider should not determine their outputs or how they are measured. These are determined by understanding the business requirements of users and customers and ensuring that they can be met by the capabilities of the external service provider.

Even if the external service provider becomes an integral part of the organization, they are still a third party with a different set of business objectives, policies and practices. Security standards must be upheld and both parties must clearly understand their respective roles and contributions.

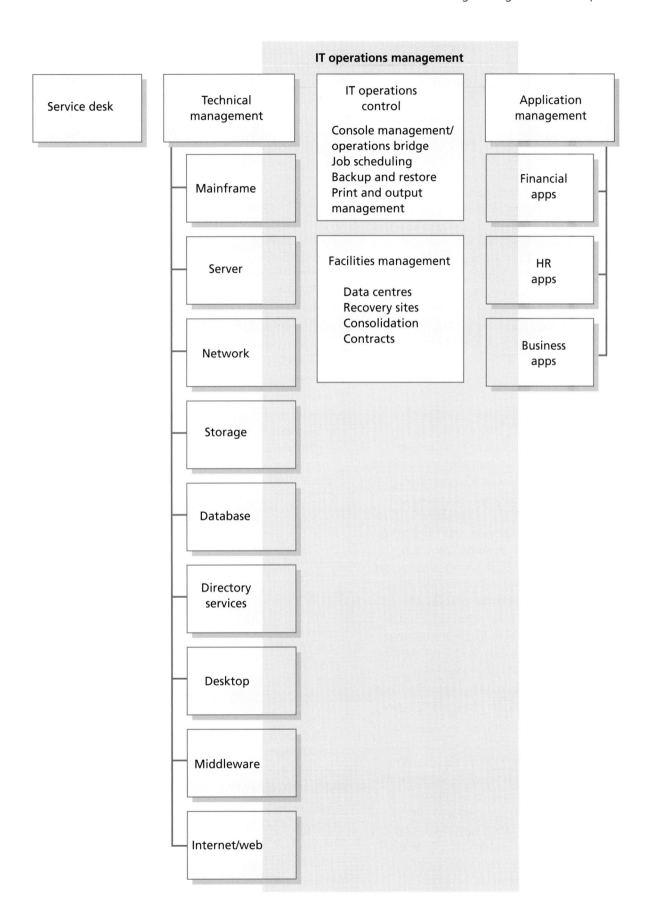

Figure 6.1 Service operation functions

The ISO/IEC 20000 management standard can be referenced for details of the above objectives. More information on this can be found in section A.6 in Appendix A.

The service operation functions shown in Figure 6.1 are needed to manage the 'steady state' operational IT environment. These are logical functions and do not necessarily have to be performed by an equivalent organizational structure. This means that technical and application management can be organized in any combination and into any number of departments. The second-level groupings in Figure 6.1 are examples of typical groups of activities performed by technical management (see Chapter 5) and are not a suggested organization structure.

The following is an overview of the service operation functions in Figure 6.1.

6.2.1.1 Service desk

The service desk is the single point of contact for users when there is a service disruption, for service requests or even for some categories of request for change (RFC). The service desk provides a point of communication to the users and a point of coordination for several IT groups and processes. To enable them to perform these actions effectively the service desk is usually separate from the other service operation functions. In some cases, e.g. where detailed technical support is offered to users on the first call, it may be necessary for technical or application management staff to be on the service desk. This does not mean that the service desk becomes part of the technical management function. In fact, while they are on the service desk, they cease to be a part of the technical management or application management functions and become part of the service desk, even if only temporarily.

6.2.1.2 Technical management

Technical management provides detailed technical skills and the resources needed to support the ongoing operation of IT services and the management of the IT infrastructure. Technical management also plays an important role in the design, testing, release and improvement of IT services. In small organizations, it is possible to manage this expertise in a single department, but larger organizations are typically split into a number of technically specialized departments

(see section 6.10.1). In many organizations, the technical management departments are also responsible for the daily operation of a subset of the IT infrastructure. Figure 6.1 shows that, although they are part of a technical management department, staff who perform these activities are logically part of the IT operations management function.

6.2.1.3 IT operations management

IT operations management is the function responsible for the daily operational activities needed to manage IT services and the supporting IT infrastructure. This is done according to the performance standards defined during service design. In some organizations this is a single, centralized department, while in others some activities and staff are centralized and some are provided by distributed or specialized departments. This is illustrated in Figure 6.1 by the overlap between the technical and application management functions. IT operations management has two sub-functions that are unique and are generally organizationally distinct. These are:

- **IT operations control** This is generally staffed by shifts of operators which ensures that routine operational tasks are carried out. IT operations control will also provide centralized monitoring and control activities, usually using an operations bridge or network operations centre.
- **Facilities management** This refers to the management of the physical IT environment, usually data centres or computer rooms. In many organizations technical and application management are co-located with IT operations in large data centres. In some organizations many physical components of the IT infrastructure have been outsourced and facilities management may include the management of the outsourcing contracts.

6.2.1.4 Application management

Application management is responsible for managing applications throughout their lifecycle. The application management function supports and maintains operational applications and also plays an important role in the design, testing and improvement of applications that form part of IT services. Application management is usually divided into departments based on the application portfolio of the organization (see the examples in Figure 6.1), thus allowing easier specialization and more focused support. In many organizations application management departments have staff who perform daily operations for those applications. As with technical management, these staff logically form part of the IT operations management function.

Special note on information security management

Although most would agree that information security management is a function, it is highly specialized and spans several stages of the lifecycle. It is also responsible for the oversight of many activities within all service operation functions. For a more in-depth description of information security management, please refer to *ITIL Service Design*.

6.3   SERVICE DESK FUNCTION

A service desk is a functional unit made up of a dedicated number of staff responsible for dealing with a variety of service activities, usually made via telephone calls, web interface, or automatically reported infrastructure events.

The service desk is a vitally important part of an IT organization and should be the single point of contact for IT users on a day-by-day basis. It not only handles incidents, escalates incidents to problem management staff, manages service requests and answers questions, it may also provide an interface for other activities such as customer change requests, maintenance contracts, software licences, SLM, service asset and configuration management, availability management, financial management for IT services, and IT service continuity management.

The value of an effective service desk should not be underestimated – a good service desk can often compensate for deficiencies elsewhere in the IT organization, but a poor service desk (or the lack of a service desk) can give a poor impression of an otherwise very effective IT organization!

It is therefore very important that the correct calibre of staff be used on the service desk and that IT managers do their best to make the desk an attractive place to work to improve staff retention.

The exact nature, type, size and location of a service desk will vary, depending upon the type of business, number of users, geography, complexity of calls, scope of services and many other factors.

In alignment to customer and business requirements, the IT organization's senior managers should decide the exact nature of its required service desk (and whether it should be internal or outsourced to a third party) as part of its overall ITSM strategy (see *ITIL Service Strategy*). Subsequent planning must then be done to prepare for and then implement the appropriate service desk function (either when implementing a new function, or more likely these days when making necessary amendments to an existing function – see *ITIL Service Design* and *ITIL Service Transition*).

6.3.1 Justification and role of the service desk

Very little justification is needed today for a service desk, as many organizations have become convinced that this is by far the best approach for dealing with first-line IT support issues. One only needs ask the question 'What is the alternative?' to make a compelling case for the service desk concept. Where further justification is needed, the following benefits should be considered:

■ Improved customer service, perception and satisfaction
■ Increased accessibility through a single point of contact, communication and information
■ Better quality and faster turnaround of customer or user requests
■ Improved teamwork and communication
■ Enhanced focus and a proactive approach to service provision
■ A reduced negative business impact
■ Better managed infrastructure and control
■ Improved usage of IT support resources and increased productivity of business personnel
■ More meaningful management information for decision support
■ It is common practice that the service desk provides entry-level positions for ITSM staff. Working on the service desk is an excellent grounding for anyone wishing to pursue a career in service management. However, this could also present challenges with people who do not understand the business or technology.

Users calling the service desk should be able to speak to someone who is able to address their needs, and service desk analysts should not be burned out in less than a year because of undue stress. Care should be taken to select appropriately skilled individuals with a good understanding of the business and to provide adequate training – thus preventing reduction in levels of support due to a lack of knowledge at the first line.

6.3.2 Service desk objectives

The primary aim of the service desk is to provide a single point of contact between the services being provided and the users. A typical service desk manages incidents and service requests, and also handles communication with the users. Service desk staff execute the incident management and request fulfilment processes to restore the normal-state service operation to the users as quickly as possible. In this context 'restoration of service' is meant in the widest possible sense. While this could involve fixing a technical fault, it could equally involve fulfilling a service request or answering a query – anything that is needed to allow the users to return to working satisfactorily.

Specific responsibilities will include:

- Logging all relevant incident/service request details, allocating categorization and prioritization codes
- Providing first-line investigation and diagnosis
- Resolving incidents/service requests when first contacted whenever possible
- Escalating incidents/service requests that they cannot resolve within agreed timescales
- Keeping users informed of progress
- Closing all resolved incidents, requests and other calls
- Conducting customer/user satisfaction call-backs/surveys as agreed
- Communication with users – keeping them informed of incident progress, notifying them of impending changes or agreed outages etc.
- Updating the CMS under the direction and approval of service asset and configuration management if so agreed.

Note that these activities are explained and set in context with the fuller incident management and request fulfilment process in sections 4.2 and 4.3, respectively.

6.3.3 Service desk organizational structure

There are many ways of structuring service desks and locating them – and the correct solution will vary for different organizations. The primary options are detailed below, but in reality an organization may need to implement a structure that combines a number of these options in order to fully meet the business needs.

6.3.3.1 Local service desk

This is where a desk is co-located within or physically close to the user community it serves (see Figure 6.2). This often aids communication and gives a clearly visible presence, which some users like, but can often be inefficient and expensive to resource as local staff are tied up waiting to deal with incidents when the volume and arrival rate of calls may not justify this.

There may, however, be some valid reasons for maintaining a local desk, even where call volumes alone do not justify this. Reasons might include:

- Language and cultural or political differences
- Different time zones
- Specialized groups of users
- The existence of customized or specialized services that require specialist knowledge
- VIP/criticality status of users.

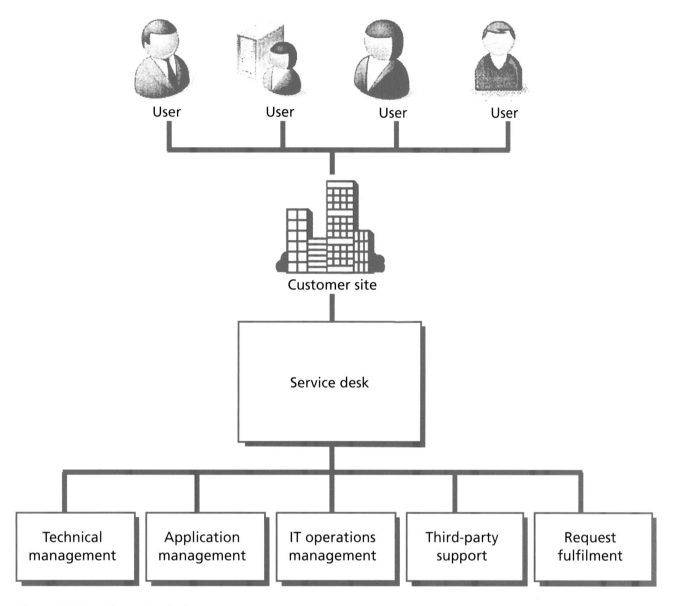

Figure 6.2 Local service desk

6.3.3.2 Centralized service desk

It is possible to reduce the number of service desks by merging them into a single location (or into a smaller number of locations) by drawing the staff into one or more centralized service desk structures (see Figure 6.3). This can be more efficient and cost-effective, allowing fewer overall staff to deal with a higher volume of calls, and can also lead to higher skill levels through greater familiarization from more frequent occurrence of events. It might still be necessary to maintain some form of local presence to handle physical support requirements, but such staff can be controlled and deployed from the central desk.

Figure 6.3 Centralized service desk

6.3.3.3 Virtual service desk

Through the use of technology, particularly the internet, and the use of corporate support tools, it is possible to give the impression of a single, centralized service desk when in fact the personnel may be spread or located in any number or type of geographical or structural locations (see Figure 6.4). This brings in the option of home working, secondary support groups, offshoring or outsourcing – or any combination necessary to meet user demand. It is important to note, however, that safeguards are needed in all of these circumstances to ensure consistency and uniformity in service quality and cultural terms.

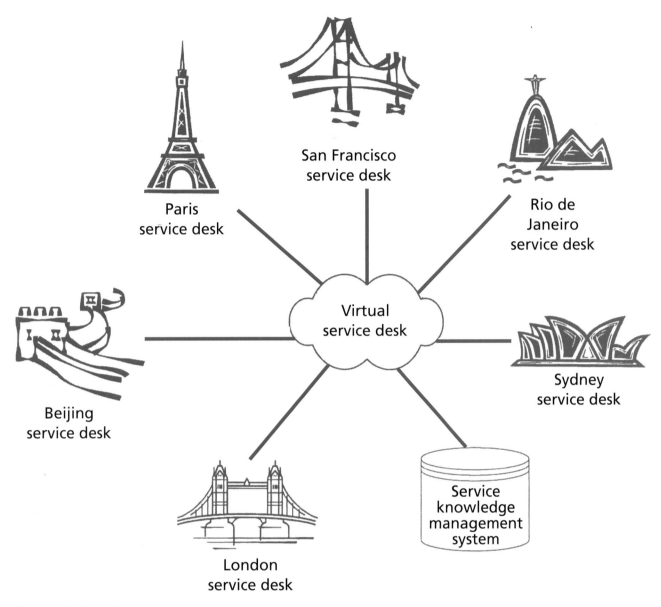

Figure 6.4 Virtual service desk

6.3.3.4 Follow the sun

Some global or international organizations may wish to combine two or more of their geographically dispersed service desks to provide a 24-hour follow-the-sun service. For example, a service desk in the Asia-Pacific may handle calls during its standard office hours and at the end of this period it may hand over responsibility for any open incidents to a European-based desk. That desk will handle these calls alongside its own incidents during its standard day and then hand over to a USA-based desk – which finally hands back responsibility to the Asia-Pacific desk to complete the cycle.

This can give 24-hour coverage at relatively low cost, as no desk has to work more than a single shift. However, the same safeguards of common processes, tools, shared databases of information and culture must be addressed for this approach to proceed – and well-controlled escalation and handover processes are needed.

6.3.3.5 Specialized service desk groups

For some organizations it might be beneficial to create specialist groups within the overall service desk structure, so that incidents relating to a particular IT service can be routed directly (normally via telephony selection or a web-based interface) to the specialist group. This can allow faster resolution of these incidents, through greater familiarity and specialist training.

The selection would be made using a script along the lines of 'If your call is about the X service, please press 1 now, otherwise please hold for a service desk analyst'.

Care is needed not to overcomplicate the selection, so specialist groups should only be considered for a very small number of key services where these exist, and where call rates about that service justify a separate specialist group.

Note on building a single point of contact

Regardless of the combination of options chosen to fulfil an organization's overall service desk structure, individual users should be in no doubt about who to contact if they need assistance or where they can access self-help support. A single telephone number (or a single number for each group if separate desks are chosen) should be provided and well publicized, as well as a single email address and a single web service desk contact page.

There are several ways to help publicize the service desk telephone number and email address, and make them easily available when users are likely to need them, such as:

- Including the service desk telephone number on hardware CI labels, attached to the components the user is likely to be calling about
- Printing service desk contact details on telephones
- For PCs and laptops, using a customized background or desktop with the service desk contact details, together with information read from the system that will be needed when calling (such as IP address, OS build number etc.) in one corner
- Printing the service desk number on 'freebies' (pens, pencils, mugs, mouse mats etc.)
- Prominently placing these details on service desk internet/intranet sites
- Including them on any calling cards or satisfaction survey cards left with users when a desk visit has been necessary
- Repeating the details on all correspondence sent to users (together with call reference numbers)
- Placing the details on notice boards or physical locations that users are likely to regularly visit (entrances, canteens, refreshment areas etc.).

6.3.4 Service desk staffing

The issues involved in, and criteria for, establishing the appropriate staffing model and levels are discussed in this section. Details of typical service desk roles and responsibilities can be found in section 6.7.10. They include the service desk manager, supervisor, analysts and, in some organizations, these roles are complemented by business users ('super users') who provide first-line support.

6.3.4.1 Staffing levels

An organization must ensure that the correct number of staff are available at any given time to match the demand being placed upon the desk by the business. Call rates can be very volatile and often in the same day the arrival rate may go from very high to very low and back again. An organization planning a new desk should attempt to predict the call arrival rate and profile, and to staff accordingly. Statistical analysis of call arrival rates under current support arrangements must be undertaken and then closely monitored and adjusted as necessary.

Many organizations will find that call rates peak during the start of the office day and then fall off quickly, perhaps with another burst in the early part of the afternoon – this obviously varies depending upon the organization's business but is often a recurring pattern for many organizations. In such circumstances it may be possible to utilize part-time staff, home-workers, second-line support staff or third parties to cover the peaks.

The following factors should be considered when deciding staffing levels:

- Customer service expectations
- Business requirements, such as budget, call response times etc.
- The level of self-help tools available and automation of service request handling (i.e. password resets etc.)
- Size, relative age, design and complexity of the IT infrastructure and service catalogue – for example, the number and type of incidents, the extent of customized versus standard off-the-shelf software deployed etc.
- The number of customers and users to support, and associated factors such as:

- Number of customers and users speaking a different language
- Skill level.

Incident and service request types (and types of RFC if appropriate):

- Duration of time required for call types (e.g. simple queries, specialist application queries, hardware etc.)
- Local or external expertise required
- The volume and types of incidents and service requests
- The period of support cover required, based on:
  - Hours covered
  - Out-of-hours support requirements
  - Time zones to be covered
  - Locations to be supported (particularly if service desk staff also conduct desk-side support)
  - Travel time between locations
  - Workload pattern of requests (e.g. daily, month end etc.)
  - The service level targets in place (response levels etc.)
- The type of response required:
  - Telephone
  - Email/fax/voice mail/video
  - Online chat
  - Texting
  - Physical attendance
  - Online access/control
- The level of training required
- The support technologies available (e.g. phone systems, remote support tools etc.)
- The existing skill levels of staff
- The processes and procedures in use.

All these items should be carefully considered before making any decision on staffing levels. This should also be reflected in the levels of documentation required. Remember that the better the service, the more the business will use it.

A number of tools are available to help determine the appropriate number of staff for the service desk. These workload modelling tools are dependent on detailed local knowledge of the organization such as call volumes and patterns, service and user profiles etc.

6.3.4.2 Skill levels

An organization must decide on the level and range of skills it requires of its service desk staff, and then ensure that these skills are available at the appropriate times.

A range of skill options are possible, starting from a call logging service only – where staff need only very basic technical skills – right through to a technical service desk where the organization's most technically skilled staff are used. In the case of the former, there will be a high handling but low resolution rate, while in the latter case this will be reversed.

The decision on the required skills level will often be driven by target resolution times (agreed with the business and captured in service level targets), the complexity of the systems supported and 'what the business is prepared to pay'.

There is a strong correlation between response and resolution targets and costs – generally speaking, the shorter the target times, the higher the cost because more resources are required.

While there may be instances when business dependency or criticality make a highly technically skilled desk an imperative, the optimum and most cost-effective approach is generally to have a 'call logging' first line of support via the service desk, with quick and effective escalations to more skilled second- and third-line resolution groups where skilled staff can be concentrated and more effectively utilized (see section 4.2 for more details and guidance on end-to-end support structures). However, this basic starting point can be improved over time by providing the first-line staff with an effective knowledge base, diagnostic scripts and integrated support tools (including a CMS), as well as ongoing training and awareness, so that first-line resolution rates can gradually be increased.

This can also be achieved by locating second-level staff on the service desk, effectively creating a two-tier structure. This has the advantage of making second-level staff available to help deal with peak call periods and to train more junior personnel, and it will often increase the first-call resolution rate. However, second-line staff often have duties outside of the service desk – resulting in rosters having to be managed or second-line staff positions being duplicated. In addition, having to deal with routine calls may be demotivating for more experienced staff. A further potential drawback is that the service desk becomes really good at resolving calls, whereas second-line staff should be focused on removing the root cause instead.

Another factor to consider when deciding on the skills requirements for service desk staff is the level of customization or specialization of the supported services. Standardized services require less specific knowledge to provide quality customer support. The more specialized the service, the more likely it is that specialist knowledge will be required on the first call.

Note that first-line resolution rates can be reduced by effective problem management, which will reduce a number of the simpler, repetitive incidents. In such cases, although the resolution rates appear to be going down, the overall service quality will have improved by the complete removal of many incidents. While this is good, if service desk staff are paid incentives or bonuses for first-call resolution, it could prove disastrous for morale and process effectiveness, unless the bonus threshold is reviewed.

Improvements in resolution times/rates should not be left to chance, but should instead be part of an ongoing approach to service improvement (see *ITIL Continual Service Improvement* for more details).

Once the required skill levels have been identified, there is an ongoing task to ensure that the service desk is operated in such a way that the necessary staff obtain and maintain the necessary skills – and that staff with the correct balance of skills are on duty at appropriate times so that consistency is maintained.

This will involve an ongoing training and awareness programme which should cover:

- Interpersonal skills, such as telephony skills, communication skills, active listening and customer care training
- Business awareness: specific knowledge of the organization's business areas, drivers, structure, priorities etc.
- Service awareness of all the organization's key IT services for which support is being provided
- Technical awareness (and deeper technical training to the appropriate level, depending upon the resolution rate sought)
- Depending on level of support provided, some diagnosis skills (e.g. Kepner and Tregoe)

- Support tools and techniques
- Awareness training and tutorials in new systems and technologies, prior to their introduction
- Processes and procedures (most particularly incident, change and service asset and configuration management – but an overview of all ITSM processes and procedures)
- Typing skills to ensure quick and accurate entry of incident or service request details.

For such a programme to be effective, skill requirements and levels should be evaluated periodically and training records maintained.

Careful formulation of staffing rotations or schedules should be maintained so that a consistent balance of staff experience and appropriate skill levels are present during all critical operational periods. It is not sufficient to have only the right number of staff on duty – the correct blend of skills should also be available.

6.3.4.3 Training

It is vital that all service desk staff are adequately trained before they are called upon to staff the service desk. A formal induction programme should be undertaken by all new staff, the exact content of which will vary depending upon the existing skill levels and experience of the new recruit, but is likely to include many of the required skills as described above.

Where possible, a business awareness programme, including short periods of secondment into key business areas, should be provided for new staff who do not already have this level of business awareness.

When starting on the service desk, new staff should initially 'shadow' experienced staff – sit with them and listen in on calls – before starting to take calls themselves with a mentor listening in and able to intervene and provide support where necessary. The mentor should initially review each call with the trainee after it concludes to learn any lessons. The frequency of such reviews should be gradually reduced as experience and confidence grows but the mentor should still be available to provide ongoing support even when the trainee has reached the stage of going solo.

Mentors may need to be trained on how to mentor. Service desk experience and technical skills are not the only requirements for mentoring. Effective knowledge-transfer skills and the ability to teach without being condescending or threatening are equally important.

A programme will be necessary to keep service desk staff knowledge up to date – and to make them aware of new developments, services and technologies. The timing of such events is critical so as not to impact upon normal duties. Many service desks find that it is best to organize short tutorials during quiet periods when staff are less likely to be needed for call handling.

Note on training and professional development

Investment should also be made in the professional development of service desk staff. Internal mentoring and shadowing second- and third-level support staff is a good start, but best-of-breed service desks benefit from a formalized programme of staff development. Organizational commitment to professional development helps instil a sense of accomplishment and opportunity to staff. This often leads to innovation in service desk operation (such as specialized services) which in turn drive operational efficiencies at all tier levels of support. It helps to build skills that can be used in their current role as well as it jump-starts the training for a new role. While it is important to develop their core competencies in their current role, having a clear career path and recognizing future requirements and development needs are also important.

6.3.4.4 Staff retention

It is very important that all IT managers recognize the importance of the service desk and the staff who work on it, and give this special attention. Any significant loss of staff can be disruptive and lead to inconsistency of service, so efforts should be made to make the service desk an attractive place to work.

Ways in which this can be done include proper recognition of the role, with reward packages recognizing this, team-building exercises and staff rotation onto other activities (projects, second-line support etc.).

The service desk can often be used as a stepping stone into other more technical or supervisory/ managerial roles. If this is done, care is needed to ensure that proper succession planning takes place so that the desk does not lose all of its key

expertise in any area at one time. Also, good documentation and cross-training can mitigate this risk.

6.3.4.5 Super users

Many organizations find it useful to appoint or designate a number of 'super users' throughout the user community, to act as liaison points with IT in general and the service desk in particular.

Super users can be given some additional training and awareness and used as a conduit for communications flow in both directions. They can be asked to filter requests and issues raised by the user community (in some cases even going as far as to have incidents or requests raised by the super user); this can help prevent 'incident storms' when a key service or component fails, affecting many users.

They can also be used to cascade information from the service desk outwards throughout their local user community, which can be very useful in disseminating service details to all users very quickly.

It is important to note that super users should log all calls that they deal with, and not just those that they pass on to IT. This will mean access to, and training on how to use, the incident logging tools. This will help to measure the activity of the super user and also to ensure that their position is not abused. In addition, it will ensure that valuable history regarding incidents and service quality are not lost.

It may also be possible for super users to be involved in:

- Staff training for users in their area
- Providing support for minor incidents or simple request fulfilment
- Involvement with new releases and deployments.

Super users do not necessarily provide support for the whole of IT. In many cases a super user will only provide support for a specific application, module or business unit area. As a business user the super user often has in-depth knowledge of how key business processes run and how services work in practice. This is very useful knowledge to share with the service desk, so that it can provide higher-quality services in future.

Before selection and training begins, potential super users, and specifically their management, will need to make a firm commitment that they will have the time and interest to perform this role.

A super user, while a valuable interface to the business and the service desk, must be given proper training, accountability and expectation. The role of a super user can be vulnerable to misuse if the responsibilities and the process governing the role activities are not clearly communicated to the users. It is imperative that a super user is not seen as a replacement for, or a means to circumvent, the service desk.

6.3.5 Measuring service desk performance

Metrics should be established so that performance of the service desk can be evaluated at regular intervals. This is important to assess the health, maturity, efficiency, effectiveness and any opportunities to improve service desk operations.

Metrics for service desk performance must be realistic and carefully chosen. It is common to select those metrics that are easily available and that may seem to be a possible indication of performance; however, this can be misleading. For example, the total number of calls received by the service desk is not in itself an indication of either good or bad performance and may in fact be caused by events completely outside the control of the service desk, for example a particularly busy period for the organization, or the release of a new version of a major corporate system.

An increase in the number of calls to the service desk can indicate less reliable services over that period of time – but may also indicate increased user confidence in a service desk that is maturing, resulting in a higher likelihood that users will seek help rather than try to cope alone. For this type of metric to be reliable for reaching either conclusion, further comparison of previous periods for any service desk improvements implemented since the last measurement baseline, or service reliability changes, problems etc. to isolate the true cause for the increase is needed.

Further analysis and more detailed metrics are therefore needed and must be examined over a period of time. These will include the call-handling statistics previously mentioned under telephony, and also the first-line resolution rate. This is the percentage of calls resolved at first line, without the need for escalation to other support groups. It is the figure often quoted by organizations as the primary measure of the service desk's performance – and used for comparison purposes with the performance of other desks – but care is needed when making any comparisons. For greater accuracy and more valid comparisons this can be broken down further as follows:

- The percentage of calls resolved during the first contact with the service desk, i.e. while the user is still on the telephone to report the call.
- The percentage of calls resolved by the service desk staff themselves, without having to seek deeper support from other groups. Note that some desks will choose to co-locate or embed more technically skilled second-line staff with the service desk. In such cases it is important when making comparisons to also separate out: (i) the percentage resolved by the service desk staff alone; and (ii) the percentage resolved by the first-line service desk staff and second-line support staff combined.
- Average time to resolve an incident (when resolved at first line).
- Average time to escalate an incident (where first-line resolution is not possible).
- Average service desk cost of handling an incident. Three metrics should be considered here:
  - Total cost of the service desk divided by the number of calls. This will provide an average figure which is useful as an index and for planning purposes but does not accurately represent the relative costs of different types of calls.
  - Percentage of call duration time on the desk overall and cost per minute (total costs for the period divided by total call duration minutes). This can be used to calculate the cost for individual calls and give a more accurate figure.
  - Cost per call by type. By evaluating the types of incidents with call duration, a more refined picture arises and gives an indication of which incident types tend to cost more to resolve. These should become possible targets when looking for improvements.
  - Percentage of customer or user updates conducted within target times, as defined in SLA targets.

Table 6.1 Survey techniques and tools

Technique/Tool	Advantages	Disadvantages
After-call survey Callers are asked to remain on the phone after the call and then asked to rate the service they were provided	High response rate because the caller is already on the phone Caller is surveyed immediately after the call so their experience is recent	People may feel pressured into taking the survey, resulting in a negative service experience The surveyor is seen as part of the service desk being surveyed, which may discourage open answers
Outbound telephone survey Customers and users who have previously used the service desk are contacted some time after their experience with the service desk	Higher response rate because the caller is interviewed directly Specific categories of user or customer can be targeted for feedback (e.g. people who requested a specific service, or people who experienced a disruption to a particular service)	This method could be seen as intrusive, if the call disrupts the user or customer from their work The survey is conducted some time after the user or customer used the service desk, so their perception may have changed
Personal interviews Customers and users are interviewed personally by the person doing the survey. This is especially effective for customers or users who use the service desk extensively or who have had a very negative experience	The interviewer is able to observe non-verbal signals as well as listening to what the user or customer is saying Users and customers feel a greater degree of personal attention and a sense that their answers are being taken seriously	Interviews are time-consuming for both the interviewer and the respondent Users and customers could turn the interviews into complaint sessions
Group interviews Customers and users are interviewed in small groups. This is good for gathering general impressions and for determining whether there is a need to change certain aspects of the service desk, e.g. service hours or location	A larger number of users and customers can be interviewed Questions are more generic and therefore more consistent between interviews	People may not express themselves freely in front of their peers or managers People's opinions can easily be changed by others in the group during the interview
Postal/email surveys Survey questionnaires are mailed to a target set of customers and users. They are asked to return their responses by email or post	Specific or all customers or users can be targeted Postal surveys can be anonymous, allowing people to express themselves more freely Email surveys are not anonymous, but can be created using automated forms that make it convenient and easy for the user to reply and increase the likelihood it will be completed	Postal surveys are labour-intensive to process The percentage of people responding to postal surveys tends to be small Misinterpretation of a question could affect the result
Online surveys Questionnaires are posted on a website and users and customers encouraged via email or links from a popular site to participate in the survey	The potential audience of these surveys is fairly large Respondents can complete the questionnaire in their own time The links on popular websites are good reminders without being intrusive	The type and percentage of respondents cannot be predicted

- Average time to review and close a resolved call.
- The number of calls broken down by time of day and day of week, combined with the average call-time metric, is critical in determining the number of staff required.

Further general details on metrics and how they should be used to drive forward service quality is included in *ITIL Continual Service Improvement*.

6.3.5.1 Customer/user satisfaction surveys

As well as tracking the 'hard' measures of the service desk's performance (via the metrics described above), it is also important to assess 'soft' measures, such as how well the customers and users feel their calls have been answered, whether they feel the service desk operator was courteous and professional, and whether they instilled confidence in the user.

This type of measure is best obtained from the users themselves. This can be done as part of a wider customer/user satisfaction survey covering all of IT or can be specifically targeted at the service desk issues alone.

One effective way of achieving the latter is through a call-back telephone survey, where an independent service desk operator or supervisor rings back a small percentage of users shortly after their incident has been resolved, to ask the specific questions needed.

Care should be taken to keep the number of questions to a minimum (five to six at the most) so that users will have the time to cooperate. Also survey questions should be designed so that the user or customer knows what area or subject questions are about and which incident or service they are referring to. The service desk must act on low satisfaction levels and any feedback received.

To allow adequate comparisons, the same percentage of calls should be selected in each period and they should be rigorously carried out despite any other time pressures.

Surveys are a complex and specialized area, requiring a good understanding of statistics and survey techniques. This publication will not attempt to provide an overview of all of these, but a summary of some of the more widely used techniques and tools is listed in Table 6.1.

6.3.5.2 Service desk environment

The environment where the service desk is to be located should be carefully chosen. Where possible, the following facilities should be provided:

- A location where the entire function can be positioned with sufficient natural light and overall space – to allow adequate desk and storage space, and room to move around if necessary
- Easy access to consoles, monitoring displays and message boards to quickly gain a picture of any key operating or service events, or issues that may be taking place
- A quiet environment with adequate acoustic control so that one telephone conversation is not disrupted by another
- Pleasant surroundings and comfortable furniture so as to lighten the mood (the service desk can be a very stressful place to work, so every little bit helps!)
- A separate rest-room and refreshment area nearby so that staff can take short breaks when necessary, without being away for too long.

Anecdote

One company found that there was a 'them and us' culture existing between the service desk and the other support teams. The third-line teams often believed themselves to be better than the service desk. Hiding the service desk away in an isolated room helped to reinforce this culture. The company found that creating an open-plan office with the service desk in the middle encouraged closer working and helped to break down these barriers. Additionally, having members of the support teams at various times act as service desk agents can further break down the barriers and increase respect for IT support capabilities.

6.3.6 Outsourcing the service desk

The decision to outsource is a strategic issue for senior managers – and is addressed in detail in *ITIL Service Strategy* and *ITIL Service Design*. Many of the guidelines in this section are not unique to the service desk and can be applied to any function, support area or service being outsourced (or out-tasked).

Regardless of the reasons for, or the extent of, the outsourcing contract, it is vital that the organization retains accountability for the activities and services provided by the service desk. The organization is ultimately accountable for the outcomes of the decision and must therefore determine what service the outsourcer provides, not the other way round.

If the outsourcing route is chosen, some safeguards are needed to ensure that the outsourced service desk works effectively and efficiently with the organization's other IT teams and departments and that end-to-end service management control is maintained (this is particularly important for organizations seeking ISO/IEC 20000 certification as overall management control has to be demonstrated). Some of these safeguards are set out below.

6.3.6.1 Common tools and processes

The service desk does not have responsibility for all the processes and procedures that it initiates. For example, a service request is received by the service desk but the request is fulfilled by the internal IT operational team.

If the service desk is outsourced, care must be taken that the tools are consistent with those still being used in the customer organization. Outsourcing is often seen as an opportunity to replace outdated or inadequate tools, only to find that there are severe integration problems between the new tool and the legacy tools and processes.

For this reason it is important to ensure that these issues are properly researched and the customer's requirements are adequately scoped and specified before the outsourcing contract. Service desk tools must not only support the outsourced service desk, they must also support the customer organization's processes and business requirements.

Ideally the outsourced desk should use the same tools and processes (or, as a minimum, interfacing tools and processes) to allow smooth process flow between the service desk and second- and third-line support groups.

In addition, the outsourced service desk should have access to:

- All incident records and information
- Problem records and information
- Known error data
- Change schedule

- Sources of internal knowledge (especially technical or application experts)
- SKMS
- CMS
- Alerts from monitoring tools.

It is often a challenge integrating processes and tools in a less mature organization with those in a more mature organization. A common but incorrect assumption is that the maturity of the one organization will somehow result in higher maturity in the other. Active involvement to ensure alignment of processes and tools is essential to a smooth transition and ongoing management of services between the internal and external organizations. In fact, if this is not directly addressed, it could result in the failure of the contract.

It is also often incorrectly assumed that the proof of service management quality and maturity in an external outsource partner can be guaranteed by stating requirements in the procurement process for 'ITIL conformance' and/or 'ISO/IEC 20000 certification'. These statements may indicate that a potential supplier uses the ITIL framework in its delivery of services to customers, or that they have achieved standards certification for their internal practices, but it is equally important to have the enabling technology in place and being used that demonstrates a service provider's capability to manage services and interface to internal practices harmoniously. There is no standard of compliance that ensures this and so procurement efforts should include specific queries to satisfy this requirement. More information on outsource provider acquisition can be found in *ITIL Service Design*.

6.3.6.2 SLA targets

The SLA targets for overall incident handling and resolution times need to be agreed with the customers and between all teams and departments – and OLA/UC targets need to be coordinated and agreed with individual support groups so that they underpin and support the SLA targets.

Examples of these can be seen in section 4.2.5.4 and in *ITIL Service Design*.

6.3.6.3 Good communications

The lines of communication between the outsourced service desk and the other support groups need to work very effectively. This can be helped by some or all of the following steps:

- Close physical co-location
- Regular liaison/review meetings
- Cross-training tutorials between the teams and departments
- Partnership arrangements when staff from both organizations are used jointly to staff the desk
- Communication plans and performance targets are documented in a consistent manner in OLAs and UCs.

In cases where the service desk is located offshore, not all of these measures will be possible. However, the need for training and communication of the service desk staff is still critical, even more so in cases where there are language and cultural differences.

As a rule, outsourcing companies who offer offshore service desk solutions should take the following into account:

- Training programmes focused on cultural understanding of the customer market
- Language skills – especially the understanding of idiomatic use of the language in the customer market. This is not so that the service desk staff sound like natives of the customer's country (that type of insincerity is very quickly detected by customers), but to facilitate better understanding of the customer and the better to appreciate their priorities
- Regular visits by representatives of the customer organization to provide training and appropriate feedback directly to the service desk management and staff
- Training in the use of the customer organizations tools and methods of work. This is especially effective if similar training materials are presented by the same instructors as those used by the customer organization.

6.3.6.4 Ownership of data

Clear ownership of the data collected by the outsourced service desk must be established. Ownership of all data relative to users, customers, affected CIs, services, incidents, service requests, changes etc. must remain with the organization that is outsourcing the activity, but both organizations will require access to it.

Data that is related specifically to performance of employees of the outsourcing company will remain the property of that company, which is often legally prevented from sharing the data with the customer organization. This may also be true of other data that is used purely for internal management of the service desk, such as head count, optimization activities, service desk cost information etc.

All reporting requirements and issues around ownership of data must be specified in the UC with the company providing the outsourcing service.

6.4 TECHNICAL MANAGEMENT FUNCTION

Technical management refers to the groups, departments or teams that provide technical expertise and overall management of the IT infrastructure.

6.4.1 Technical management role

Technical management plays a dual role:

- It is the custodian of technical knowledge and expertise related to managing the IT infrastructure. In this role, technical management ensures that the knowledge required to design, test, manage and improve IT services is identified, developed and refined.
- It provides the actual resources to support the service lifecycle. In this role technical management ensures that resources are effectively trained and deployed to design, build, transition, operate and improve the technology required to deliver and support IT services.

By performing these two roles, technical management is able to ensure that the organization has access to the right type and level of human resources to manage technology and thus to meet business objectives. Defining the requirements for these roles starts in service strategy and is expanded in service design, validated in service transition and refined in CSI (see other ITIL publications in this series).

Part of this role is also to ensure a balance between the skill level, utilization and cost of these resources. For example, hiring a top-level resource at the higher end of the salary scale and then only using that skill for 10% of the time is not effective.

A better technical management strategy would be to identify the times that the skill is needed and then hire a contractor for only those tasks.

Another strategy in larger organizations is to leverage specialist staff out of central pools so that specialists can be well utilized and provide an economy of scale to the organization and minimize the need to hire in contractors. Specialized skills should be identified among resources in the IT organization, and then leveraged for specific needs as they arise, analogous to a special tactical unit, whose members also perform regular duties but who are assigned to tasks needing their specialized skills. This type of resource utilization is particularly useful both for project teams and problem resolution.

An additional but very important role played by technical management is to provide guidance to IT operations about how best to carry out the ongoing operational management of technology. This role is partly carried out during the service design process, but it is also a part of everyday communication with IT operations management as they seek to achieve stability and optimum performance.

The objectives, activities and structures that enable technical management to perform these roles effectively are discussed below.

6.4.2 Technical management objectives

The objectives of technical management are to help plan, implement and maintain a stable technical infrastructure to support the organization's business processes through:

- Well designed and highly resilient, cost-effective technical topology
- The use of adequate technical skills to maintain the technical infrastructure in optimum condition
- Swift use of technical skills to speedily diagnose and resolve any technical failures that do occur.

6.4.3 Generic technical management activities

Technical management is involved in two types of activity:

- Activities that are generic to the technical management function as a whole. These are

discussed in this section as they enable technical management to execute its role.

- A set of discrete activities and processes that are performed by all three functions of technical, application and IT operations management. These are covered in Chapter 5.

Generic technical management activities are highlighted as follows:

- Identifying the knowledge and expertise required to manage and operate the IT infrastructure and to deliver IT services. This process starts during the service strategy stage, is expanded in detail in service design and is executed in service operation. Ongoing assessment and updating of these skills is done during CSI.
- Documenting the skills that exist in the organization, as well as those skills that need to be developed. This will include the development of skills inventories and the performance of training needs analyses.
- Initiating training programmes to develop and refine the skills in the appropriate technical resources and maintaining training records for all technical resources.
- Designing and delivering training for users, the service desk and other groups. Although training requirements must be defined in service design, they are executed in service operation. Where technical management does not deliver training, it is responsible for identifying organizations that can provide it.
- Recruiting or contracting resources with skills that cannot be developed internally, or where there are insufficient people to perform the required technical management activities.
- Procuring skills for specific activities where the required skills are not available internally or in the open market, or where it is more cost-efficient to do so.
- Defining the standards to be used in the design of new architectures and participation in the definition of technology architectures during the service strategy and design stages.
- Researching and developing solutions that can help expand the service portfolio or which can be used to simplify or automate IT operations, reduce costs or increase levels of IT service.
- Participating in the design and development of new services. Technical management will

contribute to the design of the technical architecture and performance standards for IT services. In addition, it will also be responsible for specifying the operational activities required to manage the IT infrastructure on an ongoing basis.

■ Participating in projects, not only during service design and service transition, but also for CSI or operational projects, such as operating system upgrades, server consolidation projects or physical moves.

■ Engineering availability and capacity management for IT services to meet the levels of service required by the business. This means that modelling and workload forecasting are often done with technical management resources.

■ Assessing risk, identifying critical service and system dependencies and defining and implementing countermeasures.

■ Designing and performing tests for the functionality, performance and manageability of IT services to support service transition activities.

■ Managing suppliers – many technical management departments or groups are the only ones who know exactly what is required of a supplier and how to measure and manage them. For this reason, many organizations rely on technical management departments to manage contracts with suppliers of specific CIs. If this is the case, it is important to ensure that these relationships are managed as part of the SLM and supplier management processes.

■ Defining and managing event management standards and tools. Technical management should also test event mechanisms during service transition and will also monitor and respond to many categories of events during service operation.

■ Participating in resolution of incidents. Technical management departments or groups are integral to the performance of incident management. They receive incidents through functional escalation and provide second- and higher-level support. They are also involved in maintaining categories and defining the escalation procedures that are executed in incident management.

■ Participating in resolution of problems. Technical management as a function provides resources that contribute to the execution of the problem management process. It provides technical expertise and knowledge that is used to diagnose and resolve problems. It also maintains relationships with the suppliers and their support teams that are used to escalate and follow up on technical issues, changes, incidents and problems.

■ Defining coding systems that are used in incident and problem management (e.g. incident categories).

■ Supporting problem management in validating and maintaining the KEDB.

■ Supporting the change management process where reliance on the technical knowledge and expertise may be needed to evaluate changes.

■ Assisting with the deployment of releases.

■ Providing information for, and operationally maintaining, the CMS and its data. This will be done in cooperation with application management to ensure that the correct CI attributes and relationships are created from the deployment of services and the ongoing maintenance over the life of CIs.

■ Identifying opportunities for improvement. Technical management is involved in the CSI activities, particularly in highlighting areas for improvement and then in helping to evaluate alternative solutions.

■ Ensuring that all system and operating documentation is up to date and properly utilized. This includes ensuring that all management, administration and user manuals are up to date and complete and that technical staff are familiar with their contents.

■ Updating and maintaining data used for reporting on technical and service capabilities, e.g. capacity and performance management, availability management, problem management etc.

■ Assisting financial management for IT services to identify the cost of technology and IT human resources used to manage IT services.

■ Defining the operational activities performed as part of IT operations management. Many technical management departments, groups or teams also perform the operational activities as part of an organization's IT operations management function.

6.4.4 Technical management organization

Technical management is not normally provided by a single department or group. One or more technical support teams or departments will be needed to provide technical management and support for the IT infrastructure. In all but the smallest organizations, where a single combined team or department may suffice, separate teams or departments will be needed for each type of infrastructure being used.

Technical management consists of a number of technological areas. Each of these requires a specific set of skills to manage and operate it. Some skill sets are related and can be performed by generalists, whereas others are specific to a component, system or platform.

The primary criterion of technical management organizational structure is that of specialization or division of labour. The principle is that people are grouped according to their technical skill sets, and that these skill sets are determined by the technology that needs to be managed.

Section 6.10 covers the organizational aspects of technical management in more detail, but this list provides some examples of typical technical management teams or departments:

- Mainframe team or department – if one or more mainframe types are still being used by the organization
- Server team or department – often split again by technology types (e.g. Unix server, Wintel server)
- Storage team or department, responsible for the management of all data storage devices, storage area networks (SANs) and media
- Network support team or department, looking after the organization's internal WANs/LANs and managing any external network suppliers
- Virtualization team or department, responsible for designing, implementing, tuning and administering virtualized processing environments
- Desktop team or department, responsible for all installed desktop equipment
- Database team or department, responsible for the creation, maintenance and support of the organization's databases

- Middleware team or department, responsible for the integration, testing and maintenance of all middleware in use in the organization
- Directory services team or department, responsible for maintaining access and rights to service elements in the infrastructure
- Internet or web team or department, responsible for managing the availability and security of access to servers and content by external customers, users and partners
- Messaging team or department, responsible for email services
- IP-based telephony team or department.

6.4.5 Technical design and technical maintenance and support

Technical management consists of specialist technical architects and designers (who are primarily involved during service design) and specialist maintenance and support staff (who are primarily involved during service operation).

In this publication, they are viewed as being part of the same function, but many organizations see them as two separate teams or even departments. The problem with this approach is that good design needs input from the people who are required to manage the solution – and good operation requires involvement from the people who designed the solution.

The problems that need to be overcome are similar to those faced in managing the application lifecycle (see section 6.6 for a more detailed discussion). The solution will include the following elements:

- Support staff should be involved during the design or architecture of a solution. Design staff should be involved in setting maintenance objectives and resolving support issues.
- A change in how both design and support staff are measured. Designers should be held accountable for their portion of the design flaws that create operational outages. Support staff should be held accountable for their contribution to the technical architecture.

6.4.6 Measuring technical management performance

Performance metrics for technical management will largely depend on which technology is being managed, but some generic metrics are listed here.

6.4.6.1 Measurement of agreed outputs

These could include:

- Contribution to achievement of services to the business. Although many of the technical management teams will not be in direct contact with the business, the technology they manage impacts the business. Metrics should reflect both negative (incidents traced to their team) and positive (system performance and availability) contributions
- Transaction rates and availability for critical business transactions
- Service desk training
- Recording problem resolutions into the KEDB
- User measures of the quality of outputs as defined in the SLAs
- Installation and configuration of components under their control.

6.4.6.2 Process metrics

Technical management teams execute many service management process activities. Their ability to do so will be measured as part of the process metrics where appropriate (see section on each process for more details). Examples include:

- Response time to events and event completion rates
- Incident resolution times for second- and third-line support
- Problem resolution statistics
- Number of escalations and reason for those escalations
- Number of changes implemented and backed out
- Number of unauthorized changes detected
- Number of releases deployed, total and successful
- Security issues detected and resolved
- Actual resource utilization, transaction volumes and demand loads against capacity plan forecasts (where the team has contributed to the development of the plan)

- Tracking against service improvement plans (SIPs)
- Costs expended for service improvements versus the planned service improvement budget.

6.4.6.3 Technology performance

These metrics are based on service design specifications and technical performance standards set by vendors, and will typically be contained in OLAs or SOPs. Actual metrics will vary by technology, but are likely to include:

- Utilization rates (e.g. memory or processor for server, bandwidth for networks etc.)
- Availability (of systems, network, devices etc.), which is helpful for measuring team or system performance, but is not to be confused with service availability – which requires the ability to measure the overall availability of the service and may use the availability figures for a number of individual systems or components
- Accuracy of information and data that is being presented
- Performance (e.g. response times, queuing rates etc.).

6.4.6.4 Mean time between failures of specified equipment

This metric is used to ensure that good purchasing decisions are being made and, when compared with maintenance schedules, whether the equipment is being properly maintained.

6.4.6.5 Measurement of maintenance activity

Measurement includes:

- Maintenance performed per schedule
- Number of maintenance windows exceeded
- Maintenance objectives achieved (number and percentage).

6.4.6.6 Training and skills development

These metrics ensure that staff have the skills and training to manage the technology that is under their control, and will also identify areas where training is still required. Metrics include:

- Achieved skills performance levels
- Number of calls and escalations to third-party or other internal subject matter experts for additional help and support

■ Percentage of incidents caused by skills issues.

6.4.7 Technical management documentation

Technical management is involved in drafting and maintaining several documents as part of other processes (e.g. capacity planning, change management, problem management etc.). These documents are discussed in some detail in the relevant process descriptions.

However, there are some documents that are specific to the technical management groups or teams who will document management and control for documents relating to the technology under their control. Technical management documentation includes the following.

6.4.7.1 Technical documentation

The sourcing and maintenance of technical documentation for all CIs is the responsibility of technical management. These include:

■ Technical manuals
■ Management and administration manuals
■ User manuals for CIs. These will typically exclude application user manuals, which are maintained by application management.

6.4.7.2 Maintenance schedules

These schedules are drawn up and agreed during the service design stage related to availability and capacity management, but they are essentially the property of the various technical management departments, groups or teams. This is because they have the technical expertise for specific technologies and are most likely to know what is needed to keep them in working order.

For more details on the definition of maintenance schedules and service maintenance objectives, refer to *ITIL Service Design*.

6.4.7.3 Skills inventory

A skills inventory is a system or tool that identifies the skills and skill levels required to deliver and support IT services and also the individuals who possess those skills. Skills inventories are most effective if they are aligned with processes, architectures and performance standards.

In addition, skills inventories should identify the training available to cultivate each skill should existing staff leave the organization.

Skills inventories can also be used as part of the service portfolio to assess whether a new service can be delivered with existing staff and skill sets, or whether an investment needs to be made in new staff or training. Skills inventories can therefore contribute significantly to capacity planning.

The definition and maintenance of skills inventories requires a good interface with human resource processes and tools in the organization.

6.5 IT OPERATIONS MANAGEMENT FUNCTION

In business, the term 'operations management' is used to mean the department, group or team of people responsible for performing the organization's day-to-day operational activities – such as running the production line in a manufacturing environment or managing the distribution centres and fleet movements within a logistics organization.

Operations management generally has the following characteristics:

■ There is work to ensure that a device, system or process is actually running or working (as opposed to strategy or planning)
■ This is where plans are turned into actions
■ The focus is on daily or shorter-term activities, although it should be noted that these activities will generally be performed and repeated over a relatively long period (as opposed to one-off project-type activities)
■ These activities are executed by specialized technical staff, who often have to undergo technical training to learn how to perform each activity
■ There is a focus on building repeatable, consistent actions that – if repeated frequently enough at the right level of quality – will ensure the success of the operation
■ This is where the actual value of the organization is delivered and measured
■ There is a dependency on investment in equipment or human resources or both
■ The value generated must exceed the cost of the investment and all other organizational

overheads (such as management and marketing costs) if the business is to succeed.

In a similar way, IT operations management can be defined as the function responsible for the ongoing management and maintenance of an organization's IT infrastructure to ensure delivery of the agreed level of IT services to the business.

IT operations can be defined as the set of activities involved in the day-to-day running of the IT infrastructure for the purpose of delivering IT services at agreed levels to meet stated business objectives.

6.5.1 IT operations management role

The role of IT operations management is to execute the ongoing activities and procedures required to manage and maintain the IT infrastructure so as to deliver and support IT services at the agreed levels. These activities have already been described in Chapter 5, but are summarized here for completeness.

6.5.1.1 IT operations control

IT operations control oversees the execution and monitoring of the operational activities and events in the IT infrastructure. This can be done with the help of an operations bridge or network operations centre. In addition to executing routine tasks from all technical areas, IT operations control also performs the following specific tasks:

- Console management/operations bridge, which refers to defining central observation and monitoring capability and then using those consoles to exercise event management, monitoring and control activities
- Job scheduling, or the management of routine batch jobs or scripts
- Backup and restore on behalf of all technical and application management teams and departments and often on behalf of users
- Print and output management for the collation and distribution of all centralized printing or electronic output
- Performance of maintenance activities on behalf of technical or application management teams or departments.

6.5.1.2 Facilities management

Facilities management refers to the management of the physical IT environment, typically a data centre or computer rooms and recovery sites together with all the power and cooling equipment. Facilities management also includes the coordination of large-scale consolidation projects, e.g. data centre consolidation or server consolidation projects. In some cases the management of a data centre is outsourced, in which case facilities management refers to the management of the outsourcing contract.

As with many ITSM processes and functions, IT operations management plays a dual role:

- IT operations management is responsible for executing the activities and performance standards defined during service design and tested during service transition. In this sense the role of IT operations is primarily to maintain the status quo. The stability of the IT infrastructure and consistency of IT services is a primary concern of IT operations. Even operational improvements are aimed at finding simpler and better ways of doing the same thing.
- At the same time, IT operations is part of the process of adding value to the different lines of business and to support the value network (see *ITIL Service Strategy*). The ability of the business to meet its objectives and to remain competitive depends on the output and reliability of the day-to-day operation of IT. As such, IT operations management must be able to continually adapt to business requirements and demand. The business does not care that IT operations complied with a standard procedure or that a server performed optimally. As business demand and requirements change, IT operations management must be able to keep pace with them, often challenging the status quo.

IT operations must achieve a balance between these roles, which will require the following:

- An understanding of how technology is used to provide IT services
- An understanding of the relative importance and impact of those services on the business
- Procedures and manuals that outline the role of IT operations in both the management of technology and the delivery of IT services

- A clearly differentiated set of metrics to report to the business on the achievement of service objectives; and to report to IT managers on the efficiency and effectiveness of IT operations
- All IT operations staff understand exactly how the performance of the technology affects the delivery of IT services
- A cost strategy aimed at balancing the requirements of different business units with the cost savings available through optimization of existing technology or investment in new technology
- A value- rather than cost-based ROI strategy.

6.5.2 IT operations management objectives

The objectives of IT operations management include:

- Maintenance of the status quo to achieve stability of the organization's day-to-day processes and activities
- Regular scrutiny and improvements to achieve improved service at reduced costs, while maintaining stability
- Swift application of operational skills to diagnose and resolve any IT operations failures that occur.

6.5.3 IT operations management organization

Figure 6.1 illustrated that IT operations management is seen as a function in its own right but that, in many cases, staff from technical and application management groups form part of this function.

This means that some technical and application management departments or groups will manage and execute their own operational activities. Others will delegate these activities to a dedicated IT operations department.

There is no single method for assigning activities, as it depends on the maturity and stability of the infrastructure being managed. For example, technical and application management areas that are fairly new and unstable tend to manage their own operations. Groups where the technology or application is stable, mature and well understood tend to have standardized their operations

more and will therefore feel more comfortable delegating these activities.

Some options of how to structure IT operations are discussed in detail in section 6.10.

6.5.4 Measuring IT operations management performance

IT operations management performance is measured in terms of its effective execution of specified activities and procedures, as well as its execution of process activities. Examples of key metrics used to measure the performance of the IT operations function can include:

- Percentage of scheduled jobs completed successfully on time
- Number of exceptions to scheduled activities and jobs
- Number of data or system restores required
- Equipment installation statistics, including number of items installed by type, successful installations etc.
- Process metrics. IT operations management executes many service management process activities. Their ability to do so will be measured as part of the process metrics where appropriate (see section on each process for more details). Examples include:
  - Response time to events
  - Incident resolution times for incidents
  - Number of security-related incidents
  - Number of capacity-related incidents
  - Number of escalations and reason for those escalations
  - Number of changes implemented and backed out
  - Number of unauthorized changes detected
  - Number of releases deployed, total and successful
  - Tracking against SIPs
  - Expenditure against budget
- If maintenance activities have been delegated, then metrics related to these activities will also be appropriate:
  - Maintenance performed per schedule
  - Number of maintenance windows exceeded
  - Maintenance objectives achieved (number and percentage)
- Metrics related to facilities management are extensive, but typically include:

- Costs versus budget related to maintenance, construction, security, shipping etc.
- Incidents related to the building, e.g. repairs needed to the facility
- Reports on access to the facility
- Thresholds and monitoring results for environmental factors such as heating and air conditioning
- Number of security events and incidents and their resolution
- Power usage statistics, especially as related to changes in layout and environmental conditioning strategies
- Events or incidents related to shipping and distribution.

6.5.5 IT operations management documentation

A number of documents are produced and used during IT operations management. This list is a summary of some of the most important and does not include reports that are produced by IT operations management on behalf of other processes or functions.

6.5.5.1 Standard operating procedures

The SOPs are a set of documents containing detailed instructions and activity schedules for every IT operations management team, department or group.

These documents represent the routine work that needs to be done for every device, system or procedure. They also outline the procedures to be followed if an exception is detected or if a change is required. SOPs should also include specific security administration procedures covering all operational aspects of service, system, data and physical security that need to be performed.

SOP documents could also be used to define standard levels of performance for devices or procedures. In some organizations the SOP documents are referred to in the OLA. Instead of listing detailed performance measures in the OLA, a clause is inserted to refer to the performance standards in the SOP and how these will be measured and reported.

6.5.5.2 Operations logs

Any activity that is conducted as part of IT operations should be recorded for a number of reasons, including:

- They can be used to confirm the successful completion of specific jobs or activities
- They can be used to confirm that an IT service was delivered as agreed
- They can be used by problem management to research the root cause of incidents
- They are the basis for reports on the performance of the IT operations management teams and departments.

The format of these logs is as varied as the number of systems and operations management teams or departments. Examples of operations logs include the following:

- Operating system logs stored on each device
- Application activity logs stored in a file on the application server
- Event logs stored on the monitoring tool server
- Utilization logs for key devices
- Physical access logs recording who accessed secure buildings and when
- Shift turnover logs as a record of formal handover between one shift and the next
- Handwritten logs of actions performed by operators. This must be in a formal logbook or binder, numbered and stored in a secure environment. Checks should ensure that pages are not removed.

A policy needs to be established as part of the SOPs to state how long logs need to be kept, how they are archived and when they can be deleted. These policies will take into account statutory and compliance requirements. Policies should also specify the parameters for adequate storage and backup strategies to store and retrieve log files.

6.5.5.3 Shift schedules and reports

Shift schedules are documents that outline the exact activities that need to be carried out during the shift. They will also list all dependencies and activity sequences. There will probably be more than one shift schedule, where each team will have a version for its own systems. It is important that all schedules are coordinated before the start of the shift. This is usually done by a person who is specialized in shift scheduling, with the help of scheduling tools.

A shift schedule could consist of a number of routine items that are included in the SOP. In this case the items could simply be listed briefly with a reference to the section or page in the SOP.

Most shift schedules take the form of a checklist where operators can check off the item as it is completed, together with the time of completion. This makes it easy to see the progress of activities and also helps to identify any potential issues where jobs are taking too long.

Shift reports are a form of operations log, but have additional functions:

■ To record major events and actions that occurred during the shift
■ To form part of the handover between shift leaders
■ To report any exceptions to service maintenance objectives
■ To identify any uncompleted activity that could result in degraded performance on any service during the next service hours.

6.5.5.4 Operations schedule

The operations schedules are similar to shift schedules but cover all aspects of IT operations at a high level. This schedule will include reviews of forward schedule of changes, an overview of all planned change actions taking place, maintenance, routine jobs and additional work, together with information about upcoming business or vendor events. The operations schedule is used as the basis for the daily operations meeting and is the master reference for all IT operations managers to track progress and detect exceptions.

6.6 APPLICATION MANAGEMENT FUNCTION

Application management is responsible for managing applications throughout their lifecycle. This differs from application development as application management covers the entire ongoing lifecycle of an application, including requirements, design, build, deploy, operate and optimize. Application development is mainly concerned with the one-time activities for requirements, design and build of applications (see section 6.6.6.1 for

details on key differences between application management and application development).

The application management function is performed by any department, group or team involved in managing and supporting operational applications. Application management also plays an important role in the design, testing and improvement of applications that form part of IT services. As such, it may be involved in development projects, but is not usually the same as the applications development teams.

6.6.1 Application management roles

Application management is to applications what technical management is to the IT infrastructure. Application management activities are performed in all applications, whether purchased or developed in-house. One of the key decisions that they contribute to is the decision of whether to buy an application or build it (this is discussed in detail in *ITIL Service Design*). Once that decision is made, application management will have several roles:

■ It is the custodian of technical knowledge and expertise related to managing applications. In this role application management, working together with technical management, ensures that the knowledge required to design, test, manage and improve IT services is identified, developed and refined.
■ It provides the actual resources to support the service lifecycle. In this role, application management ensures that resources are effectively trained and deployed to design, build, transition, operate and improve the technology required to deliver and support IT services.

By performing these roles, application management is able to ensure that the organization has access to the right type and level of human resources to manage applications and thus to meet business objectives. This starts in service strategy and is expanded in service design, tested in service transition and refined in CSI (see other ITIL publications in this series). A key objective is to ensure a balance between the skill level and the cost of these resources.

Application management also performs other specific roles:

- Providing guidance to IT operations about how best to carry out the ongoing operational management of applications. This role is partly carried out during the service design process, but it is also a part of everyday communication with IT operations management as they seek to achieve stability and optimum performance.
- The integration of the application management lifecycle into the service lifecycle. This is discussed below.

The objectives, activities and structures that enable application management to play these roles effectively are discussed below.

6.6.2 Application management objectives

The objectives of application management are to support the organization's business processes by helping to identify functional and manageability requirements for application software, and then to assist in the design and deployment of those applications and the ongoing support and improvement of those applications.

These objectives are achieved through:

- Applications that are well designed, resilient and cost-effective
- Ensuring that the required functionality is available to achieve the required business outcome
- The organization of adequate technical skills to maintain operational applications in optimum condition
- Swift use of technical skills to speedily diagnose and resolve any technical failures that do occur.

6.6.3 Application management principles

6.6.3.1 Build or buy?

One of the key decisions in application management is whether to buy an application that supports the required functionality, or whether to build the application specifically for the organization's requirements. These decisions are often made by a chief technical officer (CTO) or steering committee, but they are dependent on information from a number of sources. These are discussed in detail in *ITIL Service Design*, but are summarized here from an application management function perspective.

Application management will assist in this decision during service design as follows:

- Application sizing and workload forecasts
- Specification of manageability requirements
- Identification of ongoing operational costs
- Data access requirements for reporting or integration into other applications
- Investigating to what extent the required functionality can be met by existing tools – and how much customization will be required to achieve this
- Estimating the cost of customization
- Identifying what skills will be required to support the solution (e.g. if an application is purchased, will it require a new set of employees, or can existing employees be trained to support it?)
- Administration requirements
- Security requirements.

If the decision is to build the application, a further decision needs to be made on whether the development will be outsourced or built using employees. This is detailed in *ITIL Service Strategy* and *ITIL Service Design*, but there are some important considerations affecting service operation, for example:

- How will manageability requirements be specified and agreed (e.g. designing application and transaction monitoring)? These are sometimes forgotten when the operational teams or departments are not represented in the project.
- What are the acceptance criteria for operational performance; how and where will the solution be tested and who will perform the tests?
- Who will own and manage the definitive media library (DML) for that application?
- Who will design and maintain the operational management and administration scripts for these applications?
- Who is responsible for environment set-up and owning and maintaining the different infrastructure components?
- How will the solution be instrumented so that it is capable of generating the required events?

6.6.3.2 Operational models

An operational model is the specification of the operational environment in which the application will eventually run when it goes live. This will be used during testing and transition activities to simulate and evaluate the live environment. It is a way of ensuring that the application can be sized correctly and the required environmental conditions can be documented and understood by all. The operational model should be defined and used in testing during the service design and service transition stages, respectively (see *ITIL Service Design* and *ITIL Service Transition*).

6.6.4 Application management lifecycle

The lifecycle followed to develop and manage applications has been referred to by many names, including the software lifecycle (SLC) and software development lifecycle (SDLC). These are generally used by applications development teams and their project managers to define their involvement in designing, building, testing, deploying and supporting applications. Examples of these approaches are structured systems analysis and design methodology (SSADM), dynamic systems development method (DSDM), rapid application development (RAD) etc.

ITIL is primarily interested in the overall management of applications as part of IT services, whether they are developed in-house or purchased from a third party. For this reason, the term application management lifecycle has been used, as it implies a more holistic view (see Figure 6.5).

This should not replace the SDLC, which is still a valid approach used by developers, especially by third-party software companies. However, it does mean that there should be greater alignment between the development view of applications and the ongoing lifecycle management of those applications.

This is more difficult in large-scale purchased applications, such as email, because the developers do not typically interact individually with their application's users. However, the basic lifecycle still holds true in that the application needs requirements, design, customization, operation and deployment. Optimization is achieved through better management, improvements to customization and upgrades.

The application management lifecycle is illustrated in Figure 6.5.

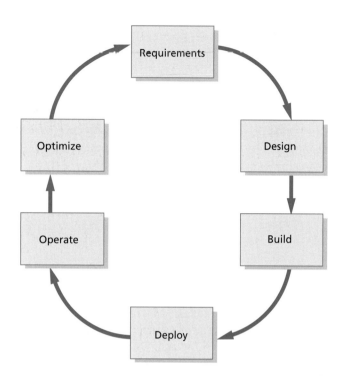

Figure 6.5 Application management lifecycle

ITSM processes and applications development processes have to be aligned as part of the overall strategy of delivering IT services in support of the business.

Applications development and operations are part of the same overall lifecycle and both should be involved at all stages, although their level of involvement will vary depending on the stage of the lifecycle.

6.6.4.1 Requirements

This is the stage during which the requirements for a new application are gathered, based on the business needs of the organization. This stage is active primarily during the service design stage of the service lifecycle.

There are six types of requirements for any application, whether being developed in-house, outsourced or purchased:

- **Functional requirements** These are specifically required to support a particular business function.
- **Manageability requirements** Looked at from a service management perspective, these

Relationship between the application management lifecycle and the service lifecycle

The application management lifecycle should not be seen as an alternative to the service lifecycle. Applications are part of services and have to be managed as such. Nevertheless, applications are a unique blend of technology and functionality and this requires a specialized focus at each stage of the service lifecycle.

Each stage of the application management lifecycle has its own specific set of objectives, activities, deliverables and dedicated teams. Each stage also has a clear responsibility to ensure that their outputs match up to the specific objectives of the service lifecycle. Different aspects of application management are covered in detail in each of the ITIL publications, as follows:

- *ITIL Service Strategy* Defines the overall architecture of applications and infrastructure. This will include defining the criteria for developing in-house, outsourcing development, or purchasing and customizing applications. Service strategy will also help define the service portfolio (including applications), which also includes information about the ROI of applications and the services they support. Thus high-level requirements are set during this stage.
- *ITIL Service Design* Helps to establish requirements for functionality and manageability of applications and works with development teams to ensure that they meet these objectives. Service design covers most of the requirements stage and is involved during the build stage of the application management lifecycle.
- *ITIL Service Transition* Application development and management teams are involved in testing and validating what has been built and deploying it operationally.
- *ITIL Service Operation* This covers the operate stage of the application management lifecycle. These processes and structures are discussed in detail in this publication.
- *ITIL Continual Service Improvement* Covers the optimize stage of the application management lifecycle. CSI measures the quality and relevance of applications in operation and provides recommendations on how to improve applications if there is a clear ROI for doing so.

requirements address the need for a responsive, available and secure service, and deal with issues such as deployment, operations, system management and security.

- **Usability requirements** These address the needs of the end user, and result in features of the system that facilitate its ease of use.
- **Architectural requirements** These are needed if a change to existing architecture standards is required.
- **Interface requirements** These are needed where there are dependencies between existing applications or tools and the new application.
- **Service level requirements** These specify how the service should perform, the quality of its output and any other qualitative aspects measured by the user or customer.

6.6.4.2 Design

This is the stage during which requirements are translated into specifications. Design includes the design of the application itself, and the design of the environment, or operational model that the application has to run on. Architectural considerations are the most important aspect of this stage, because they can impact on the structure and content of both application and operational model. Architectural considerations for the application (design of the application architecture) and architectural considerations for the operation model (design of the system architecture) are strongly related and need to be aligned.

In the case of purchased software, most organizations will not be allowed direct input to the design of the software (which has already been built). However, it is important that application management is able to provide feedback to the software vendor about the functionality, manageability and performance of the software. This will, in turn, be taken up by the software vendor as part of the continual improvement of the software.

Part of the evaluation process for purchased software should include an evaluation of whether the vendor is responsive to such feedback. At the same time, they should ensure that there is a balance between being responsive and changing their software so much that it is disruptive or that it changes some basic functionality.

Design for purchased software will also include the design of any customization that is required. Of special importance here is an evaluation of whether future versions of the software will support the customization.

6.6.4.3 Build

In the build stage, both the application and the operational model are made ready for deployment. Application components are coded or acquired, integrated and tested.

Please note that 'test' is not a separate stage in the lifecycle, even though it is a discrete activity, and even though tests are conducted independently of both the development and operational activities. Without the build and deploy stages, there would be nothing to test and, without testing, there would be no control over what is developed and deployed.

Testing is an integral component of both the build and deploy stages as a validation of the activity and output of those stages – even if it uses different environments and staff. Testing in the build stage focuses on whether the application meets its functionality and manageability specifications. Often the distinction is made between a development and test environment. The test environment allows for testing the combination of application and operational model. Testing is covered in *ITIL Service Transition*.

For purchased software, this will involve the actual purchase of the application, any required middleware and the related hardware and networking equipment. Any customization that is required will need to be done here, as will the creation of tables, categories etc. that will be used. This is often done as a pilot implementation by the relevant application management team or department.

6.6.4.4 Deploy

In this stage, both the operational model and the application are deployed. The operational model is incorporated in the existing IT environment and the application is installed on top of the operational model, using the release and deployment management process described in *ITIL Service Transition*.

Testing also takes place during this stage, although here the emphasis is on ensuring that

the deployment process and mechanisms work effectively, e.g. testing whether the application still functions to specification after it has been downloaded and installed. This is known as early life support (ELS) and covers specialized support for a new or changed IT service for a period of time after it is released. Support activities during this period can include review of KPIs, service levels and monitoring thresholds, and provision of additional resources for incident and problem management. ELS is covered in detail in *ITIL Service Transition*.

6.6.4.5 Operate

In the operate stage, the IT services organization operates the application as part of delivering a service required by the business. The performance of the application in relation to the overall service is measured continually against the service levels and key business drivers. It is important to distinguish that applications themselves do not equate to a service. It is common in many organizations to refer to applications as 'services'; however, applications are but one component of many needed to provide a business service.

The operate stage is not exclusive to applications and is discussed throughout this publication, with a more detailed list of activities given in section 6.6.5.

6.6.4.6 Optimize

In the optimize stage, the results of the service level performance measurements are measured, analysed and acted upon. Possible improvements are discussed and developments initiated if necessary. The two main strategies in this stage are to maintain and/or improve the service levels and to lower cost. This could lead to iteration in the lifecycle or to justified retirement of an application.

One important thing to remember about the application management lifecycle is that, because it is circular, the same application can reside in different stages of the lifecycle at the same time. For example, when the next version of an application is being designed, and the current version is being deployed, the previous version might still be in operation in parts of an organization. This obviously requires strong version, configuration and release control.

Particular stages might take longer or seem more significant than others, but they are all crucial. Every application must go through all of them at least once and, because of the circular nature of the lifecycle, will go through some more than once.

This approach also supports iterative development approaches, where software is continually being developed in incremental steps. Each step follows the lifecycle and the application is built in increments, using business priorities as a driver.

Good communication is the key as an application works its way through the stages of the lifecycle. It is critical that high-quality information is passed along by those handling the application in one stage of its existence to those handling it in the next stage. It is also important that an organization monitors the quality of the application management lifecycle. Changes in the lifecycle, for example in the way an organization passes information between the different stages, will affect its quality. Understanding the characteristics of every stage in the application management lifecycle is crucial to improving the quality of the whole. Methods and tools used in one stage might have an impact on others, while optimization of one stage might sub-optimize the whole.

6.6.5 Application management generic activities

While most application management teams or departments are dedicated to specific applications or sets of applications, there are a number of activities which they have in common. These include:

- Identifying the knowledge and expertise required to manage and operate applications in the delivery of IT services. This process starts during the service strategy stage, is expanded in detail in service design, transitioned to the live environment in service transition and is executed in service operation. Ongoing assessment and updating of these skills are done during CSI.
- Initiating training programmes to develop and refine the skills in the appropriate application management resources and maintaining training records for these resources.
- Recruiting or contracting resources with skills that cannot be developed internally, or where there are insufficient people to perform the required application management activities.
- Designing and delivering end-user training. Training may be developed and delivered

by either the application development or application management groups, or by a third party, but application management is responsible for ensuring that training is conducted as appropriate.

- Insourcing for specific activities where the required skills are not available internally or in the open market, or where it is more cost-efficient to do so.
- Defining standards used in the design of new architectures and participation in the definition of application architectures during the service strategy processes.
- Researching and developing solutions that can help expand the service portfolio or which can be used to simplify or automate IT operations, reduce costs or increase levels of IT service.
- Participating in the design and building of new services. All application management teams or departments will contribute to the design of the technical architecture and performance standards for IT services. They will also be responsible for specifying the operational activities required to manage applications on an ongoing basis.
- Participating in projects, not only during the service design process, but also for CSI or operational projects, such as operating system upgrades, server consolidation projects or physical moves.
- Designing and performing tests for the functionality, performance and manageability of IT services (bearing in mind that testing should be controlled and performed by an independent tester; see *ITIL Service Transition*).
- Designing applications to meet the levels of service required by the business. Availability and capacity management are dependent on application management for design expertise and guidance to assess the appropriate level of resources that will meet business demand for applications. This means that modelling and workload forecasting are often done together with technical and application management resources.
- Assistance in assessing risk, identifying critical service and system dependencies and defining and implementing countermeasures.
- Managing suppliers. Many application management departments or groups are the only ones who know exactly what is required

of a supplier and how to measure and manage them. For this reason, many organizations rely on application management to manage contracts with suppliers of specific applications. If this is the case it is important to ensure that these relationships are managed as part of the SLM and supplier management processes.

■ Being involved in the definition of event management standards and especially in the instrumentation of applications for the generation of meaningful events.

■ Providing application management resources that contribute to the execution of the problem management process. It is their technical expertise and knowledge that is used to diagnose and resolve problems. It is also their relationship with the vendors that is used to escalate and follow up with vendor support teams or departments.

■ Defining coding systems that are used in incident and problem management (e.g. incident categories).

■ Providing resources to support problem management in validating and maintaining the KEDB together with the application development teams.

■ Supporting change management with technical application knowledge and expertise to evaluate changes. Many changes may be built by application management teams.

■ Participating in release and deployment management activities. Application management is frequently the driver of the release and deployment management process for the applications they manage.

■ Defining, managing and maintaining attributes and relationships of application CIs in the CMS.

■ Identifying opportunities for improvement and assisting in the evaluation of alternative solutions.

■ Coordinating with development teams to ensure a mechanism is in place to store and maintain documentation related to applications. This includes ensuring that all design, management, SOPs and user manuals are up to date and complete and properly utilized on an ongoing basis. Application management also ensures that application management staff and users are aware of application documentation and familiar with its contents.

■ Collaborating with technical management on performing training needs analysis and maintaining skills inventories.

■ Assisting financial management for IT services to identify the cost of the ongoing management of applications.

■ Defining the operational activities related to applications that will be performed as part of IT operations management. Many application management departments, groups or teams also perform the operational activities as part of an organization's IT operations management function.

■ Providing input into, and maintenance of, software configuration policies.

Application management teams or departments will be needed for all key applications. The exact nature of the role will vary depending upon the applications being supported, but generic responsibilities are likely to include:

■ Third-level support for incidents related to the application(s) covered by that team or department

■ Involvement in operation testing plans and deployment issues

■ Application bug tracking and patch management (coding fixes for in-house code, transports/patches for third-party code)

■ Involvement in application operability and supportability issues such as error code design, error messaging, event management hooks

■ Application sizing and performance; volume metrics and load testing etc. This is in support of capacity and availability management processes

■ Involvement in developing release policies

■ Identification of enhancements to existing software, from both a functionality and manageability perspective.

6.6.6 Application management organization

Although all application management departments, groups or teams perform similar activities, each application or set of applications has a different set of management and operational requirements. Examples of these differences include:

■ **The purpose of the application** Each application was developed to meet a specific set of objectives, usually business objectives. For effective support and improvement, the group that manages that application needs to have a comprehensive understanding of the business context and how the application is used to meet its objectives. This is often achieved by business analysts who are close to the business and responsible for ensuring that business requirements are effectively translated into application specifications. Business analysts should recognize that business requirements must be translated into both functional and manageability specifications.

■ **The functionality of the application** Each application is designed to work in a different way and to perform different functions at different times.

■ **The platform on which the application runs** Although the platform is usually managed by a technical management team or department, each of them affects the way in which an application needs to be managed and operated.

■ **The type or brand of technology used** Even applications that have similar functionality operate differently on different databases or platforms. These differences have to be understood in order to manage the application effectively.

Even though the activities to manage these applications are generic, the specific schedule of activities and the way they are performed will be different. For this reason, application management teams and departments tend to be organized according to the categories of applications that they support. Typical examples of these application categories include:

■ Financial applications – in larger organizations where a number of different applications are used for different aspects of financial management, there may be several departments, groups or teams managing these applications, e.g. debtors and creditors, age analysis, general ledger etc.
■ Messaging and collaboration applications
■ Human resources applications
■ Manufacturing support applications
■ Sales force automation
■ Sales order processing applications

■ Call centre and marketing applications
■ Business-specific applications (e.g. health care, insurance, banking etc.)
■ IT applications, such as service desk, enterprise system management etc.
■ Web portals
■ Online shopping.

6.6.6.1 Application development versus application management

Often, application development and management teams and departments have acted as autonomous units. Each one manages its own environment in its own way and each has a separate interface to the business. This is illustrated in Table 6.2.

Over the past several years, these two worlds are being brought together with growing pressure from the business to be more responsive and easy to work with. This means that application development will move towards accountability for the successful operation of applications they design, while application management will move towards greater involvement in the development of applications.

This does not change the fundamental role of each group, but it does require a more integrated approach between application development and application management functions. It will also mean that the output of application development will be more commoditized and that application management will be more involved in development projects.

This will require the following changes:

■ A single interface to the business for all stages of the lifecycle and a common requirements and specification-setting process.
■ A change in how both development and management staff are measured. Development teams should be held partly accountable for design flaws that create operational outages. Management staff should be held partly accountable for contribution to the technical architecture and manageability design of applications.
■ A single change management process for both groups, with change control in each group being subordinate to the overall authority of change management (see *ITIL Service Transition*).

Table 6.2 Application development versus application management

	Application development	Application management
Nature of activities	One-time set of activities to design and construct application solutions	Ongoing set of activities to oversee and manage applications throughout their entire lifecycle
Scope of activities	Performed mostly for applications developed in house	Performed for all applications, whether purchased from third parties or developed in house
Primary focus	Utility focus	Both utility and warranty focus
	Building functionality for their customer	What the functionality is as well as how to deliver it
	What the application does is more important than how it is operated	Manageability aspects of the application, i.e. how to ensure stability and performance of the application
Management mode	Most development work is done in projects where the focus is on delivering specific units of work to specification, on time and within budget	Most work is done as part of repeatable, ongoing processes. A relatively small number of people work in projects
	This means that it is often difficult for developers to understand and build for ongoing operations, especially because they are not available for support of the application once they have moved on to the next project	This means that it is very difficult for operational staff to get involved in development projects, as that takes them away from their ongoing operational responsibilities
Measurement	Staff are typically rewarded for creativity and for completing one project so that they can move on to the next project	Staff are typically rewarded for consistency and for preventing unexpected events and unauthorized functionality (e.g. 'bells and whistles' added by developers)
Cost	Development projects are relatively easy to quantify because the resources are known and it is easy to link their expenses to a specific application or IT service	Ongoing management costs are often mixed in with the costs of other IT services because resources are often shared across multiple IT services and applications
Lifecycles	Development staff focus on software development lifecycles, which highlight the dependencies for successful operation, but do not assign accountability for these	Staff involved in ongoing management typically only control one or two stages of these lifecycles – operation and improvement

■ A clear mapping of development and management activities throughout the lifecycle, which is illustrated at a high level in Figure 6.6. The exact activities and how they interact should be defined in each organization, although some generic guidelines are given in each of the core ITIL publications.

■ Greater focus on integrating functionality and manageability requirements early in the lifecycle of applications as they are developed.

Figure 6.6 shows a common application management lifecycle with involvement from both groups. In this diagram it is clear that application development will be driving some stages with input from application management. In other cases application management will be driving the stage with input and support from application development. Both groups are subordinated to the IT service strategy of the organization and their efforts are coordinated through service transition mechanisms and processes.

6.6.7 Measuring application management performance

Performance metrics for application management will largely depend on which applications are being managed, but some generic metrics are included here.

Figure 6.6 Role of teams in the application management lifecycle

6.6.7.1 Measurement of agreed outputs

These could include:

- Percentage of users able to access the application and its functionality
- Percentage of reports and files that are transmitted accurately and on time to the users
- Percentage availability for critical business transactions
- Number of capacity and performance-related incidents compared to business transaction volumes
- Percentage of service desk staff with appropriate support skills
- Number of recorded problem resolutions in the KEDB
- User measures of the quality of outputs as defined in the SLAs.

6.6.7.2 Process metrics

Application management teams execute many service management process activities. Their ability to do so will be measured as part of the process metrics where appropriate (see section on each process for more details). Examples include:

- Response time to events and event completion rates
- Incident resolution times for second- and third-line support

- Problem resolution statistics
- Number of escalations and reason for those escalations
- Number of changes implemented and backed out
- Number of unauthorized changes detected
- Number of releases deployed, total and successful, including ensuring adherence to the release policies of the organization
- Security issues detected and resolved
- Actual application transaction volumes and demand loads against capacity plan forecasts (where the team has contributed to the development of the plan)
- Tracking against SIPs
- Expenditure against budget.

6.6.7.3 Application performance

These metrics are based on service design specifications and technical performance standards set by vendors and will typically be contained in OLAs or SOPs. Actual metrics will vary by application, but are likely to include:

- Response times
- Application availability, which is helpful for measuring team or application performance but is not to be confused with service availability – which requires the ability to measure the overall availability of the service, and may

use the availability figures for a number of individual systems or components

■ Integrity and accuracy of data and reporting.

6.6.7.4 Measurement of maintenance activity

These metrics include:

■ Maintenance performed per schedule
■ Number of maintenance windows exceeded
■ Maintenance objectives achieved (number and percentage).

6.6.7.5 Measurement of project activity

Application management teams are likely to work closely with application development teams on projects, and appropriate metrics should be used to measure this, including:

■ Time spent on projects
■ Customer and user satisfaction with the output of the project
■ Cost of involvement in the project.

6.6.7.6 Training and skills development

These metrics ensure that staff have the skills and training to manage the applications that are under their control, and will also identify areas where training is still required:

■ Achieved skills performance levels
■ Number of calls and escalations to third-party or other internal subject matter experts for additional help and support
■ Percentage of incidents caused by skills issues.

6.6.8 Application management documentation

A number of documents are produced and used during application management. This list is a summary of some of the most important and does not include reports or documents produced by application management on behalf of other processes or functions (e.g. RFC, known error documentation, release records etc.). Note that documents should be controlled as CIs and related to the relevant applications or application management teams.

6.6.8.1 Application portfolio

The application portfolio is used primarily as part of service design, but is referenced here

for completeness. The application portfolio is a list (more accurately a system or database) of all applications in use within the organization, together with the following information:

■ Key attributes of the application
■ Customers and users
■ Business purpose
■ Level of business criticality
■ Architecture (including the IT infrastructure dependencies)
■ Developers, support groups, suppliers or vendors
■ The investment made in the application to date. In this respect the application portfolio can be used as an asset register for applications.

The purpose of the application portfolio is to analyse the need for and use of applications in the organization. It can be used to link functionality and investment to business activity and is therefore an important part of ongoing IT planning and control. Another benefit of the application portfolio is that it can be used to identify duplication and excessive licensing of applications.

The application portfolio forms part of the overall IT service portfolio, which is discussed in detail in *ITIL Service Strategy*.

The application portfolio and the service catalogue

The application portfolio should not be mistaken for the service catalogue and should not be advertised as a list of services to customers or users. Applications are service assets and only one of the many components used to provide IT services. An application by itself is not a service.

The application portfolio should therefore be used as a planning document only by those managers and staff who are involved with the development and management of the organization's applications as well as other IT staff who may be tasked with managing the applications or the platforms on which the applications run.

The service catalogue should focus on listing the services that are available, rather than simply listing applications and assuming that users and customers can make the link.

6.6.8.2 Application requirements

There are two sets of documents containing requirements for applications:

■ **Business requirements documents**   These outline the utility and warranty conditions as well as any constraints for the required application. They outline what the business will do with the application. This will include the ROI for the application as well as all related improvements to the business. Business requirements will also include the service level requirements as defined by the service customers and users.

■ **Application requirements documents**   These are based on the business requirements and specify exactly how the application will meet those requirements. In short, application requirements documents gather information that will be used to commission new applications or changes to existing applications, for example:

  ● To design the architecture of the application (specification of the different components of the system, how they relate to one another and how they will be managed)

  ● To specify a request for proposal (RFP) for a commercial off the shelf (COTS) application

  ● To initiate the design and building of an application in-house.

Requirements documents are normally owned by a project leader, either of a development project team, or for a team drawing up specifications for an RFP. Requirements documents are subject to document control for the project as they form part of the overall scope of the project.

Four different types of application requirements need to be defined (for more detailed information, please refer to *ITIL Service Design* and *ITIL Service Transition*):

■ Functional requirements describe the things an application is intended to do, and can be expressed as services, tasks or functions the application is required to perform.

■ Manageability requirements are used to define what is needed to manage the application or to ensure that it performs the required functions consistently and at the right level. Manageability requirements also identify constraints on the IT system. These requirements serve as a basis for early system sizing and estimates of cost, and can support the assessment of the viability of the proposed

IT system. Most importantly, they drive design of the operational models and performance standards used in IT operations management.

■ Usability requirements are normally specified by the users of the application and refer to its ease of use. Any special requirements for handicapped users also need to be specified here.

■ Test requirements specify what is required to ensure that the test environment is representative of the operational environment and that the test is valid (i.e. that it actually tests what it is supposed to).

6.6.8.3 Use cases

Use cases are developed within service design and maintained by application management. For purchased software, it is common for the team that develops the functional specifications to maintain the use case for that application. Use cases document the intended use of the application with real-life scenarios to demonstrate its boundaries and its full functionality. Use cases can also be used as modelling and sizing scenarios and for facilitating communication between users, developers and application management staff.

For more information, refer to *ITIL Service Design*.

6.6.8.4 Design documentation

This is not one specific document, but refers to any document produced by application development or management staff that specifies how an application will be built. As these documents are generally owned and managed by the development teams, this publication will not cover them in detail. However, to ensure successful operation, application management must ensure that design documentation contains:

■ Sizing specifications
■ Workload profiles and utilization forecasts
■ Technical architecture
■ Data models
■ Coding standards
■ Performance standards
■ Software service asset and configuration management definitions
■ Support requirements
■ Environment definitions and building considerations (if appropriate).

For third-party developed applications, these documents take the form of application specifications that are used as input into the writing of RFPs. In these cases the documents are owned and managed by application management.

For more information on design documentation, refer to *ITIL Service Design*.

6.6.8.5 Manuals

Application management is responsible for the management of manuals for all applications. Although these are normally developed by the application development teams or third-party suppliers, application management is responsible for ensuring that the manuals are relevant to the operational versions of the applications.

Three types of manuals are generally maintained by application management:

- Design manuals contain information about the structure and architecture of the application. These are helpful for creating reports or defining event correlation rules. They could also help in diagnosing problems.
- Administration or management manuals describe the activities required to maintain and operate the application at the levels of performance specified in the design stage. These manuals will also provide detailed troubleshooting, known error and fault descriptions, and step-by-step instructions for common maintenance tasks.
- User manuals describe the application functionality as it is used by an end-user. These manuals contain step-by-step instructions on how to use the application, as well as descriptions of what should typically be entered into certain fields, or what to do if there is an error.

Manuals and standard operating procedures

Manuals should not be seen as a replacement for SOPs, but as input into the SOPs. SOPs should contain all aspects of applications that need to be managed as part of standard operations. If they are not extracted from the manuals, there is a high likelihood that they will be ignored or performed in a non-standard manner. Application management should ensure that any such instructions are extracted from the manuals and inserted into separate SOP documentation for operations. It is also responsible for ensuring that these instructions are updated with every change or new release of the software.

6.7 ROLES

A number of roles need to be performed in support of service operation. Please note that this section provides guidelines and examples of role descriptions. These are not exhaustive or prescriptive, and in many cases roles will need to be combined or separated. Organizations should take care to apply this guidance in a way that suits their own structure and objectives.

A role is a set of responsibilities, activities and authorities granted to a person or team. A role is defined in a process or function. One person or team may have multiple roles; for example, the roles of configuration manager and change manager may be carried out by a single person.

Roles are often confused with job titles, but it is important to realize that they are not the same. Each organization will define appropriate job titles and job descriptions that suit its needs, and individuals holding these job titles can perform one or more of the required roles.

It should also be recognized that a person may, as part of their job assignment, perform a single task that represents participation in more than one process. For example, a technical analyst who submits an RFC to add memory to a server to resolve a performance problem is participating in activities of the change management process at the same time as taking part in activities of the capacity management and problem management processes.

Roles fall into two main categories – generic roles such as process manager and process owner, and specific roles that are involved within a particular lifecycle stage, process or function. Examples of specific roles might include service desk analyst or IT operator. Roles can be combined in a number of different ways, depending on the organizational context. For example, in many organizations there will be someone with the job title of IT operations analyst who combines the roles of the IT operator, shift leader and technical operator. In a small organization the IT operations manager role may be combined with roles from incident management and the service desk function. In larger organizations there may be many different people carrying out each of these roles, split by geography, technology or other criteria. The exceptions to this are that there must be only one process owner for each process and one service owner for each service.

Roles are accountable or responsible for an activity. They may also be consulted or informed about something: for example a service owner may be consulted about a change during an impact assessment activity. The RACI model, described in section 6.8, provides a useful way of defining and communicating roles and responsibilities.

> **What is a service manager?**
>
> Service manager is a generic term for any manager within the service provider. The term is commonly used to refer to a business relationship manager, a process manager or a senior manager with responsibility for IT services overall. A service manager is often assigned several roles such as business relationship management, service level management and continual service improvement.

6.7.1 Generic service owner role

To ensure that a service is managed with a business focus, the definition of a single point of accountability is absolutely essential to provide the level of attention and focus required for its delivery.

The service owner is accountable for the delivery of a specific IT service. The service owner is responsible to the customer for the initiation, transition and ongoing maintenance and support of a particular service and accountable to the IT director or service management director for the delivery of the service. The service owner's accountability for a specific service within an organization is independent of where the underpinning technology components, processes or professional capabilities reside.

Service ownership is as critical to service management as establishing ownership for processes which cross multiple vertical silos or departments. It is possible that a single person may fulfil the service owner role for more than one service.

The service owner has the following responsibilities:

- Ensuring that the ongoing service delivery and support meet agreed customer requirements
- Working with business relationship management to understand and translate customer requirements into activities, measures or service components that will ensure that the service provider can meet those requirements
- Ensuring consistent and appropriate communication with customer(s) for service-related enquiries and issues
- Assisting in defining service models and in assessing the impact of new services or changes to existing services through the service portfolio management process
- Identifying opportunities for service improvements, discussing these with the customer and raising RFCs as appropriate
- Liaising with the appropriate process owners throughout the service lifecycle
- Soliciting required data, statistics and reports for analysis and to facilitate effective service monitoring and performance
- Providing input in service attributes such as performance, availability etc.
- Representing the service across the organization
- Understanding the service (components etc.)
- Serving as the point of escalation (notification) for major incidents relating to the service
- Representing the service in CAB meetings
- Participating in internal service review meetings (within IT)
- Participating in external service review meetings (with the business)
- Ensuring that the service entry in the service catalogue is accurate and is maintained
- Participating in negotiating SLAs and OLAs relating to the service
- Identifying improvement opportunities for inclusion in the CSI register
- Working with the CSI manager to review and prioritize improvements in the CSI register
- Making improvements to the service.

The service owner is responsible for continual improvement and the management of change affecting the service under their care. The service owner is a primary stakeholder in all of the underlying IT processes which enable or support the service they own. For example:

- **Incident management** Is involved in (or perhaps chairs) the crisis management team for high-priority incidents impacting the service owned

■ **Problem management** Plays a major role in establishing the root cause and proposed permanent fix for the service being evaluated

■ **Release and deployment management** Is a key stakeholder in determining whether a new release affecting a service in production is ready for promotion

■ **Change management** Participates in CAB decisions, authorizing changes to the services they own

■ **Service asset and configuration management** Ensures that all groups which maintain the data and relationships for the service architecture they are responsible for have done so with the level of integrity required

■ **Service level management** Acts as the single point of contact for a specific service and ensures that the service portfolio and service catalogue are accurate in relation to their service

■ **Availability management and capacity management** Reviews technical monitoring data from a domain perspective to ensure that the needs of the overall service are being met

■ **IT service continuity management** Understands and is responsible for ensuring that all elements required to restore their service are known and in place in the event of a crisis

■ **Information security management** Ensures that the service conforms to information security management policies

■ **Financial management for IT services** Assists in defining and tracking the cost models in relation to how their service is costed and recovered.

6.7.2 Generic process owner role

The process owner role is accountable for ensuring that a process is fit for purpose. This role is often assigned to the same person that carries out the process manager role, but the two roles may be separate in larger organizations. The process owner role is accountable for ensuring that their process is performed according to the agreed and documented standard and meets the aims of the process definition.

The process owner's accountabilities include:

■ Sponsoring, designing and change managing the process and its metrics

■ Defining the process strategy

■ Assisting with process design

■ Ensuring that appropriate process documentation is available and current

■ Defining appropriate policies and standards to be employed throughout the process

■ Periodically auditing the process to ensure compliance to policy and standards

■ Periodically reviewing the process strategy to ensure that it is still appropriate and change as required

■ Communicating process information or changes as appropriate to ensure awareness

■ Providing process resources to support activities required throughout the service lifecycle

■ Ensuring process technicians have the required knowledge and the required technical and business understanding to deliver the process, and understand their role in the process

■ Reviewing opportunities for process enhancements and for improving the efficiency and effectiveness of the process

■ Addressing issues with the running of the process

■ Identifying improvement opportunities for inclusion in the CSI register

■ Working with the CSI manager and process manager to review and prioritize improvements in the CSI register

■ Making improvements to the process.

Further detail on the role and responsibilities of the process owner can be found in *ITIL Service Strategy* and *ITIL Service Design*.

6.7.3 Generic process manager role

The process manager role is accountable for operational management of a process. There may be several process managers for one process, for example regional change managers or IT service continuity managers for each data centre. The process manager role is often assigned to the person who carries out the process owner role, but the two roles may be separate in larger organizations.

The process manager's accountabilities include:

■ Working with the process owner to plan and coordinate all process activities

■ Ensuring all activities are carried out as required throughout the service lifecycle

■ Appointing people to the required roles

- Managing resources assigned to the process
- Working with service owners and other process managers to ensure the smooth running of services
- Monitoring and reporting on process performance
- Identifying improvement opportunities for inclusion in the CSI register
- Working with the CSI manager and process owner to review and prioritize improvements in the CSI register
- Making improvements to the process implementation.

6.7.4 Generic process practitioner role

A process practitioner is responsible for carrying out one or more process activities.

In some organizations, and for some processes, the process practitioner role may be combined with the process manager role, in others there may be large numbers of practitioners carrying out different parts of the process.

The process practitioner's responsibilities typically include:

- Carrying out one or more activities of a process
- Understanding how their role contributes to the overall delivery of service and creation of value for the business
- Working with other stakeholders, such as their manager, co-workers, users and customers, to ensure that their contributions are effective
- Ensuring that inputs, outputs and interfaces for their activities are correct
- Creating or updating records to show that activities have been carried out correctly.

6.7.5 Incident management roles

This section describes a number of roles that need to be performed in support of the incident management process. These roles are not job titles, and each organization will have to define appropriate job titles and job descriptions for their needs.

6.7.5.1 Incident management process owner

The incident management process owner's responsibilities typically include:

- Carrying out the generic process owner role for the incident management process (see section 6.7.2 for more detail)
- Designing incident models and workflows
- Working with other process owners to ensure there is an integrated approach to the design and implementation of incident management, problem management, event management, access management and request fulfilment.

6.7.5.2 Incident management process manager

The incident management process manager's responsibilities typically include:

- Carrying out the generic process manager role for the incident management process (see section 6.7.3 for more detail)
- Planning and managing support for incident management tools and processes
- Coordinating interfaces between incident management and other service management processes
- Driving the efficiency and effectiveness of the incident management process
- Producing management information
- Managing the work of incident support staff (first- and second-line)
- Monitoring the effectiveness of incident management and making recommendations for improvement
- Developing and maintaining the incident management systems
- Managing major incidents
- Developing and maintaining the incident management process and procedures.

In many organizations the role of incident manager is assigned to the service desk supervisor, although in larger organizations with high volumes a separate role may be necessary. In either case it is important that the incident manager is given the authority to manage incidents effectively through first, second and third line analysts.

6.7.5.3 First-line analyst

This role is that of providing first-line support for incidents when they occur using the incident management process. It is common to find this role combined with the service desk analyst role as described in section 6.7.10.3. Key responsibilities include:

- Recording incidents
- Routeing incidents to support specialist groups when needed
- Analysing for correct prioritization, classification and providing initial support
- Providing ownership, monitoring, tracking and communication of incidents
- Providing resolution and recovery of incidents not assigned to support specialist groups
- Closing incidents
- Monitoring the status and progress towards resolution of assigned incidents
- Keeping users and the service desk informed about incident progress
- Escalating incidents as necessary per established escalation policies.

6.7.5.4 Second-line analyst

Many organizations choose to have a second-line support group, made up of staff with greater (though still general) technical skills than the service desk – and with additional time to devote to incident diagnosis and resolution without interference from telephone interruptions. Key responsibilities would be similar to the first-line analyst role.

Such a group can handle many of the less complicated incidents, leaving more specialist (third-line) support groups to concentrate on dealing with more deep-rooted incidents and/or new developments etc.

Where a second-line group is used, there are often advantages to locating this group close to the service desk, to enable good communications and to ease movement of staff between the groups, which may be helpful for training/awareness and during busy periods or staff shortages. A second-line support manager (or supervisor if just a small group) will normally head this group.

6.7.5.5 Third-line analyst

Third-line support will be provided by a number of internal technical groups and/or third-party suppliers/maintainers. The list will vary from organization to organization but is likely to include:

- Network support

- Voice support (if separate)
- Server support
- Desktop support
- Application management – it's likely that there may be separate teams for different applications or application types, some of which may be external supplier/maintainers. In many cases the same team will be responsible for developing applications as well as support – it is therefore important that resources are prioritized so that support is given adequate prominence
- Database support
- Hardware maintenance engineers
- Environmental equipment maintainers/suppliers.

Note that depending upon where an organization decides to source its support services, any of the above groups could be internal or external groups.

6.7.6 Problem management roles

This section describes a number of roles that need to be performed in support of the problem management process. These roles are not job titles, and each organization will have to define appropriate job titles and job descriptions for their needs.

6.7.6.1 Problem management process owner

The problem management process owner's responsibilities typically include:

- Carrying out the generic process owner role for the problem management process (see section 6.7.2 for more detail)
- Designing problem models and workflows
- Working with other process owners to ensure there is an integrated approach to the design and implementation of problem management, incident management, event management, access management and request fulfilment.

6.7.6.2 Problem management process manager

There should be a designated person (or, in larger organizations, a team) responsible for problem management. Smaller organizations may not be able to justify a full-time resource for this role, and it can be combined with other roles in such cases, but it is essential that it not just left to technical resources to perform. There needs to be a single point of coordination and an owner of problem management activities.

The problem management process manager's responsibilities typically include:

- Carrying out the generic process manager role for the problem management process (see section 6.7.3 for more detail)
- Planning and managing support for problem management tools and processes
- Coordinating interfaces between problem management and other service management processes
- Liaising with all problem resolution groups to ensure swift resolution of problems within SLA targets
- Ownership and maintenance of the KEDB
- Gatekeeper for the inclusion of all known errors and management of search algorithms
- Formal closure of all problem records
- Liaising with suppliers, contractors etc. to ensure that third parties fulfil their contractual obligations, especially with regard to resolving problems and providing problem-related information and data
- Arranging, running, documenting and all follow-up activities relating to major problem reviews.

6.7.6.3 Problem analyst

The actual solving of problems is likely to be undertaken by one or more technical support groups and/or suppliers or support contractors. These may include support resources who may work in many different areas, but will come together to undertake problem resolution activities under the coordination of the problem manager.

The problem analyst's responsibilities typically include:

- Reviewing incident data to analyse assigned problems
- Analysing problems for correct prioritization and classification
- Investigating assigned problems through to resolution or root cause
- Coordinating actions of others as necessary to assist with analysis and resolution actions for problems and known errors
- Raising RFCs to resolve problems

- Monitoring progress on the resolution of known errors and advising incident management staff on the best available workaround for incidents
- Updating the KEDB with new or updated known errors and workarounds
- Assisting with the handling of major incidents and identifying their root causes.

Where an individual problem is serious enough to warrant it, a dedicated problem management team should be formulated to work together in overcoming that particular problem. The problem resolver has a role to play in making sure that the correct number and level of resources is available in the team and for escalation and communication up the management chain of all organizations concerned.

6.7.7 Request fulfilment roles

This section describes a number of roles that need to be performed in support of the request fulfilment process. These roles are not job titles, and each organization will have to define appropriate job titles and job descriptions for their needs.

6.7.7.1 Request fulfilment process owner

The request fulfilment process owner's responsibilities typically include:

- Carrying out the generic process owner role for the request fulfilment process (see section 6.7.2 for more detail)
- Designing request fulfilment models and workflows
- Working with other process owners to ensure there is an integrated approach to the design and implementation of request fulfilment, incident management, event management, access management and problem management.

6.7.7.2 Request fulfilment process manager

The request fulfilment process manager's responsibilities typically include:

- Carrying out the generic process manager role for the request fulfilment process (see section 6.7.3 for more detail)
- Planning and managing support for request fulfilment tools and processes

- Coordinating interfaces between request fulfilment and other service management processes
- Handling staff, customer and management concerns, requests, issues and enquiries
- Ensuring request fulfilment activities operate in line with service level targets
- Reviewing and analysing all request fulfilment reports to proactively seek improvements
- Overseeing actions to obtain feedback from customers on quality of request fulfilment activities
- Assisting with activities to appropriately identify needed staffing resource levels to handle demand for request fulfilment activities and services
- Ensuring all authorized service requests are being fulfilled on a timely basis
- Representing request fulfilment activities at CAB meetings
- Reviewing the initial prioritization and authorization of service requests to determine accuracy and consistency.

6.7.7.3 Request fulfilment analyst

This role coordinates fulfilment of service requests to maintain high levels of satisfaction with IT services. It oversees, manages and coordinates all activities to respond to a service request and serves as a single point of contact until it has been fulfilled.

The request fulfilment analyst's responsibilities typically include:

- Providing a single point of contact and end-to-end responsibility to ensure submitted service requests have been processed
- Providing initial triage of service requests to determine which IT resources should be engaged to fulfil them
- Communicating service requests to other IT resources that will be involved in fulfilling them
- Escalating service requests in line with established service level targets
- Ensuring service requests are appropriately logged.

Initial handling of service requests is commonly undertaken by the service desk and incident management staff.

Eventual fulfilment of the service request will be undertaken by the appropriate service operation team(s) or departments and/or by external suppliers, as appropriate. Often, facilities management, procurement and other business areas aid in the fulfilment of the service request. In most cases there will be no need for additional roles or posts to be created.

In exceptional cases where a very high number of service requests are handled, or where the requests are of critical importance to the organization, it may be appropriate to have one or more of the incident management team dedicated to handling and managing service requests.

6.7.8 Event management roles

This section describes a number of roles that need to be performed in support of the event management process. These roles are not job titles, and each organization will have to define appropriate job titles and job descriptions for their needs.

It is unusual for an organization to appoint an 'event manager', as events tend to occur in multiple contexts and for many different reasons. However, it is important that event management procedures are coordinated to prevent duplication of effort and tools.

6.7.8.1 Event management process owner

The event management process owner's responsibilities typically include:

- Carrying out the generic process owner role for the event management process (see section 6.7.2 for more detail)
- Planning and managing support for event management tools and processes
- Working with other process owners to ensure there is an integrated approach to the design and implementation of event management, incident management, request fulfilment, access management and problem management.

6.7.8.2 Event management process manager

The event management process manager's responsibilities typically include:

- Carrying out the generic process manager role for the event management process (see section 6.7.3 for more detail)

- Planning and managing support for event management tools and processes
- Coordinating interfaces between event management and other service management processes.

6.7.8.3 Other event management roles

The role of service desk staff

The service desk is not typically involved in event management as such, unless an event requires some response that is within the scope of the service desk's defined activity, for example notifying a user that a report is ready. Generally, though, this type of activity is performed by the operations bridge, unless the service desk and operations bridge have been combined.

The investigation and resolution of events that have been identified as being incidents will initially be undertaken by the service desk and then escalated to the appropriate service operation team(s).

The service desk is also responsible for communicating information about this type of incident to the relevant technical or application management team and, where appropriate, the user.

The role of technical and application management staff

Technical and application management staff play several important roles, as follows:

- During service design, they will participate in designing the warranty aspects of the service such as classifying events, updating correlation engines, or ensuring that any auto-responses are defined.
- During service transition, they will test the service to ensure that events are properly generated and that the defined responses are appropriate.
- During service operation, these teams will typically perform event management for the systems under their control. It is unusual for teams to have a dedicated person to manage event management, but each manager or team leader will ensure that the appropriate procedures are defined and executed according to the process and policy requirements.

- Technical and application management will also be involved in dealing with incidents and problems related to events.
- If event management activities are delegated to the service desk or IT operations management, technical and application management must ensure that the staff are adequately trained and that they have access to the appropriate tools to enable them to perform these tasks.

The role of IT operations management staff

Where IT operations are separated from technical or application management, it is common for event monitoring and first-line response to be delegated to IT operations management. Operators for each area will be tasked with monitoring events, responding as required, or ensuring that incidents are created as appropriate. The instructions for how to do so must be included in the SOPs for those teams.

Event monitoring is commonly delegated to the operations bridge where it exists. The operations bridge can initiate and coordinate, or even perform, the responses required by the service, or provide first-level support for those events that generate an incident.

6.7.9 Access management roles

This section describes a number of roles that need to be performed in support of the access management process. These roles are not job titles, and each organization will have to define appropriate job titles and job descriptions for their needs.

6.7.9.1 Access management process owner

The access management process owner's responsibilities typically include:

- Carrying out the generic process owner role for the access management process (see section 6.7.2 for more detail)
- Designing access request workflows
- Working with other process owners to ensure there is an integrated approach to the design and implementation of access management, incident management, event management, request fulfilment and problem management.

6.7.9.2 Access management process manager

The access management process manager's responsibilities typically include:

- Carrying out the generic process manager role for the access management process (see section 6.7.3 for more detail)
- Planning and managing support for access management tools and processes
- Coordinating interfaces between access management and other service management processes.

6.7.9.3 Other access management roles

Because access management is an execution of security and availability management, these two areas will be responsible for defining the appropriate roles. It is important that there is a single access management process and a single set of policies related to managing rights and access. This process and the related policies are likely to be defined and maintained by information security management and executed by the various service operation functions. Their activities can be summarized as follows.

The role of service desk staff

The service desk may be used as a means to request access to a service. This is normally done using a service request. The service desk will validate the request by checking that the request has been authorized at the appropriate level of authority, that the user is a legitimate employee, contractor or customer and that they qualify for access.

Once it has performed these checks (usually by accessing the relevant databases and SLM documents) it will pass the request to the appropriate team to provide access. It is quite common for the service desk to be delegated responsibility for providing access for simple services during the call.

The service desk will also be responsible for communicating with the user to ensure that they know when access has been granted and to ensure that they receive any other required support.

The service desk is also well situated to detect and report incidents related to access. For example, users attempting to access services without authority; or users reporting incidents that indicate that a system or service has been used inappropriately, i.e. by a former employee who

used an old user name to gain access and make unauthorized changes.

The role of technical and application management staff

Technical and application management play several important roles as follows:

- During service design, they will ensure that mechanisms are created to simplify and control access management on each service that is designed. They will also specify ways in which abuse of rights can be detected and stopped.
- During service transition, they will test the service to ensure that access can be granted, controlled and prevented as designed.
- During service operation, these teams will typically perform access management for the systems under their control. It is unusual for teams to have a dedicated person to manage access management, but each manager or team leader will ensure that the appropriate procedures are defined and executed according to the process and policy requirements.
- Technical and application management will also be involved in dealing with incidents and problems related to access management.
- If access management activities are delegated to the service desk or IT operations management, technical and application management must ensure that the staff are adequately trained and that they have access to the appropriate tools to enable them to perform these tasks.

The role of IT operations management staff

Where IT operations are separated from technical or application management, it is common for operational access management tasks to be delegated to IT operations management. Operators for each area will be tasked with providing or revoking access to key systems or resources. The circumstances under which they may do so, and the instructions for how to do so, must be included in the SOPs for those teams.

The operations bridge, if it exists, can be used to monitor events related to access management and can even provide first-line support and coordination in the resolution of those events where appropriate.

6.7.10 Service desk roles

This section describes a number of roles that need to be performed in support of the service desk function. These roles are not job titles, and each organization will have to define appropriate job titles and job descriptions for their needs.

6.7.10.1 Service desk manager

In larger organizations where the service desk is of a significant size, a service desk manager role may be justified, with the service desk supervisor(s) reporting to him or her.

The service desk manager's responsibilities typically include:

- Appointing people to the required roles
- Managing resources assigned to the service desk, including the supervisor(s)
- Managing service desk activities
- Acting as an escalation point for the supervisor(s)
- Undertaking a wider customer services role
- Reporting to senior managers on any issue that could significantly impact the business
- Attending CAB meetings
- Taking overall responsibility for incident and service request handling on the service desk. This could also be expanded to any other activity taken on by the service desk, e.g. monitoring certain classes of event
- Monitoring and reporting on service desk performance
- Identifying improvement opportunities for inclusion in the CSI register
- Working with the CSI manager to review and prioritize improvements in the CSI register
- Making improvements to the service desk.

Note that in all cases, clearly defined job descriptions should be drafted and agreed so that specific responsibilities are known.

6.7.10.2 Service desk supervisor

In very small desks it is possible that the senior service desk analyst will also act as the supervisor, but in larger desks it is likely that a dedicated service desk supervisor role will be needed. Where shift hours dictate it, there may be two or more post holders who fulfil the role, usually on an overlapping basis. The service desk supervisor's responsibilities typically include:

- Ensuring that staffing and skill levels are maintained throughout operational hours by managing shift staffing schedules etc.
- Undertaking human resources activities as needed
- Acting as an escalation point where difficult or controversial calls are received
- Production of statistics and management reports
- Representing the service desk at meetings
- Arranging staff training and awareness sessions
- Liaising with senior management
- Liaising with change management
- Performing briefings to service desk staff on changes or deployments that may affect volumes at the service desk
- Assisting analysts in providing first-line support when workloads are high, or where additional experience is required.

6.7.10.3 Service desk analyst

The primary service desk analyst role is that of providing first-line support through taking calls and handling the resulting incidents or service requests using the incident reporting and request fulfilment processes, in line with the objectives described earlier. It is quite common to have this role as a combination of the first-line analyst role and request fulfilment analyst role described earlier (see sections 6.7.5.3 and 6.7.7.3).

6.7.10.4 Super user

The super user role will consist of business users who act as liaison points with IT in general and the service desk in particular.

The super user's responsibilities typically include:

- Facilitating communication between IT and the business at an operational level
- Reinforcing expectations of users regarding the service levels that have been agreed
- Staff training for users in their area
- Providing support for minor incidents or simple request fulfilment
- Escalating requests and incidents to the service desk if they cannot be resolved locally
- Assisting the service desk for ongoing issues and problems as needed (i.e. recording the number of incident instances during a specific period such as a shift etc.) for an ongoing problem and

then placing a single call with the service desk to cover all the instances)

■ Involvement with new releases and deployments.

6.7.11 Technical management roles

This section describes a number of roles that need to be performed in support of the technical management function. These roles are not job titles, and each organization will have to define appropriate job titles and job descriptions for their needs.

6.7.11.1 Technical manager/team leader

A technical manager or team leader (depending upon the size and/or importance of the team and the organization's structure and culture) may be needed for each of the technical teams or departments.

The technical manager/team leader's responsibilities typically include:

■ Taking overall responsibility for leadership, control and decision-making for the technical team or department

■ Providing technical knowledge and leadership in the specific technical areas covered by the team or department

■ Ensuring necessary technical training, awareness and experience levels are maintained within the team or department

■ Reporting to senior management on all technical issues relevant to their area of responsibility

■ Performing line management for all team or department members.

6.7.11.2 Technical analyst/architect

This term refers to any staff member in technical management who performs the activities listed in section 6.4.3, excluding the daily operational actions, which are performed by operators in either technical or IT operations management.

Based on the list of generic activities in section 6.4.3, the technical analyst/architect's responsibilities typically include:

■ Working with users, sponsors, application management and all other stakeholders to determine their evolving needs

■ Working with application management and other areas in technical management to determine the highest level of system requirements required to meet the requirements within budget and technology constraints

■ Defining and maintaining knowledge about how systems are related and ensuring that dependencies are understood and managed accordingly

■ Performing cost–benefit analyses to determine the most appropriate means to meet the stated requirements

■ Developing operational models that will ensure optimal use of resources and the appropriate level of performance

■ Ensuring that the infrastructure is configured to be effectively managed given the organization's technology architecture, available skills and tools

■ Ensuring the consistent and reliable performance of the infrastructure to deliver the required level of service to the business

■ Defining all tasks required to manage the infrastructure and ensuring that these tasks are performed appropriately

■ Providing input into the design of configuration data required to manage and track the infrastructure and applications effectively.

The ways in which technical management can be organized, and the options available, are discussed in some detail in section 6.10.

6.7.11.3 Technical operator

This term is used to refer to any staff who perform day-to-day operational tasks in technical management. Usually, these tasks are delegated to a dedicated IT operations team, and this role is therefore discussed in the IT operator role description described in section 6.7.12.4.

6.7.12 IT operations management roles

This section describes a number of roles that need to be performed in support of the IT operations management function. These roles are not job titles, and each organization will have to define appropriate job titles and job descriptions for their needs.

6.7.12.1 IT operations manager

An IT operations manager will be needed to take overall responsibility for all the activities within the IT operations management function as discussed in section 6.5.1.

The IT operations manager's responsibilities typically include:

- Providing overall leadership, control and decision-making and taking responsibility for the IT operations management teams and department
- Reporting to senior management on all IT operations issues
- Performing line management for all IT operations team or department managers/supervisors.

6.7.12.2 Shift leader

Many IT operations areas will work extended hours, on either a two- or three-shift basis. In such cases a shift leader will be needed on each of the shifts.

The shift leader's responsibilities typically include:

- Taking overall responsibility for leadership, control and decision-making during the shift period
- Ensuring that all operational activities are satisfactorily performed within agreed timescales and in accordance with company policies and procedures
- Liaising with the other shift leader(s) to ensure handover, continuity and consistency between the shifts
- Acting as line manager for all operations analysts on his/her shift
- Assuming overall health and safety, and security responsibility for the shift (unless specifically designated to other staff members).

6.7.12.3 IT operations analyst

IT operations analysts are senior IT operations staff who are able to determine the most effective and efficient way to conduct a series of operations, usually in high-volume, diverse environments.

This role is normally performed as part of technical management, but large organizations may find that the volume and diversity of operational activities requires some more in-depth planning

and execution. Examples include job scheduling and the definition of a backup strategy and schedule.

6.7.12.4 IT operator

IT operators are the staff who perform the day-to-day operational activities that are defined in technical or application management and, in some cases, IT operations analysts.

The IT operator's responsibilities typically include:

- Performing backups
- Console operations, i.e. monitoring the status of specific systems, job queues etc. and providing first-level intervention if appropriate
- Managing print devices, restocking with paper, toner etc.
- Ensuring that batch jobs, archiving etc. are performed
- Running scheduled housekeeping jobs, such as database maintenance, file clean-up etc.
- Burning images for distribution and installation on new servers, desktops or laptops
- Physical installation of standard equipment in the data centre.

6.7.13 Application management roles

This section describes a number of roles that need to be performed in support of the application management function. These roles are not job titles, and each organization will have to define appropriate job titles and job descriptions for their needs.

6.7.13.1 Applications manager/team leader

An applications manager or team leader (depending upon the size and/or importance of the team or department and the application they support, and the organization's structure and culture) will be needed for each of the applications teams or departments.

The application manager/team leader's responsibilities typically include:

- Taking overall responsibility for leadership, control and decision-making for the applications team or department
- Providing technical knowledge and leadership in the specific applications support activities covered by the team or department

- Ensuring necessary technical training, awareness and experience levels are maintained within the team or department relevant to the applications being supported and processes being used
- Ongoing communication with users and customers regarding application performance and evolving requirements of the business
- Reporting to senior management on all issues relevant to the applications being supported
- Performing line management for all team or department members.

6.7.13.2 Applications analyst/architect

Application analysts and architects are responsible for matching requirements to application specifications.

The application analyst/architect's responsibilities typically include:

- Working with users, sponsors and all other stakeholders to determine their evolving needs
- Working with technical management to determine the highest level of system requirements required to meet the business requirements within budget and technology constraints
- Performing cost–benefit analyses to determine the most appropriate means to meet the stated requirement
- Developing operational models that will ensure optimal use of resources and the appropriate level of performance
- Ensuring that applications are designed to be effectively managed given the organization's technology architecture, available skills and tools
- Developing and maintaining standards for application sizing, performance modelling etc.
- Generating a set of acceptance test requirements, together with the designers, test engineers and the user, which determine that all of the high-level requirements have been met with regard to both function and manageability
- Providing input into the design of configuration data required to manage and track applications effectively.

6.8 RESPONSIBILITY MODEL – RACI

Clear definitions of accountability and responsibility are essential for effective service management. To help with this task the RACI model or 'authority matrix' is often used within organizations to define the roles and responsibilities in relation to processes and activities. The RACI matrix provides a compact, concise, easy method of tracking who does what in each process and it enables decisions to be made with pace and confidence.

RACI is an acronym for the four main roles of being:

- **Responsible** The person or people responsible for correct execution – for getting the job done
- **Accountable** The person who has ownership of quality and the end result. Only one person can be accountable for each task
- **Consulted** The people who are consulted and whose opinions are sought. They have involvement through input of knowledge and information
- **Informed** The people who are kept up to date on progress. They receive information about process execution and quality.

When using RACI, there is only one person accountable for an activity for a defined scope of applicability. Several people may be responsible for executing parts of the activity. In this model, accountable means end-to-end accountability for the process. Accountability should remain with the same person for all activities of a process.

The RACI chart in Table 6.3 shows the structure and power of RACI modelling. The rows represent a number of required activities and the columns identify the people who make the decisions, carry out the activities or provide input.

Whether RACI or some other tool or model is used, the important thing is to not just leave the assignment of responsibilities to chance or leave it to the last minute to decide. For example, if there is a transfer of a service from one service provider to another, RACI models should be designed in the service design lifecycle stage, and tested and deployed in service transition. In service operation, people assigned to specific roles will perform the activities in the RACI matrix.

Further details on the RACI matrix are described in Chapter 3 of *ITIL Service Design*.

Table 6.3 An example of a simple RACI matrix

	Director service management	Service level manager	Problem manager	Security manager	Procurement manager
Activity 1	AR	C	I	I	C
Activity 2	A	R	C	C	C
Activity 3	I	A	R	I	C
Activity 4	I	A	R	I	
Activity 5	I	R	A	C	I

6.9 COMPETENCE AND TRAINING

6.9.1 Competence and skills for service management

Delivering service successfully depends on personnel involved in service management having the appropriate education, training, skills and experience. People need to understand their role and how they contribute to the overall organization, services and processes to be effective and motivated. As changes are made, job requirements, roles, responsibilities and competencies should be updated if necessary.

Each service lifecycle stage depends on appropriate skills and experience of people and their knowledge to make key decisions. In many organizations, personnel will deliver tasks appropriate to more than one lifecycle stage. They may well find themselves allocated (fully or partially) from operational tasks to support a design exercise and then follow that service through service transition. They may then, via early life support activities, move into support of the new or changed services that they have been involved in designing and implementing into the live environment.

The specific roles within ITIL service management all require specific skills, attributes and competencies from the people involved to enable them to work effectively and efficiently. However, whatever the role, it is imperative that the person carrying out that role has the following attributes:

- Awareness of the business priorities, objectives and business drivers
- Awareness of the role IT plays in enabling the business objectives to be met
- Customer service skills
- Awareness of what IT can deliver to the business, including latest capabilities

- The competence, knowledge and information necessary to complete their role
- The ability to use, understand and interpret the best practice, policies and procedures to ensure adherence.

The following are examples of attributes required in many of the roles, dependent on the organization and the specific roles assigned:

- Management skills – both from a person management perspective and from the overall control of process
- Ability to handle meetings – organizing, chairing, and documenting meetings and ensuring that actions are followed up
- Communication skills – an important element of all roles is raising awareness of the processes in place to ensure buy-in and conformance. An ability to communicate at all levels within the organization will be imperative
- Articulateness – both written (e.g. for reports) and verbal
- Negotiation skills are required for several aspects, such as procurement and contracts
- An analytical mind – to analyse metrics produced from the activity.

Many people working in service management are involved with continual service improvement. *ITIL Continual Service Improvement* provides specific guidance on the skill levels needed for CSI activities.

6.9.2 Competence and skills framework

Standardizing job titles, functions, roles and responsibilities can simplify service management and human resource management. Many service providers use a common framework of reference for competence and skills to support activities such as skill audits, planning future skill requirements, organizational development programmes and resource allocation. For example, resource and cost models are simpler and easier to use if jobs and roles are standard.

The Skills Framework for the Information Age (SFIA) is an example of a common reference model for the identification of the skills needed to develop effective IT services, information systems and technology. SFIA defines seven generic levels at which tasks can be performed, with the associated professional skills required for each level. A second dimension defines core competencies that can be combined with the professional skills. SFIA is used by many IT service providers to identify career development opportunities.

More information on SFIA can be found at www. sfia.org.uk

6.9.3 Training

Training in service management helps service providers to build and maintain their service management capability. Training needs must be matched to the requirements for competence and professional development.

The official ITIL qualification scheme enables organizations to develop the competence of their personnel through approved training courses. The courses help students to gain knowledge of ITIL best practices, develop their competencies and gain a recognized qualification. The scheme has four levels:

- Foundation level
- Intermediate level
- ITIL Expert
- ITIL Master.

More information on ITIL qualifications can be found at www.itil-officialsite.com

6.10 SERVICE OPERATION ORGANIZATION STRUCTURES

This section considers some specific organizational structures for all functions. There are a number of ways of organizing service operation functions, and each organization will have to make its own decisions, based upon its scale, geography, culture and business environment. Some options are discussed in the rest of this section.

6.10.1 Organization by technical specialization

In this type of organization, departments are created according to technology and the skills and activities needed to manage that technology. IT operations will follow the structure of the technical and application management departments. The implication of this is that the IT operations department is geared towards the operational agendas of the technical and application management departments.

This structure can work well, provided that these groups are fully represented in the service design, testing and improvement processes, which will ensure that their agendas are aligned with the requirements of the business.

This structure also assumes that all technical and application management departments have clearly distinguished between their management activity and operations activity. It also requires that they have standardized these operational activities so that they can be effectively managed by the IT operations manager without undue interference from the technical and application management teams or departments.

An example of an IT operations organization structure based on technical expertise is given in Figure 6.7.

The advantages of this type of organizational structure include the following:

- It is easier to set internal performance objectives because all staff in a single department have a similar set of tasks on a similar technology.
- Individual devices, systems or platforms can be managed more effectively because people with the appropriate skills are dedicated to manage these and measured according to their performance.
- Managing training programmes is easier because skill sets are clearly defined and separated into specific groups.

The disadvantages of this type of organizational structure include:

- When people are divided into separate departments the priorities of their own group tend to override the priorities of other departments. An example of this is when

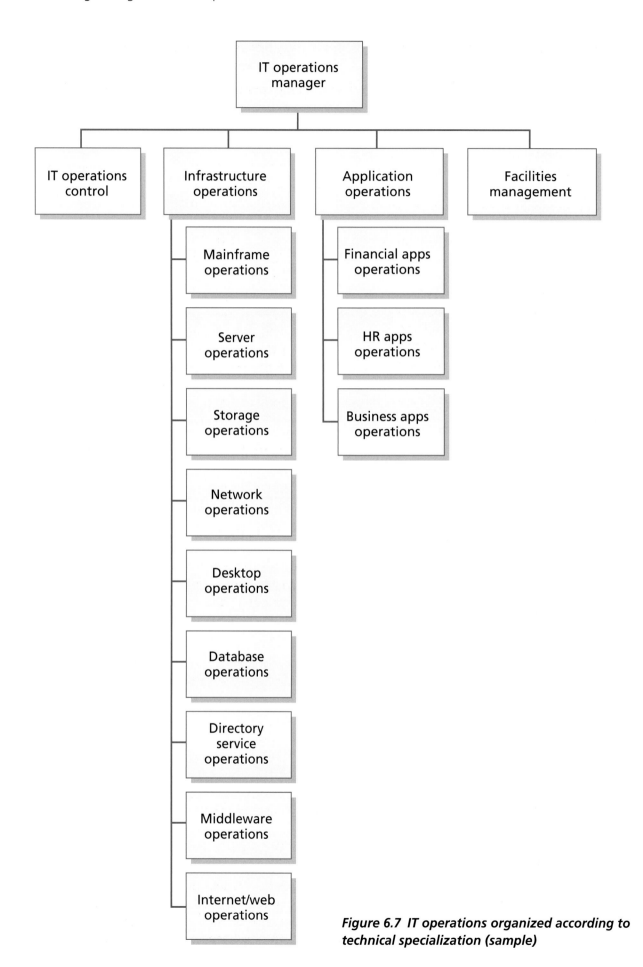

Figure 6.7 IT operations organized according to technical specialization (sample)

departments refuse to accept ownership of an incident, each one blaming the other while the business continues to be disrupted.

■ Knowledge about the infrastructure and relationships between components is difficult to collect and fragmented. Individual groups tend to collect and maintain only the data that is required to support their own function, and do not give access to it very easily.

■ Each technology managed by a group is seen as a separate entity. This becomes a problem on systems that consist of components managed by different teams, e.g. an application managed by the application management team, runs on a server managed by the server management department, using a network segment managed by the local area networking department. If a change is made by one team or department without consulting the others, this could be disastrous for the service.

■ It is more difficult to understand the impact of a single department's poor performance on the IT service because there are many different groups contributing to the same service, each with its own set of performance objectives.

■ It is more difficult to track overall IT service performance because each group is being measured on an individual basis.

■ Coordinating change assessments and schedules is more difficult because many different departments have to provide input for each change.

■ Work requiring knowledge of multiple technologies is difficult because most resources are only trained for and concerned with the management of a single technology. Projects therefore have to include cross-training, which is time-consuming and expensive.

6.10.2 Organization by activity

This type of organization structure focuses on the fact that similar activities have to be performed on all technologies in the organization. This means that people who perform similar activities, regardless of the technology, should be grouped together, although within each department there may be teams focusing on a specific technology, application etc.

In this type of organization, there is no clear differentiation between the different technical and application management areas. Similar activities

from many different areas can be grouped into a single department.

Examples of departments that have been set up to perform a specific set of activities across multiple technologies include:

■ Maintenance (this implies that one team will coordinate and perform all maintenance across all technologies)

■ Contract management or third-party management

■ Monitoring and control

■ Operations bridge/command centre

■ Network operations centre

■ Security operations centre

■ Operations strategy and planning (which, as part of the service design processes, normally defines the standards to be used in IT operations); this department can set strategy or standards for every type of technical and application management area.

The operations strategy and planning department is used to illustrate this type of structure in Figure 6.8.

The advantages of this type of organizational structure include the following:

■ It is easier to manage groups of related activities because all the people involved in these activities report to the same manager.

■ Measurement of teams or departments is based more on output than on isolated activities. This helps to build higher levels of assurance that a service can be delivered.

The disadvantages of this type of organizational structure include the following:

■ Resources with similar skills may be duplicated across different functions, which results in higher costs.

■ Although measurement is more output-based, it is still focused on the performance of internal activities rather than driven by the experience of the customer or end user.

6.10.3 Organizing to manage processes

It is not a good idea to structure the whole organization according to processes. Processes are used to overcome the 'silo effect' of departments, not to create silos. However, there are a number of processes that will need a dedicated organization

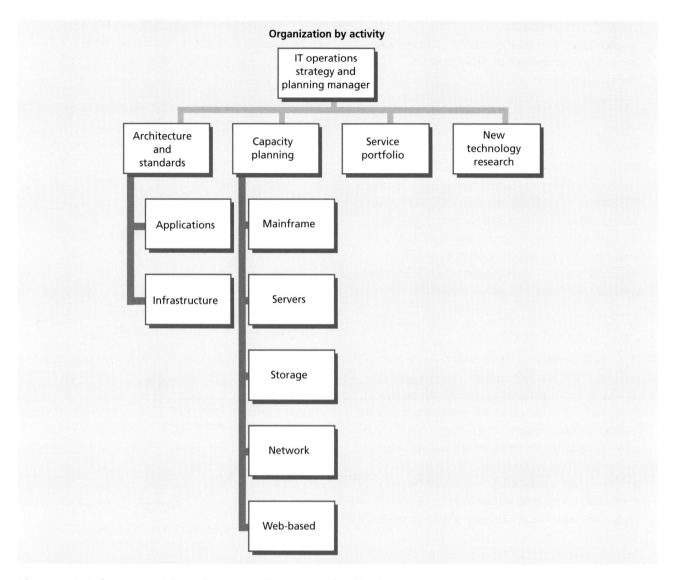

Organization by activity

Figure 6.8 A department based on executing a set of activities

structure to support and manage it. For example, it will be very difficult for financial management to be successful without a dedicated finance department – even if that department consists of a small number of staff.

In process-based organizations people are organized into groups or departments that perform or manage a specific process. This is similar to the activity-based structure, except that its departments focus on end-to-end sets of activities rather than on one individual type of activity.

It should be noted that this type of organization structure should only be used if IT operations management is responsible for more than just IT operations. In some organizations, for example, IT operations is responsible for defining SLAs and negotiating UCs.

In addition, processes specifically exist to link the activities of different groups to achieve a specific outcome. Using processes as the basis to create departments can defeat the purpose of having processes in the first place. Process-based departments are really only effective when they are able to coordinate the execution of the process through the entire organization.

This means that process-based departments should only be considered if IT operations management is to play the role of process owner for a specific process.

Examples of process-based groups or departments include:

- Capacity operations
- Availability monitoring and control
- Financial management for IT services

■ Security administration

■ Service asset and configuration management (including equipment installation and deployment).

The advantages of this type of organizational structure include the following:

■ Processes are easier to define.

■ There is less role conflict as job descriptions and process role descriptions are the same. In other structures a single job description will typically include activities for several roles.

■ Metrics of team or department performance and process performance are the same, effectively aligning 'internal' and 'external' metrics.

The disadvantages of this type of organizational structure include the following:

■ By using processes as a basis for organizational design, additional processes may need to be defined to ensure that the departments work together.

■ Even if a department is responsible for executing a process, there will still be external dependencies. Groups may not view process activities outside of their own process as being important, resulting in processes that cannot be fully executed because dependencies cannot be met.

■ While some aspects of a process can be centralized, there will always be a number of activities that will have to be performed by other groups. The relationship between the dedicated team or department and the people performing the decentralized activities is often difficult to define and manage.

6.10.4 Organizing IT operations by geography

IT operations can be physically distributed and in some cases each location needs to be organized according to its own particular context.

This structure is typically used in the following circumstances:

■ Data centres are geographically distributed.

■ Different regions or countries have different technologies or provide a different set of services.

■ There are different business models or organizational structures in the different regions, i.e. the business is decentralized by geography and each business unit is fairly autonomous.

■ Different legislation applies to different countries or regions (e.g. safety regulations).

■ Different standards apply to different countries or regions.

■ Cultural or language differences exist between staff managing IT.

An example of this type of structure is given in Figure 6.9. Note that in this example each geographical department is structured internally using technical specialization. This could be different in each region. For example one region may be structured in this way, while another region uses a process- or activity-based structure.

Figure 6.9 also illustrates that one location could perform centralized operations for all regions if they are similar enough. In this example, the American server operations department manages all server operations in all locations, Brussels manages all database operations and Singapore manages all storage operations.

The advantages of this type of organizational structure include the following:

■ Organization structure can be customized to meet local conditions.

■ IT operations can be customized to meet differing levels of IT service from region to region.

The disadvantages of this type of organizational structure include the following:

■ Reporting lines and authority structures can be confusing. For example, does network operations report into the local data centre manager or to a centralized network operations manager?

■ Operational standards are difficult to impose, resulting in inconsistent and duplicated activities and tools, resulting in reduced economies of scale, which in turn increases the overall cost of operations.

■ Duplication of roles, activities, tools and facilities across multiple locations could be very costly.

Figure 6.9 IT operations organized according to geography

- Shared services, such as email, are more difficult to deliver as each regional organization operates differently.
- Communication with customers and inside IT will be more difficult as they are not co-located and it may be difficult for staff in one location to understand the priorities of customers or staff in another location.

6.10.5 Hybrid organization structures

It is unlikely that IT operations management will be organized using only one type of organization structure. Some organizations use a technical specialization structure combined with some additional activity- or process-based structures.

The type of structure used and the exact combination of technical specialization, activity-based and process-based departments will depend on a number of organizational variables.

6.10.6 Combined functions

One final type of organization should be discussed. This structure incorporates IT operations, technical and application management departments into a single structure. This is sometimes the case where all groups are co-located in a single data centre. Here, the IT operations manager takes responsibility for all technical, application and IT operations management.

Organizational structure variables

The exact criteria chosen and the resulting organizational structure will depend on a number of variables, which may include:

- The nature of the business
- Business requirements and expectations
- The technological and technical architecture
- The stability of the current IT infrastructure and the availability of skills to manage it
- The governance of the organization (i.e. the way in which authority is assigned and decisions are made – as well as any formal governance framework that is used, such as COBIT or SOX)
- The legislative, political and socioeconomic environment of the organization
- The type and level of skills available to the organization
- The size, age and maturity of the organization
- The management style of the organization
- Dependence on IT for business-critical activities, processes and functions
- The way in which IT participates in the value network (i.e. the way IT interacts with the business and its partners, suppliers and customers)
- The relationship between IT and its vendors.

For a more complete description of how these factors influence organizational design, please refer to Chapter 6 in *ITIL Service Strategy*.

This type of organization structure is illustrated in Figure 6.10. In this structure, IT operations management is responsible for the technical and application management functions, which in turn are responsible for managing their own operational activities. Each department is able to delegate some of these activities to the operations control department.

The advantages of this organization structure are:

- There is greater consistency and control between the more tactical and more operational technical management activities.
- It is easier to enforce the performance standards and technical architectures that are created in service design, because the people who were involved in design are managing the

activities of the people who are executing those activities.
- As there is no duplication between location or activity, this structure is often more cost-effective.

The disadvantage of this organization structure is:

- The scope of this structure makes it very difficult to manage effectively in large organizations or in organizations with multiple data centres.

6.10.6.1 Organizing application and technical management

Technical and application management organizations tend to be fairly straightforward. Technical management departments are usually based on the technology they manage (see section 6.4.4) and application management departments are usually based on the applications and sets of applications they manage (see section 6.6.6).

However, there are some alternative organization structures and variations, which are discussed in this section.

Organizing by geography

In organizations with multiple locations, it is common for the technical and application management departments to be represented in each physical location. However, this does not mean that each location will have all the same departments, or that they are all responsible for the same actions.

As support tools mature, more and more IT infrastructure and application CIs can be managed remotely. This means that each department will have a strong, centralized technical or application management support team, with local members to provide specialized, on-site activities or support.

For example, a central server support team might help create standards for server configurations, monitoring and controlling remote devices, performing backups, performing operating system upgrades etc. Assisting them would be local teams that may provide basic on-site support, hardware maintenance and repair and configuration and installation of new servers.

In application management, the central team could participate in ongoing design and testing of the application, monitoring and control; perform

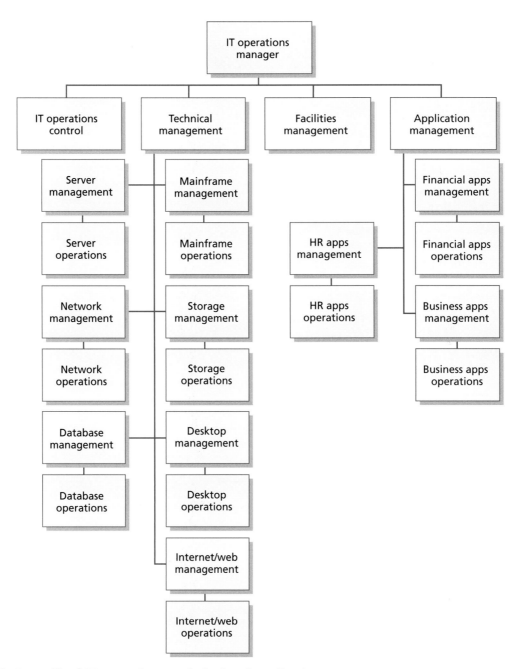

Figure 6.10 Centralized IT operations, technical and application management structure

backups, data integrity checks etc. The local team could provide on-site support and education to end users and work with the local technical management team to resolve more complex problems involving local equipment.

There is one potential issue that needs to be resolved, however, and that is who the local team reports to. In some organizations they report to the manager of the centralized team. This has the added advantage of consistent performance and management across the whole enterprise.

In other organizations the local teams report to the most senior IT manager at that site. This has the added advantage that IT services can be customized to meet local conditions, but it creates a lot of confusion about who the local teams should take direction from.

The advantages of this type of organizational structure include the following:

■ Organization structure can be customized to meet local conditions.

■ Technical and application management can be customized to meet differing levels of IT service from region to region.

The disadvantages of this type of organizational structure include the following:

■ Reporting lines and authority structures can be confusing.
■ Standards are difficult to impose, resulting in inconsistent and duplicated activities and tools, resulting in reduced economies of scale, which in turn increases the overall cost of operations.
■ Duplication of roles, activities, tools and facilities across multiple locations could be very costly.

Organizing by system

Some organizations organize their technical and application management functions according to systems. This means that each department will consist of application specialists and IT infrastructure technical specialists, all geared towards managing the services based on that set of systems. Components that are shared across all these systems, such as the network, will be managed by dedicated technical management departments.

The advantage of this organization structure is:

■ It is easier to produce high-quality output to the end user because all department members are focused on the success of the system as a whole, rather than the performance of an individual technology component or application.

The disadvantages of this organization structure are:

■ Duplication of skills and resources across several departments will increase the cost of the organization. For example, each group is likely to have an individual or team dedicated to managing servers – each of which will be doing very similar tasks.
■ Communication between staff who are managing similar technology is reduced. This reduces the amount of learning by experience and increases reliance on collaborative knowledge management tools.

■ When people with similar skills are in the same department, the department will compensate for members with lower skill and competency levels. When there is only one person with server management skills on a system-based department, and their competency is minimal, it will affect the performance of the entire department.

Technology
considerations

7

7 Technology considerations

Each function and process is defined in the relevant section in Chapters 4 and 6. This chapter brings all technology requirements together to define the overall requirement of an integrated set of service management technologies for service operation.

The same technology, with some possible additions, should be used for the other stages of the service lifecycle – service strategy, service design, service transition and CSI – to give consistency and to allow the service lifecycle to be properly managed.

The main requirements for service operation are as set out in this chapter.

7.1 GENERIC REQUIREMENTS

An integrated ITSM technology (or toolset, as some suppliers sell their technology as 'modules' whereas some organizations may choose to integrate products from alternative suppliers) is needed that includes the following core functionality.

7.1.1 Self-help

Many organizations find it beneficial to offer self-help capabilities to their users. The technology should therefore support this capability with some form of web front-end allowing web pages to be defined offering a menu-driven range of self-help and service requests – with a direct interface into the back-end process-handling software.

7.1.2 Workflow or process engine

A workflow or process control engine is needed to allow the pre-definition and control of defined processes such as an incident lifecycle, request fulfilment lifecycle, problem lifecycle, change model etc. This should allow responsibilities, activities, timescales, escalation paths and alerting to be predefined and then automatically managed.

7.1.3 Integrated configuration management system

Toolsets should have an integrated CMS to allow the organization's IT infrastructure assets, components, services and any ancillary CIs (such as contracts, locations, licences, suppliers – anything that the IT organization wishes to control) to be held, together with all relevant attributes, in a centralized location, and to allow relationships between each to be stored and maintained, and linked to incident, problem, known error and change records as appropriate.

7.1.4 Discovery/deployment/licensing technology

In order to populate or verify the CMS data and to assist in licence management, discovery or automated audit tools will be required. Such tools should be capable of being run from any location on the network and allow interrogation and recovery of information relating to all components that make up, or are connected to, the IT infrastructure.

Such technology should allow 'filtering' so that the data being carried forward can be vetted and only required data extracted. It is also very helpful if 'changes only' since the last audit can be extracted and reported upon.

The same technology can often be used to deploy new software to target locations – this is an essential requirement for all service operation teams or departments, to allow patches, transports etc. to be distributed to the correct users.

An interface to 'self-help' capabilities is desirable to allow authorized software downloads to be requested in this way but automatically handled by the deployment software.

Tools that allow automatic comparison of the details of software licences held (in the CMS, ideally) and actual licence numbers deployed – with reporting of any discrepancies – are extremely desirable.

7.1.5 Remote control

It is often helpful for the service desk analysts and other support groups to be able to take control of the user's desktop (under properly controlled security conditions) so as to allow them to conduct investigations or correct settings etc. Facilities to allow this level of remote control will be needed.

7.1.6 Diagnostic utilities

It could be extremely useful for the service desk and other support groups if the technology incorporated the capability to create and use diagnostic scripts and other diagnostic utilities (such as, for example, case-based reasoning tools) to help with earlier diagnosis of incidents. Ideally, these should be 'context sensitive' and presentation of the scripts automated as far as possible.

7.1.7 Reporting

There is no use storing data unless it can be easily retrieved and used to meet the organization's purposes. The technology should therefore incorporate good reporting capabilities, as well as allowing standard interfaces which can be used to input data to industry-standard reporting packages, dashboards etc. Ideally, instant on-screen as well as printed reporting can be provided through the use of context-sensitive 'top ten' reports.

7.1.8 Dashboards

Dashboard-type technology is useful to allow 'see at a glance' visibility of overall IT service performance and availability levels. Such displays can be included in management-level reports to users and customers – but can also give real-time information for inclusion in IT web pages to give dynamic reporting, and can be used for support and investigation purposes. Capabilities to support customized views of information to meet specific levels of interest can be particularly useful.

However, they sometimes represent a technical rather than service view of the infrastructure and in such cases they may be of less interest to customers and users. For IT management and executives, use of a balanced scorecard approach (see section A.14) summarized into a dashboard view may be desired as a way of reporting on overall IT quality and performance.

7.1.9 Integration with the business

To facilitate greater business alignment, business applications and tools need to be able to interface with ITSM support tools to give the required functionality.

Example of interfacing

An Eastern European telecoms company was able to interface its telephone cell-net monitoring and billing system to its event management, incident management and service asset and configuration management processes. In this way it was able to detect any unusual usage/billing patterns and interpret these such that it could identify, with a high degree of certainty, that a telephone had been stolen and was being used to make illicit calls.

It was able to raise events for such patterns and automate actions to suspend usage of the mobile phone devices and, in parallel, identify the exact location of the illicit user (using GPRS technology) and raise incidents so that the police were able to find the suspected thief and recover the device.

More advanced tools integration capabilities are needed to allow greater exploitation of this sort of business and IT integration.

7.1.10 Software as a Service (SaaS) technologies

SaaS technologies offer hosted service management capabilities over the internet (see section C.2 in *ITIL Service Strategy*). The key benefits are that management functionality can be put into place without capital expenditures on hardware, software and labour for installation. With SaaS technologies, management services need only be accessed through a web browser. Key benefits can include lower capital and start-up costs and faster implementation of management solutions, as well as a ready-built approach for handling service continuity of those solutions in the event of a major business disruption.

While initially attractive, care must be taken to consider possible constraints such as:

- The level of customization and changes to functionality that will be allowed (i.e. whether IT can use their desired incident classification schema or be forced to use only what the vendor allows)
- Whether the tooling provider will provide a dedicated environment specific to the IT functions of the business or utilize a shared environment that may limit the kinds of tailoring and customization that can be done

- The hours of service availability that will be provided (i.e. whether the vendor has periods of time when services are unavailable due to maintenance)
- Upgrade flexibility to handle new functionality or manage newer technologies
- Licensing schemes that may become restrictive or expensive when taking a total-cost-of-ownership view
- Limits on storage size for items such as incident records and history or how frequently these may be accessed
- Security and access management constraints or risk exposures related to the management solutions being used
- Integration of the vendor solution with other service management tools.

7.2 EVENT MANAGEMENT

The following features are desirable for any event management technology:

- Multi-environmental, open interface to allow monitoring and alerting across heterogeneous services and an organization's entire IT infrastructure
- Easy to deploy, with minimal set-up costs
- 'Standard' agents to monitor most common environments/components/systems
- Open interfaces to accept any standard (e.g. SNMP) event input and generation of multiple alerting
- Centralized routeing of all events to a single location, programmable to allow different location(s) at various times
- Configurable and programmable functionality to correlate similar/identical events
- Capability to manipulate events programmatically after they are generated and before they are communicated and presented
- Capability to suppress or flag events during periods of scheduled outages such that those needing to respond to events recognize that no action may be needed during those times
- Support for design/test stages – so that new applications/services can be monitored during design/test stages and results fed back into the design and transition
- Programmable assessment and handling of alerts depending upon symptoms and impact

- The ability to allow an operator to acknowledge an alert, and if no response is entered within a defined timeframe, to escalate the alert
- Good reporting functionality to allow feedback into design and transition stages as well as a meaningful management information and business user 'dashboard'.

Such technology should allow a direct interface into the organization's incident management processes (via entry into the incident log), as well as the capability to escalate to support staff, third-party suppliers, engineers, and so on via email, SMS messaging etc.

Specialist facilities, or perhaps separate specialist tools, will be required for website monitoring. Such facilities must be able to simulate customer traffic onto the website and to report on availability and performance in relation to the 'customer experience'.

7.3 INCIDENT MANAGEMENT

7.3.1 Integrated ITSM technology

Integrated ITSM technology is required that has the following functionality:

- Incident logging capabilities that allow for efficient entry of incident data (see section 4.2.5.2), categorization, prioritization, tracking and reporting of incidents
- An integral CMS to allow automated relationships to be made and maintained between incidents, service requests, problems, known errors, workarounds, and all other CIs
- The CMS that can be used to assist in determining priority and aid in investigation and diagnosis
- A process flow engine to allow processes to be predefined (including predefined incident models, see section 4.2.4.2) and automatically controlled – with flexible internal routeing to all relevant support groups and external interfaces (e.g. email)
- Automated alerting and escalation capabilities to prevent an incident being overlooked or delayed
- Open interfacing to event management tools, so that any failures can be automatically raised as incidents

- A web interface to allow self-help and service requests to be input via internet/intranet screens
- An integrated KEDB so that diagnosed and/or resolved incidents/problems can be recorded and searched to help speed up future incident resolution
- Easy-to-use reporting facilities to allow incident metrics to be produced and to facilitate incident analysis for problem management and availability management purposes
- Diagnostic tools (either integrated or interfaces to separate products), as already mentioned under service desk
- Reporting capabilities that allow for efficient access to incident histories and summarizing of incidents by category, priority, status (i.e. open, closed, in progress etc.), CIs impacted, or other means to provide data and support for reactive and proactive problem management activities.

7.3.2 Workflow and automated escalation

The target times should be included in support tools, which should be used to automate the workflow control and escalation paths.

If, for example, a second-line support group has not resolved an incident within a 60-minute agreed target, the incident must be automatically routed to the appropriate (determined by incident categorization) third-line support group, and any necessary hierarchic escalation should be automatically undertaken (e.g. alert message to the service desk manager, incident manager and/ or IT services manager and perhaps to the user, if appropriate). The second-line support group must be informed of the escalation action as part of the automated process.

7.4 REQUEST FULFILMENT

Integrated ITSM technology is needed so that service requests can be linked to incidents or events that have initiated them (and been stored in the same CMS, which can be interrogated to report against SLAs). Some organizations will be content to use the incident management element of such tools and to treat service requests as a subset and defined category of incidents. Where an organization chooses to raise separate service requests, it will require a tool that allows this capability.

Front-end self-help capabilities will be needed to allow users to submit requests via some form of web-based, menu-driven selection process. This may be integrated with an IT service catalogue and access controls to ensure service requests are issued only by those authorized to do so.

Workflow engine capabilities will be needed to automate work steps and authorization tasks for supporting service request models and fulfilment activities.

In all other respects the facilities needed to manage service requests are very similar to those for managing incidents and changes: predefined workflow control of models, priority levels, automated escalation, effective reporting etc.

7.5 PROBLEM MANAGEMENT

7.5.1 Integrated service management technology

An integrated ITSM tool is needed that differentiates between incidents and problems – so that separate problem records can be raised to deal with the underlying causes of incidents, but linked to the related incidents. The functionality of problem records should be similar to those needed for incident records and also allow for multiple incident matching against problem records.

7.5.2 Change management

Integration with change management is very important, so that request, event, incident and problem records can be related to RFCs that have caused problems. This is to evaluate the success of the change management process – as well as incident and known error records – and so that RFCs can be readily raised to control the activities needed to overcome problems that have been identified through root cause analysis or proactive trend analysis.

7.5.3 Integrated CMS

It is also important to have an integrated CMS which allows problem records to be linked to the components affected and the services impacted – and to any other relevant CIs.

Service asset and configuration management forms part of a larger SKMS which includes linkages to many of the data repositories used in service operation. The process and practices of service asset and configuration management and its underlying technology requirements are included in *ITIL Service Transition*.

7.5.4 Known error database

An effective KEDB will be an essential requirement, which should allow easy storage and retrieval of known error data.

Good reporting facilities are needed to ease the production of management reports, allowing the data to be incorporated automatically without the need for re-keying of data – and to allow drill-down capabilities for incident and problem analysis.

Note that in some cases, components or systems being investigated by problem management may be provided by third-party vendors or manufacturers. To address this, vendors' support tools and/or KEDBs may also need to be used.

7.6 ACCESS MANAGEMENT

Access management uses a variety of technologies, mainly:

- Human resource management technology, to authenticate the identity of users, authorize their access, and track their status
- Directory services technology (see section 5.7 for a description of directory services). This technology enables technology managers to assign names to resources on a network and then provide access to those resources based on the profile of the user. Directory services tools also enable access management to create roles and groups and to link these to both users and resources
- Access management features in applications, middleware, operating systems and network operating systems
- Change management systems
- Request fulfilment technology (see section 7.4).

7.7 SERVICE DESK

Adequate tools and technology support should be provided to enable service desk staff to perform their roles as efficiently and effectively as possible. This will include the following.

7.7.1 Telephony

Because a high percentage of incidents are likely to be raised by telephone calls from users, the service desk should be provided with good, modern telephony services. This should include:

- An automatic call distribution (ACD) system to allow a single telephone number (or numbers if a distributed or segmented service desk is the preferred option) and group pick-up capabilities. Warning: If options are offered via the ACD, via keyboard or interactive voice response (IVR) selection, do not use too many levels of options or offer ambiguous options. Also do not include any 'dead ends' or options which, once chosen, do not allow the caller to go back to previous menus.
- Computer telephony integration (CTI) software to allow caller recognition (via the linked ACD) and automated population of the users' details into the incident record from the CMS.
- Voice over internet protocol (VoIP) – use of this technology can significantly reduce telephony costs when dealing with remote and international users.
- Statistical software to allow telephony statistics to be gathered and easily interrogated/printed for analysis – this should allow the following information to be obtained for any selected period:
  - Number of calls received, in total and broken down by any 'splits' – where any call routeing has been chosen and is being provided by an IVR system/keypad response
  - Call arrival profiles and answer times
  - Call abandon rates
  - Call handling rates by individual service desk call handlers
  - Average call durations.
- Hands-free headsets, with dual-user access capabilities (on at least some of the headsets) for use during training of new staff etc.

7.7.2 Support tools

There are a range of free-standing service desk support tools available in the marketplace – and some organizations may choose to produce their own simple incident logging/management systems. If an organization seriously intends to implement ITSM, then a fully integrated ITSM toolset will be required that has a CMS at the centre and provides integrated support for all the ITIL-defined processes.

Specific elements of such a tool that will be particularly beneficial for the service desk include the following.

7.7.2.1 Known error database

An integrated KEDB should be used to store details of previous incidents, problems, workarounds, root causes and their resolutions, so that any incident recurrences can be more quickly diagnosed and fixed.

To facilitate this, functionality is needed to categorize and quickly retrieve previous known errors, using pattern matching and keyword searching against symptoms. Management of the KEDB is the responsibility of problem management, but the service desk will use it to help speed incident handling.

7.7.2.2 Diagnostic scripts

Multi-level diagnostic scripts should be developed, stored and managed to allow service desk staff to pinpoint the cause of failures. Specialist support groups and suppliers should be asked to provide details of the likely failures and the key questions to be asked to identify exactly what has gone wrong – and for details of the resolution actions to be taken.

These details should then be included in context-sensitive scripts that should appear on screen, dependent upon the multi-level categorization of the incident, and should be driven by the user's answers to diagnostic questions.

7.7.2.3 Self-help web interface

It is often cost-effective and expedient to provide some form of automated 'self-help' functionality, so users can seek and obtain assistance which will enable them to resolve their own difficulties. Ideally this should be via a 24/7 web interface that is driven by menu selection and might include, as appropriate:

- Frequently asked questions (FAQs) and solutions
- 'How to do' search capabilities – to guide users through a context-sensitive list of tasks or activities

- A bulletin-type service containing details of outstanding service issues/problems together with anticipated restoration times
- Password change capabilities – using secure password protection software to check identities, perform authorization and change passwords without the need for service desk intervention
- Software fix downloads (patches, service packs, bug fixes etc. where it is determined that the user has the wrong version or a fix is needed); tools are available to automate the checking process, to compare the actual desktop image with the agreed 'standard' builds and to allow upgrades to be offered and accepted where necessary
- Software repairs – where it is detected that a corruption may have occurred, to allow software fixes, removal and/or reinstallation
- Software removal requests – automatically completed with any licence being returned to the pool
- Downloads of additional software packages – tools are available to check a predefined software policy and to allow the download of additional software packages, if covered by the policy. This can include automated software licence checks and financial approvals as well as CMS updating
- Advance notice of any planned downtime or services outages or degradations.

The self-help solution should include the capability for users to log incidents themselves, which can be used during periods that the service desk is closed (if not operating 24/7) and attended to by service desk staff at the start of the next shift.

Some care has to be exercised to ensure that the self-help activities selected for inclusion are not too advanced for the average user, and that safeguards are included to prevent a 'little knowledge being a dangerous thing'! It may be possible to offer slightly more advanced self-help facilities to 'super users' who have had extra training. It is also necessary to be very careful about assumptions made when staffing a service desk about the amount of use that users will make of self-help facilities.

Note that, as already covered in the list above, it is possible to combine some simpler request fulfilment activities as part of an overall self-help system – which can also be of significant benefit in reducing calls to the service desk (see section 7.1.1 for further details).

7.7.2.4 Remote control

It is often helpful for the service desk analysts to be able to take control of the user's desktop so as to allow them to conduct investigations or correct settings etc. Facilities to allow this level of remote control will be needed.

7.7.3 IT service continuity planning for ITSM support tools

Organizations are likely to become quickly dependent upon their ITSM tools and will find it difficult to work without them. A full business impact analysis and risk assessment should be performed and plans then developed to ensure appropriate IT service continuity and resilience levels.

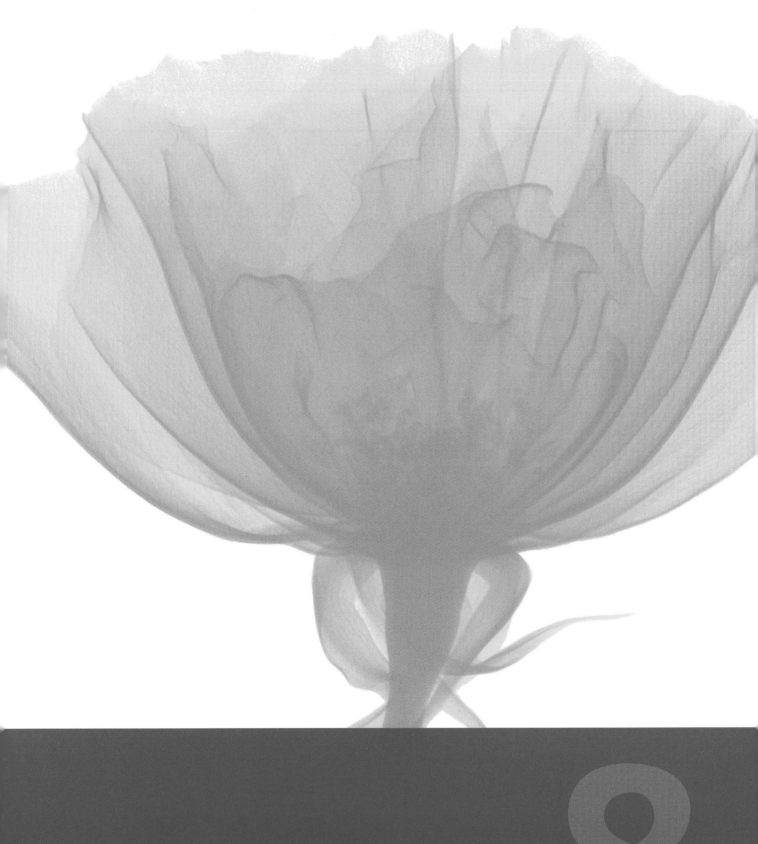

Implementation of
service operation

8

8 Implementation of service operation

It should be noted that service operation is a stage in a lifecycle and not an entity in its own right. By the time a service, process, organization structure or technology is operating, it has already been implemented. However, there are a number of processes and functions described in this publication, and it is therefore important to address the implementation considerations which should have been addressed by the time they come into operation.

A number of these have been covered in the relevant section – for example guidance is given about organization structures and roles in Chapter 6. This will not be repeated here. Rather, this section will focus on some generic implementation guidance for service operation as a whole.

8.1 MANAGING CHANGE IN SERVICE OPERATION

Service operation should strive to achieve stability – but not stagnation! There are many valid and advantageous reasons why 'change is a good thing', but service operation staff must ensure that any changes are absorbed without adverse impact upon the stability of the IT services being offered.

8.1.1 Change triggers

There are many things that may trigger a change in the service operation environment. These include:

- New or upgraded hardware or network components
- New or upgraded applications software
- New or upgraded system software (operating systems, utilities, middleware etc., including patches and bug fixes
- Legislative, conformance or governance changes
- Obsolescence – some components may become obsolete and require replacement or cease to be supported by the supplier/maintainer
- Business imperative – you have to be flexible to work in ITSM, particularly during service operation, and there will be many occasions when the business needs IT changes to meet dynamic business requirements

- Enhancements to processes, procedures and/or underpinning tools to improve IT delivery or reduce financial costs
- Changes of management or personnel (ranging from loss or transfer of individuals right through to major takeovers or acquisitions)
- Change of service levels or in service provision – outsourcing, insourcing, partnerships etc.

8.1.2 Change assessment

Service operation staff must be involved in the assessment of all changes to ensure that operational issues are fully taken into account. This involvement should start as soon as possible, not just at the later stages of change (i.e. CAB and ECAB membership) by which time many fundamental decisions will have been made and influence is likely to be very limited. The change manager should inform all affected parties of the change being assessed so input can be prepared and available prior to CAB meetings.

However, it is important that service operation staff are involved at these latter stages as they may be involved in the actual implementation and they will wish to ensure that careful scheduling takes place to avoid potential contentions or particularly sensitive periods.

8.1.3 Measurement of successful change

The ultimate measure of success in respect of changes made to service operation is that customers and users do not experience any unexpected variation or outage of service. As far as possible, the effects of changes should be invisible, apart from any enhanced functionality, quality or financial savings resulting from the change.

8.2 SERVICE OPERATION AND PROJECT MANAGEMENT

Because service operation is generally viewed as 'business as usual' and often focused on executing defined procedures in a standard way, there is a tendency not to use project management processes when they would in fact be appropriate. For example, major infrastructure upgrades, or the deployment of new or changed procedures, are significant tasks where formal project management can be used to improve control and manage costs/resources.

Using project management to manage these types of activity would have the following benefits:

- The project benefits are clearly stated and agreed
- There is more visibility of what is being done and how it is being managed, which makes it easier for other IT groups and the business to quantify the contributions made by operational teams
- This in turn makes it easier to obtain funding for projects that have traditionally been difficult to cost justify
- Greater consistency and improved quality
- Achievement of objectives results in higher credibility for operational groups.

8.3 ASSESSING AND MANAGING RISK IN SERVICE OPERATION

There will be a number of occasions where it is imperative that risk assessment to service operation is quickly undertaken and acted upon.

The most obvious area is in assessing the risk of potential changes or known errors (already covered elsewhere) but in addition service operation staff may need to be involved in assessing the risk and impact of:

- Failures, or potential failures – either reported by event management or incident/problem management, or warnings raised by manufacturers, suppliers or contractors
- New projects that will ultimately result in delivery into the live environment
- Environmental risk (encompassing IT service continuity-type risks to the physical environment and locale as well as political, commercial or industrial relations related risks)
- Suppliers, particularly where new suppliers are involved or where key service components are under the control of third parties
- Security risks – both theoretical or actual arising from security-related incidents or events
- New customers/services to be supported.

8.4 OPERATIONAL STAFF IN SERVICE DESIGN AND TRANSITION

All IT groups will be involved during service design and service transition to ensure that new components or services are designed, tested and implemented to provide the correct levels of functionality, usability, availability, capacity etc.

Additionally, service operation staff must be involved during the early stages of service design and service transition to ensure that when new services reach the live environment they are fit for purpose, from a service operation perspective, and are 'supportable' in the future.

In this context, 'supportable' means:

- Capable of being supported from a technical and operational viewpoint from within existing or pre-agreed additional resources and skills levels
- Without adverse impact on other existing technical or operational working practices, processes or schedules
- Without any unexpected operational costs or ongoing or escalating support expenditure
- Without any unexpected contractual or legal complications
- No complex support paths between multiple support departments of third-party organizations.

Note that change is not just about technology. It also requires training, awareness, cultural change, motivational issues and a lot more. Further details regarding wider management of change are covered in *ITIL Service Transition*.

8.5 PLANNING AND IMPLEMENTING SERVICE MANAGEMENT TECHNOLOGIES

There are a number of factors that organizations need to plan for in readiness for, and during deployment and implementation of, ITSM support tools. These include the following.

8.5.1 Licences

The overall cost of ITSM tools, particularly the integrated tool that will form the heart of the required toolset, is usually determined by the number and type of user licences that the organization needs.

Such tools are often sold in modular format, so the exact functionality of each module needs to be well understood and some initial sizing must be conducted to determine how many – and what type – of users will need access to each module.

Licences are often available in the following types (the exact terminology may vary depending upon the software supplier).

8.5.1.1 Dedicated licences

For use by those staff that require frequent and prolonged use of the module (e.g. service desk staff would need a dedicated licence to use an incident management module).

8.5.1.2 Shared licences

For staff who make fairly regular use of the module, but with significant intervals in between, so can usually manage with a shared licence (e.g. third-line support staff may need regular access to an incident management module, but only at times when they are actively updating an incident record). The ratio of required licences to users needs to be estimated, so the correct number of licences can be purchased – this will depend upon the number of potential users, the length of periods of use and the expected frequency between usages to give an estimated concurrency level. The cost of a shared licence is usually higher than that of dedicated licences – but the overall cost is less as users are sharing and fewer licences are therefore needed in total.

8.5.1.3 Web licences

Usually allowing some form of 'light interface' via web access to the tool's capabilities (e.g. Software as a Service (SaaS) based solutions – *see ITIL Service Strategy*, section C.2), web licences are usually suitable for staff requiring remote access, only occasional access, or usage of just a small subset of the functionality (e.g. engineering staff wishing to log details of actions taken on incidents or users just wanting to log an incident directly). Web licences usually cost a lot less than other licences (they may even be free with other licences) and the ratio of use is also often lower, so overall costs are reduced further.

Some staff may require access to multiple licences (e.g. support staff may require a dedicated or shared licence when in the office during the day, but may require a web licence when providing

out of hours support from home). Keep in mind that licences may be required for customers/users/suppliers using the same tool to input, view or update records or reports. Note that some licence agreements (of any of the types mentioned) may restrict usage of the software to an individual device or CPU.

8.5.1.4 Service on demand

There has been a trend within the IT industry for suppliers to offer IT applications 'on demand', where access is given to the application for a period of demand and then severed when it is no longer needed – and charged on the basis of the time spent using the application. This type of access may be offered by some ITSM tool suppliers – which could be attractive to smaller organizations or if the tools in question are very specialized and used relatively infrequently.

An alternative to this is where the use of a tool is offered as part of a specific consultancy assignment (e.g. a specialist capacity management consultancy, say, who may offer a regular but relatively infrequent capacity planning consultancy package and provide use of the tools for the duration of the assignment). In such cases the licence fees are likely to be included as part of, or an addendum to, the consultancy fee.

A further variation is where software is licensed and charged on an agent/activity basis. An example of this is interrogation/monitoring and/or simulation software (e.g. agent software that can simulate predefined customer paths through an organization's website, to assess and report upon performance and availability). Such software is typically charged on the basis of the number of agents, their location and/or the amount of activity generated.

In all cases, full investigations of the licensing structure must be investigated and well understood during the procurement investigations and well before tools are deployed, so that the ultimate costs do not come as any sort of surprise.

8.5.2 Deployment

Many ITSM tools, particularly discovery and event monitoring tools, will require some client/agent software deploying to all target locations before they can be used. This will need careful planning and execution, and should be handled through formal release and deployment management (see *ITIL Service Transition*).

Even where network deployment is possible, this needs careful scheduling and testing – and records must be maintained throughout the deployment so that support staff know who has been upgraded and who has not. Some form of interim change management may be necessary and the CMS should be updated as the deployment progresses.

It is often necessary to reboot devices for the client software to be recognized – and this needs to be arranged in advance, otherwise long delays can occur if staff do not generally switch off their desktops overnight.

There may be particular problems deploying to laptops and other portable equipment, and special arrangements may be necessary for staff to log on and receive the new software.

8.5.3 Capacity checks

Some capacity management may be necessary in advance to ensure that all of the target locations have sufficient storage and processing capacity to host and run the new software – any that cannot will need upgrading or replacing, and lead times for these actions need to be included in the plans.

The capacity of the network should also be checked to establish whether it can handle the transmission of management information, the transmission of log files and the distribution of clients, and also possibly software and configuration files.

8.5.4 Timing of technology deployment

Care is needed to ensure that tools are deployed at the appropriate time in relation to the organization's level of ITSM sophistication and knowledge. If tools are deployed too soon, they may be seen as an immediate panacea and any necessary action to change processes, working practices or attitudes may be hindered or overlooked.

A tool alone is usually not enough to make things work better. There is an old adage: 'A fool with a tool is still a fool'!

The organization must first examine the processes that the tool is seeking to address and also ensure that staff are 'bought in' to the new processes and way of working and have adopted a 'service culture'.

However, tools can and often do make things a reality for many people – they are tangible and technical staff can immediately see how the new processes can work and how they may improve their way of working.

Some processes just cannot be done without adequate tooling, so there is a careful balance to be maintained to ensure tools are introduced when they are needed – but not before! Similarly, care is needed to ensure that training is provided at the correct point – not too early or knowledge will diminish or be lost, but early enough so that staff can be formally trained and familiarize themselves with the operation of the tools in advance of live deployment. Extra training should be planned for an additional period when the tools go live and into the future, as needed.

8.5.5 Type of introduction

A decision is needed on what type of introduction is needed – whether to go for a 'Big Bang' introduction or some sort of phased approach. As most organizations will not start from a 'greenfield' situation, and will have live services to keep running during the introduction, a phased approach is more likely to be necessary.

In many cases a new tool will be replacing an older, probably less sophisticated, tool and the switchover between the two is another factor to be planned. This will often involve deciding what data needs to be carried forward from the old tool to the new one – and this may require significant reformatting to achieve the required results. Ideally this transfer should be done electronically, but in some cases a small amount of rekeying of live data may be inevitable and should be factored into the plans.

Caution: older tools generally rely on more manual entry and maintenance of data so if electronic data migration is being used, an audit should be performed to verify data quality.

Where data transfer is complicated or time-consuming to achieve, an alternative might be to allow a period of parallel running – with the old tool being available for an initial period alongside the new one, so that historical data can be referenced if needed. In such cases it will be prudent to make the old tool 'read only' so that no mistakes can be made by logging new data in the old tool. Complete details on the release and deployment management process can be found in *ITIL Service Transition*.

Challenges, risks and critical success factors

9

9 Challenges, risks and critical success factors

9.1 CHALLENGES

There are a number of challenges faced within service operation that need to be overcome. These include those set out in this section.

9.1.1 Lack of engagement with development and project staff

Traditionally, there has been a separation between service operation staff and those staff involved in developing new applications or running projects that will eventually deliver new functionality into the operational environment.

This separation was originally deliberate and driven by the desire to prevent collusion and avoid potential security risks (in some organizations it is still a legislative requirement). However, instead of using this separation of duties to create positive contributions, in many organizations it is a source of rivalry and political manoeuvring.

All too often, ITSM is seen as something that has been initiated in the operational areas and is nothing to do with development or projects.

This view is very damaging as the appropriate time to be thinking of service operation issues is at the outset of new developments or projects – when there is still time to include these factors in the planning stages.

ITIL Service Design and *ITIL Service Transition* describe the steps needed to ensure that IT operations issues are considered from the outset of new developments and projects.

9.1.2 Justifying funding

It is often difficult to justify expenditure in the area of service operation, as money spent in this sphere is often regarded as 'infrastructure costs', with nothing new to show for the investment.

ITIL Service Strategy discusses how to ensure an ROI and eliminate the perception of investment as a purely infrastructure 'overhead'. Good guidance is offered on how to justify investment.

Anecdotes

One organization uses an 'operation transition-in policy' to ensure that services being deployed have had the appropriate level of input from the operational teams. This is basically a policy that clearly shows under what circumstances an application is 'ready' to transition into operations. This helped with communication to development and project teams and also provided a clear set of guidelines on how to work with the operational teams.

Another organization uses operational use cases to get development teams to include requirements that should be fulfilled by the application to be run in production under the control of operations personnel.

In reality, many investments in ITSM, particularly in the service operation areas, can save money and show a positive ROI – as well as resulting improvement in service quality. Some examples of potential areas of savings include:

- Reduced software licence costs through the better management of licences and deployed copies
- Reduced support costs due to fewer incidents and problems and reduced resolution times
- Reduced headcount through better aligned processes, leading to less duplication of activities and better usage of existing resources
- Less 'lost business' due to poor IT service quality
- Better utilization of existing infrastructure equipment and deferral of further expenditure due to better capacity management.

9.1.3 Challenges for service operation managers

The following is a list of some of the challenges that managers in service operation should expect to face. There is no easy solution to these challenges, mainly because they are by-products of the organization culture and the decisions made during the process of deciding the organizational structure. The purpose of including the list is to ensure that service operation managers are conscious of them and can create a plan to deal with them.

The differences between design activities and operational activities will continue to present challenges. This is for a number of reasons, including the following:

- Service design may tend to focus on an individual service at a time, whereas service operation tends to focus on delivering and supporting all services at the same time. Operation managers should work closely with service design and service transition to provide the operation perspective to ensure that design and transition outcomes support the overall operational needs.

- Service design will often be conducted in projects, while service operation focuses on ongoing, repeatable management processes and activities. The result of this is that operational staff are often not available to participate in service design project activities, which in turn results in IT services that are difficult to operate, or which do not include adequate manageability design elements. In addition, once project staff have finished the design of one IT service they could move on to the next project and not be available to support difficulties in the operational environment. Overcoming this challenge requires service operation to plan for its staff to be actively involved in design projects, to resource the transition activities and participate in early life support of services introduced in the operational environment.

- The two stages in the lifecycle have different metrics, which encourages service design to complete the project on time, to specification and in budget. In many cases it is difficult to forecast what the service will look like and how much it will cost after it has been deployed and operated for some time. When it does not run as expected, IT operations management is held responsible. While this challenge will always be a reality in service management, this can be addressed by active involvement in the service transition stage of the lifecycle. The objective of service transition is to ensure that designed services will operate as expected and the operations manager can provide the knowledge needed to service transition to assess, and remedy, issues before they become issues in the operational environment.

- Service transition that is not used effectively to manage the transition between the design and operation stages. For example, some organizations may only use change management to schedule the deployment of changes that have already been made – rather than testing to see whether the change will successfully make the transition between design and operation. It is imperative that the practices of service transition are followed and organization policies to prevent poorly managed change practices are in place. Operation, change and transition managers must have the authority to deny any changes into the operational environment, without exception, that are not thoroughly tested.

These challenges can only be dealt with if service operation staff are involved in service design and transition, and this will require that they are formally tasked and measured to do this. Roles identified in the service design processes should be included in technical and IT application management staff job descriptions and their time allocated on a project-by-project basis.

Another set of challenges relates to measurement. Each alternative structure will introduce different combinations of items that are easy or difficult to measure. For example measuring the performance of a device or team could be relatively easy, but determining whether that performance is good or bad for the overall IT service is another matter altogether. A good SLM process will help to resolve this, but this means that service operation teams must be an integral part of that process (see *ITIL Continual Service Improvement*).

A third set of challenges relates to the use of virtual teams. Traditional, hierarchical management structures are becoming inadequate because of the complexity and diversity of most organizations. A management paradigm (matrix management) has emerged where employees report to different sources for different tasks. This has resulted in a complex web of accountability and an increased risk of activities falling through the cracks. On the other hand, it also enables the organization to make skills and knowledge available where they are most needed to support the business. Knowledge management and the mapping of authority structures will become increasingly important as organizations expand and diversify. This is discussed in *ITIL Service Strategy*.

One of the most significant challenges faced by service operation managers is the balancing of many internal and external relationships. Most IT organizations today are complex and as services become more commoditized there is an increased use of value networks, partnerships and shared services models. While a significant advantage to dynamically evolving business needs, this increases the complexity of managing services cohesively and efficiently and providing the invisible seam between the customer and the intricate web of how services are actually delivered. A service operation manager should invest in relationship management knowledge and skills to help deal with the complexity of this challenge.

9.2 CRITICAL SUCCESS FACTORS

9.2.1 Management support

Senior and middle management support is needed for all ITSM activities and processes, particularly in service operation.

Senior management support is critical for obtaining and maintaining adequate funding and resourcing. Rather than seeing service operation as a 'black hole' for investment, senior management should quantify and champion the benefits of good service operation. They should also be fully informed of the dire results that can result because of poor service operation.

Senior management must provide visible support during the launch of new service operation initiatives (such as through appearances at seminars, signatories to memos and announcements etc.) and their ongoing support must be equally well demonstrated. The wrong message may be given if a senior manager fails to turn up to an important project meeting or launch seminar. Even worse are senior managers who support the initiative verbally, but abuse their authority to encourage circumvention of the service operation practice.

Senior managers should also empower the middle managers who will be directly responsible for service operation. Supporting the initiative publicly, but then overriding budget requirements or necessary changes, will harm both the

implementation and ongoing service operation initiative.

Middle managers must also provide the necessary support – and in particular this should be demonstrated by their actions. If a middle manager is seen to be circumventing or overriding an agreed procedure (e.g. implementing a change that has not been through the change management process) then this gives the clear message that others can do the same – and that the procedure is worthless and can be ignored by all. Middle managers should go out of their way to make their support known, not just by their words but also by their actions and adherence to the organization's agreed processes and procedures.

Middle managers should also give their full support to hiring staff to support the process, instead of accepting the need for formalized service operation and then simply increasing the workload of existing staff to get it done.

9.2.2 Business support

It is important that the business units also support service operation. This level of support can be far better achieved if the service operation staff involve the business in all of their activities and are open in their reporting of both successes and failures – and their efforts to improve.

It is equally important that the business units understand, accept and carry out the role they play in service operation. Good service requires good customers! Adhering to the policies, processes and procedures, such as using the service desk for logging all requests, is a direct responsibility of the customer to support and promote within the business.

Regular communications with the business to understand their concerns and aspirations and to give feedback on efforts to meet their needs are essential in building the correct relationships and ensuring ongoing support.

Also the business should agree to the costs for implementing service operation and understand the return on the investment, unless this has already been agreed as part of the design process.

9.2.3 Champions

ITSM projects and the resulting ongoing practice (performed by service operation staff) are often more successful if one or more 'champions' are forthcoming who can lead others through their enthusiasm and commitment for ITSM.

In some cases these champions may be senior managers who are leading from the top. But champions can also be successful if they come from other tiers of the organization. One or two junior staff can still have a significant beneficial influence on a successful conclusion.

Champions are often created or heavily influenced through formal service management training, particularly at more advanced levels where the potential benefits to an organization, and to the individuals who make a career path in service management, can be fully explored.

Champions emerge over time. They cannot be created or appointed. Often it is users or customers who provide the most help in creating good service management processes as they are acutely aware of needed improvements from a business perspective. It is important to recognize that these are usually highly motivated staff who often voluntarily take on the greatest workloads. If their input is to be most effective they must be given time to work as the champion.

9.2.4 Staffing and retention

Having the appropriate number of staff with the appropriate skills is critical to the success of service operation. Some challenges that need to be overcome include the following:

■ Projects for new services are usually quite good about specifying required new skills, but often underestimate the number of staff required and how to retain the new skills. See Appendix B for some ideas on how to facilitate better communication about requirements.

■ Scarcity of resources (staff) who have a good understanding of service management. Having good technical people is necessary, but there needs to be a number of key people who are able to move between technology issues and service issues.

■ Because these key people are fairly scarce, it is quite common to train them, only to have them resign and join another company for a better salary. Clear career paths and good incentives should be part of every service management initiative.

■ Attempting to assign too much, too soon, to existing staff. Achieving efficient service operation will take time, but if approached correctly it will be achieved. Unfortunately, some managers try to expedite the savings by assigning the interim work of implementing the new processes and tools to existing, very busy, staff. Invariably either the project fails, or service suffers and sometimes valuable staff will leave. Successful service management projects often require a short-term investment in either temporary staff or contractors, and this should not be underestimated.

■ Coaching and ongoing mentoring should always be available to proactively support staff needs, and address concerns and issues.

■ Capabilities, automated or otherwise, should be in place that foster a teaming culture and enable individuals to work well as teams.

9.2.5 Service management training

Adequate training and awareness can have much wider overall benefits. As well as creating champions of a few, they can be used to win the 'hearts and minds' of many. Service operation staff must all be aware of the consequences of their actions, both good and bad, on the organization – and all must be instilled with a 'service management culture'.

It is possible to have the finest service operation practice and tools in the world – but service management will not be successful unless the people are also attuned to the overall service management objectives. Buy-in and support of all staff are therefore very important – and the role of training and awareness, and even formal qualifications that benefit the individual, should not be underestimated.

Training required for successful service management includes:

■ Training IT staff on the processes that have been implemented. This will include generic training so that they understand the concepts fully, as well as training specially targeted at the organization's own processes

■ Training on 'soft' or 'people' skills, especially for those staff in customer-facing positions

■ Training about understanding the business, and the importance of achieving a service culture

- Where tools have been implemented, training on how to use and manage those tools
- Also, customers and users need appropriate training on how to work with IT – access services, request changes, submit requests, use tools etc.
- Training on tools and techniques that enable individuals to work well within teams.

9.2.6 Suitable tools

Many service operation processes and activities cannot be performed effectively without adequate support tools (as outlined in Chapter 7). Senior management must ensure that funding for such tools is included in ongoing budgets and support their procurement, deployment and ongoing maintenance.

9.2.7 Validity of testing

The quality of IT services that can be provided in service operation is dependent upon the quality of systems and components delivered into the operational environment.

The quality level will be significantly enhanced if adequate and complete testing of new components and releases is carried out in good time. Documentation should also be tested for completeness and quality.

A comprehensive and realistic testing environment should be in place for all systems/components, which mirrors the operational environment in terms of volume as well as characteristics. There should be independent testers wherever possible. Funding for such testing environments is essential if high-quality services are to be achieved.

Additionally, sufficient time and effort are needed to ensure that testing is properly planned and designed – and adequate time is included for testing, and re-testing should some parts fail! The best way to ensure this is by following the guidance in *ITIL Service Transition*.

9.2.8 Measurement and reporting

A clear definition is needed of how things will be measured and reported (as outlined in Appendix B), so that all staff have clear targets to aim for and IT and business managers are able to quickly and easily review progress and pinpoint any areas for attention.

9.3 RISKS

Failure to meet the challenges already described in section 9.1 or to address the CSFs outlined in section 9.2 are obvious risks, but others are described as set out below.

9.3.1 Service loss

The ultimate risk to the business of weaknesses in service operation is the loss of critical IT services with subsequent adverse impact on its employees, customers and finances. In extreme cases there may be potential loss to life and limb where the IT services affected are used for critical health or safety purposes – such as emergency vehicle deployment or health scanning etc.

9.3.2 Risks to successful service operation

The risks to achieving successful service operation are numerous – and in many cases are the opposite of the CSFs as described earlier – but also include:

- **Inadequate funding and resources** Funding must be justified, allocated and held in reserve for its original purpose.
- **Loss of momentum** Where staff see service management as 'flavour of the month' rather than permanently changing the way they work for the future, any impetus is lost as a result: it must be made clear from the outset that a new way of working is required. Also, mechanisms should be in place to ensure that the initiative survives organizational changes.
- **Loss of key personnel** Sometimes the loss of one or two key personnel can have a severe impact: to try to minimize this effect, organizations should seek to cross-train staff and reduce dependencies upon individuals. This is especially true in less mature organizations where knowledge has still not been formalized into processes, documents and tools. These organizations tend to be dependent on 'heroic' efforts of a few knowledgeable people, and are devastated when they leave.
- **Resistance to change** Sometimes people object to new things and are reluctant to take them on board. Education, training, communication and highlighting benefits will help.
- **Lack of management support** This often occurs among middle managers who may not see the overall vision or gain the hands-on benefits that more junior staff may gain. See

section 9.2.1 for more information on this, but managers need to support service management and participate in the appropriate stages and processes of service design, transition and operation to provide tangible support.

- **Faulty design**   If the initial design is faulty, a successful implementation will never give the required results – and redesign will ultimately be necessary.

- **Distrust**   In some organizations service management can be viewed with suspicion by both IT and the business. IT staff see it as an attempt to control them, while the business perceives it as an attempt by IT to gain more funding without actually improving anything. The benefits of service management should be clearly articulated for all stakeholders.

- **Differing customer expectations**   While operational staff are encouraged to execute against standards, customer and user expectations sometimes differ. In other cases one customer may have paid more for a superior service, but when a user from a different area sees the superior service, they feel cheated. This problem should be resolved through clear SLM and careful communication during service design. Complaints of this nature should be taken up through business relationship management and service level management, and should not simply involve service operation automatically increasing service upon request.

Afterword

Afterword

A simple truth must guide us all in service operation. Business and technology will continue to evolve into the future. What was innovative last year is common this year. What is best practice today will be common tomorrow. Achieving excellence in service operation requires flexibility, balance and good judgement in the use of ITIL practices. The guidance in this publication is a key to achieving knowledge, wisdom, future vision and the ability to balance today's business needs and tomorrow's demand.

Common, good, best and future practices all contribute to the goal of service excellence. ITIL provides these as the basis for guiding you towards this goal.

Stability in a changing world is the reality for service providers. Those who excel, and remain the best of breed, understand this and know that the way to achieve is to adapt, learn, innovate and lead.

ITIL Service Operation is an integral part of the service lifecycle, and when used together with the other ITIL lifecycle publications forms a powerful tool in the hands of any IT service provider.

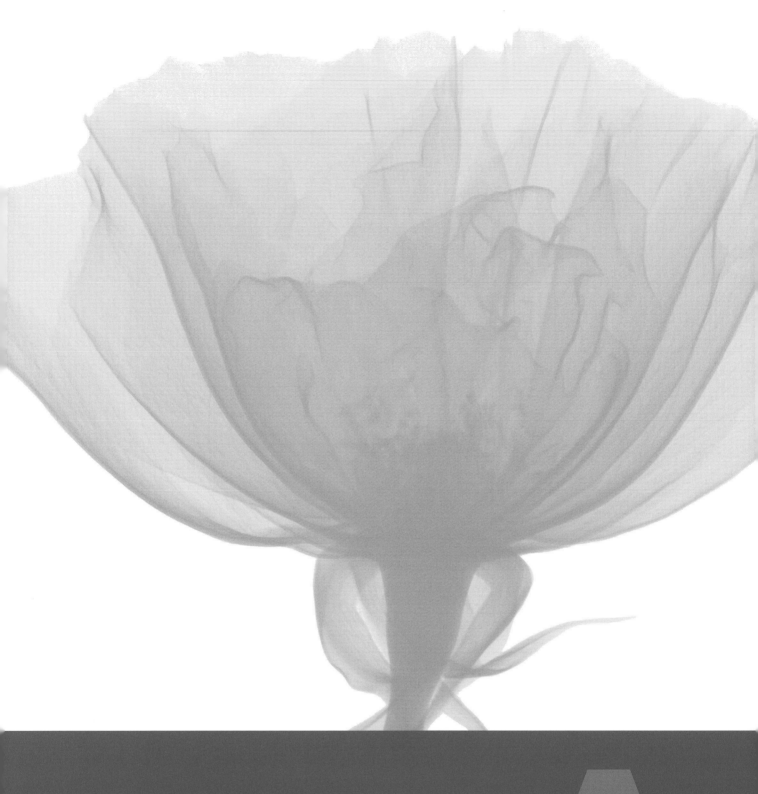

Appendix A:
Related guidance

Appendix A: Related guidance

This is a common appendix across the ITIL core publications. It includes frameworks, best practices, standards, models and quality systems that complement and have synergy with the ITIL service lifecycle.

Section 2.1.7 describes the role of best practices in the public domain and references some of the publications in this appendix. Each core publication references this appendix where relevant.

Related guidance may also be referenced within a single ITIL core publication where the topic is specific to that publication.

A.1 ITIL GUIDANCE AND WEB SERVICES

ITIL is part of the Best Management Practice (BMP) portfolio of best-practice guidance (see section 1.3). BMP products present flexible, practical and effective guidance, drawn from a range of the most successful global business experiences. Distilled to its essential elements, the guidance can then be applied to every type of business and organization.

The BMP website (www.best-management-practice.com) includes news, reviews, case studies and white papers on ITIL and all other BMP best-practice guidance.

The ITIL official website (www.itil-officialsite.com) contains reliable, up-to-date information on ITIL – including information on accreditation and the ITIL software scheme for the endorsement of ITIL-based tools.

Details of the core publications are as follows:

- Cabinet Office (2011). *ITIL Service Strategy*. TSO, London.
- Cabinet Office (2011). *ITIL Service Design*. TSO, London.
- Cabinet Office (2011). *ITIL Service Transition*. TSO, London.
- Cabinet Office (2011). *ITIL Service Operation*. TSO, London.
- Cabinet Office (2011). *ITIL Continual Service Improvement*. TSO, London.

The full ITIL glossary, in English and other languages, can be accessed through the ITIL official site at:

www.itil-officialsite.com/InternationalActivities/ITILGlossaries.aspx

The range of translated glossaries is always growing, so check this website for the most up-to-date list.

Details of derived and complementary publications can be found in the publications library of the Best Management Practice website at:

www.best-management-practice.com/Publications-Library/IT-Service-Management-ITIL/

A.2 QUALITY MANAGEMENT SYSTEM

Quality management focuses on product/service quality as well as the quality assurance and control of processes to achieve consistent quality. Total Quality Management (TQM) is a methodology for managing continual improvement by using a quality management system. TQM establishes a culture involving all people in the organization in a process of continual monitoring and improvement.

ISO 9000:2005 describes the fundamentals of quality management systems that are applicable to all organizations which need to demonstrate their ability to consistently provide products that meet customer and applicable statutory and regulatory requirements. ISO 9001:2008 specifies generic requirements for a quality management system.

Many process-based quality management systems use the methodology known as 'Plan-Do-Check-Act' (PDCA), often referred to as the Deming Cycle, or Shewhart Cycle, that can be applied to all processes. PDCA can be summarized as:

- **Plan** Establish the objectives and processes necessary to deliver results in accordance with customer requirements and the organization's policies.
- **Do** Implement the processes.
- **Check** Monitor and measure processes and product against policies, objectives and

requirements for the product and report the results.

- **Act** Take actions to continually improve process performance.

There are distinct advantages of tying an organization's ITSM processes, and service operation processes in particular, to its quality management system. If an organization has a formal quality management system that complies with ISO 9001, then this can be used to assess progress regularly and drive forward agreed service improvement initiatives through regular reviews and reporting.

Visit www.iso.org for information on ISO standards.

See www.deming.org for more information on the W. Edwards Deming Institute and the Deming Cycle for process improvement.

A.3 RISK MANAGEMENT

A number of different methodologies, standards and frameworks have been developed for the assessment and management of risk. Some focus more on generic techniques widely applicable to different levels and needs, while others are specifically concerned with risk management relating to important assets used by the organization in the pursuit of its objectives. Each organization should determine the approach to risk management that is best suited to its needs and circumstances. It is possible that the approach adopted will leverage the ideas reflected in more than one of the recognized standards and/or frameworks.

Appendix G gives more information on risk management. See also:

- Office of Government Commerce (2010). *Management of Risk: Guidance for Practitioners*. TSO, London.
- ISO 31000:2009 Risk management – principles and guidelines.
- ISO/IEC 27001: 2005 Information technology – security techniques – information security management systems – requirements.
- ISACA (2009). *The Risk IT Framework* (based on COBIT, see section A.5).

A.4 GOVERNANCE OF IT

Corporate governance refers to the rules, policies, processes (and in some cases, laws) by which businesses are operated, regulated and controlled. These are often defined by the board or shareholders, or the constitution of the organization; but they can also be defined by legislation, regulation or consumer groups.

ISO 9004 (Managing for the sustained success of an organization – a quality management approach) provides guidance on governance for the board and executive of an organization.

The standard for corporate governance of IT is ISO/IEC 38500. The purpose of this standard is to promote effective, efficient and acceptable use of IT in all organizations by:

- Assuring stakeholders (including consumers, shareholders and employees) that, if the standard is followed, they can have confidence in the organization's corporate governance of IT
- Informing and guiding directors in governing the use of IT in their organization
- Providing a basis for objective evaluation of the corporate governance of IT.

Typical examples of regulations that impact IT include: financial, safety, data protection, privacy, software asset management, environment management and carbon emission targets.

Further details are available at www.iso.org

ITIL Service Strategy references the concepts of ISO/IEC 38500 and how the concepts can be applied.

A.5 COBIT

The Control OBjectives for Information and related Technology (COBIT) is a governance and control framework for IT management created by ISACA and the IT Governance Institute (ITGI).

COBIT is based on the analysis and harmonization of existing IT standards and good practices and conforms to generally accepted governance principles. It covers five key governance focus areas: strategic alignment, value delivery, resource management, risk management and performance management. COBIT is primarily aimed at internal and external stakeholders within an enterprise who wish to generate value from IT investments;

those who provide IT services; and those who have a control/risk responsibility.

COBIT and ITIL are not 'competitive', nor are they mutually exclusive – on the contrary, they can be used in conjunction as part of an organization's overall governance and management framework. COBIT is positioned at a high level, is driven by business requirements, covers the full range of IT activities, and concentrates on *what* should be achieved rather than *how* to achieve effective governance, management and control. ITIL provides an organization with best-practice guidance on *how* to manage and improve its processes to deliver high-quality, cost-effective IT services. The following COBIT guidance supports strategy management and continual service improvement (CSI):

■ COBIT maturity models can be used to benchmark and drive improvement.
■ Goals and metrics can be aligned to the business goals for IT and used to create an IT management dashboard.
■ The COBIT 'monitor and evaluate' (ME) process domain defines the processes needed to assess current IT performance, IT controls and regulatory compliance.

Further details are available at www.isaca.org and www.itgi.org

A.6 ISO/IEC 20000 SERVICE MANAGEMENT SERIES

ISO/IEC 20000 is an internationally recognized standard for ITSM covering service providers who manage and deliver IT-enabled services to internal or external customers. ISO/IEC 20000-1 is aligned with other ISO management systems standards such as ISO 9001 and ISO/IEC 27001.

One of the most common routes for an organization to achieve the requirements of ISO/IEC 20000 is by adopting ITIL best practices. ISO/IEC 20000-1 is based on a service management system (SMS). The SMS is defined as a management system to direct and control the service management activities of the service provider. ISO/IEC 20000 includes:

■ ISO/IEC 20000-1:2005 – Information technology – Service management – Part 1: Specification

■ ISO/IEC 20000-1:2011 – Information technology – Service management – Part 1: Requirements for a service management system (the most recent edition of the ISO/IEC 20000 standard)
■ ISO/IEC 20000-2:2005 – Information technology – Service management – Part 2: Code of practice (being updated to include guidance on the application of service management systems and to support ISO/IEC 20000-1:2011)
■ ISO/IEC 20000-3:2005 – Information technology – Service management – Part 3: Scope and applicability
■ ISO/IEC TR 20000-4 – Information technology – Service management – Part 4: Process reference model
■ ISO/IEC TR 20000-5:2010 – Information technology – Service management – Part 5: Exemplar implementation plan for ISO/IEC 20000-1.

A closely related publication that is under development is ISO/IEC TR 15504-8 – Process assessment model for IT service management.

Further details can be found at www.iso.org or www.isoiec20000certification.com

Organizations using ISO/IEC 20000-1: 2005 for certification audits will transfer to the new edition, ISO/IEC 20000-1: 2011.

ITIL guidance supports organizations that are implementing service management practices to achieve the requirements of ISO/IEC 20000-1: 2005 and the new edition ISO/IEC 20000-1: 2011.

Other references include:

■ Dugmore, J. and Lacy, S. (2011). *Introduction to ISO/IEC 20000 Series: IT Service Management.* British Standards Institution, London.
■ Dugmore, J. and Lacy, S. (2011). *BIP 0005: A Manager's Guide to Service Management* (6th edition). British Standards Institution, London.

A.7 ENVIRONMENTAL MANAGEMENT AND GREEN/SUSTAINABLE IT

The transition to a low-carbon economy is a global challenge. Many governments have set targets to reduce carbon emissions or achieve carbon neutrality. IT is an enabler for environmental and cultural change that will help governments to achieve their targets – for example, through enabling tele- and video-conferencing, and remote and home working. However, IT is also a major user of energy and natural resources. Green IT refers to environmentally sustainable computing where the use and disposal of computers and printers are carried out in sustainable ways that do not have a negative impact on the environment.

Appendix E in *ITIL Service Design* includes further information on environmental architectures and standards. Appendix E in this publication also provides useful considerations for facilities management, including environmental aspects.

The ISO 14001 series of standards for an environment management system is designed to assure internal and external stakeholders that the organization is an environmentally responsible organization. It enables an organization of any size or type to:

■ Identify and control the environmental impact of its activities, products or services
■ Improve its environmental performance continually
■ Implement a systematic approach to setting and achieving environmental objectives and targets, and then demonstrating that they have been achieved.

Further details are available at www.iso.org

A.8 ISO STANDARDS AND PUBLICATIONS FOR IT

ISO 9241 is a series of standards and guidance on the ergonomics of human system interaction that cover people working with computers. It covers aspects that impact the utility of a service (whether it is fit for purpose) such as:

■ ISO 9241-11:1999 Guidance on usability
■ ISO 9241-210:2010 Human-centred design for interactive systems
■ ISO 9241-151:2008 Guidance on world wide web user interfaces.

ISO/IEC JTC1 is Joint Technical Committee 1 of ISO and the International Electrotechnical Commission (IEC). It deals with information technology standards and other publications.

SC27 is a subcommittee under ISO/IEC JTC1 that develops ISO/IEC 27000, the information security management system (ISMS) family of standards. For further details, Appendix G includes information

on ISO/IEC 27001. SC7 is a subcommittee under ISO/IEC JTC1 that covers the standardization of processes, supporting tools and supporting technologies for the engineering of systems, services and software. SC7 publications include:

■ ISO/IEC 20000 Information technology – service management (see section A.6)
■ ISO/IEC 19770-1 Information technology – software asset management processes. ISO/IEC 19770-2:2009 establishes specifications for tagging software to optimize its identification and management
■ ISO/IEC 15288 Systems and software engineering – systems life cycle processes. The processes can be used as a basis for establishing business environments – e.g. methods, procedures, techniques, tools and trained personnel
■ ISO/IEC 12207 Systems and software engineering – software life cycle processes
■ ISO/IEC 15504 Process assessment series. Also known as SPICE (software process improvement and capability determination), it aims to ensure consistency and repeatability of the assessment ratings with evidence to substantiate the ratings. The series includes exemplar process assessment models (PAM), related to one or more conformant or compliant process reference model (PRM). ISO/IEC 15504-8 is an exemplar process assessment model for IT service management that is under development
■ ISO/IEC 25000 series – provides guidance for the use of standards named Software product Quality Requirements and Evaluation (SQuaRE)
■ ISO/IEC 42010 Systems and software engineering — recommended practice for architectural description of software-intensive systems.

SC7 is working on the harmonization of standards in the service management, software and IT systems domains. Further details are available at www.iso.org

A.9 ITIL AND THE OSI FRAMEWORK

At around the time that ITIL V1 was being written, the International Standards Organization launched an initiative that resulted in the Open Systems Interconnection (OSI) framework. Since this initiative covered many of the same areas as ITIL

V1, it is not surprising that there was considerable overlap.

However, it is also not surprising that they classified their processes differently, used different terminology, or used the same terminology in different ways. To confuse matters even more, it is common for different groups in an organization to use terminology from both ITIL and the OSI framework.

The OSI framework made significant contributions to the definition and execution of ITSM programmes and projects around the world. It has also caused a great deal of debate between teams that do not realize the origins of the terminology that they are using. For example, some organizations have two change management departments – one following the ITIL change management process and the other using the OSI installation, moves, additions and changes (IMAC) model. Each department is convinced that it is completely different from the other, and that it is performing a different role. Closer examination will reveal that there are several areas of commonality.

In service operation, the management of known errors may be mapped to fault management. There is also a section related to operational capacity management, which can be related to the OSI concept of performance management.

Information on the set of ISO standards for the OSI framework is available at: www.iso.org

A.10 PROGRAMME AND PROJECT MANAGEMENT

Large, complex deliveries are often broken down into manageable, interrelated projects. For those managing this overall delivery, the principles of programme management are key to delivering on time and within budget. Best management practice in this area is found in *Managing Successful Programmes* (MSP).

Guidance on effective portfolio, programme and project management is brought together in *Portfolio, Programme and Project Offices* (P3O), which is aimed at helping organizations to establish and maintain appropriate business support structures with proven roles and responsibilities.

Structured project management methods, such as PRINCE2 (PRojects IN Controlled Environments) or the Project Management Body of Knowledge (PMBOK) developed by the Project Management Institute (PMI), can be used when improving IT services. Not all improvements will require a structured project approach, but many will, due to the sheer scope and scale of the improvement. Project management is discussed in more detail in *ITIL Service Transition*.

Visit www.msp-officialsite.com for more information on MSP.

Visit www.p3o-officialsite.com for more information on P3O.

Visit www.prince-officialsite.com for more information on PRINCE2.

Visit www.pmi.org for more information on PMI and PMBOK.

See also the following publications:

- Cleland, David I. and Ireland, Lewis R. (2006). *Project Management: Strategic Design and Implementation* (5th edition). McGraw-Hill Professional.
- Haugan, Gregory T. (2006). *Project Management Fundamentals*. Management Concepts.
- Office of Government Commerce (2009). *Managing Successful Projects with PRINCE2*. TSO, London.
- Cabinet Office (2011). *Managing Successful Programmes*. TSO, London.
- Office of Government Commerce (2008). *Portfolio, Programme and Project Offices*. TSO, London.
- The Project Management Institute (2008). *A Guide to the Project Management Body of Knowledge* (PMBOK Guide) (4th edition). Project Management Institute.

A.11 ORGANIZATIONAL CHANGE

There is a wide range of publications that cover organizational change including the related guidance for programme and project management referred to in the previous section.

Chapter 5 in *ITIL Service Transition* covers aspects of organizational change elements that are an essential part of, or a strong contributor towards, service transition. *ITIL Service Transition* and *ITIL*

Continual Service Improvement refer to Kotter's 'eight steps for organizational change'.

Visit www.johnkotter.com for more information. See also the following publications:

■ Kotter, John P. (1996). *Leading Change*. Harvard Business School Press.
■ Kotter, John P. (1999) *What Leaders Really Do*. Harvard Business School Press.
■ Kotter, J. P. (2000). Leading change: why transformation efforts fail. *Harvard Business Review* January–February.
■ Kotter, John P. and Cohen, Dan S. (2002) *The Heart of Change: Real-Life Stories of How People Change their Organizations*. Harvard Business School Press.
■ Kotter, J. P. and Schlesinger, L. C. (1979). Choosing strategies for change. *Harvard Business Review* Vol. 57, No. 2, p.106.
■ Kotter, John P., Rathgeber, Holger, Mueller, Peter and Johnson, Spenser (2006). *Our Iceberg Is Melting: Changing and Succeeding Under Any Conditions*. St. Martin's Press.

A.12 SKILLS FRAMEWORK FOR THE INFORMATION AGE

The Skills Framework for the Information Age (SFIA) enables employers of IT professionals to carry out a range of human resource activities against a common framework including a skills audit, planning future skill requirements, development programmes, standardization of job titles and functions, and resource allocation.

SFIA provides a standardized view of the wide range of professional skills needed by people working in IT. SFIA is constructed as a simple two-dimensional matrix consisting of areas of work on one axis and levels of responsibility on the other. It uses a common language and a sensible, logical structure that can be adapted to the training and development needs of a very wide range of businesses.

Visit www.sfia.org.uk for further details.

A.13 CARNEGIE MELLON: CMMI AND ESCM FRAMEWORK

The Capability Maturity Model Integration (CMMI) is a process improvement approach developed by the Software Engineering Institute (SEI) of Carnegie Mellon University. CMMI provides organizations with the essential elements of effective processes. It can be used to guide process improvement across a project, a division or an entire organization. CMMI helps integrate traditionally separate organizational functions, sets process improvement goals and priorities, provides guidance for quality processes, and suggests a point of reference for appraising current processes. There are several CMMI models covering different domains of application.

The eSourcing Capability Model for Service Providers (eSCM-SP) is a framework developed by ITSqc at Carnegie Mellon to improve the relationship between IT service providers and their customers.

Organizations can be assessed against CMMI models using SCAMPI (Standard CMMI Appraisal Method for Process Improvement).

For more information, see www.sei.cmu.edu/cmmi/

A.14 BALANCED SCORECARD

A new approach to strategic management was developed in the early 1990s by Drs Robert Kaplan (Harvard Business School) and David Norton. They named this system the 'balanced scorecard'. Recognizing some of the weaknesses and vagueness of previous management approaches, the balanced scorecard approach provides a clear prescription as to what companies should measure in order to 'balance' the financial perspective. The balanced scorecard suggests that the organization be viewed from four perspectives, and it is valuable to develop metrics, collect data and analyse the organization relative to each of these perspectives:

■ The learning and growth perspective
■ The business process perspective
■ The customer perspective
■ The financial perspective.

Some organizations may choose to use the balanced scorecard method as a way of assessing and reporting their IT quality performance in general and their service operation performance in particular.

Further details are available through the balanced scorecard user community at www.scorecardsupport.com

A.15 SIX SIGMA

Six Sigma is a data-driven process improvement approach that supports continual improvement. It is business-output-driven in relation to customer specification. The objective is to implement a measurement-oriented strategy focused on process improvement and defects reduction. A Six Sigma defect is defined as anything outside customer specifications.

Six Sigma focuses on dramatically reducing process variation using statistical process control (SPC) measures. The fundamental objective is to reduce errors to fewer than 3.4 defects per million executions (regardless of the process). Service providers must determine whether it is reasonable to expect delivery at a Six Sigma level given the wide variation in IT deliverables, roles and tasks within IT operational environments.

There are two primary sub-methodologies within Six Sigma: DMAIC (Define, Measure, Analyse, Improve, Control) and DMADV (Define, Measure, Analyse, Design, Verify). DMAIC is an improvement method for existing processes for which performance does not meet expectations, or for which incremental improvements are desired. DMADV focuses on the creation of new processes. For more information, see:

- George, Michael L. (2003). *Lean Six Sigma for Service: How to Use Lean Speed and Six Sigma Quality to Improve Services and Transactions*. McGraw-Hill.
- Pande, Pete and Holpp, Larry (2001) *What Is Six Sigma?* McGraw-Hill.
- Pande, Peter S., Neuman, Robert P. and Cavanagh, Roland R. (2000). *The Six Sigma Way: How GE, Motorola, and Other Top Companies are Honing their Performance*. McGraw-Hill.

Appendix B:
Communication in
service operation

B

Appendix B: Communication in service operation

B.1 ROUTINE OPERATIONAL COMMUNICATION

Most communication in service operation has to do with ensuring that all teams and departments are able to execute the standard activities involved in delivering IT services and managing the IT infrastructure.

Serious consideration should be given during service design to defining the content, type and format of communication that is required

to operate IT services. General communication requirements are described in Table B.1.

B.2 COMMUNICATION BETWEEN SHIFTS

Not all organizations work in shifts, but for those who do, Table B.2 summarizes the communication that needs to take place between shifts.

B.3 PERFORMANCE REPORTING

Performance reporting in the context of communication refers to three main areas, as set

Table B.1 Communication requirements in IT services

Purpose	To coordinate the regular activities of service operation at all levels
	To ensure that all staff are aware of the scheduled activity at all times and that they are aware of any changes or initiatives that may affect the normal operation of the IT environment
Frequency	This type of communication is regular and is communicated in daily, weekly and monthly cycles
Audience	All managers and staff involved in service operation
	All process managers for processes executed by service operation staff, especially change, incident and problem management
	Customers and users
	Vendor staff involved in service operation
Content	Summarize events since the previous communication to ensure that everyone is aware of any follow-up that needs to occur. Also to ensure that all batches have completed and the teams or departments are ready for standard operational activity
	A report on the health of major systems
	Inform operations management staff of any news or events that may affect operations that period
	Discuss any outstanding problems or incidents and ensure that an action plan is in place for each
	Discuss the schedule of changes that are expected to be made during the day, together with a briefing of potential incidents that may occur as a result and the appropriate action to be taken. This should not be confused with the CAB meeting. This is an opportunity to check whether changes that were agreed and scheduled by the CAB, or through a change model, are still on track
	Any planned maintenance or other outages that have been scheduled for the next operational period
	Announcement of the results of any post mortem or crisis meetings that were held since the previous communication
	Announcement or reminder of training that may be available over the next week or month to give staff and their supervisors time to schedule the training into the operations schedule
Context/ sources	Operations logs
	Incident reports
	Problem reports
	Maintenance schedules
	Change schedule

Table B.2 Communication requirements between shifts

Purpose	This communication ensures that the handover between outgoing and incoming shifts is smooth and also makes the new shift aware of any potential difficulties; they also ensure that the new shift is aware of any tasks that need to be completed
Frequency	At the handover of every shift
Audience	Shift leaders of each shift
	Staff from each shift who perform similar tasks
Content	A summary report on operations undertaken during the previous shift
	A summary of all exceptions and alerts that were resolved during the shift
	Details of any outstanding exceptions and alerts, with information about all actions taken to the current point and any information about anticipated future actions (e.g. a vendor is expected to be on site to provide support during the next 4 hours)
Context/ sources	Communication between shifts will usually be based on the following sources: ■ Shift logs ■ Shift leader's report ■ Interpersonal verbal or electronic 'chat' communication where shift personnel are in different facilities

Table B.3 Performance reporting requirements: IT service

Shift logs	To provide information to the groups responsible for IT service reporting to customers and users, which they can use to demonstrate the achievement of service targets and as input to service level review meetings. The information can also be used as a basis for charging for IT services
Frequency	As defined in the SLAs and OLAs. This information is usually communicated regularly on a daily, monthly and quarterly basis
Audience	Service operation teams and departments, usually IT operations staff
	SLM staff
	Service design teams (who help to define performance standards and refine these through CSI)
	CSI teams, especially those tasked with service reporting
Content	Examples of the type of service performance information that needs to be communicated to enable reporting on service performance are: ■ Achievement of specific activities as defined in OLAs ■ Achievement of targets for delivery of specified outputs ■ Service or system availability achievements ■ Ability to meet service maintenance objectives within targeted times and impact levels
Content/ sources	Monitoring and reporting tools Event logs Shift logs

out below. Tables B.3–B.5 also illustrate the three approaches.

B.3.1 IT service performance

This category of performance reporting is generally done as part of SLM and is covered in *ITIL Continual Service Improvement*. However, there is a very important aspect of service reporting that concerns service operation, namely that it is the service operation teams or departments that are required to record and communicate the information that goes into these reports.

However, service operation staff are not in the best position to decide on the content, format and frequency of service performance reporting. The requirements for this type of communication have to be clearly defined during service design and refined during CSI.

Table B.4 Performance reporting requirements: service operation team or department

Purpose	There are three main purposes of service operation team or department performance communication: ■ Proactively, to ensure that service operation staff are executing the activities required to deliver IT services and to support the IT infrastructure ■ To detect potential issues with resource levels, capability and circumvention of procedures ■ To ensure that corrective action has been correctly implemented and adhered to.
Frequency	There is no set frequency for this type of communication. Although some performance reports may be produced daily, weekly or monthly, most managers are involved in ongoing communication with their teams or departments as the situation requires. Under normal operating situations, this communication will tend to be less frequent than in situations where there is a high degree of change or where the organization is experiencing high numbers and severity of incidents.
Audience	Service operation managers Service operation staff Performance issues may be escalated to the service owner or chief information officer (CIO)
Content	Comparison between required and actual performance Trends of performance over time Specific reports of misconduct or failure to perform a required action
Context/ sources	Regular performance reports, e.g. incident logs, maintenance records, process metrics Interpersonal and verbal communication during working situations Team or department meetings Coaching by a team leader or manager Investigation following a poor service report may initiate a series of communications in service operation Individual performance appraisals, usually using KPIs documented in the individual's job description

B.3.2 Service operation team or department performance

This is an 'internal' communication in that it takes place between the members of a team or department and their manager, or a process manager and the team that executes the process. People outside of these teams or departments should not be involved in this type of communication as it is aimed at managing people rather than measuring the quality of a service.

However, it is a common mistake for IT organizations to communicate this type of information to customers as if it were the same as reporting on service quality. For example, a manager might report that their department solves 80% of all problems. As far as the average user is concerned, however, this information is irrelevant. They are more concerned with whether their IT service performed as agreed. In addition, disclosing internal information to customers and users could be embarrassing for the service operation teams and departments and could result in high levels of interference from the business to 'correct' perceived problems.

B.3.3 Infrastructure or process performance

As with team or department performance, this is an 'internal' communication that takes place between the members of a team or department who are responsible for managing an infrastructure component or system, or the members of a process team. People outside of these teams should not be involved in this type of communication as it is aimed at managing people rather than measuring the quality of a service.

B.4 COMMUNICATION IN PROJECTS

Service operation staff are often involved in projects. This may be to provide input to a new design, or to help verify utilization or throughput rates, or to assist in conducting tests of new or changed services. In other cases the projects may affect existing OLAs and their feedback will be required. It must be recognized that this involvement will add to the level of communication that these individuals will be receiving and transmitting. This will require additional time and focus, which should be allowed for by managers assigning resources to projects on a part-time basis.

B.5 COMMUNICATION RELATED TO CHANGES

Change management is covered in detail in *ITIL Service Transition* and includes information about change communication. However, it is necessary to stress the nature of operational communication about changes.

B.6 COMMUNICATION RELATED TO EXCEPTIONS

In this context an exception refers to any occurrence that is outside normal or expected activity or performance. The most common form of exception is an incident (which is covered in detail in section 4.2). There are other exceptions that do not necessarily go through incident management, such as a process exception (which will be handled in the context of that process or by a quality assurance process); a team, department or individual whose performance is not up to standard (which will be handled through human resources disciplinary procedures); or an exception to a vendor's contractual performance. Although these are not all directly related to service management, they will add overheads to the level

Table B.5 Performance reporting requirements: infrastructure or process

Purpose	There are at least three purposes of this type of communication:
	■ To ensure normal operation of the infrastructure or a process
	■ To detect potential issues with the infrastructure or process concerned
	■ To ensure that corrective action has been taken and that it was effective.
Frequency	The frequency of this type of communication will vary depending on the nature of the system(s) being managed or the process being executed.
	Some components of the infrastructure are more volatile and will require frequent communications and even meetings to ensure that they perform predictably. More stable components will simply require a confirmation that everything is still working as expected.
	Some processes have a requirement of frequent reporting and communication. For example, incident management may require updates every five minutes for a high-impact incident. Other processes do not need to communicate that frequently. For example capacity planning needs to communicate changes on a monthly or even quarterly basis.
Audience	Staff who manage key CIs
	Staff who execute processes
	Process owners and technology managers
	Potential escalation to more senior managers, the service owner
Content	Comparison between required and actual performance
	Trends of performance over time
	Specific reports of missed targets or unexpected levels of performance
Context/ sources	Event logs
	System performance records
	Process performance reports
	Incident and problem records
	Exception reports and audit reports
	Review with vendor
	Service reporting may indicate a problem with one or more technology areas or processes

Table B.6 Project team communications

Purpose	Project team communication has multiple purposes, including: ■ To gain support from project stakeholders – this communication will focus on the scope, cost and benefits of the project and will seek to demonstrate an overall return on the project's investment ■ To ensure that all members of the project team understand and are aligned to the objectives of the project ■ To assign work to individuals or teams ■ To schedule activities and ensure that resources are ready to begin their stage of the project ■ To check on and report the progress of the project ■ To detect and escalate potential exceptions or delays in the project ■ To prepare project customers and audiences for the deployment of the solution being built.
Frequency	The frequency will depend on the nature of the project and the type of project management methodology being used. Formal project communication tends to follow the cycle of project meetings. For example: ■ Weekly or monthly project meetings may be held with the project manager and the individual team leaders ■ A monthly status update may be sent to the project's executive sponsor and possibly other key stakeholders.
Audience	Project manager and project administrative and coordination staff Project sponsor Key project stakeholders (e.g. customers, IT managers, board members, users etc.) Project teams and individual contributors Vendor sales and technical staff where the purchase of services or solutions are part of the project
Content	Gathering requirements for the solution being built by the project Project scheduling Project 'marketing' information including ROI or business case information Status updates Gathering information to complete a task Events that could affect the scope, cost or timely completion of the project Progress reporting within teams or between teams Information about the results of testing Notifications to teams or individuals that the project is approaching 'their' stage or activity and that they should make the appropriate preparations Reporting on the successful completion of activities Review of the overall success of the project Exceptions and the result of quality assurance checks are reported into project assurance teams, who in turn may communicate the need for corrective action as necessary. Inside each team, communication will be more focused on completing project tasks and may generally be more frequent than the project-wide communication. There is likely to be a high level of less formal communication inside each team and also between teams to ensure that tasks are completed on time and promised resources are available when and where they are supposed to be. Extensive communication is also required as part of the handover from one team to another as the project moves from one stage or phase to another. An important rule of thumb is to document any communication that could potentially affect the outcome or the cost of the project.
Context/ sources	Project charter Project budget Statement of requirements Project schedule Project meetings Team meetings Status and progress reports Test reports Customer sign-off documentation Post-implementation review

Table B.7 Communication about changes

Purpose	To support change, release and deployment management processes by: ■ Assessing the potential impact of and resources required for the change ■ Ensuring that each team is aware of the nature and schedule of changes that have been assigned to them ■ Building, testing and deploying changes in their environment ■ Ensuring that each team reports its progress on each change ■ Notifying change management that a change is ready for deployment ■ Backing out changes that were unsuccessful and communicating the results to change management ■ Assisting in the assessment of changes to ensure that they have been implemented correctly.
Frequency	The frequency of communication related to changes is determined by the nature of the change and the times set forth in the change schedule. Most teams or departments will review changes on a daily or weekly basis. Each day they will discuss and prioritize all new changes assigned to them and report on the progress of changes they are working on. After each change they will report on the success of each change and ensure that any remedial action required is initiated.
Audience	Change manager, administrators and coordinators Team leaders, department heads, shift managers or project managers Service operation staff involved in building, testing and deploying changes (usually technical, application and IT operations management teams or department) Managers of test environments and teams Change or release deployment teams
Content	Requests for and authorization of changes Reports on the feasibility of a change Reports on the resources required to build, test or deploy a change Change activity scheduling Detailed descriptions of the change and the activities required of each team or department Progress and status reporting of change activity Test results Exception reports, including details of the execution of back-out plans
Context/ sources	RFCs Change control communication (during daily or weekly operational meetings, or by email, conference call or using the change management tools) CAB meetings Release plans Projected service outage reports Change reviews

of communication required of staff during the service operation stage.

B.7 COMMUNICATION RELATED TO EMERGENCIES

Although ITIL specifies how to deal with urgent, high-impact situations such as disasters (IT service continuity management) and major incidents (incident management), managers in the service operation stage will find themselves dealing with various types and scales of emergency not covered in these processes. It is important to note that this is not a separate process; rather it is a view of several processes and situations from a communication perspective.

Table B.8 Communication during exceptions

Purpose	Communication during or after exceptions is aimed at:
	▪ Informing the appropriate people of the exception
	▪ Assessing the significance, severity and impact of the exception
	▪ Ensuring that resources with the appropriate skills and seniority are involved in resolving the exception and taking action to prevent future recurrence
	▪ Providing updates to stakeholders that are affected by the exception.
Frequency	This type of communication is reactive and ad hoc, in that it does not occur unless there is an identified exception or the risk of an exception. The frequency is thus directly proportional to the frequency of exceptions.
	Once an exception is detected, the frequency and content of communication will be determined by the impact, urgency and severity of the exception.
Audience	The exact audience will depend on the type and extent of the exception, but could include:
	▪ Incident management support staff
	▪ The service desk
	▪ Problem management support staff
	▪ Process owners (if the exception relates to process performance)
	▪ Departmental managers or team leaders
	▪ SLM staff
	▪ Human resource managers and staff
	▪ Technology managers and experts
	▪ Vendor account management staff
	▪ Vendor technical experts.
Content	Description and assessment of the exception
	Assessment of the impact. This will typically involve communication with the stakeholders who are affected by the exception
	Estimation and then confirmation of the cost of resolution
	A decision on what action will be taken
	Communication of the decision taken. This is likely to be in a number of formats. For example the communication to customers is likely to contain an apology and a high-level overview of what is being done to resolve the exception. A communication to the people who are expected to resolve the exception will be more detailed and will contain clear actions and timelines
	Confirmation that the exception has been resolved
	Escalation actions taken to date and next steps to be taken per the appropriate escalation procedure
Context/ sources	Process reviews
	Change reviews
	Service level reviews
	Events
	Trend analysis of processes, devices, team performance etc.
	Incident, problem and change records
	Customer satisfaction surveys

Communication during emergencies is similar in purpose and content to communication during exceptions. The main differences are in the level of urgency and impact of the exception.

Emergency communications are usually initiated by the incident manager (see section 4.2.5 for a discussion on major incidents) or by a senior IT manager who has been designated as the escalation point for all such emergencies.

Table B.9 Communication during emergencies

Purpose	The purpose of communication in an emergency is to immediately investigate and confirm the impact and severity of the incident to confirm that it is indeed an emergency situation. It should also confirm that this incident does not represent a disaster or any contingency covered in the IT service continuity plans.
	As soon as the scope of the emergency has been identified, the team responsible for managing the situation will allocate resources to create an action plan and to begin resolving the emergency and restoring service.
Frequency	This type of communication does not occur unless there is a major incident or emergency situation.
	Once an exception is detected, the frequency and content of communication will be determined by the impact and severity of the exception, and potentially by a service recovery plan.
Audience	Incident manager
	Senior managers of groups responsible for the IT staff that will be required to resolve the situation
	Business managers and executives (possibly including legal staff if the organization is exposed to potential legal action as a result of the incident)
	Customers and users
	IT service continuity manager and central coordination team
	Senior vendor staff and managers (depending on the extent and nature of the situation)·
	Technical management staff and managers
	Application management staff and managers
	IT operations management staff and managers
Content	The nature and extent of the emergency
	Assessment of the impact. This will typically involve communication with the stakeholders who are affected by the exception
	Estimation and then confirmation of the cost of resolution
	A decision on what action will be taken
	Communication of the decision taken. This is likely to be in a number of formats. For example the communication to customers is likely to contain an apology and a high-level overview of what is being done to resolve the exception. A communication to the people who are expected to resolve the exception will be more detailed and will contain clear actions and timelines
	Confirmation that the exception has been resolved
	Escalation actions taken to date and next steps to be taken per the appropriate escalation procedure
Context/ sources	Incident record for major incidents
	Events
	Crisis or emergency meetings called by the incident manager, the designated manager, or the IT service continuity manager

In the case where an IT service continuity plan is invoked, this will include a detailed communication plan to be executed by the appropriate authority.

The incident manager or designated manager will often form a response team, and the communication is initiated and coordinated by this team.

B.8 GLOBAL COMMUNICATIONS

Many IT organizations have service operation activities that physically take place in more than one country. In addition, they may also be serving users and customers that may also be located in different countries. For these organizations, a comprehensive global communications strategy needs to be in place. Failure to do this may incur operating risks or low customer satisfaction levels related to differences in language, culture, or regulatory requirements that may differ from country to country.

Table B.10 Global communications

Purpose	A clear strategy and policy would be put in place to handle service operation activities that may take place in multiple countries. Failure to do this may incur operating risks or low customer satisfaction levels related to differences in language, culture, or regulatory requirements that may differ from country to country.
Frequency	Communication with users, customers and IT staff across different countries will be ongoing. It must ensure that service operation activities are not negatively impacted by differences between countries.
Audience	Considerations for the kinds of global issues that may exist will drive the need for the audience that might be required. Some examples of these might include: ■ Negotiators who deal with specific country labour laws and issues such as a national union or mandatory requirements for military service that may impact desired availability of support staff. ■ Subject matter experts with expertise of country-specific labour laws and cost recovery regulations. For example, some countries will accept charges for labour to be recovered by hour – others will only accept labour charges by day. This has direct impact on service operation activities in situations such as despatching on-site support or repair staff. ■ Translators who provide communications across multiple languages. Some countries may have requirements for an 'official' language that must be used when conducting business. While some organizations choose to identify a 'standard' language that must be used across the global enterprise, this may not work in all countries. ■ Cultural supporters and coordinators who understand and coordinate impact of country-specific holidays, limits in work week hours or other issues that could impact availability of service operation staff.
Content	The content of this communication will vary depending on the context. However, it is important to develop an overall global communications strategy and associated policies that recognize and address global communication concerns. Specific areas of impact may include: ■ Service desk operations where communications may need to provide support in additional languages ■ On-site technical support and repair technicians that need to be despatched to locations other than their home country ■ Written communications such as operation reports, incident descriptions, email communications or other items that are used to support service operation workflows that span more than one country.
Context/ sources	The context of this communication is the day-to-day executing of operational activities and the delivery and support of services. Sources can include: ■ Company legal experts knowledgeable on international labour laws ■ Management staff local to each country where service operation activities are performed ■ Financial experts knowledgeable on international taxes, tariffs and exchange rates ■ Support staff or others with bilingual skills and capabilities.

Service desk international communications

Operating a service desk across multiple countries is a particular challenge for many IT organizations. Should support services only be provided in one language? Multiple languages? As an example, one strategy used by IT organizations will utilize a global service desk that communicates in one language, but provides translation available for the users, when necessary. Others may choose to route calls to separate service desks each devoted to one or more specific languages. Another option chosen by some companies is to mandate that a single language be used across all service desks regardless of what country users may be calling from.

There are pros and cons to each strategy that an IT organization may wish to make. A strategy and policy needs to be put into place for these kinds of situation that makes it clear how the service desk will operate across multiple countries.

B.9 COMMUNICATION WITH USERS AND CUSTOMERS

This section appears last, not because it is the least important, but because it incorporates several of the areas discussed above. An important principle in communicating with customers is that communication should not focus on internal aspects of service operation. The focus is on the

Table B.11 Communication with users and customers

Purpose	There are a number of reasons for user and customer communication in service operation. These include: ■ Ensuring that services have been delivered as agreed ■ Communication around fulfilling service requests ■ Reporting incidents and keeping users and customers updated on their status until resolved ■ Notifying users and customers of changes that may impact them ■ Providing access to services ■ Dealing with potential security issues ■ Scheduling activities that involve users or customers, e.g. maintenance ■ Notification of special business events that require additional support or changed priorities ■ Review of customer and user satisfaction ■ Coordination during contingency situations.
Frequency	Communication with users and customers is ongoing. The format and content of communication will be defined by the processes that are being executed. For example, communication about an incident will be determined by the incident management process. Some communication will be formal and scheduled, e.g. providing reports on the performance of a service during a review meeting. Other communication will be formal, but ad hoc, e.g. communication about the status of an incident.
Audience	The identity of the exact audience and their number will depend on which process is being executed, the type of situation that has occurred and the scope of what is being communicated, e.g. providing an update about the status of a service request will have a very different audience than when participating in a service level review meeting. Communications should be carefully tailored to the specific audience attributes and needs.
Content	The content of this communication will vary depending on the context. However, it is important to gear the communication to the audience. This means using service names rather than server or application names, being professional, avoiding technical jargon, not being condescending and treating customers and users with respect.
Context/ sources	The context of this communication is the day-to-day executing of operational activities and the delivery and support of services. Service operation teams should not be communicating with customers or users on planning issues, strategy, design or testing – unless they have been assigned to a project team which is dealing with one of these areas.

customer or user's requirements and what IT is doing to meet them. This should not involve technical descriptions and detailed information about internal processes.

Appendix C:
Kepner and Tregoe

Appendix C: Kepner and Tregoe

Charles Kepner and Benjamin Tregoe developed a useful method to analyse problems. In this appendix, their method is presented as an example of a problem analysis method.

Kepner and Tregoe state that problem analysis should be a systematic process of problem solving and should take maximum advantage of knowledge and experience. They distinguish the following five phases for problem analysis (described further below):

■ Defining the problem
■ Describing the problem with regard to identity, location, time and size
■ Establishing possible causes
■ Testing the most probable cause
■ Verifying the true cause.

Depending on time and available information, these phases can be realized to a greater or lesser extent. Even in situations where only a limited amount of information is available, or time pressure is high, it is worthwhile adopting a structured approach to problem analysis to improve the chances of success.

C.1 DEFINING THE PROBLEM

Because the investigation is based on the definition of the problem, this definition has to state precisely which deviation(s) from the agreed service levels have occurred.

Often, during the definition of a problem, the most likely problem cause is already indicated. Take care not to jump to conclusions, which can guide the investigation in the wrong direction from the beginning.

In practice, problem definition is often a difficult task because of a complicated IT infrastructure and non-transparent agreements on service levels.

C.2 DESCRIBING THE PROBLEM

The following aspects are used to describe the problem, i.e. what the problem is:

■ **Identity**   Which part does not function well? What is the problem?
■ **Location**   Where does the problem occur?
■ **Time**   When did the problem start to occur? How frequently has the problem occurred?
■ **Size**   What is the size of the problem? How many parts are affected?

The '*is*' situation is determined by the answers to these questions. The next step is to investigate which similar parts in a similar environment are functioning properly. With this, an answer is formulated to the question 'What *could be* but *is not*?' (Which parts could be showing the same problem but do not?).

It is then possible to search effectively for relevant differences in both situations. Furthermore, past changes, which could be the cause of these differences, can be identified.

C.3 ESTABLISHING POSSIBLE CAUSES

The list of differences and changes mentioned above most likely hold the cause of the problem so possible causes can be extracted from this list.

C.4 TESTING THE MOST PROBABLE CAUSE

Each possible cause needs to be assessed to determine whether it could be the cause of all the symptoms of the problem.

C.5 VERIFYING THE TRUE CAUSE

The remaining possible causes have to be verified as being the source of the problem. This can only be done by proving this in one way or another – for example by implementing a change or replacing a part. Address the possible causes that can be verified quickly and simply first.

Appendix D:
Ishikawa diagrams

Appendix D: Ishikawa diagrams

The Ishikawa diagram, also known as the fishbone, cause-and-effect or tree diagram, is a tool used to systematically identify and present all the possible causes of a particular problem on a chart. The technique is named after its developer, Kaoru Ishikawa (1915–89), a leader in Japanese quality control. An example is shown below.

The main goal is represented by the spine or trunk of the diagram and primary factors are represented as branches. Secondary factors are then added as stems, and so on. Creating the diagram stimulates discussion and often leads to increased understanding of a complex problem. These diagrams are extensively used in identifying solutions to systemic problems, such as identifying the cause of productivity loss on assembly lines, or lower customer satisfaction levels in a service organization.

The basic technique of developing these diagrams, together with a very simple example, is shown here. A problem-solving team will use the Ishikawa diagram as follows:

1 Prepare a blank diagram in a format that can be viewed by the entire group. This could be a flip chart, board, projected through a data projector from a PC etc.

2 Define the problem that the group is trying to solve in clear and specific terms and write it in the box at the 'fish head' box of the diagram.

3 Write the cause categories into the tips of the 'fish bones'. These should be fairly broad categories as the exact causes are not yet known. An example is shown in Figure D.1 in which the group is trying to find the cause for unacceptable levels of network downtime.

4 Use brainstorming techniques to get participants to suggest possible causes, and note these on the relevant branch of the diagram. A simple diagram has been completed in Figure D.2.

5 Interpret the diagram. This could be done by ranking the top causes based on experience and available data. Once the top causes have been

Figure D.1 Sample of starting an Ishikawa diagram

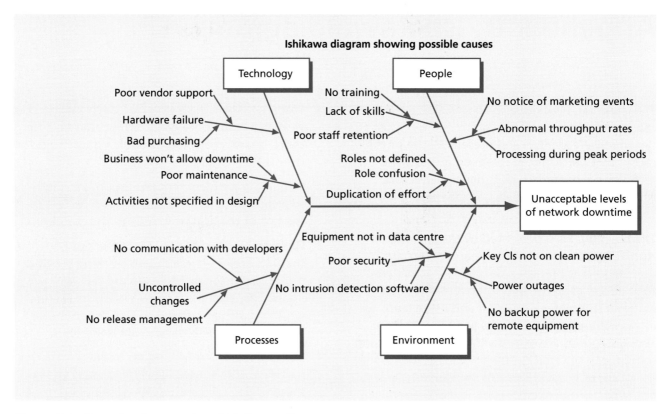

Figure D.2 Sample of a completed Ishikawa diagram

selected, each one will be investigated further according to its rank and priority.

Appendix E:
Considerations for
facilities management

E

Appendix E: Considerations for facilities management

The purpose of this appendix is not to provide a detailed explanation of all aspects of facilities management. Rather, it will highlight the most important activities to help in positioning some of the other functions and in identifying where specific processes impact on good facilities management and vice versa.

Facilities management will provide information to service asset and configuration management regarding the location and status of CIs, and will also be an integral part of change management, capacity and availability planning and IT service continuity management.

Every organization should produce an environmental policy for equipment location, with minimum agreed standards for particular concentrations of equipment. Additionally, minimum standards should be agreed for the protection of buildings containing equipment and equipment room shells. The following sections cover the major aspects that need to be considered, with example characteristics.

E.1 BUILDING MANAGEMENT

Although many building management activities are outsourced or contracted to other suppliers, they are still the responsibility of facilities management. Typical activities include:

- **Cleaning** This could be done by employees or by third parties. It is very important here to ensure that cleaning staff comply with all access control and confidentiality policies.
- **Waste disposal** This includes separation of items for recycling, hazardous items (e.g. batteries, liquids and gases such as refrigerant for air-conditioning units) and confidential documentation.
- **Installation of physical facilities** This includes facilities such as cabling, power, raised floors, secure entry and exit systems, offices, furniture etc.
- **Parking** This should include allocation of staff and contractor parking, visitor parking

and parking for handicapped staff or visitors. Facilities management will also include documenting and enforcing any policies around who should park where.

- **Signage** This should ensure that the building can be found but is not obviously a key location worthy of attack.
- **Access control and security monitoring** Secure perimeters and secure entrances, need to be established and audited. This is covered in more detail in section E.6 below and also in Appendix F.
- **Building site and protection** Consideration should be given to security fencing, video cameras, movement and intruder detectors, window and door alarms, and lightning protectors to provide a safe and secure working environment.
- **Entry** This might include providing multiple controlled points of entry.
- **External environment** Provide safeguards to minimize external risks such as floods, electrical storms or hurricanes.
- **Services** Provide alternate routes and suppliers for all essential services, including network services.

E.2 EQUIPMENT ROOMS

Facilities are not managed simply because they exist and are owned by an organization. They are managed so that the people and equipment they contain can be used for specific purposes. In the case of IT facilities, such as data centres, this adds some very specific demands to the manager of that facility.

One of these is the hosting of IT equipment. This is not just a case of providing a room and allowing the technical management teams to install and manage equipment. Different types of equipment have very specific requirements of the facility in which it is housed, for example:

- Water-cooled equipment needs access to cool water – which has to be supplied by the facility.

- The weight of equipment varies and has to be distributed so as not to place too much stress on the floor.
- Electrical supply may vary for different types of equipment.

If equipment is simply placed in the data centre in the order in which it is received, it will be very difficult to find anything and staff may have to cross the floor several times to tend to similar equipment. This traffic jeopardizes the integrity and security of other equipment on the floor.

This means that facilities management has to own the responsibility of planning and designing the layout of the data centre for optimal access and security of the equipment that will be hosted there. At the same time, it should be remembered that this equipment is being used to deliver IT services, and any requirements for that service need to be taken into account in hosting the equipment. For example, data centre standards may have to be changed in order to accommodate a non-standard server. Other considerations can include:

- Room access, such as providing secure controlled entry, combination lock, swipe card, video camera (if business critical and unattended)
- Room location, such as locating rooms on the first floor wherever possible, with no water, gas, chemical or fire hazards within the vicinity, above, below or adjacent
- Room visibility, such as ensuring that no signage or external windows are in place
- Shell, such as providing an external shell that is waterproof, airtight, soundproofed, and fire-resistant (0.5 hours to 4 hours depending on criticality)
- Equipment delivery, such as providing adequate provisions for the delivery and positioning of large delicate equipment
- Internal floor, ensuring it is sealed
- Separate plant room, such as supplying separate space for an uninterruptible power supply (UPS), electrical supply and switching, air-handling units, dual units and rooms if business critical
- False floors, such as providing antistatic, liftable floor tiles 600 × 600 mm on pedestals, with alternate pedestals screwed to the solid floor with a minimum of 600 mm clearance to solid floor. Floor loadings of up to 5 kN/m2 with a recommended minimum of 3 m between false floor and ceiling
- Internal walls, such as ensuring false floor to ceiling is fire-resistant, but with air flow above and below floor level
- Fire detection/prevention, such as providing a high sensitivity smoke detector (HSSD) or multi-level alarm with alternative halon replacement or release on 'double-knock' detection
- Lighting, ensuring that normal levels of ceiling lighting with emergency lighting on power failure are in place
- Fire extinguishers, ensuring that sufficient electrical fire extinguishers are in place with adequate signage and procedures
- Vibration, ensuring that vibrations should be minimal within the complete area
- Electromagnetic interference, ensuring that minimal interference is present (1.5 V/m ambient field strength)
- Installations, ensuring that all room equipment is provided and installed by qualified suppliers and installers to appropriate electrical and health and safety standards
- Network connections, ensuring that equipment space is flood-wired with adequate capacity for reasonable growth. All cables should be positioned and secured to appropriate cable trays
- Disaster recovery, ensuring that fully tested recovery plans should be developed for all major data centres including the use of standby sites and equipment
- Clearance, ensuring enough open floor space is available between physical components to allow for access to equipment for repair and maintenance activities.

In addition, most data centres also offer the following hosting activities:

- Receipt of new equipment
- Unpacking, configuring and installing standard equipment
- Producing and maintaining data centre layout diagrams
- Managing the schedule of any maintenance activity to equipment hosted in the data centre
- Disposing of retired equipment
- Provisioning appropriate containers for the disposal of environmentally hazardous materials

such as batteries or potentially toxic waste produced from computing equipment.

From this list of activities, it is clear that facilities management should not be seen as a separate function, but very much part of the overall operation of IT in the organization.

E.3 POWER MANAGEMENT

Power management refers to managing the sourcing and utilization of power sources that are used to keep the facility functional. This definition of power management has a number of implications, which are discussed below.

Facilities management's first task in managing power is to determine the power requirements for the facility. This includes defining:

- What the power is going to be needed for, e.g. office space, equipment in the data centre, the cafeteria etc.
- When that power is going to be needed. Some operations require a consistent supply of electricity 24 hours a day. Others, such as office space, will use more electricity during the day and very little at night. Others only need electricity at a specific time
- How much power is going to be needed
- What type of power will be used. Although most organizations use electricity, in many locations the heating systems are dependent on natural gas.

Other considerations can also include:

- Power, such as providing a power distribution unit (PDU), with three-phase supply to non-switched boxes, one per piece of equipment, with appropriate rated circuit-breakers for each supply. Alternatively, approved power distribution strips can be used. Balanced three-phase loadings. UPS (online or line interactive with SNMP management) to ensure voltage supplied is within ± 5% of rating with minimal impulse, sags, surges and over/under voltage conditions
- External power supply, such as supplying an external generator for major data centres and use of redundant power grids
- Power safety, such as ensuring that clean earth is provided on the PDU and for all equipment with clearly marked remote power-off buttons

on each exit. Dirty power outlets, clearly marked, should also be supplied.

Facilities management will also be responsible for establishing a contract with utility companies, or in many cases the local authority or municipality that provides that service. This will include an agreed rate and a level of availability. This has become very important in locations where the electricity supply is variable due to lack of infrastructure or due to over-utilization by general consumers.

Facilities management will be responsible for establishing standby power sources for power failures, disasters and other contingencies. This is generally in the form of UPSs for key equipment, and also generators powered by an alternative energy source (usually diesel). Facilities management is responsible not only for supplying these alternatives, but also for testing them, keeping supplies of the fuel and maintaining them.

Alternative power sources should be modelled and tested to ensure that they are able to handle required demand loads and can be automatically activated following a power failure.

Another key activity of facilities management is to manage the utilization of power. Traditionally, the role of facilities management was just to ensure that power was available. However, as natural resources become scarcer and more expensive, more attention is being focused on techniques to manage utilization more responsibly.

One such approach is the dynamic management of power in data centres. The principle is that during peak processing periods, more computers will be used to do the work. As the workload reduces, the work is centralized onto fewer computers, while those that are not being utilized are powered down or placed into standby mode. This requires a significant integration between the activities of IT operations management, technical management and all the service design processes.

E.4 ENVIRONMENTAL CONDITIONING AND ALERT SYSTEMS

Facilities management ensures that physical conditions within the data centres or computer rooms are maintained at the correct levels for optimal IT operations. Examples of these conditions might include:

- Temperature, providing strict control, 22° (± 3°) and up to 550 W/m^2. 6° variation throughout the room and a maximum of 6° per hour
- Humidity control, providing strict control: 50% (± 10%)
- Air quality, providing positive pressure, filtered intake low gaseous pollution (e.g. sulphur dioxide ≤ 0.14 ppm), dust levels for particles > 1 micron, < 5 × 106 particles/m3 and auto shut-down on smoke or fire detection
- Environmental detectors, such as providing for smoke, temperature, power, humidity, water and intruder with automated alarm capability and local alarm panels with repeater panels and also remote alarm capabilities.

Temperature is maintained through heating and cooling systems, as well as the layout of the equipment in the facility. This will require the following activities:

- Ascertaining the heat output for CIs and their optimal operating temperature
- Identifying the total cooling requirement for all equipment in the facility as well as for specific items. For example, an air conditioner may be able to keep a data centre at a constant temperature, but there may be equipment that needs to be kept at a lower temperature
- Modelling the overall heating and cooling requirements as well as mapping specific areas in the facility that may be naturally warmer or cooler. This information is used to identify where the best location is for specific equipment. It is important to note that when new equipment is installed in a facility, it will change the mapping of cooler and warmer areas in the facility, hence the requirement for more sophisticated mapping and modelling techniques. These models will also need to take into account seasonal variances in temperature. For example, some facilities may need to be heated in winter and cooled in summer
- Purchase and maintenance of air conditioning units with sufficient capacity, and maintaining these units regularly
- Investing in backup air-conditioning units that can be used if a main unit fails, or to provide extra cooling capacity on exceptionally hot days (although this should be a rare exception – if the backup unit is used too frequently this implies that initial planning was inadequate)

- Ongoing monitoring of the temperature and adjustment of cooling settings according to changes in season and equipment layout. These monitors could be linked to the operations bridge, which would be able to respond to any significant deviation from normal temperatures
- Identifying and avoiding 'obvious' errors, such as locating the heat output of a major server close to the intake of an air-conditioning unit; or preventing airflow by stacking manuals in 'free' space
- Similar steps should be taken to identify ideal humidity levels and specify whether dehumidifying equipment is required
- Smoke detection equipment is usually installed as part of the overall fire control strategy of the facility and is linked to automated fire-fighting systems. However, facilities management should not assume that an automated response to fire threats will be adequate. Smoke detection units should be linked to the operations bridge and any exceptions should be investigated.

Movement detection units should be installed in all unattended operating areas. These will ensure that unauthorized access is detected and reported to facilities security and possibly also the operations bridge. This will help to enforce proper scheduling of maintenance or installation activities.

Dust and particle detection can help in maintaining air quality around systems that are particularly sensitive. Again, monitors should be routed to the operations bridge so that deviations can be investigated and corrected before any significant damage occurs.

There are also a number of other types of facilities monitoring, which are based on the location of the facility. For example, building movement monitors installed in locations with high levels of seismic activity. These act as early warning systems to indicate that a system needs to be shut down or failed over to an alternative site before a significant earth tremor or earthquake affects sensitive equipment. Similar monitors and safeguards are also being installed in facilities where there is high electrical storm activity.

These systems are collectively referred to as building management systems (BMSs), although as these tools are integrated, the term is being used to refer to a single integrated management system, rather than a loose collection of tools performing similar functions. Thought should be given to using monitoring tools that can be integrated into, or at least consistent with, existing monitoring tools and event management systems (see Chapter 7 for more details on tools).

E.5 SAFETY

A major concern of facilities management is the safety of the people working in the building. Facilities management is therefore responsible for understanding and enforcing compliance with relevant safety standards and legislation.

Safety is enforced in the following areas:

- Building design and construction
- Layout of the rooms and equipment in the facility
- Education of all personnel about safety standards in force in the facility
- Definition of evacuation procedures and routes and gathering points in the event of a fire or other life-threatening situation
- Posting notices and information regarding any safety information of which personnel need to be aware.

E.6 PHYSICAL ACCESS CONTROL

This is a very important part of facilities management and has grown into a specialized field. As such, the content is summarized here for convenience, but is discussed in detail in Appendix F.

The major components of physical access control (as discussed in Appendix F) are:

- Assistance in defining and maintaining physical access controls as part of the organization's security policies
- Maintenance of floor plans indicating which areas are restricted
- Installation and maintenance of physical access control devices
- Monitoring and control of access to facilities
- Security staffing
- Installation and maintenance of surveillance equipment
- Protection against social engineering.

E.7 SHIPPING AND RECEIVING

Large facilities require special areas where delivery can be taken of furniture, computer equipment, racks etc. This area needs to be secured so that delivery personnel do not gain access to the rest of the facility. There also needs to be a secure store near the receiving area where items can be stored until they can be moved to their final location.

A process needs to be in place to ensure that items to be shipped are accounted for and that only those items are removed by the delivery or despatch contractor. Wherever possible, these items should be marshalled into the secure store in the shipping and delivery area before being despatched. This will prevent unauthorized access to the facility.

Delivery and despatch documentation has to be completed, inspected and signed for each consignment that is delivered or despatched. A central log of all consignments should also be maintained as a control.

E.8 INVOLVEMENT IN SUPPLIER MANAGEMENT

Most facilities are supplied, managed and serviced by a number of entities. Although the actual contracts with these entities would typically be managed by the appropriate commercial and legal departments, facilities management will play a key role in specifying and negotiating these contracts. Typical contracts include:

- **Management of leases for leased properties**   This is quite rare, as most organizations view their data centre as a key asset. Leasing such facilities would be seen as a risk because of the potential that the building is sold, the landlord goes out of business or the landlord does not fulfil the contract in terms of proper maintenance.
- **Leasing or maintenance of environmental equipment**   This could include air-conditioning units, environmental monitoring and alert (e.g. smoke detection and fire-fighting or suppression equipment).
- **Building maintenance contracts**   These include servicing of elevators, flooring, plumbing and electrical supply.
- **Telecommunications facilities**   Although telecommunications is usually managed by

a dedicated team or department or as part of wide area networking, they are often dependent on third parties to supply and maintain telecommunication equipment located in or just outside the data centre. In many countries these are provided by government or para-state telecommunications organizations. Management of these types of contracts requires a special skill set.

■ **Security services**   These are engaged for the provision of physical access control and armed response services.

A very important part of supplier management is to ensure that all third-party staff are aware of, and comply with, the security policies of the organization. This includes physical access control, confidentiality and unauthorized use of the organization's facilities or equipment. Regular audits should be held to ensure that this is being enforced.

E.9   MAINTENANCE

Facilities management is responsible for coordinating all routine maintenance activity within the building. This refers to both building maintenance as well as to the maintenance of equipment in the data centre.

The reason for including equipment maintenance is simply to prevent the building being exposed to too much unusual activity at any one time. Multiple teams working in different places in the data centre at the same time represents a security and safety risk.

It is important to note that the actual maintenance of IT equipment is carried out by the technical management staff, but under the coordination of change management and facilities management.

The facilities manager should maintain a master schedule of all planned maintenance activity to ensure that maintenance activity is properly coordinated. This schedule forms part of the overall change management change schedule and is used to ensure that there are no conflicts between routine maintenance activity and the deployment of changes.

E.10   OFFICE ENVIRONMENTS

Facilities management may also coordinate and support office environments. These may be located within, adjacent or externally to equipment rooms. Examples of considerations for these kinds of environment can include:

■ Access, ensuring that all offices have the appropriate secure access depending on the business, the information and the equipment contained within them.

■ Lighting, temperature, humidity and air quality, providing a normal clean, comfortable and tidy office environment, conforming to the organization's health, safety and environmental requirements.

■ Power, providing a clean power supply for all computer equipment, with UPS facilities if appropriate.

■ False floors, optional, but preferred if possible. At a minimum, all cables should be contained within appropriate trunking.

■ Fire detection/prevention and extinguishers, providing normal office smoke/fire detection systems and intruder alerting systems, unless there are major concentrations of equipment. Sufficient fire extinguishers of the appropriate type should also be provided with adequate signage and procedures.

■ Network connections, ensuring that offices are flood-wired with adequate capacity for reasonable growth. All cables should be positioned and secured to appropriate cable trays. All network equipment should be secured in secure cupboards or cabinets.

■ Disaster recovery, ensuring that fully tested recovery plans are in place where appropriate.

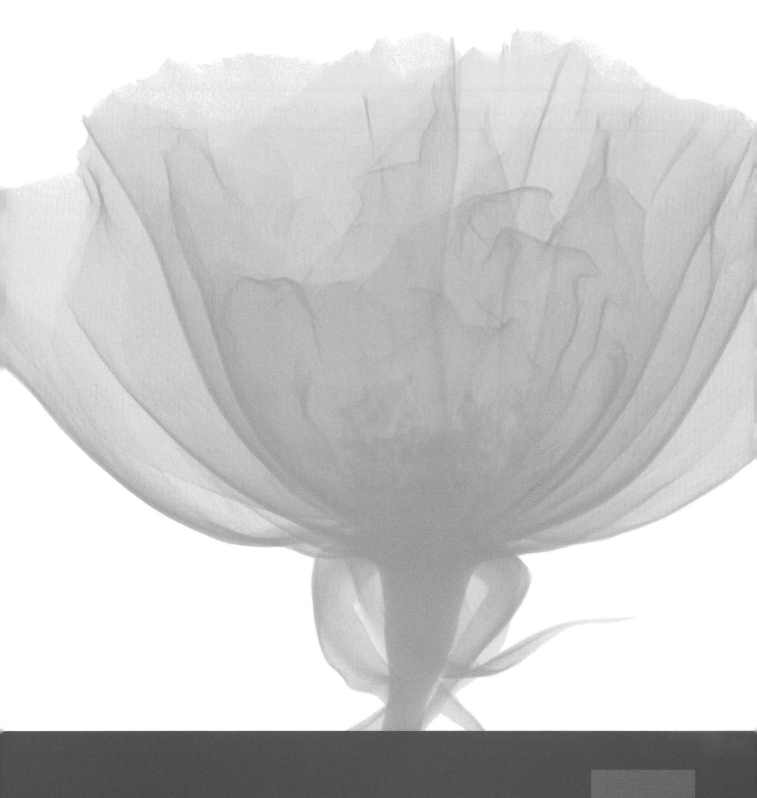

Appendix F:
Physical access control

Appendix F: Physical access control

Section 5.11 and Appendix E introduced the area of physical access control as part of facilities management. This section provides a more detailed discussion of this area.

Information security management is responsible for defining and documenting all access control policies. These policies will identify all physical security measures that need to be taken and which groups of employee should have access to what type of facility. Facilities management will ensure that these policies are properly enforced. Policies should include:

- Which areas are restricted and to whom
- What access controls will be put in place
- Under what circumstances access will be allowed to specific restricted areas. For example, preventing all access to a data centre floor unless an authorized RFC number is typed into a keypad
- How access control will be monitored
- A statement of privacy policies and what information has to be known in order to permit access
- Policies regarding the surveillance of personnel, e.g. what may be recorded, where and whether there are any exceptions.

Most organizations use multiple levels of access control, starting with access to the property, then moving to access to specific areas in the building and then to specific functions, equipment or rooms. Each level of security is enforced using different mechanisms and personnel, thus providing additional security.

All facilities should have a documented, current floor plan which indicates exactly which areas are restricted and which are not. This plan will also indicate which security measures are implemented and where. This will aid in security audits and also for the maintenance of access control equipment.

Access control devices need to be installed on all entrances and exits. The aim of these devices is to ensure that only authorized personnel have access to the restricted area. Although this appears at first glance to be a fairly straightforward subject, there are a number of items that need to be taken into account (see Table F.1).

As most physical access control mechanisms are not foolproof, it is important to ensure that access can be monitored and controlled. This is done by specialized security staff and by electronic surveillance equipment.

Because security is all about managing the access of people to a facility, it is fitting that people are used to enforce security measures. Larger organizations sometimes provide their own security staff, but most tend to outsource physical access control to specialized companies. This is usually for the following reasons:

- Security guards require specialized training and are usually subject to a different (almost military) disciplinary code from most company employees. This is often in conflict with the more commercial type of disciplinary code and is best managed by a different set of managers using a different management culture.
- External companies are less likely to be influenced by social engineering situations, as they have specialized training and are unlikely to understand some of the organization's internal nuances that could be used by an experienced social engineer.

Surveillance equipment is used to extend the effectiveness of both the physical access control mechanisms and the security personnel. It is important to note that no surveillance equipment can replace the presence of a trained, aware security guard, merely extend their effectiveness. Examples of commonly used surveillance equipment include:

- Video cameras to monitor key access points and also in less used access points, thus allowing a security guard to monitor several locations at once. These are usually recorded and the videos stored for some time before being used again. This is to ensure that if any wrongdoing is discovered, the video files and recording media can be used in the investigation. This means that the quality of images must be good

Table F.1 Access control devices

Access control	Example	Advantages	Disadvantages
Mechanical	Lock and key	Stable and reliable Inexpensive	Requires key control Locks have to be replaced every time someone leaves the organization Can easily be compromised by anyone with knowledge of a few simple techniques
Code access	Mechanical (e.g. a push button device mounted into the door) Electronic (e.g. a keypad used to arm or disarm a security alarm)	Stable Relatively inexpensive	Someone observing personnel using the device can obtain the code easily Code has to be changed every time someone leaves the organization People tend to write the code down
Electronic access	Key cards	Easy to use Can be used to track personnel's access Can be cancelled or changed centrally to suit changed requirements Can be cancelled even where staff do not return their card	Relatively expensive, although costs have decreased, and often cheaper than using human resources to physically guard each access point Dependent on power availability Can be compromised by people using specialized copying equipment
Biometric	Retinal scanner or voice analysis	Very reliable mechanism for identifying specific individuals Difficult to forge access More effective at countering social engineering	Dependent on the availability of power Requires more sophisticated access control systems Relatively expensive
Multiple access	Door with a key card. One person opens the door and permits access to any number of people accompanying them	Easy to move from one place to another, especially where groups are working together	Difficult to control 'tailgating' Dependent on the security awareness of authorized personnel Extremely vulnerable to social engineering Should not be used in highly secured areas
Single access	Turnstile permits only one person to enter. The same key card cannot be used to enter a second person	Easier to control access Prevents social engineering more effectively	Could become a bottleneck at peak hours Requires more intensive surveillance and staffing
Uni-directional access	Revolving door allowing only access or only exit. Typically used in airports where security personnel are only concerned about people entering the airport, but not about those exiting	Good for situations where there is no need to monitor what people take out, but where things they take in could cause significant damage	Requires more monitoring to ensure that people do not attempt to go through the wrong direction Typically uni-directional; also implies additional scanning equipment and surveillance

Table F.1 Access control devices *continued*

Access control	Example	Advantages	Disadvantages
Bi-directional access	Access-controlled door	Good for general access to restricted areas	People exiting can provide access to unauthorized personnel moving in Could be a bottleneck (e.g. in bi-directional turnstiles people going out have to wait for people coming in)
Active	Requires action by personnel to gain access, e.g. swiping a key card or punching a code	Easier to control access More secure	Requires personnel to remember a code or to bring a key card
Passive	Passive detector unlocks an exit from inside whenever someone approaches	Provides safer exit in the event of a fire Does not require key cards for people moving to non-secure areas	Easy for unauthorized personnel to gain access simply by waiting outside the door Can be triggered from the outside by inserting something under the door and moving it within range of the sensor

enough to facilitate identification of people, but it also has to be in a format that makes it easy to store vast quantities of visual data.

- Access event logs. These typically log every entrance and exit by personnel using electronic access mechanisms.
- Passive detection units to detect the presence of personnel in an area that should not be staffed.
- Alarms that will notify security staff of unauthorized access or exit, often linked to an audible alarm.

No matter how secure the environment, it is dependent on the security awareness of the employees and contractors who work in the facility. Social engineering is still one of the most common breaches of physical security. Social engineering refers to the practice of gaining entry to a facility by using interpersonal and communication skills to convince someone to allow unauthorized access to a building, restricted area, restricted equipment and data; or to cabinets containing confidential documents.

Examples of social engineering include:

- Posing as a legitimate contractor or employee of the organization. The usual technique is to approach security personnel and state that they have forgotten their access card. An access log is signed and a visitor's card produced. There is often no real checking of whether the person

is a legitimate employee, especially in busy reception areas
- Posing as someone who has a reason to gain authorized access to the facility, e.g. a utilities worker or fire inspector
- An ex-employee or contractor approaching people with whom they are familiar to allow them access
- 'Tailgating', where a person simply follows an authorized employee through an entrance that they have opened.

Social engineering is best countered by enforcing strict compliance with access control procedures, continuing education programmes, regular briefings of security personnel and stringent audits.

A growing number of companies offer services to test the rigour of access control with people who specialize in using social engineering techniques.

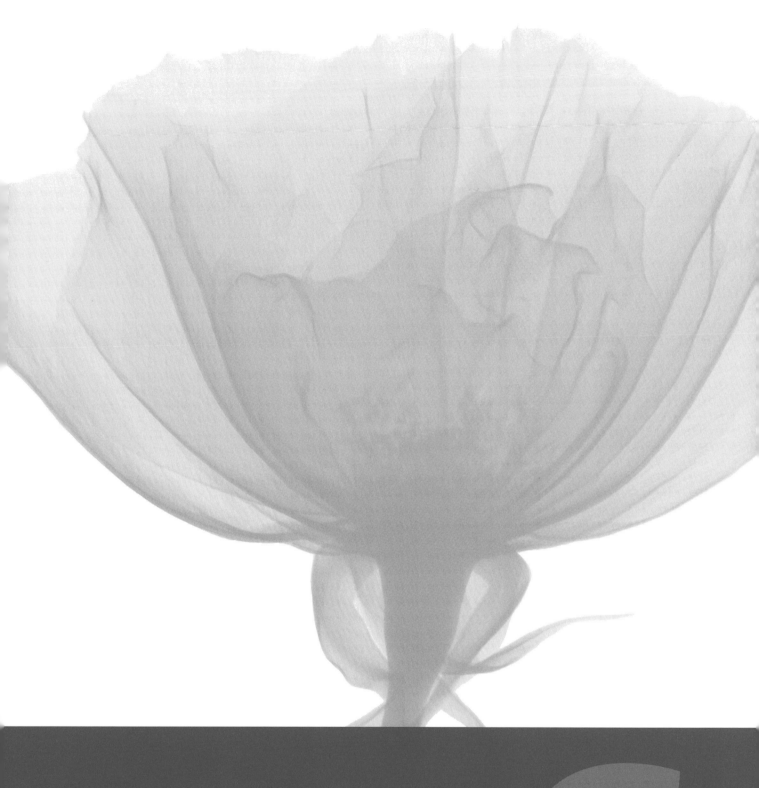

Appendix G:
Risk assessment
and management

G

Appendix G: Risk assessment and management

This appendix contains basic information about several broadly known and used approaches to the assessment and management of risk. It is not intended to be a comprehensive study of the subject, but rather to provide an awareness of some of the methods in use.

G.1 DEFINITION OF RISK AND RISK MANAGEMENT

Risk may be defined as uncertainty of outcome, whether a positive opportunity or negative threat. It is the fact that there is uncertainty that creates the need for attention and formal management of risk. After all, if an organization were absolutely certain that a negative threat would materialize, there would be little difficulty in determining an appropriate course of action. Likewise, if an organization could be guaranteed that the positive opportunity would be realized, then its path would be clear. Managing risks requires the identification and control of the exposure to those risks which may have an impact on the achievement of an organization's business objectives.

Every organization manages its risk, but not always in a way that is visible, repeatable and consistently applied to support decision-making. The purpose of formal risk management is to enable better decision-making based on a sound understanding of risks and their likely impact on the achievement of objectives. An organization can gain this understanding by ensuring that it makes cost-effective use of a risk framework that has a series of well-defined steps. Decision-making should include determining any appropriate actions to take to manage the risks to a level deemed to be acceptable by the organization.

A number of different methodologies, standards and frameworks have been developed for risk management. Some focus more on generic techniques widely applicable to different levels and needs, while others are specifically concerned with risk management relating to important assets used by the organization in the pursuit of its objectives. Each organization should determine the approach to risk management that is best suited to its needs and circumstances, and it is possible that the approach adopted will leverage the ideas reflected in more than one of the recognized standards and/or frameworks.

In this appendix the following approaches to managing risks are briefly explained:

- Management of Risk (M_o_R)
- ISO 31000
- ISO/IEC 27001
- Risk IT.

G.2 MANAGEMENT OF RISK (M_o_R)

Management of Risk (M_o_R) is intended to help organizations put in place an effective framework for risk management. This will help them take informed decisions about the risks that affect their strategic, programme, project and operational objectives.

M_o_R provides a route map of risk management, bringing together principles, an approach, a process with a set of interrelated steps and pointers to more detailed sources of advice on risk management techniques and specialisms. It also provides advice on how these principles, approach and process should be embedded, reviewed and applied differently depending on the nature of the objectives at risk.

The M_o_R framework is illustrated in Figure G.1.

The M_o_R framework is based on four core concepts:

- **M_o_R principles** Principles are essential for the development and maintenance of good risk management practice. They are informed by corporate governance principles and the international standard for risk management, ISO 31000: 2009. They are high-level and universally applicable statements that provide guidance to organizations as they design an appropriate approach to risk management as part of their internal controls.

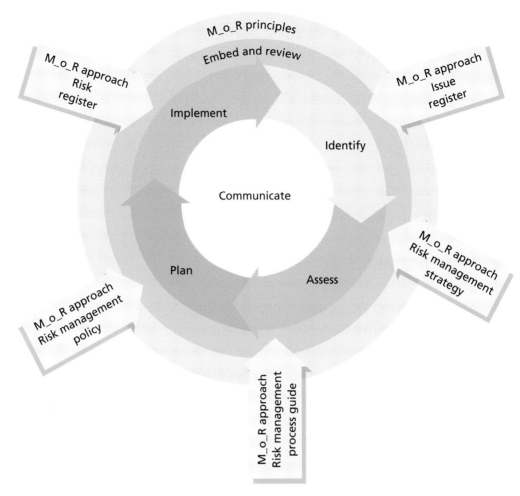

Figure G.1 The M_o_R framework

- **M_o_R approach** Principles need to be adapted and adopted to suit each individual organization. An organization's approach to the principles needs to be agreed and defined within a risk management policy, process guide and strategies.
- **M_o_R process** The process is divided into four main steps: identify, assess, plan and implement. Each step describes the inputs, outputs, tasks and techniques involved to ensure that the overall process is effective.
- **Embedding and reviewing M_o_R** Having put in place an approach and process that satisfy the principles, an organization should ensure that they are consistently applied across the organization and that their application undergoes continual improvement in order for them to be effective.

There are several common techniques which support risk management, including a summary risk profile. A summary risk profile is a graphical representation of information normally found in an existing risk register, and helps to increase the visibility of risks. For more information on summary risk profiles and other M_o_R techniques, see *Management of Risk: Guidance for Practitioners* (OGC, 2010).

G.3   ISO 31000

ISO 31000 was published in November 2009 and is the first set of international guidelines for risk management, intended to be applicable and adaptable for 'any public, private or community enterprise, association, group or individual.' ISO 31000 is a process-oriented rather than a control-oriented approach to risk management, and provides guidance on a broader, more conceptual basis, rather than specifying all aspects of an organization's risk assessment and management approach. For example, ISO 31000 does not define how an organization will create risk data or measure risk, nor does it ensure that an organization will include a review of all risk areas relevant to the achievement of their objectives.

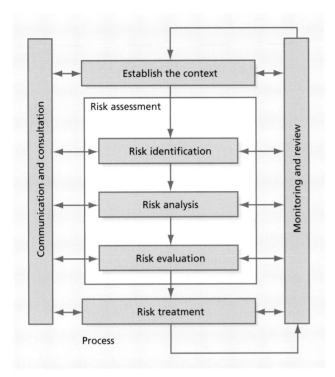

Figure G.2 ISO 31000 risk management process flow

ISO 31000 was published as a standard without certification.

ISO 31000 defines risk as 'the effect of uncertainty on objectives'. Risk management should be performed within a framework that provides the foundations and provisions which will embed the management of risk throughout all levels of the organization. ISO 31000 identifies the necessary components of such a framework as:

- Mandate and commitment
- Design of framework for managing risk
- Understanding the organization and its context
- Establishing risk management policy
- Accountability
- Integration into organizational processes
- Resources
- Establishing internal communication and reporting mechanisms
- Establishing external communication and reporting mechanisms
- Implementing risk management
- Monitoring and review of the framework
- Continual improvement of the framework.

Within this context the risk management process is seen at a high level in Figure G.2.

Once the framework has been established and the context understood, risk assessment is undertaken.

This consists of three steps: risk identification, risk analysis and risk evaluation. The risk identification step is intended to create a comprehensive list of risks based on those events that might create, enhance, prevent, degrade, accelerate or delay the achievement of the organization's objectives. Risk analysis involves developing a full understanding of the risks as an input to risk evaluation and the decisions regarding the plan for treating the risks. Risk evaluation is to make decisions about which risks require treatment and the relative priorities amongst them.

Risk treatment involves the modification of risks using one or more approaches. These approaches are not necessarily mutually exclusive and may include:

- Avoiding the risk by deciding not to start or continue with the activity that gives rise to the risk
- Taking or increasing the risk in order to pursue an opportunity
- Removing the risk source
- Changing the likelihood
- Changing the consequences
- Sharing the risk with another party or parties (including contracts and risk financing)
- Retaining the risk by informed decision.

The approach described in ISO 31000 provides broad scope for each organization to adopt the high-level principles and adapt them to their specific needs and circumstances.

G.4 ISO/IEC 27001

ISO/IEC 27001 was published in October 2005 and is an information security management system (ISMS) standard which formally specifies a management system that is intended to bring information security under explicit management control. While ISO/IEC 27001 is a security standard, not a risk management standard, it mandates specific requirements for security, including requirements relating to risk management. The risk management methods described in this context may be applied to general risk management activities as well.

ISO/IEC 27001 requires that management:

- Systematically examines the organization's information security risks, taking account of the threats, vulnerabilities and impacts

- Designs and implements a coherent and comprehensive suite of information security controls and/or other forms of risk treatment (such as risk avoidance or risk transfer) to address those risks that are deemed unacceptable
- Adopts an overarching management process to ensure that the information security controls continue to meet the organization's information security needs on an ongoing basis.

The key risk management-related steps described in ISO/IEC 27001 include:

- Define the risk assessment approach of the organization
- Identify a risk assessment methodology that is suited to the ISMS, and the identified business information security, legal and regulatory requirements
- Develop criteria for accepting risks and identify acceptable levels of risk
- Identify the risks
- Identify the assets within the scope of the ISMS, and the owners of these assets
- Identify the threats to these assets
- Identify the vulnerabilities that might be exploited by the threats
- Identify the impact that losses of confidentiality, integrity and availability may have on these assets
- Analyse and evaluate the risks
- Assess the business impacts on the organization that might result from security failures, taking into account the consequences of a loss of confidentiality, integrity or availability of the assets
- Assess the realistic likelihood of security failures occurring in the light of prevailing threats and vulnerabilities, and impacts associated with these assets, and the controls currently implemented
- Estimate the levels of risk
- Determine whether the risks are acceptable or require treatment using the previously established criteria for accepting risks
- Identify and evaluate options for the treatment of risks. Possible actions may include:
  - Applying appropriate controls

- Knowingly and objectively accepting risks, providing they clearly satisfy the organization's policies and the criteria for accepting risks
- Avoiding risks
- Transferring the associated business risks to other parties, e.g. insurers, suppliers
- Select control objectives and controls for the treatment of risks
- Obtain management approval of the proposed residual risks
- Obtain management authorization to implement and operate the ISMS.

During the implementation and operation of the ISMS, a plan for risk treatment is formulated (identifying the appropriate management action, resources, responsibilities and priorities for managing information security risks) and implemented. ISO/IEC 27001 also calls for the ongoing monitoring and reviewing of the risks and risk treatment and the formal maintenance of the ISMS to ensure that the organization's goals are met.

This approach is focused specifically on the assets involved in organizational information security, but the general principles can be applied to overall service provision.

G.5 RISK IT

Risk IT is part of the IT governance product portfolio of ISACA that provides a framework for effective governance and management of IT risk, based on a set of guiding principles. Risk IT is about IT risk, including business risk related to the use of IT. The publications in which Risk IT is documented include *The Risk IT Framework* (ISACA, 2009) and *The Risk IT Practitioner Guide* (ISACA, 2009) (available from www.isaca.org).

The key principles in Risk IT are that effective enterprise governance and management of IT risk:

- Always connect to the business objectives
- Align the management of IT-related business risk with overall enterprise risk management
- Balance the costs and benefits of managing IT risk
- Promote fair and open communication of IT risk

■ Establish the right tone from the top while defining and enforcing personal accountability for operating within acceptable and well-defined tolerance levels

■ Are continuous processes and part of daily activities.

The framework provides for three domains, each containing three processes, as shown in Figure G.3. The Risk IT Framework describes the key activities of each process, the responsibilities for the process, information flows between the processes and the performance management of each process.

Risk governance ensures that IT risk management practices are embedded in the enterprise, enabling it to secure optimal risk-adjusted return. Risk evaluation ensures that IT-related risks and opportunities are identified, analysed and presented in business terms. Risk response ensures that IT-related risk issues, opportunities and events are addressed in a cost-effective manner and in line with business priorities.

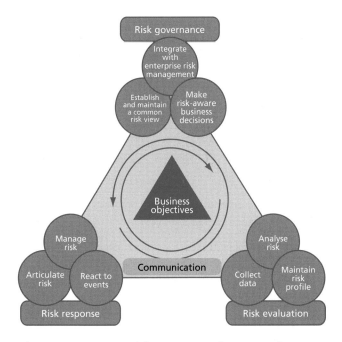

Figure G.3 ISACA Risk IT process framework

Appendix H:
Pareto analysis

H

Appendix H: Pareto analysis

This is a technique for analysing and separating important causes of failure from more trivial issues. The technique identifies those underlying causes of failures that occur the most – essentially answering the question: 'What causes 80% of the failures?' The following steps can be taken to use this approach:

1 Form a table listing the causes and their frequency as a percentage.
2 Arrange the rows in decreasing order of importance of the causes, i.e. the most important cause first.
3 Add a cumulative percentage column to the table. By this step, the chart should look something like Table H.1, which illustrates 10 causes of network failure in an organization.
4 Create a bar chart with the causes, in order of their percentage of total.
5 Superimpose a line chart of the cumulative percentages. The completed graph is illustrated in Figure H.1.
6 Draw a line at 80% on the y-axis parallel to the x-axis. Then drop the line at the point of intersection with the curve on the x-axis. This point on the x-axis separates the important causes and trivial causes. This line is represented as a dotted line in Figure H.1.

Table H.1 Pareto cause ranking chart

Network failures

Causes	Percentage of total	Computation	Cumulative (%)
Network controller	35	0 + 35%	35
File corruption	26	35% + 26%	61
Addressing conflicts	19	61% + 19%	80
Server OS	6	80% + 6%	86
Scripting error	5	86% + 5%	91
Untested change	3	91% + 3%	94
Operator error	2	94% + 2%	96
Backup failure	2	96% + 2%	98
Intrusion attempts	1	98% + 1%	99
Disk failure	1	99% + 1%	100

From Table H.1 it is clear that there are three primary causes for network failure in the organization. These are causing 80% of the failures and should therefore be targeted first.

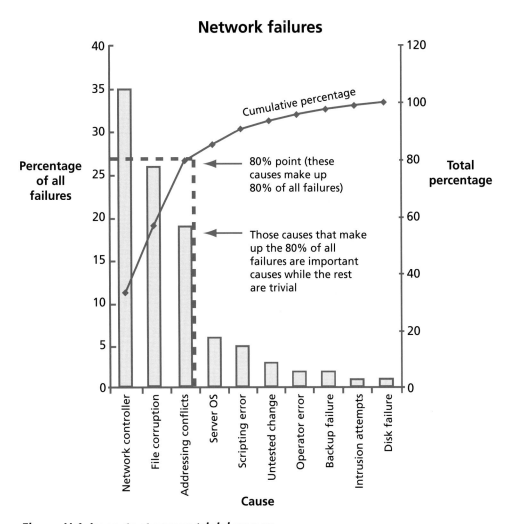

Figure H.1 *Important versus trivial causes*

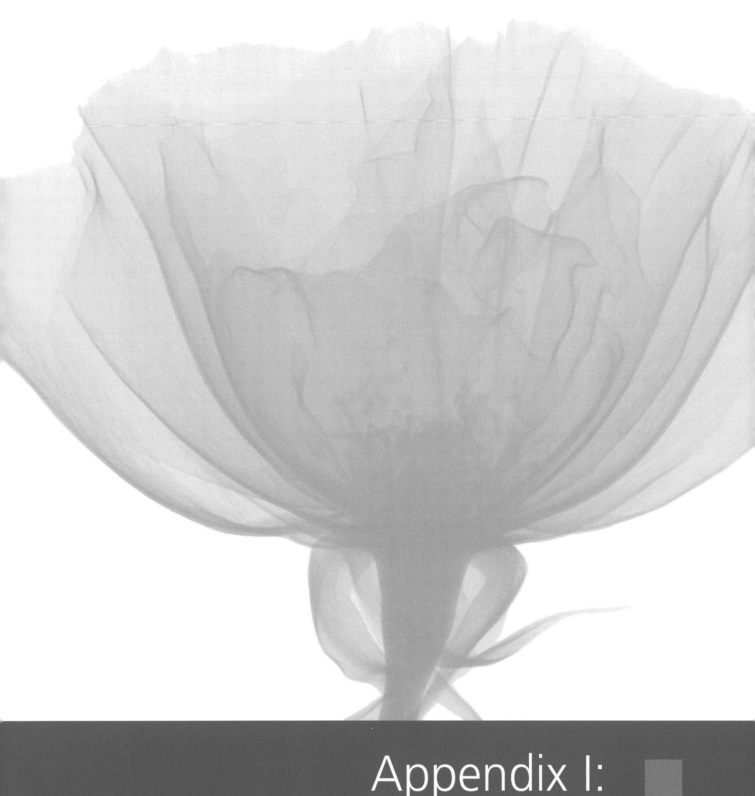

Appendix I: Examples of inputs and outputs across the service lifecycle

Appendix I: Examples of inputs and outputs across the service lifecycle

This appendix identifies some of the major inputs and outputs between each stage of the service lifecycle. This is not an exhaustive list and is designed to help understand how the different lifecycle stages interact. See Table 3.5 for more detail on the inputs and outputs of the service operation stage.

Lifecycle stage	Examples of inputs from other service lifecycle stages	Examples of outputs to other service lifecycle stages
Service strategy	Information and feedback for business cases and service portfolio Requirements for strategies and plans Inputs and feedback on strategies and policies Financial reports, service reports, dashboards, and outputs of service review meetings Response to change proposals Service portfolio updates including the service catalogue Change schedule Knowledge and information in the service knowledge management system (SKMS)	Vision and mission Strategies, strategic plans and policies Financial information and budgets Service portfolio Change proposals Service charters including service packages, service models, and details of utility and warranty Patterns of business activity and demand forecasts Updated knowledge and information in the SKMS Achievements against metrics, KPIs and CSFs Feedback to other lifecycle stages Improvement opportunities logged in the CSI register
Service design	Vision and mission Strategies, strategic plans and policies Financial information and budgets Service portfolio Service charters including service packages, service models, and details of utility and warranty Feedback on all aspects of service design and service design packages Requests for change (RFCs) for designing changes and improvements Input to design requirements from other lifecycle stages Service reports, dashboards, and outputs of service review meetings Knowledge and information in the SKMS	Service portfolio updates including the service catalogue Service design packages, including: ■ Details of utility and warranty ■ Acceptance criteria ■ Updated service models ■ Designs and interface specifications ■ Transition plans ■ Operation plans and procedures Information security policies Designs for new or changed services, management information systems and tools, technology architectures, processes, measurement methods and metrics SLAs, OLAs and underpinning contracts RFCs to transition or deploy new or changed services Financial reports Updated knowledge and information in the SKMS Achievements against metrics, KPIs and CSFs Feedback to other lifecycle stages Improvement opportunities logged in the CSI register

Lifecycle stage	Examples of inputs from other service lifecycle stages	Examples of outputs to other service lifecycle stages
Service transition	Vision and mission Strategies, strategic plans and policies Financial information and budgets Service portfolio Change proposals, including utility and warranty requirements and expected timescales RFCs for implementing changes and improvements Service design packages, including: ■ Details of utility and warranty ■ Acceptance criteria ■ Service models ■ Designs and interface specifications ■ Transition plans ■ Operation plans and procedures Input to change evaluation and change advisory board (CAB) meetings Knowledge and information in the SKMS	New or changed services, management information systems and tools, technology architectures, processes, measurement methods and metrics Responses to change proposals and RFCs Change schedule Known errors Standard changes for use in request fulfilment Knowledge and information in the SKMS (including the configuration management system) Financial reports Updated knowledge and information in the SKMS Achievements against metrics, KPIs and CSFs Feedback to other lifecycle stages Improvement opportunities logged in the CSI register
Service operation	Vision and mission Strategies, strategic plans and policies Financial information and budgets Service portfolio Service reports, dashboards, and outputs of service review meetings Service design packages, including: ■ Details of utility and warranty ■ Operations plans and procedures ■ Recovery procedures Service level agreements (SLAs), operational level agreements (OLAs) and underpinning contracts Known errors Standard changes for use in request fulfilment Information security policies Change schedule Patterns of business activity and demand forecasts Knowledge and information in the SKMS	Achievement of agreed service levels to deliver value to the business Operational requirements Operational performance data and service records RFCs to resolve operational issues Financial reports Updated knowledge and information in the SKMS Achievements against metrics, KPIs and CSFs Feedback to other lifecycle stages Improvement opportunities logged in the CSI register
Continual service improvement	Vision and mission Strategies, strategic plans and policies Financial information and budgets Service portfolio Achievements against metrics, key performance indicators (KPIs) and critical success factors (CSFs) from each lifecycle stage Operational performance data and service records Improvement opportunities logged in the CSI register Knowledge and information in the SKMS	RFCs for implementing improvements across all lifecycle stages Business cases for significant improvements Updated CSI register Service improvement plans Results of customer and user satisfaction surveys Service reports, dashboards, and outputs of service review meetings Financial reports Updated knowledge and information in the SKMS Achievements against metrics, KPIs and CSFs Feedback to other lifecycle stages

References and further reading

References and further reading

Note that this list does not include the publications in the Best Management Practice (BMP) portfolio which are cited in full in Appendix A.

Alexander, H. (1990). *The Vest-Pocket CEO – Decision Making Tools for Executives*. Prentice Hall.

Argyris, Chris (1976). *Increasing Leadership Effectiveness*. Wiley, New York.

Brown, Aaron B. and Hellerstein, Joseph L. (2005). *Reducing the Cost of IT Operations – Is Automation Always the Answer? White Paper*. IBM Thomas J. Watson Research Center.

Brown, Carol V. and Ross, Jeanne, W. (1999). *The IT Organization of the 21st Century: Moving to a Process Based Orientation, Working Paper*. MIT Sloan School of Management.

Brown, Carol V. and Topi, H. (2003). *Information Systems Management Handbook*. CRC Press LLC.

Currie, Wendy L. and Galliers, Bob (2003). *Rethinking Management Information Systems*. Oxford University Press.

Dugmore, J. and Lacy, S. (2006). *Achieving ISO/IEC 20000*. British Standards Institution, London.

Forrester Research Report (2005). *31 Best Practices for the Service Desk.*

Golden, Bernard (2008). *Virtualization for Dummies* (discusses IT operation management issues for managing virtualized environments). Wiley Publishing.

Hackman, J. R. and Oldham, G. R. (1980). *Work Redesign (Organization Development)*. Addison-Wesley, Reading, MA.

Magretta, J. (2002). *What Management Is: How it Works and Why it's Everyone's Business*. The Free Press, New York.

Orlikowski, W. (2010). *Leveraging Social Media for Customer Engagement: An Experiment at BT, Research Briefing*. MIT Sloan School of Management.

Peters, T. and Waterman, R. (1982). *In Search of Excellence*. Harper & Row, New York and London.

Schiesser, R. (2002) *IT Systems Management*. Prentice Hall.

Velte, Anthony T., Velte, Toby J. and Elsenpeter, Robert (2010). *Cloud Computing – A Practical Approach*. McGraw-Hill.

Abbreviations and
glossary

Abbreviations

ACD	automatic call distribution
AM	availability management
AMIS	availability management information system
ASP	application service provider
AST	agreed service time
BCM	business continuity management
BCP	business continuity plan
BIA	business impact analysis
BMP	Best Management Practice
BRM	business relationship manager
BSI	British Standards Institution
CAB	change advisory board
CAPEX	capital expenditure
CCM	component capacity management
CFIA	component failure impact analysis
CI	configuration item
CMDB	configuration management database
CMIS	capacity management information system
CMM	capability maturity model
CMMI	Capability Maturity Model Integration
CMS	configuration management system
COBIT	Control OBjectives for Information and related Technology
COTS	commercial off the shelf
CSF	critical success factor
CSI	continual service improvement
CTI	computer telephony integration
DIKW	Data-to-Information-to-Knowledge-to-Wisdom
DML	definitive media library
ECAB	emergency change advisory board

ELS	early life support
eSCM-CL	eSourcing Capability Model for Client Organizations
eSCM-SP	eSourcing Capability Model for Service Providers
FTA	fault tree analysis
IRR	internal rate of return
ISG	IT steering group
ISM	information security management
ISMS	information security management system
ISO	International Organization for Standardization
ISP	internet service provider
IT	information technology
ITSCM	IT service continuity management
ITSM	IT service management
itSMF	IT Service Management Forum
IVR	interactive voice response
KEDB	known error database
KPI	key performance indicator
LOS	line of service
MIS	management information system
M_o_R	Management of Risk
MTBF	mean time between failures
MTBSI	mean time between service incidents
MTRS	mean time to restore service
MTTR	mean time to repair
NPV	net present value
OLA	operational level agreement
OPEX	operational expenditure
PBA	pattern of business activity
PDCA	Plan-Do-Check-Act
PFS	prerequisite for success

PIR	post-implementation review
PMBOK	Project Management Body of Knowledge
PMI	Project Management Institute
PMO	project management office
PRINCE2	PRojects IN Controlled Environments
PSO	projected service outage
QA	quality assurance
QMS	quality management system
RACI	responsible, accountable, consulted and informed
RCA	root cause analysis
RFC	request for change
ROA	return on assets
ROI	return on investment
RPO	recovery point objective
RTO	recovery time objective
SAC	service acceptance criteria
SACM	service asset and configuration management
SAM	software asset management
SCM	service capacity management
SCMIS	supplier and contract management information system
SDP	service design package
SFA	service failure analysis
SIP	service improvement plan
SKMS	service knowledge management system
SLA	service level agreement
SLM	service level management
SLP	service level package
SLR	service level requirement
SMART	specific, measurable, achievable, relevant and time-bound
SMIS	security management information system
SMO	service maintenance objective
SoC	separation of concerns

SOP	standard operating procedure
SOR	statement of requirements
SOX	Sarbanes-Oxley (US law)
SPI	service provider interface
SPM	service portfolio management
SPOF	single point of failure
TCO	total cost of ownership
TCU	total cost of utilization
TO	technical observation
TOR	terms of reference
TQM	total quality management
UC	underpinning contract
UP	user profile
VBF	vital business function
VOI	value on investment
WIP	work in progress

Glossary

The core ITIL publications (*ITIL Service Strategy*, *ITIL Service Design*, *ITIL Service Operation*, *ITIL Service Transition*, *ITIL Continual Service Improvement*) referred to in parentheses at the beginning of a definition indicate where a reader can find more information. Terms without such a reference may either be used generically across all five core publications, or simply may not be explained in any greater detail elsewhere in the ITIL series. In other words, readers are only directed to other sources where they can expect to expand on their knowledge or to see a greater context.

acceptance

Formal agreement that an IT service, process, plan or other deliverable is complete, accurate, reliable and meets its specified requirements. Acceptance is usually preceded by change evaluation or testing and is often required before proceeding to the next stage of a project or process. *See also* service acceptance criteria.

access management

(*ITIL Service Operation*) The process responsible for allowing users to make use of IT services, data or other assets. Access management helps to protect the confidentiality, integrity and availability of assets by ensuring that only authorized users are able to access or modify them. Access management implements the policies of information security management and is sometimes referred to as rights management or identity management.

account manager

(*ITIL Service Strategy*) A role that is very similar to that of the business relationship manager, but includes more commercial aspects. Most commonly used by Type III service providers when dealing with external customers.

accounting

(*ITIL Service Strategy*) The process responsible for identifying the actual costs of delivering IT services, comparing these with budgeted costs, and managing variance from the budget.

accredited

Officially authorized to carry out a role. For example, an accredited body may be authorized to provide training or to conduct audits.

active monitoring

(*ITIL Service Operation*) Monitoring of a configuration item or an IT service that uses automated regular checks to discover the current status. *See also* passive monitoring.

activity

A set of actions designed to achieve a particular result. Activities are usually defined as part of processes or plans, and are documented in procedures.

agreement

A document that describes a formal understanding between two or more parties. An agreement is not legally binding, unless it forms part of a contract. *See also* operational level agreement; service level agreement.

alert

(*ITIL Service Operation*) A notification that a threshold has been reached, something has changed, or a failure has occurred. Alerts are often created and managed by system management tools and are managed by the event management process.

application

Software that provides functions which are required by an IT service. Each application may be part of more than one IT service. An application runs on one or more servers or clients. *See also* application management; application portfolio.

application management

(*ITIL Service Operation*) The function responsible for managing applications throughout their lifecycle.

application portfolio

(*ITIL Service Design*) A database or structured document used to manage applications throughout their lifecycle. The application portfolio contains key attributes of all applications. The application portfolio is sometimes implemented as part of the service portfolio, or as part of the configuration management system.

application sizing

(*ITIL Service Design*) The activity responsible for understanding the resource requirements needed to support a new application, or a major change to an existing application. Application sizing helps to ensure that the IT service can meet its agreed service level targets for capacity and performance.

architecture

(*ITIL Service Design*) The structure of a system or IT service, including the relationships of components to each other and to the environment they are in. Architecture also includes the standards and guidelines that guide the design and evolution of the system.

assembly

(*ITIL Service Transition*) A configuration item that is made up of a number of other CIs. For example, a server CI may contain CIs for CPUs, disks, memory etc.; an IT service CI may contain many hardware, software and other CIs. *See also* build; component CI.

assessment

Inspection and analysis to check whether a standard or set of guidelines is being followed, that records are accurate, or that efficiency and effectiveness targets are being met. *See also* audit.

asset

(*ITIL Service Strategy*) Any resource or capability. The assets of a service provider include anything that could contribute to the delivery of a service. Assets can be one of the following types: management, organization, process, knowledge, people, information, applications, infrastructure or financial capital. *See also* customer asset; service asset; strategic asset.

asset management

(*ITIL Service Transition*) A generic activity or process responsible for tracking and reporting the value and ownership of assets throughout their lifecycle. *See also* service asset and configuration management; fixed asset management; software asset management.

asset register

(*ITIL Service Transition*) A list of fixed assets that includes their ownership and value. *See also* fixed asset management.

attribute

(*ITIL Service Transition*) A piece of information about a configuration item. Examples are name, location, version number and cost. Attributes of CIs are recorded in a configuration management database (CMDB) and maintained as part of a configuration management system (CMS). *See also* relationship; configuration management system.

audit

Formal inspection and verification to check whether a standard or set of guidelines is being followed, that records are accurate, or that efficiency and effectiveness targets are being met. An audit may be carried out by internal or external groups. *See also* assessment; certification.

authority matrix

See RACI.

automatic call distribution (ACD)

(*ITIL Service Operation*) Use of information technology to direct an incoming telephone call to the most appropriate person in the shortest possible time. ACD is sometimes called automated call distribution.

availability

(*ITIL Service Design*) Ability of an IT service or other configuration item to perform its agreed function when required. Availability is determined by reliability, maintainability, serviceability, performance and security. Availability is usually calculated as a percentage. This calculation is often based on agreed service time and downtime. It is best practice to calculate availability of an IT service using measurements of the business output.

availability management (AM)

(*ITIL Service Design*) The process responsible for ensuring that IT services meet the current and future availability needs of the business in a cost-effective and timely manner. Availability management defines, analyses, plans, measures and improves all aspects of the availability of IT services, and ensures that all IT infrastructures, processes, tools, roles etc. are appropriate for the agreed service level targets for availability. *See also* availability management information system.

availability management information system (AMIS)

(*ITIL Service Design*) A set of tools, data and information that is used to support availability management. *See also* service knowledge management system.

availability plan

(*ITIL Service Design*) A plan to ensure that existing and future availability requirements for IT services can be provided cost-effectively.

back-out

(*ITIL Service Transition*) An activity that restores a service or other configuration item to a previous baseline. Back-out is used as a form of remediation when a change or release is not successful.

backup

(*ITIL Service Design*) (*ITIL Service Operation*) Copying data to protect against loss of integrity or availability of the original.

balanced scorecard

(*ITIL Continual Service Improvement*) A management tool developed by Drs Robert Kaplan (Harvard Business School) and David Norton. A balanced scorecard enables a strategy to be broken down into key performance indicators. Performance against the KPIs is used to demonstrate how well the strategy is being achieved. A balanced scorecard has four major areas, each of which has a small number of KPIs. The same four areas are considered at different levels of detail throughout the organization.

baseline

(*ITIL Continual Service Improvement*) (*ITIL Service Transition*) A snapshot that is used as a reference point. Many snapshots may be taken and recorded over time but only some will be used as baselines. For example:

- An ITSM baseline can be used as a starting point to measure the effect of a service improvement plan
- A performance baseline can be used to measure changes in performance over the lifetime of an IT service
- A configuration baseline can be used as part of a back-out plan to enable the IT infrastructure to be restored to a known configuration if a change or release fails.

See also benchmark.

benchmark

(*ITIL Continual Service Improvement*) (*ITIL Service Transition*) A baseline that is used to compare related data sets as part of a benchmarking exercise. For example, a recent snapshot of a process can be compared to a previous baseline of that process, or a current baseline can be compared to industry data or best practice. *See also* benchmarking; baseline.

benchmarking

(*ITIL Continual Service Improvement*) The process responsible for comparing a benchmark with related data sets such as a more recent snapshot, industry data or best practice. The term is also used to mean creating a series of benchmarks over time, and comparing the results to measure progress or improvement. This process is not described in detail within the core ITIL publications.

Best Management Practice (BMP)

The Best Management Practice portfolio is owned by the Cabinet Office, part of HM Government. Formerly owned by CCTA and then OGC, the BMP functions moved to the Cabinet Office in June 2010. The BMP portfolio includes guidance on IT service management and project, programme, risk, portfolio and value management. There is also a management maturity model as well as related glossaries of terms.

best practice

Proven activities or processes that have been successfully used by multiple organizations. ITIL is an example of best practice.

billing

(*ITIL Service Strategy*) Part of the charging process. Billing is the activity responsible for producing an invoice or a bill and recovering the money from customers. *See also* pricing.

brainstorming

(*ITIL Service Design*) (*ITIL Service Operation*) A technique that helps a team to generate ideas. Ideas are not reviewed during the brainstorming session, but at a later stage. Brainstorming is often used by problem management to identify possible causes.

British Standards Institution (BSI)

The UK national standards body, responsible for creating and maintaining British standards. See www.bsi-global.com for more information. *See also* International Organization for Standardization.

budget

A list of all the money an organization or business unit plans to receive, and plans to pay out, over a specified period of time. *See also* budgeting; planning.

budgeting

The activity of predicting and controlling the spending of money. Budgeting consists of a periodic negotiation cycle to set future budgets (usually annual) and the day-to-day monitoring and adjusting of current budgets.

build

(*ITIL Service Transition*) The activity of assembling a number of configuration items to create part of an IT service. The term is also used to refer to a release that is authorized for distribution – for example, server build or laptop build. *See also* configuration baseline.

business

(*ITIL Service Strategy*) An overall corporate entity or organization formed of a number of business units. In the context of ITSM, the term includes public sector and not-for-profit organizations, as well as companies. An IT service provider provides IT services to a customer within a business. The IT service provider may be part of the same business as its customer (internal service provider), or part of another business (external service provider).

business case

(*ITIL Service Strategy*) Justification for a significant item of expenditure. The business case includes information about costs, benefits, options, issues, risks and possible problems. *See also* cost benefit analysis.

business customer

(*ITIL Service Strategy*) A recipient of a product or a service from the business. For example, if the business is a car manufacturer, then the business customer is someone who buys a car.

business impact analysis (BIA)

(*ITIL Service Strategy*) Business impact analysis is the activity in business continuity management that identifies vital business functions and their dependencies. These dependencies may include suppliers, people, other business processes, IT services etc. Business impact analysis defines the recovery requirements for IT services. These requirements include recovery time objectives, recovery point objectives and minimum service level targets for each IT service.

business objective

(*ITIL Service Strategy*) The objective of a business process, or of the business as a whole. Business objectives support the business vision, provide guidance for the IT strategy, and are often supported by IT services.

business operations

(*ITIL Service Strategy*) The day-to-day execution, monitoring and management of business processes.

business perspective

(*ITIL Continual Service Improvement*) An understanding of the service provider and IT services from the point of view of the business, and an understanding of the business from the point of view of the service provider.

business process

A process that is owned and carried out by the business. A business process contributes to the delivery of a product or service to a business customer. For example, a retailer may have a purchasing process that helps to deliver services to its business customers. Many business processes rely on IT services.

business relationship management

(*ITIL Service Strategy*) The process responsible for maintaining a positive relationship with customers. Business relationship management identifies customer needs and ensures that the service provider is able to meet these needs with an appropriate catalogue of services. This process has strong links with service level management.

business relationship manager (BRM)

(*ITIL Service Strategy*) A role responsible for maintaining the relationship with one or more customers. This role is often combined with the service level manager role.

business service

A service that is delivered to business customers by business units. For example, delivery of financial services to customers of a bank, or goods to the customers of a retail store. Successful delivery of business services often depends on one or more IT services. A business service may consist almost entirely of an IT service – for example, an online banking service or an external website where product orders can be placed by business customers. *See also* customer-facing service.

business service management

The management of business services delivered to business customers. Business service management is performed by business units.

business unit

(*ITIL Service Strategy*) A segment of the business that has its own plans, metrics, income and costs. Each business unit owns assets and uses these to create value for customers in the form of goods and services.

call

(*ITIL Service Operation*) A telephone call to the service desk from a user. A call could result in an incident or a service request being logged.

call centre

(*ITIL Service Operation*) An organization or business unit that handles large numbers of incoming and outgoing telephone calls. *See also* service desk.

call type

(*ITIL Service Operation*) A category that is used to distinguish incoming requests to a service desk. Common call types are incident, service request and complaint.

capability

(*ITIL Service Strategy*) The ability of an organization, person, process, application, IT service or other configuration item to carry out an activity. Capabilities are intangible assets of an organization. *See also* resource.

Capability Maturity Model Integration (CMMI)

(*ITIL Continual Service Improvement*) A process improvement approach developed by the Software Engineering Institute (SEI) of Carnegie Mellon University, US. CMMI provides organizations with the essential elements of effective processes. It can be used to guide process improvement across a project, a division or an entire organization. CMMI helps integrate traditionally separate organizational functions, set process improvement goals and priorities, provide guidance for quality processes, and provide a point of reference for appraising current processes. See www.sei.cmu.edu/cmmi for more information. *See also* maturity.

capacity

(*ITIL Service Design*) The maximum throughput that a configuration item or IT service can deliver. For some types of CI, capacity may be the size or volume – for example, a disk drive.

capacity management

(*ITIL Continual Service Improvement*) (*ITIL Service Design*) The process responsible for ensuring that the capacity of IT services and the IT infrastructure is able to meet agreed capacity- and performance-related requirements in a cost-effective and timely manner. Capacity management considers all resources required to deliver an IT service, and is concerned with meeting both the current and future capacity and performance needs of the business. Capacity management includes three sub-processes: business capacity management, service capacity management, and component capacity management. *See also* capacity management information system.

capacity management information system (CMIS)

(*ITIL Service Design*) A set of tools, data and information that is used to support capacity management. *See also* service knowledge management system.

capacity plan

(*ITIL Service Design*) A plan used to manage the resources required to deliver IT services. The plan contains details of current and historic usage of IT services and components, and any issues that need to be addressed (including related improvement activities). The plan also contains scenarios for different predictions of business demand and costed options to deliver the agreed service level targets.

capacity planning

(*ITIL Service Design*) The activity within capacity management responsible for creating a capacity plan.

capital cost

(*ITIL Service Strategy*) The cost of purchasing something that will become a financial asset – for example, computer equipment and buildings. The value of the asset depreciates over multiple accounting periods. *See also* operational cost.

capital expenditure (CAPEX)

See capital cost.

category

A named group of things that have something in common. Categories are used to group similar things together. For example, cost types are used to group similar types of cost. Incident categories are used to group similar types of incident, while CI types are used to group similar types of configuration item.

certification

Issuing a certificate to confirm compliance to a standard. Certification includes a formal audit by an independent and accredited body. The term is also used to mean awarding a certificate to provide evidence that a person has achieved a qualification.

change

(*ITIL Service Transition*) The addition, modification or removal of anything that could have an effect on IT services. The scope should include changes to all architectures, processes, tools, metrics and documentation, as well as changes to IT services and other configuration items.

change advisory board (CAB)

(*ITIL Service Transition*) A group of people that support the assessment, prioritization, authorization and scheduling of changes. A change advisory board is usually made up of representatives from: all areas within the IT service provider; the business; and third parties such as suppliers.

change evaluation

(*ITIL Service Transition*) The process responsible for formal assessment of a new or changed IT service to ensure that risks have been managed and to help determine whether to authorize the change.

change management

(*ITIL Service Transition*) The process responsible for controlling the lifecycle of all changes, enabling beneficial changes to be made with minimum disruption to IT services.

change model

(*ITIL Service Transition*) A repeatable way of dealing with a particular category of change. A change model defines specific agreed steps that will be followed for a change of this category. Change models may be very complex with many steps that require authorization (e.g. major software release) or may be very simple with no requirement for authorization (e.g. password reset). *See also* change advisory board; standard change.

change proposal

(*ITIL Service Strategy*) (*ITIL Service Transition*) A document that includes a high level description of a potential service introduction or significant change, along with a corresponding business case and an expected implementation schedule. Change proposals are normally created by the service portfolio management process and are passed to change management for authorization. Change management will review the potential impact on other services, on shared resources, and on the overall change schedule. Once the change proposal has been authorized, service portfolio management will charter the service.

change record

(*ITIL Service Transition*) A record containing the details of a change. Each change record documents the lifecycle of a single change. A change record is created for every request for change that is received, even those that are subsequently rejected. Change records should reference the configuration items that are affected by the change. Change records may be stored in the configuration management system, or elsewhere in the service knowledge management system.

change request

See request for change.

change schedule

(*ITIL Service Transition*) A document that lists all authorized changes and their planned implementation dates, as well as the estimated dates of longer-term changes. A change schedule is sometimes called a forward schedule of change, even though it also contains information about changes that have already been implemented.

change window

(*ITIL Service Transition*) A regular, agreed time when changes or releases may be implemented with minimal impact on services. Change windows are usually documented in service level agreements.

charging

(*ITIL Service Strategy*) Requiring payment for IT services. Charging for IT services is optional, and many organizations choose to treat their IT service provider as a cost centre. *See also* charging process; charging policy.

charging policy

(*ITIL Service Strategy*) A policy specifying the objective of the charging process and the way in which charges will be calculated. *See also* cost.

charging process

(*ITIL Service Strategy*) The process responsible for deciding how much customers should pay (pricing) and recovering money from them (billing). This process is not described in detail within the core ITIL publications.

charter

(*ITIL Service Strategy*) A document that contains details of a new service, a significant change or other significant project. Charters are typically authorized by service portfolio management or by a project management office. The term charter is also used to describe the act of authorizing the work required to complete the service change or project. *See also* change proposal; service charter; project portfolio.

chronological analysis

(*ITIL Service Operation*) A technique used to help identify possible causes of problems. All available data about the problem is collected and sorted by date and time to provide a detailed timeline. This can make it possible to identify which events may have been triggered by others.

CI type

(*ITIL Service Transition*) A category that is used to classify configuration items. The CI type identifies the required attributes and relationships for a configuration record. Common CI types include hardware, document, user etc.

classification

The act of assigning a category to something. Classification is used to ensure consistent management and reporting. Configuration items, incidents, problems, changes etc. are usually classified.

client

A generic term that means a customer, the business or a business customer. For example, client manager may be used as a synonym for business relationship manager. The term is also used to mean:

■ A computer that is used directly by a user – for example, a PC, a handheld computer or a work station
■ The part of a client server application that the user directly interfaces with – for example, an email client.

closed

(*ITIL Service Operation*) The final status in the lifecycle of an incident, problem, change etc. When the status is closed, no further action is taken.

closure

(*ITIL Service Operation*) The act of changing the status of an incident, problem, change etc. to closed.

COBIT

(*ITIL Continual Service Improvement*) Control OBjectives for Information and related Technology (COBIT) provides guidance and best practice for the management of IT processes. COBIT is published by ISACA in conjunction with the IT Governance Institute (ITGI). See www.isaca.org for more information.

code of practice

A guideline published by a public body or a standards organization, such as ISO or BSI. Many standards consist of a code of practice and a specification. The code of practice describes recommended best practice.

commercial off the shelf (COTS)

(*ITIL Service Design*) Pre-existing application software or middleware that can be purchased from a third party.

compliance

Ensuring that a standard or set of guidelines is followed, or that proper, consistent accounting or other practices are being employed.

component

A general term that is used to mean one part of something more complex. For example, a computer system may be a component of an IT service; an application may be a component of a release unit. Components that need to be managed should be configuration items.

component CI

(*ITIL Service Transition*) A configuration item that is part of an assembly. For example, a CPU or memory CI may be part of a server CI.

component failure impact analysis (CFIA)

(*ITIL Service Design*) A technique that helps to identify the impact of configuration item failure on IT services and the business. A matrix is created with IT services on one axis and CIs on the other. This enables the identification of critical CIs (that could cause the failure of multiple IT services) and fragile IT services (that have multiple single points of failure).

computer telephony integration (CTI)

(*ITIL Service Operation*) Computer telephony integration is a general term covering any kind of integration between computers and telephone systems. It is most commonly used to refer to systems where an application displays detailed screens relating to incoming or outgoing telephone calls. *See also* automatic call distribution; interactive voice response.

concurrency

A measure of the number of users engaged in the same operation at the same time.

confidentiality

(*ITIL Service Design*) A security principle that requires that data should only be accessed by authorized people.

configuration

(*ITIL Service Transition*) A generic term used to describe a group of configuration items that work together to deliver an IT service, or a recognizable part of an IT service. Configuration is also used to describe the parameter settings for one or more configuration items.

configuration baseline

(*ITIL Service Transition*) The baseline of a configuration that has been formally agreed and is managed through the change management process. A configuration baseline is used as a basis for future builds, releases and changes.

configuration control

(*ITIL Service Transition*) The activity responsible for ensuring that adding, modifying or removing a configuration item is properly managed – for example, by submitting a request for change or service request.

configuration item (CI)

(*ITIL Service Transition*) Any component or other service asset that needs to be managed in order to deliver an IT service. Information about each configuration item is recorded in a configuration record within the configuration management system and is maintained throughout its lifecycle by service asset and configuration management. Configuration items are under the control of change management. They typically include IT services, hardware, software, buildings, people and formal documentation such as process documentation and service level agreements.

configuration management

See service asset and configuration management.

configuration management database (CMDB)

(*ITIL Service Transition*) A database used to store configuration records throughout their lifecycle. The configuration management system maintains one or more configuration management databases, and each database stores attributes of configuration items, and relationships with other configuration items.

configuration management system (CMS)

(*ITIL Service Transition*) A set of tools, data and information that is used to support service asset and configuration management. The CMS is part of an overall service knowledge management system and includes tools for collecting, storing, managing, updating, analysing and presenting data about all configuration items and their relationships. The CMS may also include information about incidents, problems, known errors, changes and releases. The CMS is maintained by service asset and configuration management and is used by all IT service management processes. *See also* configuration management database.

continual service improvement (CSI)

(*ITIL Continual Service Improvement*) A stage in the lifecycle of a service. Continual service improvement ensures that services are aligned with changing business needs by identifying and implementing improvements to IT services that support business processes. The performance of the IT service provider is continually measured and improvements are made to processes, IT services and IT infrastructure in order to increase efficiency, effectiveness and cost effectiveness. Continual service improvement includes the seven-step improvement process. Although this process is associated with continual service improvement, most processes have activities that take place across multiple stages of the service lifecycle. *See also* Plan-Do-Check-Act.

contract

A legally binding agreement between two or more parties.

control

A means of managing a risk, ensuring that a business objective is achieved or that a process is followed. Examples of control include policies, procedures, roles, RAID, door locks etc. A control is sometimes called a countermeasure or safeguard. Control also means to manage the utilization or behaviour of a configuration item, system or IT service.

Control OBjectives for Information and related Technology

See COBIT.

control perspective

(*ITIL Service Strategy*) An approach to the management of IT services, processes, functions, assets etc. There can be several different control perspectives on the same IT service, process etc., allowing different individuals or teams to focus on what is important and relevant to their specific role. Examples of control perspective include reactive and proactive management within IT operations, or a lifecycle view for an application project team.

core service

(*ITIL Service Strategy*) A service that delivers the basic outcomes desired by one or more customers. A core service provides a specific level of utility and warranty. Customers may be offered a choice of utility and warranty through one or more service options. *See also* enabling service; enhancing service; IT service; service package.

cost

The amount of money spent on a specific activity, IT service or business unit. Costs consist of real cost (money), notional cost (such as people's time) and depreciation.

cost benefit analysis

An activity that analyses and compares the costs and the benefits involved in one or more alternative courses of action. *See also* business case; internal rate of return; net present value; return on investment; value on investment.

cost element

(*ITIL Service Strategy*) The middle level of category to which costs are assigned in budgeting and accounting. The highest-level category is cost type. For example, a cost type of 'people' could have cost elements of payroll, staff benefits, expenses, training, overtime etc. Cost elements can be further broken down to give cost units. For example, the cost element 'expenses' could include cost units of hotels, transport, meals etc.

cost model

(*ITIL Service Strategy*) A framework used in budgeting and accounting in which all known costs can be recorded, categorized and allocated to specific customers, business units or projects. *See also* cost type; cost element; cost unit.

cost type

(*ITIL Service Strategy*) The highest level of category to which costs are assigned in budgeting and accounting – for example, hardware, software, people, accommodation, external and transfer. *See also* cost element; cost unit.

cost unit

(*ITIL Service Strategy*) The lowest level of category to which costs are assigned, cost units are usually things that can be easily counted (e.g. staff numbers, software licences) or things easily measured (e.g. CPU usage, electricity consumed). Cost units are included within cost elements. For example, a cost element of 'expenses' could include cost units of hotels, transport, meals etc. *See also* cost type.

cost effectiveness

A measure of the balance between the effectiveness and cost of a service, process or activity. A cost-effective process is one that achieves its objectives at minimum cost. *See also* key performance indicator; return on investment; value for money.

countermeasure

Can be used to refer to any type of control. The term is most often used when referring to measures that increase resilience, fault tolerance or reliability of an IT service.

course corrections

Changes made to a plan or activity that has already started to ensure that it will meet its objectives. Course corrections are made as a result of monitoring progress.

crisis management

Crisis management is the process responsible for managing the wider implications of business continuity. A crisis management team is responsible for strategic issues such as managing media relations and shareholder confidence, and decides when to invoke business continuity plans.

critical success factor (CSF)

Something that must happen if an IT service, process, plan, project or other activity is to succeed. Key performance indicators are used to measure the achievement of each critical success factor. For example, a critical success factor of 'protect IT services when making changes' could be measured by key performance indicators such as 'percentage reduction of unsuccessful changes', 'percentage reduction in changes causing incidents' etc.

CSI register

(*ITIL Continual Service Improvement*) A database or structured document used to record and manage improvement opportunities throughout their lifecycle.

culture

A set of values that is shared by a group of people, including expectations about how people should behave, their ideas, beliefs and practices. *See also* vision.

customer

Someone who buys goods or services. The customer of an IT service provider is the person or group who defines and agrees the service level targets. The term is also sometimes used informally to mean user – for example, 'This is a customer-focused organization.'

customer asset

Any resource or capability of a customer. *See also* asset.

customer agreement portfolio

(*ITIL Service Strategy*) A database or structured document used to manage service contracts or agreements between an IT service provider and its customers. Each IT service delivered to a customer should have a contract or other agreement that is listed in the customer agreement portfolio. *See also* customer-facing service; service catalogue; service portfolio.

customer-facing service

(*ITIL Service Design*) An IT service that is visible to the customer. These are normally services that support the customer's business processes and facilitate one or more outcomes desired by the customer. All live customer-facing services, including those available for deployment, are recorded in the service catalogue along with customer-visible information about deliverables, prices, contact points, ordering and request processes. Other information such as relationships to supporting services and other CIs will also be recorded for internal use by the IT service provider.

dashboard

(*ITIL Service Operation*) A graphical representation of overall IT service performance and availability. Dashboard images may be updated in real time, and can also be included in management reports and web pages. Dashboards can be used to support service level management, event management and incident diagnosis.

Data-to-Information-to-Knowledge-to-Wisdom (DIKW)

(*ITIL Service Transition*) A way of understanding the relationships between data, information, knowledge and wisdom. DIKW shows how each of these builds on the others.

definitive media library (DML)

(*ITIL Service Transition*) One or more locations in which the definitive and authorized versions of all software configuration items are securely stored. The definitive media library may also contain associated configuration items such as licences and documentation. It is a single logical storage area even if there are multiple locations. The definitive media library is controlled by service asset and configuration management and is recorded in the configuration management system.

deliverable

Something that must be provided to meet a commitment in a service level agreement or a contract. It is also used in a more informal way to mean a planned output of any process.

demand management

(*ITIL Service Design*) (*ITIL Service Strategy*) The process responsible for understanding, anticipating and influencing customer demand for services. Demand management works with capacity management to ensure that the service provider has sufficient capacity to meet the required demand. At a strategic level, demand management can involve analysis of patterns of business activity and user profiles, while at a tactical level, it can involve the use of differential charging to encourage customers to use IT services at less busy times, or require short-term activities to respond to unexpected demand or the failure of a configuration item.

Deming Cycle

See Plan-Do-Check-Act.

dependency

The direct or indirect reliance of one process or activity on another.

deployment

(*ITIL Service Transition*) The activity responsible for movement of new or changed hardware, software, documentation, process etc. to the live environment. Deployment is part of the release and deployment management process.

design

(*ITIL Service Design*) An activity or process that identifies requirements and then defines a solution that is able to meet these requirements. *See also* service design.

design coordination

(*ITIL Service Design*) The process responsible for coordinating all service design activities, processes and resources. Design coordination ensures the consistent and effective design of new or changed IT services, service management information systems, architectures, technology, processes, information and metrics.

detection

(*ITIL Service Operation*) A stage in the expanded incident lifecycle. Detection results in the incident becoming known to the service provider. Detection can be automatic or the result of a user logging an incident.

development

(*ITIL Service Design*) The process responsible for creating or modifying an IT service or application ready for subsequent release and deployment. Development is also used to mean the role or function that carries out development work. This process is not described in detail within the core ITIL publications.

development environment

(*ITIL Service Design*) An environment used to create or modify IT services or applications. Development environments are not typically subjected to the same degree of control as test or live environments. *See also* development.

diagnosis

(*ITIL Service Operation*) A stage in the incident and problem lifecycles. The purpose of diagnosis is to identify a workaround for an incident or the root cause of a problem.

diagnostic script

(*ITIL Service Operation*) A structured set of questions used by service desk staff to ensure they ask the correct questions, and to help them classify, resolve and assign incidents. Diagnostic scripts may also be made available to users to help them diagnose and resolve their own incidents.

directory service

(*ITIL Service Operation*) An application that manages information about IT infrastructure available on a network, and corresponding user access rights.

document

Information in readable form. A document may be paper or electronic – for example, a policy statement, service level agreement, incident record or diagram of a computer room layout. *See also* record.

downtime

(*ITIL Service Design*) (*ITIL Service Operation*) The time when an IT service or other configuration item is not available during its agreed service time. The availability of an IT service is often calculated from agreed service time and downtime.

driver

Something that influences strategy, objectives or requirements – for example, new legislation or the actions of competitors.

early life support (ELS)

(*ITIL Service Transition*) A stage in the service lifecycle that occurs at the end of deployment and before the service is fully accepted into operation. During early life support, the service provider reviews key performance indicators, service levels and monitoring thresholds and may implement improvements to ensure that service targets can be met. The service provider may also provide additional resources for incident and problem management during this time.

economies of scale

(*ITIL Service Strategy*) The reduction in average cost that is possible from increasing the usage of an IT service or asset. *See also* economies of scope.

economies of scope

(*ITIL Service Strategy*) The reduction in cost that is allocated to an IT service by using an existing asset for an additional purpose. For example, delivering a new IT service from an existing IT infrastructure. *See also* economies of scale.

effectiveness

(*ITIL Continual Service Improvement*) A measure of whether the objectives of a process, service or activity have been achieved. An effective process or activity is one that achieves its agreed objectives. *See also* key performance indicator.

efficiency

(*ITIL Continual Service Improvement*) A measure of whether the right amount of resource has been used to deliver a process, service or activity. An efficient process achieves its objectives with the minimum amount of time, money, people or other resources. *See also* key performance indicator.

emergency change

(*ITIL Service Transition*) A change that must be introduced as soon as possible – for example, to resolve a major incident or implement a security patch. The change management process will normally have a specific procedure for handling emergency changes. *See also* emergency change advisory board.

emergency change advisory board (ECAB)

(*ITIL Service Transition*) A subgroup of the change advisory board that makes decisions about emergency changes. Membership may be decided at the time a meeting is called, and depends on the nature of the emergency change.

enabling service

(*ITIL Service Strategy*) A service that is needed in order to deliver a core service. Enabling services may or may not be visible to the customer, but they are not offered to customers in their own right. *See also* enhancing service.

enhancing service

(*ITIL Service Strategy*) A service that is added to a core service to make it more attractive to the customer. Enhancing services are not essential to the delivery of a core service but are used to encourage customers to use the core services or to differentiate the service provider from its competitors. *See also* enabling service; excitement factor.

enterprise financial management

(*ITIL Service Strategy*) The function and processes responsible for managing the overall organization's budgeting, accounting and charging requirements. Enterprise financial management is sometimes referred to as the 'corporate' financial department. *See also* financial management for IT services.

environment

(*ITIL Service Transition*) A subset of the IT infrastructure that is used for a particular purpose – for example, live environment, test environment, build environment. Also used in the term 'physical environment' to mean the accommodation, air conditioning, power system etc. Environment is used as a generic term to mean the external conditions that influence or affect something.

error

(*ITIL Service Operation*) A design flaw or malfunction that causes a failure of one or more IT services or other configuration items. A mistake made by a person or a faulty process that impacts a configuration item is also an error.

escalation

(*ITIL Service Operation*) An activity that obtains additional resources when these are needed to meet service level targets or customer expectations. Escalation may be needed within any IT service management process, but is most commonly associated with incident management, problem management and the management of customer complaints. There are two types of escalation: functional escalation and hierarchic escalation.

eSourcing Capability Model for Client Organizations (eSCM-CL)

(*ITIL Service Strategy*) A framework to help organizations in their analysis and decision-making on service sourcing models and strategies. It was developed by Carnegie Mellon University in the US. *See also* eSourcing Capability Model for Service Providers.

eSourcing Capability Model for Service Providers (eSCM-SP)

(*ITIL Service Strategy*) A framework to help IT service providers develop their IT service management capabilities from a service sourcing perspective. It was developed by Carnegie Mellon University in the US. *See also* eSourcing Capability Model for Client Organizations.

estimation

The use of experience to provide an approximate value for a metric or cost. Estimation is also used in capacity and availability management as the cheapest and least accurate modelling method.

event

(*ITIL Service Operation*) A change of state that has significance for the management of an IT service or other configuration item. The term is also used to mean an alert or notification created by any IT service, configuration item or monitoring tool. Events typically require IT operations personnel to take actions, and often lead to incidents being logged.

event management

(*ITIL Service Operation*) The process responsible for managing events throughout their lifecycle. Event management is one of the main activities of IT operations.

exception report

A document containing details of one or more key performance indicators or other important targets that have exceeded defined thresholds. Examples include service level agreement targets being missed or about to be missed, and a performance metric indicating a potential capacity problem.

excitement factor

(*ITIL Service Strategy*) An attribute added to something to make it more attractive or more exciting to the customer. For example, a restaurant may provide a free drink with every meal. *See also* enhancing service.

expanded incident lifecycle

(*ITIL Continual Service Improvement*) (*ITIL Service Design*) Detailed stages in the lifecycle of an incident. The stages are detection, diagnosis, repair, recovery and restoration. The expanded incident lifecycle is used to help understand all contributions to the impact of incidents and to plan for how these could be controlled or reduced.

external customer

A customer who works for a different business from the IT service provider. *See also* external service provider; internal customer.

external metric

A metric that is used to measure the delivery of IT service to a customer. External metrics are usually defined in service level agreements and reported to customers. *See also* internal metric.

external service provider

(*ITIL Service Strategy*) An IT service provider that is part of a different organization from its customer. An IT service provider may have both internal and external customers. *See also* outsourcing; Type III service provider.

facilities management

(*ITIL Service Operation*) The function responsible for managing the physical environment where the IT infrastructure is located. Facilities management includes all aspects of managing the physical environment – for example, power and cooling, building access management, and environmental monitoring.

failure

(*ITIL Service Operation*) Loss of ability to operate to specification, or to deliver the required output. The term may be used when referring to IT services, processes, activities, configuration items etc. A failure often causes an incident.

fault

See error.

fault tolerance

(*ITIL Service Design*) The ability of an IT service or other configuration item to continue to operate correctly after failure of a component part. *See also* countermeasure; resilience.

fault tree analysis (FTA)

(*ITIL Continual Service Improvement*) (*ITIL Service Design*) A technique that can be used to determine a chain of events that has caused an incident, or may cause an incident in the future. Fault tree analysis represents a chain of events using Boolean notation in a diagram.

financial management

(*ITIL Service Strategy*) A generic term used to describe the function and processes responsible for managing an organization's budgeting, accounting and charging requirements. Enterprise financial management is the specific term used to describe the function and processes from the perspective of the overall organization. Financial management for IT services is the specific term used to describe the function and processes from the perspective of the IT service provider.

financial management for IT services

(*ITIL Service Strategy*) The function and processes responsible for managing an IT service provider's budgeting, accounting and charging requirements. Financial management for IT services secures an appropriate level of funding to design, develop and deliver services that meet the strategy of the organization in a cost-effective manner. *See also* enterprise financial management.

first-line support

(*ITIL Service Operation*) The first level in a hierarchy of support groups involved in the resolution of incidents. Each level contains more specialist skills, or has more time or other resources. *See also* escalation.

fishbone diagram

See Ishikawa diagram.

fit for purpose

(*ITIL Service Strategy*) The ability to meet an agreed level of utility. Fit for purpose is also used informally to describe a process, configuration item, IT service etc. that is capable of meeting its objectives or service levels. Being fit for purpose requires suitable design, implementation, control and maintenance.

fit for use

(*ITIL Service Strategy*) The ability to meet an agreed level of warranty. Being fit for use requires suitable design, implementation, control and maintenance.

fixed asset management

(*ITIL Service Transition*) The process responsible for tracking and reporting the value and ownership of fixed assets throughout their lifecycle. Fixed asset management maintains the asset register and is usually carried out by the overall business, rather than by the IT organization. Fixed asset management is sometimes called financial asset management and is not described in detail within the core ITIL publications.

follow the sun

(*ITIL Service Operation*) A methodology for using service desks and support groups around the world to provide seamless 24/7 service. Calls, incidents, problems and service requests are passed between groups in different time zones.

fulfilment

Performing activities to meet a need or requirement – for example, by providing a new IT service, or meeting a service request.

function

A team or group of people and the tools or other resources they use to carry out one or more processes or activities – for example, the service desk. The term also has two other meanings:

- An intended purpose of a configuration item, person, team, process or IT service. For example, one function of an email service may be to store and forward outgoing mails, while the function of a business process may be to despatch goods to customers.
- To perform the intended purpose correctly, as in 'The computer is functioning.'

functional escalation

(*ITIL Service Operation*) Transferring an incident, problem or change to a technical team with a higher level of expertise to assist in an escalation.

governance

Ensures that policies and strategy are actually implemented, and that required processes are correctly followed. Governance includes defining roles and responsibilities, measuring and reporting, and taking actions to resolve any issues identified.

guideline

A document describing best practice, which recommends what should be done. Compliance with a guideline is not normally enforced. *See also* standard.

hierarchic escalation

(*ITIL Service Operation*) Informing or involving more senior levels of management to assist in an escalation.

high availability

(*ITIL Service Design*) An approach or design that minimizes or hides the effects of configuration item failure from the users of an IT service. High availability solutions are designed to achieve an agreed level of availability and make use of techniques such as fault tolerance, resilience and fast recovery to reduce the number and impact of incidents.

identity

(*ITIL Service Operation*) A unique name that is used to identify a user, person or role. The identity is used to grant rights to that user, person or role. Example identities might be the username SmithJ or the role 'change manager'.

immediate recovery

(*ITIL Service Design*) A recovery option that is also known as hot standby. Provision is made to recover the IT service with no significant loss of service to the customer. Immediate recovery typically uses mirroring, load balancing and split-site technologies.

impact

(*ITIL Service Operation*) (*ITIL Service Transition*) A measure of the effect of an incident, problem or change on business processes. Impact is often based on how service levels will be affected. Impact and urgency are used to assign priority.

incident

(*ITIL Service Operation*) An unplanned interruption to an IT service or reduction in the quality of an IT service. Failure of a configuration item that has not yet affected service is also an incident – for example, failure of one disk from a mirror set.

incident management

(*ITIL Service Operation*) The process responsible for managing the lifecycle of all incidents. Incident management ensures that normal service operation is restored as quickly as possible and the business impact is minimized.

incident record

(*ITIL Service Operation*) A record containing the details of an incident. Each incident record documents the lifecycle of a single incident.

indirect cost

(*ITIL Service Strategy*) The cost of providing an IT service which cannot be allocated in full to a specific customer – for example, the cost of providing shared servers or software licences. Also known as overhead. *See also* direct cost.

information security management (ISM)

(*ITIL Service Design*) The process responsible for ensuring that the confidentiality, integrity and availability of an organization's assets, information, data and IT services match the agreed needs of the business. Information security management supports business security and has a wider scope than that of the IT service provider, and includes handling of paper, building access, phone calls etc. for the entire organization. *See also* security management information system.

information security management system (ISMS)

(*ITIL Service Design*) The framework of policy, processes, functions, standards, guidelines and tools that ensures an organization can achieve its information security management objectives. *See also* security management information system.

information security policy

(*ITIL Service Design*) The policy that governs the organization's approach to information security management.

information system

See management information system.

information technology (IT)

The use of technology for the storage, communication or processing of information. The technology typically includes computers, telecommunications, applications and other software. The information may include business data, voice, images, video etc. Information technology is often used to support business processes through IT services.

insourcing

(*ITIL Service Strategy*) Using an internal service provider to manage IT services. The term insourcing is also used to describe the act of transferring the provision of an IT service from an external service provider to an internal service provider. *See also* service sourcing.

integrity

(*ITIL Service Design*) A security principle that ensures data and configuration items are modified only by authorized personnel and activities. Integrity considers all possible causes of modification, including software and hardware failure, environmental events, and human intervention.

interactive voice response (IVR)

(*ITIL Service Operation*) A form of automatic call distribution that accepts user input, such as key presses and spoken commands, to identify the correct destination for incoming calls.

internal customer

A customer who works for the same business as the IT service provider. *See also* external customer; internal service provider.

internal metric

A metric that is used within the IT service provider to monitor the efficiency, effectiveness or cost effectiveness of the IT service provider's internal processes. Internal metrics are not normally reported to the customer of the IT service. *See also* external metric.

internal rate of return (IRR)

(*ITIL Service Strategy*) A technique used to help make decisions about capital expenditure. It calculates a figure that allows two or more alternative investments to be compared. A larger internal rate of return indicates a better investment. *See also* net present value; return on investment.

internal service provider

(*ITIL Service Strategy*) An IT service provider that is part of the same organization as its customer. An IT service provider may have both internal and external customers. *See also* insourcing; Type I service provider; Type II service provider.

International Organization for Standardization (ISO)

The International Organization for Standardization (ISO) is the world's largest developer of standards. ISO is a non-governmental organization that is a network of the national standards institutes of 156 countries. See www.iso.org for further information about ISO.

International Standards Organization

See International Organization for Standardization.

internet service provider (ISP)

An external service provider that provides access to the internet. Most ISPs also provide other IT services such as web hosting.

Ishikawa diagram

(*ITIL Continual Service Improvement*) (*ITIL Service Operation*) A technique that helps a team to identify all the possible causes of a problem. Originally devised by Kaoru Ishikawa, the output of this technique is a diagram that looks like a fishbone.

ISO 9000

A generic term that refers to a number of international standards and guidelines for quality management systems. See www.iso.org for more information. *See also* International Organization for Standardization.

ISO 9001

An international standard for quality management systems. *See also* ISO 9000; standard.

ISO/IEC 20000

An international standard for IT service management.

ISO/IEC 27001

(*ITIL Continual Service Improvement*) (*ITIL Service Design*) An international specification for information security management. The corresponding code of practice is ISO/IEC 27002. *See also* standard.

IT infrastructure

All of the hardware, software, networks, facilities etc. that are required to develop, test, deliver, monitor, control or support applications and IT services. The term includes all of the information technology but not the associated people, processes and documentation.

IT operations

(*ITIL Service Operation*) Activities carried out by IT operations control, including console management/ operations bridge, job scheduling, backup and restore, and print and output management. IT operations is also used as a synonym for service operation.

IT operations control

(*ITIL Service Operation*) The function responsible for monitoring and control of the IT services and IT infrastructure. *See also* operations bridge.

IT operations management

(*ITIL Service Operation*) The function within an IT service provider that performs the daily activities needed to manage IT services and the supporting IT infrastructure. IT operations management includes IT operations control and facilities management.

IT service

A service provided by an IT service provider. An IT service is made up of a combination of information technology, people and processes. A customer-facing IT service directly supports the business processes of one or more customers and its service level targets should be defined in a service level agreement. Other IT services, called supporting services, are not directly used by the business but are required by the service provider to deliver customer-facing services. *See also* core service; enabling service; enhancing service; service; service package.

IT service continuity management (ITSCM)

(*ITIL Service Design*) The process responsible for managing risks that could seriously affect IT services. IT service continuity management ensures that the IT service provider can always provide minimum agreed service levels, by reducing the risk to an acceptable level and planning for the recovery of IT services. IT service continuity management supports business continuity management.

IT service continuity plan

(*ITIL Service Design*) A plan defining the steps required to recover one or more IT services. The plan also identifies the triggers for invocation, people to be involved, communications etc. The IT service continuity plan should be part of a business continuity plan.

IT service management (ITSM)

The implementation and management of quality IT services that meet the needs of the business. IT service management is performed by IT service providers through an appropriate mix of people, process and information technology. *See also* service management.

IT service provider

(*ITIL Service Strategy*) A service provider that provides IT services to internal or external customers.

ITIL

A set of best-practice publications for IT service management. Owned by the Cabinet Office (part of HM Government), ITIL gives guidance on the provision of quality IT services and the processes, functions and other capabilities needed to support them. The ITIL framework is based on a service lifecycle and consists of five lifecycle stages (service strategy, service design, service transition, service operation and continual service improvement), each of which has its own supporting publication. There is also a set of complementary ITIL publications providing guidance specific to industry sectors, organization types, operating models and technology architectures. See www.itil-officialsite. com for more information.

job description

A document that defines the roles, responsibilities, skills and knowledge required by a particular person. One job description can include multiple roles – for example, the roles of configuration manager and change manager may be carried out by one person.

job scheduling

(*ITIL Service Operation*) Planning and managing the execution of software tasks that are required as part of an IT service. Job scheduling is carried out by IT operations management, and is often automated using software tools that run batch or online tasks at specific times of the day, week, month or year.

Kepner and Tregoe analysis

(*ITIL Service Operation*) A structured approach to problem solving. The problem is analysed in terms of what, where, when and extent. Possible causes are identified, the most probable cause is tested, and the true cause is verified.

key performance indicator (KPI)

(*ITIL Continual Service Improvement*) (*ITIL Service Design*) A metric that is used to help manage an IT service, process, plan, project or other activity. Key performance indicators are used to measure the achievement of critical success factors. Many metrics may be measured, but only the most important of these are defined as key performance indicators and used to actively manage and report on the process, IT service or activity. They should be selected to ensure that efficiency, effectiveness and cost effectiveness are all managed.

knowledge base

(*ITIL Service Transition*) A logical database containing data and information used by the service knowledge management system.

knowledge management

(*ITIL Service Transition*) The process responsible for sharing perspectives, ideas, experience and information, and for ensuring that these are available in the right place and at the right time. The knowledge management process enables informed decisions, and improves efficiency by reducing the need to rediscover knowledge. *See also* Data-to-Information-to-Knowledge-to-Wisdom; service knowledge management system.

known error

(*ITIL Service Operation*) A problem that has a documented root cause and a workaround. Known errors are created and managed throughout their lifecycle by problem management. Known errors may also be identified by development or suppliers.

known error database (KEDB)

(*ITIL Service Operation*) A database containing all known error records. This database is created by problem management and used by incident and problem management. The known error database may be part of the configuration management system, or may be stored elsewhere in the service knowledge management system.

known error record

(*ITIL Service Operation*) A record containing the details of a known error. Each known error record documents the lifecycle of a known error, including the status, root cause and workaround. In some implementations, a known error is documented using additional fields in a problem record.

lifecycle

The various stages in the life of an IT service, configuration item, incident, problem, change etc. The lifecycle defines the categories for status and the status transitions that are permitted. For example:

- The lifecycle of an application includes requirements, design, build, deploy, operate, optimize
- The expanded incident lifecycle includes detection, diagnosis, repair, recovery and restoration
- The lifecycle of a server may include: ordered, received, in test, live, disposed etc.

live

(*ITIL Service Transition*) Refers to an IT service or other configuration item that is being used to deliver service to a customer.

live environment

(*ITIL Service Transition*) A controlled environment containing live configuration items used to deliver IT services to customers.

major incident

(*ITIL Service Operation*) The highest category of impact for an incident. A major incident results in significant disruption to the business.

manageability

An informal measure of how easily and effectively an IT service or other component can be managed.

management information

Information that is used to support decision making by managers. Management information is often generated automatically by tools supporting the various IT service management processes. Management information often includes the values of key performance indicators, such as 'percentage of changes leading to incidents' or 'first-time fix rate'.

management information system (MIS)

(*ITIL Service Design*) A set of tools, data and information that is used to support a process or function. Examples include the availability management information system and the supplier and contract management information system. *See also* service knowledge management system.

Management of Risk (M_o_R)

M_o_R includes all the activities required to identify and control the exposure to risk, which may have an impact on the achievement of an organization's business objectives. See www.mor-officialsite.com for more details.

management system

The framework of policy, processes, functions, standards, guidelines and tools that ensures an organization or part of an organization can achieve its objectives. This term is also used with a smaller scope to support a specific process or activity – for example, an event management system or risk management system. *See also* system.

market space

(*ITIL Service Strategy*) Opportunities that an IT service provider could exploit to meet the business needs of customers. Market spaces identify the possible IT services that an IT service provider may wish to consider delivering.

maturity

(*ITIL Continual Service Improvement*) A measure of the reliability, efficiency and effectiveness of a process, function, organization etc. The most mature processes and functions are formally aligned to business objectives and strategy, and are supported by a framework for continual improvement.

mean time between failures (MTBF)

(*ITIL Service Design*) A metric for measuring and reporting reliability. MTBF is the average time that an IT service or other configuration item can perform its agreed function without interruption. This is measured from when the configuration item starts working, until it next fails.

metric

(*ITIL Continual Service Improvement*) Something that is measured and reported to help manage a process, IT service or activity. *See also* key performance indicator.

middleware

(*ITIL Service Design*) Software that connects two or more software components or applications. Middleware is usually purchased from a supplier, rather than developed within the IT service provider. *See also* commercial off the shelf.

mission

A short but complete description of the overall purpose and intentions of an organization. It states what is to be achieved, but not how this should be done. *See also* vision.

model

A representation of a system, process, IT service, configuration item etc. that is used to help understand or predict future behaviour.

modelling

A technique that is used to predict the future behaviour of a system, process, IT service, configuration item etc. Modelling is commonly used in financial management, capacity management and availability management.

monitor control loop

(*ITIL Service Operation*) Monitoring the output of a task, process, IT service or other configuration item; comparing this output to a predefined norm; and taking appropriate action based on this comparison.

monitoring

(*ITIL Service Operation*) Repeated observation of a configuration item, IT service or process to detect events and to ensure that the current status is known.

near-shore

(*ITIL Service Strategy*) Provision of services from a country near the country where the customer is based. This can be the provision of an IT service, or of supporting functions such as a service desk. *See also* offshore; onshore.

net present value (NPV)

(*ITIL Service Strategy*) A technique used to help make decisions about capital expenditure. It compares cash inflows with cash outflows. Positive net present value indicates that an investment is worthwhile. *See also* internal rate of return; return on investment.

normal service operation

(*ITIL Service Operation*) An operational state where services and configuration items are performing within their agreed service and operational levels.

objective

The outcomes required from a process, activity or organization in order to ensure that its purpose will be fulfilled. Objectives are usually expressed as measurable targets. The term is also informally used to mean a requirement.

off the shelf

See commercial off the shelf.

Office of Government Commerce (OGC)

OGC (former owner of Best Management Practice) and its functions have moved into the Cabinet Office as part of HM Government. See www.cabinetoffice.gov.uk

offshore

(*ITIL Service Strategy*) Provision of services from a location outside the country where the customer is based, often in a different continent. This can be the provision of an IT service, or of supporting functions such as a service desk. *See also* near-shore; onshore.

onshore

(*ITIL Service Strategy*) Provision of services from a location within the country where the customer is based. *See also* near-shore; offshore.

operate

To perform as expected. A process or configuration item is said to operate if it is delivering the required outputs. Operate also means to perform one or more operations. For example, to operate a computer is to do the day-to-day operations needed for it to perform as expected.

operation

(*ITIL Service Operation*) Day-to-day management of an IT service, system or other configuration item. Operation is also used to mean any predefined activity or transaction – for example, loading a magnetic tape, accepting money at a point of sale, or reading data from a disk drive.

operational

The lowest of three levels of planning and delivery (strategic, tactical, operational). Operational activities include the day-to-day or short-term planning or delivery of a business process or IT service management process. The term is also a synonym for live.

operational cost

The cost resulting from running the IT services, which often involves repeating payments – for example, staff costs, hardware maintenance and electricity (also known as current expenditure or revenue expenditure). *See also* capital expenditure.

operational expenditure (OPEX)

See operational cost.

operational level agreement (OLA)

(*ITIL Continual Service Improvement*) (*ITIL Service Design*) An agreement between an IT service provider and another part of the same organization. It supports the IT service provider's delivery of IT services to customers and defines the goods or services to be provided and the responsibilities of both parties. For example, there could be an operational level agreement:

- Between the IT service provider and a procurement department to obtain hardware in agreed times
- Between the service desk and a support group to provide incident resolution in agreed times.

See also service level agreement.

operations bridge

(*ITIL Service Operation*) A physical location where IT services and IT infrastructure are monitored and managed.

operations control

See IT operations control.

operations management

See IT operations management.

optimize

Review, plan and request changes, in order to obtain the maximum efficiency and effectiveness from a process, configuration item, application etc.

organization

A company, legal entity or other institution. The term is sometimes used to refer to any entity that has people, resources and budgets – for example, a project or business unit.

outcome

The result of carrying out an activity, following a process, or delivering an IT service etc. The term is used to refer to intended results as well as to actual results. *See also* objective.

outsourcing

(*ITIL Service Strategy*) Using an external service provider to manage IT services. *See also* service sourcing.

overhead

See indirect cost.

pain value analysis

(*ITIL Service Operation*) A technique used to help identify the business impact of one or more problems. A formula is used to calculate pain value based on the number of users affected, the duration of the downtime, the impact on each user, and the cost to the business (if known).

Pareto principle

(*ITIL Service Operation*) A technique used to prioritize activities. The Pareto principle says that 80% of the value of any activity is created with 20% of the effort. Pareto analysis is also used in problem management to prioritize possible problem causes for investigation.

partnership

A relationship between two organizations that involves working closely together for common goals or mutual benefit. The IT service provider should have a partnership with the business and with third parties who are critical to the delivery of IT services. *See also* value network.

passive monitoring

(*ITIL Service Operation*) Monitoring of a configuration item, an IT service or a process that relies on an alert or notification to discover the current status. *See also* active monitoring.

pattern of business activity (PBA)

(*ITIL Service Strategy*) A workload profile of one or more business activities. Patterns of business activity are used to help the IT service provider understand and plan for different levels of business activity. *See also* user profile.

performance

A measure of what is achieved or delivered by a system, person, team, process or IT service.

performance management

Activities to ensure that something achieves its expected outcomes in an efficient and consistent manner.

pilot

(*ITIL Service Transition*) A limited deployment of an IT service, a release or a process to the live environment. A pilot is used to reduce risk and to gain user feedback and acceptance. *See also* change evaluation; test.

plan

A detailed proposal that describes the activities and resources needed to achieve an objective – for example, a plan to implement a new IT service or process. ISO/IEC 20000 requires a plan for the management of each IT service management process.

Plan-Do-Check-Act (PDCA)

(*ITIL Continual Service Improvement*) A four-stage cycle for process management, attributed to Edward Deming. Plan-Do-Check-Act is also called the Deming Cycle. **Plan** – design or revise processes that support the IT services; **Do** – implement the plan and manage the processes; **Check** – measure the processes and IT services, compare with objectives and produce reports; **Act** – plan and implement changes to improve the processes.

planned downtime

(*ITIL Service Design*) Agreed time when an IT service will not be available. Planned downtime is often used for maintenance, upgrades and testing. *See also* change window; downtime.

planning

An activity responsible for creating one or more plans – for example, capacity planning.

policy

Formally documented management expectations and intentions. Policies are used to direct decisions, and to ensure consistent and appropriate development and implementation of processes, standards, roles, activities, IT infrastructure etc.

post-implementation review (PIR)

A review that takes place after a change or a project has been implemented. It determines if the change or project was successful, and identifies opportunities for improvement.

practice

A way of working, or a way in which work must be done. Practices can include activities, processes, functions, standards and guidelines. *See also* best practice.

pricing

(*ITIL Service Strategy*) Pricing is the activity for establishing how much customers will be charged.

PRINCE2

See PRojects IN Controlled Environments.

priority

(*ITIL Service Operation*) (*ITIL Service Transition*) A category used to identify the relative importance of an incident, problem or change. Priority is based on impact and urgency, and is used to identify required times for actions to be taken. For example, the service level agreement may state that Priority 2 incidents must be resolved within 12 hours.

proactive monitoring

(*ITIL Service Operation*) Monitoring that looks for patterns of events to predict possible future failures. *See also* reactive monitoring.

proactive problem management

(*ITIL Service Operation*) Part of the problem management process. The objective of proactive problem management is to identify problems that might otherwise be missed. Proactive problem management analyses incident records, and uses data collected by other IT service management processes to identify trends or significant problems.

problem

(*ITIL Service Operation*) A cause of one or more incidents. The cause is not usually known at the time a problem record is created, and the problem management process is responsible for further investigation.

problem management

(*ITIL Service Operation*) The process responsible for managing the lifecycle of all problems. Problem management proactively prevents incidents from happening and minimizes the impact of incidents that cannot be prevented.

problem record

(*ITIL Service Operation*) A record containing the details of a problem. Each problem record documents the lifecycle of a single problem.

procedure

A document containing steps that specify how to achieve an activity. Procedures are defined as part of processes. *See also* work instruction.

process

A structured set of activities designed to accomplish a specific objective. A process takes one or more defined inputs and turns them into defined outputs. It may include any of the roles, responsibilities, tools and management controls required to reliably deliver the outputs. A process may define policies, standards, guidelines, activities and work instructions if they are needed.

process control

The activity of planning and regulating a process, with the objective of performing the process in an effective, efficient and consistent manner.

process manager

A role responsible for the operational management of a process. The process manager's responsibilities include planning and coordination of all activities required to carry out, monitor and report on the process. There may be several process managers for one process – for example, regional change managers or IT service continuity managers for each data centre. The process manager role is often assigned to the person who carries out the process owner role, but the two roles may be separate in larger organizations.

process owner

The person who is held accountable for ensuring that a process is fit for purpose. The process owner's responsibilities include sponsorship, design, change management and continual improvement of the process and its metrics. This role can be assigned to the same person who carries out the process manager role, but the two roles may be separate in larger organizations.

production environment

See live environment.

programme

A number of projects and activities that are planned and managed together to achieve an overall set of related objectives and other outcomes.

project

A temporary organization, with people and other assets, that is required to achieve an objective or other outcome. Each project has a lifecycle that typically includes initiation, planning, execution, and closure. Projects are usually managed using a formal methodology such as PRojects IN Controlled Environments (PRINCE2) or the Project Management Body of Knowledge (PMBOK). *See also* charter; project management office; project portfolio.

project charter

See charter.

Project Management Body of Knowledge (PMBOK)

A project management standard maintained and published by the Project Management Institute. See www.pmi.org for more information. *See also* PRojects IN Controlled Environments (PRINCE2).

Project Management Institute (PMI)

A membership association that advances the project management profession through globally recognized standards and certifications, collaborative communities, an extensive research programme, and professional development opportunities. PMI is a not-for-profit membership organization with representation in many countries around the world. PMI maintains and publishes the Project Management Body of Knowledge (PMBOK). See www.pmi.org for more information. *See also* PRojects IN Controlled Environments (PRINCE2).

project management office (PMO)

(*ITIL Service Design*) (*ITIL Service Strategy*) A function or group responsible for managing the lifecycle of projects. *See also* charter; project portfolio.

project portfolio

(*ITIL Service Design*) (*ITIL Service Strategy*) A database or structured document used to manage projects throughout their lifecycle. The project portfolio is used to coordinate projects and ensure that they meet their objectives in a cost-effective and timely manner. In larger organizations, the project portfolio is typically defined and maintained by a project management office. The project portfolio is important to service portfolio management as new services and significant changes are normally managed as projects. *See also* charter.

projected service outage (PSO)

(*ITIL Service Transition*) A document that identifies the effect of planned changes, maintenance activities and test plans on agreed service levels.

PRojects IN Controlled Environments (PRINCE2)

The standard UK government methodology for project management. See www.prince-officialsite.com for more information. *See also* Project Management Body of Knowledge (PMBOK).

qualification

(*ITIL Service Transition*) An activity that ensures that the IT infrastructure is appropriate and correctly configured to support an application or IT service. *See also* validation.

quality

The ability of a product, service or process to provide the intended value. For example, a hardware component can be considered to be of high quality if it performs as expected and delivers the required reliability. Process quality also requires an ability to monitor effectiveness and efficiency, and to improve them if necessary. *See also* quality management system.

quality assurance (QA)

(*ITIL Service Transition*) The process responsible for ensuring that the quality of a service, process or other service asset will provide its intended value. Quality assurance is also used to refer to a function or team that performs quality assurance. This process is not described in detail within the core ITIL publications. *See also* service validation and testing.

quality management system (QMS)

(*ITIL Continual Service Improvement*) The framework of policy, processes, functions, standards, guidelines and tools that ensures an organization is of a suitable quality to reliably meet business objectives or service levels. *See also* ISO 9000.

RACI

(*ITIL Service Design*) A model used to help define roles and responsibilities. RACI stands for responsible, accountable, consulted and informed.

reactive monitoring

(*ITIL Service Operation*) Monitoring that takes place in response to an event. For example, submitting a batch job when the previous job completes, or logging an incident when an error occurs. *See also* proactive monitoring.

record

A document containing the results or other output from a process or activity. Records are evidence of the fact that an activity took place and may be paper or electronic – for example, an audit report, an incident record or the minutes of a meeting.

recovery

(*ITIL Service Design*) (*ITIL Service Operation*) Returning a configuration item or an IT service to a working state. Recovery of an IT service often includes recovering data to a known consistent state. After recovery, further steps may be needed before the IT service can be made available to the users (restoration).

recovery option

(*ITIL Service Design*) A strategy for responding to an interruption to service. Commonly used strategies are manual workaround, reciprocal arrangement, gradual recovery, intermediate recovery, fast recovery, and immediate recovery. Recovery options may make use of dedicated facilities or third-party facilities shared by multiple businesses.

recovery point objective (RPO)

(*ITIL Service Design*) (*ITIL Service Operation*) The maximum amount of data that may be lost when service is restored after an interruption. The recovery point objective is expressed as a length of time before the failure. For example, a recovery point objective of one day may be supported by daily backups, and up to 24 hours of data may be lost. Recovery point objectives for each IT service should be negotiated, agreed and documented, and used as requirements for service design and IT service continuity plans.

recovery time objective (RTO)

(*ITIL Service Design*) (*ITIL Service Operation*) The maximum time allowed for the recovery of an IT service following an interruption. The service level to be provided may be less than normal service level targets. Recovery time objectives for each IT service should be negotiated, agreed and documented. *See also* business impact analysis.

redundancy

(*ITIL Service Design*) Use of one or more additional configuration items to provide fault tolerance. The term also has a generic meaning of obsolescence, or no longer needed.

relationship

A connection or interaction between two people or things. In business relationship management, it is the interaction between the IT service provider and the business. In service asset and configuration management, it is a link between two configuration items that identifies a dependency or connection between them. For example, applications may be linked to the servers they run on, and IT services have many links to all the configuration items that contribute to that IT service.

release

(*ITIL Service Transition*) One or more changes to an IT service that are built, tested and deployed together. A single release may include changes to hardware, software, documentation, processes and other components.

release and deployment management

(*ITIL Service Transition*) The process responsible for planning, scheduling and controlling the build, test and deployment of releases, and for delivering new functionality required by the business while protecting the integrity of existing services.

release record

(*ITIL Service Transition*) A record that defines the content of a release. A release record has relationships with all configuration items that are affected by the release. Release records may be in the configuration management system or elsewhere in the service knowledge management system.

reliability

(*ITIL Continual Service Improvement*) (*ITIL Service Design*) A measure of how long an IT service or other configuration item can perform its agreed function without interruption. Usually measured as MTBF or MTBSI. The term can also be used to state how likely it is that a process, function etc. will deliver its required outputs. *See also* availability.

remediation

(*ITIL Service Transition*) Actions taken to recover after a failed change or release. Remediation may include back-out, invocation of service continuity plans, or other actions designed to enable the business process to continue.

repair

(*ITIL Service Operation*) The replacement or correction of a failed configuration item.

request for change (RFC)

(*ITIL Service Transition*) A formal proposal for a change to be made. It includes details of the proposed change, and may be recorded on paper or electronically. The term is often misused to mean a change record, or the change itself.

request fulfilment

(*ITIL Service Operation*) The process responsible for managing the lifecycle of all service requests.

request model

(*ITIL Service Operation*) A repeatable way of dealing with a particular category of service request. A request model defines specific agreed steps that will be followed for a service request of this category. Request models may be very simple, with no requirement for authorization (e.g. password reset), or may be more complex with many steps that require authorization (e.g. provision of an existing IT service). *See also* request fulfilment.

requirement

(*ITIL Service Design*) A formal statement of what is needed – for example, a service level requirement, a project requirement or the required deliverables for a process. *See also* statement of requirements.

resilience

(*ITIL Service Design*) The ability of an IT service or other configuration item to resist failure or to recover in a timely manner following a failure. For example, an armoured cable will resist failure when put under stress. *See also* fault tolerance.

resolution

(*ITIL Service Operation*) Action taken to repair the root cause of an incident or problem, or to implement a workaround. In ISO/IEC 20000, resolution processes is the process group that includes incident and problem management.

resource

(*ITIL Service Strategy*) A generic term that includes IT infrastructure, people, money or anything else that might help to deliver an IT service. Resources are considered to be assets of an organization. *See also* capability; service asset.

response time

A measure of the time taken to complete an operation or transaction. Used in capacity management as a measure of IT infrastructure performance, and in incident management as a measure of the time taken to answer the phone, or to start diagnosis.

responsiveness

A measurement of the time taken to respond to something. This could be response time of a transaction, or the speed with which an IT service provider responds to an incident or request for change etc.

restoration of service

See restore.

restore

(*ITIL Service Operation*) Taking action to return an IT service to the users after repair and recovery from an incident. This is the primary objective of incident management.

retire

(*ITIL Service Transition*) Permanent removal of an IT service, or other configuration item, from the live environment. Being retired is a stage in the lifecycle of many configuration items.

return on investment (ROI)

(*ITIL Continual Service Improvement*) (*ITIL Service Strategy*) A measurement of the expected benefit of an investment. In the simplest sense, it is the net profit of an investment divided by the net worth of the assets invested. *See also* net present value; value on investment.

review

An evaluation of a change, problem, process, project etc. Reviews are typically carried out at predefined points in the lifecycle, and especially after closure. The purpose of a review is to ensure that all deliverables have been provided, and to identify opportunities for improvement. *See also* change evaluation; post-implementation review.

rights

(*ITIL Service Operation*) Entitlements, or permissions, granted to a user or role – for example, the right to modify particular data, or to authorize a change.

risk

A possible event that could cause harm or loss, or affect the ability to achieve objectives. A risk is measured by the probability of a threat, the vulnerability of the asset to that threat, and the impact it would have if it occurred. Risk can also be defined as uncertainty of outcome, and can be used in the context of measuring the probability of positive outcomes as well as negative outcomes.

risk assessment

The initial steps of risk management: analysing the value of assets to the business, identifying threats to those assets, and evaluating how vulnerable each asset is to those threats. Risk assessment can be quantitative (based on numerical data) or qualitative.

risk management

The process responsible for identifying, assessing and controlling risks. Risk management is also sometimes used to refer to the second part of the overall process after risks have been identified and assessed, as in 'risk assessment and management'. This process is not described in detail within the core ITIL publications. *See also* risk assessment.

role

A set of responsibilities, activities and authorities assigned to a person or team. A role is defined in a process or function. One person or team may have multiple roles – for example, the roles of configuration manager and change manager may be carried out by a single person. Role is also used to describe the purpose of something or what it is used for.

root cause

(*ITIL Service Operation*) The underlying or original cause of an incident or problem.

root cause analysis (RCA)

(*ITIL Service Operation*) An activity that identifies the root cause of an incident or problem. Root cause analysis typically concentrates on IT infrastructure failures. *See also* service failure analysis.

scalability

The ability of an IT service, process, configuration item etc. to perform its agreed function when the workload or scope changes.

scope

The boundary or extent to which a process, procedure, certification, contract etc. applies. For example, the scope of change management may include all live IT services and related configuration items; the scope of an ISO/IEC 20000 certificate may include all IT services delivered out of a named data centre.

second-line support

(*ITIL Service Operation*) The second level in a hierarchy of support groups involved in the resolution of incidents and investigation of problems. Each level contains more specialist skills, or has more time or other resources.

security

See information security management.

security management

See information security management.

security management information system (SMIS)

(*ITIL Service Design*) A set of tools, data and information that is used to support information security management. The security management information system is part of the information security management system. *See also* service knowledge management system.

security policy

See information security policy.

server

(*ITIL Service Operation*) A computer that is connected to a network and provides software functions that are used by other computers.

service

A means of delivering value to customers by facilitating outcomes customers want to achieve without the ownership of specific costs and risks. The term 'service' is sometimes used as a synonym for core service, IT service or service package. *See also* utility; warranty.

service acceptance criteria (SAC)

(*ITIL Service Transition*) A set of criteria used to ensure that an IT service meets its functionality and quality requirements and that the IT service provider is ready to operate the new IT service when it has been deployed. *See also* acceptance.

service asset

Any resource or capability of a service provider. *See also* asset.

service asset and configuration management (SACM)

(*ITIL Service Transition*) The process responsible for ensuring that the assets required to deliver services are properly controlled, and that accurate and reliable information about those assets is available when and where it is needed. This information includes details of how the assets have been configured and the relationships between assets. *See also* configuration management system.

service catalogue

(*ITIL Service Design*) (*ITIL Service Strategy*) A database or structured document with information about all live IT services, including those available for deployment. The service catalogue is part of the service portfolio and contains information about two types of IT service: customer-facing services that are visible to the business; and supporting services required by the service provider to deliver customer-facing services. *See also* customer agreement portfolio; service catalogue management.

service catalogue management

(*ITIL Service Design*) The process responsible for providing and maintaining the service catalogue and for ensuring that it is available to those who are authorized to access it.

service change

See change.

service charter

(*ITIL Service Design*) (*ITIL Service Strategy*) A document that contains details of a new or changed service. New service introductions and significant service changes are documented in a charter and authorized by service portfolio management. Service charters are passed to the service design lifecycle stage where a new or modified service design package will be created. The term charter is also used to describe the act of authorizing the work required by each stage of the service lifecycle with respect to the new or changed service. *See also* change proposal; service portfolio; service catalogue.

service continuity management

See IT service continuity management.

service culture

A customer-oriented culture. The major objectives of a service culture are customer satisfaction and helping customers to achieve their business objectives.

service design

(*ITIL Service Design*) A stage in the lifecycle of a service. Service design includes the design of the services, governing practices, processes and policies required to realize the service provider's strategy and to facilitate the introduction of services into supported environments. Service design includes the following processes: design coordination, service catalogue management, service level management, availability management, capacity management, IT service continuity management, information security management, and supplier management. Although these processes are associated with service design, most processes have activities that take place across multiple stages of the service lifecycle. *See also* design.

service design package (SDP)

(*ITIL Service Design*) Document(s) defining all aspects of an IT service and its requirements through each stage of its lifecycle. A service design package is produced for each new IT service, major change or IT service retirement.

service desk

(*ITIL Service Operation*) The single point of contact between the service provider and the users. A typical service desk manages incidents and service requests, and also handles communication with the users.

service failure analysis (SFA)

(*ITIL Service Design*) A technique that identifies underlying causes of one or more IT service interruptions. Service failure analysis identifies opportunities to improve the IT service provider's processes and tools, and not just the IT infrastructure. It is a time-constrained, project-like activity, rather than an ongoing process of analysis.

service hours

(*ITIL Service Design*) An agreed time period when a particular IT service should be available. For example, 'Monday–Friday 08:00 to 17:00 except public holidays'. Service hours should be defined in a service level agreement.

service improvement plan (SIP)

(*ITIL Continual Service Improvement*) A formal plan to implement improvements to a process or IT service.

service knowledge management system (SKMS)

(*ITIL Service Transition*) A set of tools and databases that is used to manage knowledge, information and data. The service knowledge management system includes the configuration management system, as well as other databases and information systems. The service knowledge management system includes tools for collecting, storing, managing, updating, analysing and presenting all the knowledge, information and data that an IT service provider will need to manage the full lifecycle of IT services. *See also* knowledge management.

service level

Measured and reported achievement against one or more service level targets. The term is sometimes used informally to mean service level target.

service level agreement (SLA)

(*ITIL Continual Service Improvement*) (*ITIL Service Design*) An agreement between an IT service provider and a customer. A service level agreement describes the IT service, documents service level targets, and specifies the responsibilities of the IT service provider and the customer. A single agreement may cover multiple IT services or multiple customers. *See also* operational level agreement.

service level management (SLM)

(*ITIL Service Design*) The process responsible for negotiating achievable service level agreements and ensuring that these are met. It is responsible for ensuring that all IT service management processes, operational level agreements and underpinning contracts are appropriate for the agreed service level targets. Service level management monitors and reports on service levels, holds regular service reviews with customers, and identifies required improvements.

service level package (SLP)

See service option.

service level requirement (SLR)

(*ITIL Continual Service Improvement*) (*ITIL Service Design*) A customer requirement for an aspect of an IT service. Service level requirements are based on business objectives and used to negotiate agreed service level targets.

service level target

(*ITIL Continual Service Improvement*) (*ITIL Service Design*) A commitment that is documented in a service level agreement. Service level targets are based on service level requirements, and are needed to ensure that the IT service is able to meet business objectives. They should be SMART, and are usually based on key performance indicators.

service lifecycle

An approach to IT service management that emphasizes the importance of coordination and control across the various functions, processes and systems necessary to manage the full lifecycle of IT services. The service lifecycle approach considers the strategy, design, transition, operation and continual improvement of IT services. Also known as service management lifecycle.

service maintenance objective (SMO)

(*ITIL Service Operation*) The expected time that a configuration item will be unavailable due to planned maintenance activity.

service management

A set of specialized organizational capabilities for providing value to customers in the form of services.

service manager

A generic term for any manager within the service provider. Most commonly used to refer to a business relationship manager, a process manager or a senior manager with responsibility for IT services overall.

service model

(*ITIL Service Strategy*) A model that shows how service assets interact with customer assets to create value. Service models describe the structure of a service (how the configuration items fit together) and the dynamics of the service (activities, flow of resources and interactions). A service model can be used as a template or blueprint for multiple services.

service operation

(*ITIL Service Operation*) A stage in the lifecycle of a service. Service operation coordinates and carries out the activities and processes required to deliver and manage services at agreed levels to business users and customers. Service operation also manages the technology that is used to deliver and support services. Service operation includes the following processes: event management, incident management, request fulfilment, problem management, and access management. Service operation also includes the following functions: service desk, technical management, IT operations management, and application management. Although these processes and functions are associated with service operation, most processes and functions have activities that take place across multiple stages of the service lifecycle. *See also* operation.

service option

(*ITIL Service Design*) (*ITIL Service Strategy*) A choice of utility and warranty offered to customers by a core service or service package. Service options are sometimes referred to as service level packages.

service owner

(*ITIL Service Strategy*) A role responsible for managing one or more services throughout their entire lifecycle. Service owners are instrumental in the development of service strategy and are responsible for the content of the service portfolio. *See also* business relationship management.

service package

(*ITIL Service Strategy*) Two or more services that have been combined to offer a solution to a specific type of customer need or to underpin specific business outcomes. A service package can consist of a combination of core services, enabling services and enhancing services. A service package provides a specific level of utility and warranty. Customers may be offered a choice of utility and warranty through one or more service options. *See also* IT service.

service pipeline

(*ITIL Service Strategy*) A database or structured document listing all IT services that are under consideration or development, but are not yet available to customers. The service pipeline provides a business view of possible future IT services and is part of the service portfolio that is not normally published to customers.

service portfolio

(*ITIL Service Strategy*) The complete set of services that is managed by a service provider. The service portfolio is used to manage the entire lifecycle of all services, and includes three categories: service pipeline (proposed or in development), service catalogue (live or available for deployment), and retired services. *See also* customer agreement portfolio; service portfolio management.

service portfolio management (SPM)

(*ITIL Service Strategy*) The process responsible for managing the service portfolio. Service portfolio management ensures that the service provider has the right mix of services to meet required business outcomes at an appropriate level of investment. Service portfolio management considers services in terms of the business value that they provide.

service provider

(*ITIL Service Strategy*) An organization supplying services to one or more internal customers or external customers. Service provider is often used as an abbreviation for IT service provider. *See also* Type I service provider; Type II service provider; Type III service provider.

service reporting

(*ITIL Continual Service Improvement*) Activities that produce and deliver reports of achievement and trends against service levels. The format, content and frequency of reports should be agreed with customers.

service request

(*ITIL Service Operation*) A formal request from a user for something to be provided – for example, a request for information or advice; to reset a password; or to install a workstation for a new user. Service requests are managed by the request fulfilment process, usually in conjunction with the service desk. Service requests may be linked to a request for change as part of fulfilling the request.

service sourcing

(*ITIL Service Strategy*) The strategy and approach for deciding whether to provide a service internally, to outsource it to an external service provider, or to combine the two approaches. Service sourcing also means the execution of this strategy. *See also* insourcing; internal service provider; outsourcing.

service strategy

(*ITIL Service Strategy*) A stage in the lifecycle of a service. Service strategy defines the perspective, position, plans and patterns that a service provider needs to execute to meet an organization's business outcomes. Service strategy includes the following processes: strategy management for IT services, service portfolio management, financial management for IT services, demand management, and business relationship management. Although these processes are associated with service strategy, most processes have activities that take place across multiple stages of the service lifecycle.

service transition

(*ITIL Service Transition*) A stage in the lifecycle of a service. Service transition ensures that new, modified or retired services meet the expectations of the business as documented in the service strategy and service design stages of the lifecycle. Service transition includes the following processes: transition planning and support, change management, service asset and configuration management, release and deployment management, service validation and testing, change evaluation, and knowledge management. Although these processes are associated with service transition, most processes have activities that take place across multiple stages of the service lifecycle. *See also* transition.

service validation and testing

(*ITIL Service Transition*) The process responsible for validation and testing of a new or changed IT service. Service validation and testing ensures that the IT service matches its design specification and will meet the needs of the business.

seven-step improvement process

(*ITIL Continual Service Improvement*) The process responsible for defining and managing the steps needed to identify, define, gather, process, analyse, present and implement improvements. The performance of the IT service provider is continually measured by this process and improvements are made to processes, IT services and IT infrastructure in order to increase efficiency, effectiveness and cost effectiveness. Opportunities for improvement are recorded and managed in the CSI register.

shift

(*ITIL Service Operation*) A group or team of people who carry out a specific role for a fixed period of time. For example, there could be four shifts of IT operations control personnel to support an IT service that is used 24 hours a day.

single point of contact

(*ITIL Service Operation*) Providing a single consistent way to communicate with an organization or business unit. For example, a single point of contact for an IT service provider is usually called a service desk.

single point of failure (SPOF)

(*ITIL Service Design*) Any configuration item that can cause an incident when it fails, and for which a countermeasure has not been implemented. A single point of failure may be a person or a step in a process or activity, as well as a component of the IT infrastructure. *See also* failure.

snapshot

(*ITIL Continual Service Improvement*) (*ITIL Service Transition*) The current state of a configuration item, process or any other set of data recorded at a specific point in time. Snapshots can be captured by discovery tools or by manual techniques such as an assessment. *See also* baseline; benchmark.

software asset management (SAM)

(*ITIL Service Transition*) The process responsible for tracking and reporting the use and ownership of software assets throughout their lifecycle. Software asset management is part of an overall service asset and configuration management process. This process is not described in detail within the core ITIL publications.

source

See service sourcing.

specification

A formal definition of requirements. A specification may be used to define technical or operational requirements, and may be internal or external. Many public standards consist of a code of practice and a specification. The specification defines the standard against which an organization can be audited.

stakeholder

A person who has an interest in an organization, project, IT service etc. Stakeholders may be interested in the activities, targets, resources or deliverables. Stakeholders may include customers, partners, employees, shareholders, owners etc. *See also* RACI.

standard

A mandatory requirement. Examples include ISO/IEC 20000 (an international standard), an internal security standard for Unix configuration, or a government standard for how financial records should be maintained. The term is also used to refer to a code of practice or specification published by a standards organization such as ISO or BSI. *See also* guideline.

standard change

(*ITIL Service Transition*) A pre-authorized change that is low risk, relatively common and follows a procedure or work instruction – for example, a password reset or provision of standard equipment to a new employee. Requests for change are not required to implement a standard change, and they are logged and tracked using a different mechanism, such as a service request. *See also* change model.

standard operating procedures (SOP)

(*ITIL Service Operation*) Procedures used by IT operations management.

standby

(*ITIL Service Design*) Used to refer to resources that are not required to deliver the live IT services, but are available to support IT service continuity plans. For example, a standby data centre may be maintained to support hot standby, warm standby or cold standby arrangements.

statement of requirements (SOR)

(*ITIL Service Design*) A document containing all requirements for a product purchase, or a new or changed IT service. *See also* terms of reference.

status

The name of a required field in many types of record. It shows the current stage in the lifecycle of the associated configuration item, incident, problem etc.

storage management

(*ITIL Service Operation*) The process responsible for managing the storage and maintenance of data throughout its lifecycle.

strategic

(*ITIL Service Strategy*) The highest of three levels of planning and delivery (strategic, tactical, operational). Strategic activities include objective setting and long-term planning to achieve the overall vision.

strategic asset

(*ITIL Service Strategy*) Any asset that provides the basis for core competence, distinctive performance or sustainable competitive advantage, or which allows a business unit to participate in business opportunities. Part of service strategy is to identify how IT can be viewed as a strategic asset rather than an internal administrative function.

strategy

(*ITIL Service Strategy*) A strategic plan designed to achieve defined objectives.

strategy management for IT services

(*ITIL Service Strategy*) The process responsible for defining and maintaining an organization's perspective, position, plans and patterns with regard to its services and the management of those services. Once the strategy has been defined, strategy management for IT services is also responsible for ensuring that it achieves its intended business outcomes.

super user

(*ITIL Service Operation*) A user who helps other users, and assists in communication with the service desk or other parts of the IT service provider. Super users are often experts in the business processes supported by an IT service and will provide support for minor incidents and training.

supplier

(*ITIL Service Design*) (*ITIL Service Strategy*) A third party responsible for supplying goods or services that are required to deliver IT services. Examples of suppliers include commodity hardware and software vendors, network and telecom providers, and outsourcing organizations. *See also* supply chain; underpinning contract.

supplier and contract management information system (SCMIS)

(*ITIL Service Design*) A set of tools, data and information that is used to support supplier management. *See also* service knowledge management system.

supplier management

(*ITIL Service Design*) The process responsible for obtaining value for money from suppliers, ensuring that all contracts and agreements with suppliers support the needs of the business, and that all suppliers meet their contractual commitments. *See also* supplier and contract management information system.

supply chain

(*ITIL Service Strategy*) The activities in a value chain carried out by suppliers. A supply chain typically involves multiple suppliers, each adding value to the product or service. *See also* value network.

support group

(*ITIL Service Operation*) A group of people with technical skills. Support groups provide the technical support needed by all of the IT service management processes. *See also* technical management.

support hours

(*ITIL Service Design*) (*ITIL Service Operation*) The times or hours when support is available to the users. Typically these are the hours when the service desk is available. Support hours should be defined in a service level agreement, and may be different from service hours. For example, service hours may be 24 hours a day, but the support hours may be 07:00 to 19:00.

supporting service

(*ITIL Service Design*) An IT service that is not directly used by the business, but is required by the IT service provider to deliver customer-facing services (for example, a directory service or a backup service). Supporting services may also include IT services only used by the IT service provider. All live supporting services, including those available for deployment, are recorded in the service catalogue along with information about their relationships to customer-facing services and other CIs.

system

A number of related things that work together to achieve an overall objective. For example:

- A computer system including hardware, software and applications
- A management system, including the framework of policy, processes, functions, standards, guidelines and tools that are planned and managed together – for example, a quality management system
- A database management system or operating system that includes many software modules which are designed to perform a set of related functions.

system management

The part of IT service management that focuses on the management of IT infrastructure rather than process.

tactical

The middle of three levels of planning and delivery (strategic, tactical, operational). Tactical activities include the medium-term plans required to achieve specific objectives, typically over a period of weeks to months.

technical management

(*ITIL Service Operation*) The function responsible for providing technical skills in support of IT services and management of the IT infrastructure. Technical management defines the roles of support groups, as well as the tools, processes and procedures required.

technical observation (TO)

(*ITIL Continual Service Improvement*) (*ITIL Service Operation*) A technique used in service improvement, problem investigation and availability management. Technical support staff meet to monitor the behaviour and performance of an IT service and make recommendations for improvement.

technical support

See technical management.

terms of reference (TOR)

(*ITIL Service Design*) A document specifying the requirements, scope, deliverables, resources and schedule for a project or activity.

test

(*ITIL Service Transition*) An activity that verifies that a configuration item, IT service, process etc. meets its specification or agreed requirements. *See also* acceptance; service validation and testing.

test environment

(*ITIL Service Transition*) A controlled environment used to test configuration items, releases, IT services, processes etc.

third party

A person, organization or other entity that is not part of the service provider's own organization and is not a customer – for example, a software supplier or a hardware maintenance company. Requirements for third parties are typically specified in contracts that underpin service level agreements. *See also* underpinning contract.

third-line support

(*ITIL Service Operation*) The third level in a hierarchy of support groups involved in the resolution of incidents and investigation of problems. Each level contains more specialist skills, or has more time or other resources.

threat

A threat is anything that might exploit a vulnerability. Any potential cause of an incident can be considered a threat. For example, a fire is a threat that could exploit the vulnerability of flammable floor coverings. This term is commonly used in information security management and IT service continuity management, but also applies to other areas such as problem and availability management.

threshold

The value of a metric that should cause an alert to be generated or management action to be taken. For example, 'Priority 1 incident not solved within four hours', 'More than five soft disk errors in an hour', or 'More than 10 failed changes in a month'.

throughput

(*ITIL Service Design*) A measure of the number of transactions or other operations performed in a fixed time – for example, 5,000 e-mails sent per hour, or 200 disk I/Os per second.

total cost of ownership (TCO)

(*ITIL Service Strategy*) A methodology used to help make investment decisions. It assesses the full lifecycle cost of owning a configuration item, not just the initial cost or purchase price. *See also* total cost of utilization.

total cost of utilization (TCU)

(*ITIL Service Strategy*) A methodology used to help make investment and service sourcing decisions. Total cost of utilization assesses the full lifecycle cost to the customer of using an IT service. *See also* total cost of ownership.

total quality management (TQM)

(*ITIL Continual Service Improvement*) A methodology for managing continual improvement by using a quality management system. Total quality management establishes a culture involving all people in the organization in a process of continual monitoring and improvement.

transaction

A discrete function performed by an IT service – for example, transferring money from one bank account to another. A single transaction may involve numerous additions, deletions and modifications of data. Either all of these are completed successfully or none of them is carried out.

transition

(*ITIL Service Transition*) A change in state, corresponding to a movement of an IT service or other configuration item from one lifecycle status to the next.

transition planning and support

(*ITIL Service Transition*) The process responsible for planning all service transition processes and coordinating the resources that they require.

trend analysis

(*ITIL Continual Service Improvement*) Analysis of data to identify time-related patterns. Trend analysis is used in problem management to identify common failures or fragile configuration items, and in capacity management as a modelling tool to predict future behaviour. It is also used as a management tool for identifying deficiencies in IT service management processes.

tuning

The activity responsible for planning changes to make the most efficient use of resources. Tuning is most commonly used in the context of IT services and components. Tuning is part of capacity management, which also includes performance monitoring and implementation of the required changes. Tuning is also called optimization, particularly in the context of processes and other non-technical resources.

Type I service provider

(*ITIL Service Strategy*) An internal service provider that is embedded within a business unit. There may be several Type I service providers within an organization.

Type II service provider

(*ITIL Service Strategy*) An internal service provider that provides shared IT services to more than one business unit. Type II service providers are also known as shared service units.

Type III service provider

(*ITIL Service Strategy*) A service provider that provides IT services to external customers.

underpinning contract (UC)

(*ITIL Service Design*) A contract between an IT service provider and a third party. The third party provides goods or services that support delivery of an IT service to a customer. The underpinning contract defines targets and responsibilities that are required to meet agreed service level targets in one or more service level agreements.

unit cost

(*ITIL Service Strategy*) The cost to the IT service provider of providing a single component of an IT service. For example, the cost of a single desktop PC, or of a single transaction.

urgency

(*ITIL Service Design*) (*ITIL Service Transition*) A measure of how long it will be until an incident, problem or change has a significant impact on the business. For example, a high-impact incident may have low urgency if the impact will not affect the business until the end of the financial year. Impact and urgency are used to assign priority.

usability

(*ITIL Service Design*) The ease with which an application, product or IT service can be used. Usability requirements are often included in a statement of requirements.

use case

(*ITIL Service Design*) A technique used to define required functionality and objectives, and to design tests. Use cases define realistic scenarios that describe interactions between users and an IT service or other system.

user

A person who uses the IT service on a day-to-day basis. Users are distinct from customers, as some customers do not use the IT service directly.

user profile (UP)

(*ITIL Service Strategy*) A pattern of user demand for IT services. Each user profile includes one or more patterns of business activity.

utility

(*ITIL Service Strategy*) The functionality offered by a product or service to meet a particular need. Utility can be summarized as 'what the service does', and can be used to determine whether a service is able to meet its required outcomes, or is 'fit for purpose'. The business value of an IT service is created by the combination of utility and warranty. *See also* service validation and testing.

validation

(*ITIL Service Transition*) An activity that ensures a new or changed IT service, process, plan or other deliverable meets the needs of the business. Validation ensures that business requirements are met even though these may have changed since the original design. *See also* acceptance; qualification; service validation and testing; verification.

value chain

(*ITIL Service Strategy*) A sequence of processes that creates a product or service that is of value to a customer. Each step of the sequence builds on the previous steps and contributes to the overall product or service. *See also* value network.

value for money

An informal measure of cost effectiveness. Value for money is often based on a comparison with the cost of alternatives. *See also* cost benefit analysis.

value network

(*ITIL Service Strategy*) A complex set of relationships between two or more groups or organizations. Value is generated through exchange of knowledge, information, goods or services. *See also* partnership; value chain.

value on investment (VOI)

(*ITIL Continual Service Improvement*) A measurement of the expected benefit of an investment. Value on investment considers both financial and intangible benefits. *See also* return on investment.

variance

The difference between a planned value and the actual measured value. Commonly used in financial management, capacity management and service level management, but could apply in any area where plans are in place.

verification

(*ITIL Service Transition*) An activity that ensures that a new or changed IT service, process, plan or other deliverable is complete, accurate, reliable and matches its design specification. *See also* acceptance; validation; service validation and testing.

version

(*ITIL Service Transition*) A version is used to identify a specific baseline of a configuration item. Versions typically use a naming convention that enables the sequence or date of each baseline to be identified. For example, payroll application version 3 contains updated functionality from version 2.

vision

A description of what the organization intends to become in the future. A vision is created by senior management and is used to help influence culture and strategic planning. *See also* mission.

vital business function (VBF)

(*ITIL Service Design*) Part of a business process that is critical to the success of the business. Vital business functions are an important consideration of business continuity management, IT service continuity management and availability management.

vulnerability

A weakness that could be exploited by a threat – for example, an open firewall port, a password that is never changed, or a flammable carpet. A missing control is also considered to be a vulnerability.

warranty

(*ITIL Service Strategy*) Assurance that a product or service will meet agreed requirements. This may be a formal agreement such as a service level agreement or contract, or it may be a marketing message or brand image. Warranty refers to the ability of a service to be available when needed, to provide the required capacity, and to provide the required reliability in terms of continuity and security. Warranty can be summarized as 'how the service is delivered', and can be used to determine whether a service is 'fit for use'. The business value of an IT service is created by the combination of utility and warranty. *See also* service validation and testing.

work in progress (WIP)

A status that means activities have started but are not yet complete. It is commonly used as a status for incidents, problems, changes etc.

work instruction

A document containing detailed instructions that specify exactly what steps to follow to carry out an activity. A work instruction contains much more detail than a procedure and is only created if very detailed instructions are needed.

work order

A formal request to carry out a defined activity. Work orders are often used by change management and by release and deployment management to pass requests to technical management and application management functions.

workaround

(*ITIL Service Operation*) Reducing or eliminating the impact of an incident or problem for which a full resolution is not yet available – for example, by restarting a failed configuration item. Workarounds for problems are documented in known error records. Workarounds for incidents that do not have associated problem records are documented in the incident record.

workload

The resources required to deliver an identifiable part of an IT service. Workloads may be categorized by users, groups of users, or functions within the IT service. This is used to assist in analysing and managing the capacity, performance and utilization of configuration items and IT services. The term is sometimes used as a synonym for throughput.

Index

Index